Mapping Identity

Mapping Identity

The Creation of the Coeur d'Alene Indian Reservation, 1805–1902

Laura Woodworth-Ney

UNIVERSITY PRESS OF COLORADO
Louisville

© 2004 by the University Press of Colorado

Published by the University Press of Colorado
245 Century Circle, Suite 202
Louisville, Colorado 80027

All rights reserved
First paperback edition 2020

 The University Press of Colorado is a proud member of the Association of University Presses.

The University Press of Colorado is a cooperative publishing enterprise supported, in part, by Adams State University, Colorado State University, Fort Lewis College, Metropolitan State University of Denver, Regis University, University of Colorado, University of Northern Colorado, University of Wyoming, Utah State University, and Western Colorado University.

Library of Congress Cataloging-in-Publication Data

Woodworth-Ney, Laura.
   Mapping identity : the creation of the Coeur d'Alene Indian Reservation, 1805–1902 / Laura Woodworth-Ney.
    p. cm.
   Includes bibliographical references and index.
   ISBN 0-87081-761-2 (hardcover) — ISBN 978-1-64642-157-2 (pbk)
   1. Coeur d'Alene Indian Reservation (Idaho)—History—Sources. 2. Skitswish Indians—History Sources. 3. Skitswish Indians—Ethnic identity. 4. Skitswish Indians—Cultural assimilation. 5. Jesuits—Missions—Idaho—Coeur d'Alene Indian Reservation—History—Sources. 6. Idaho—Race relations. 7. Idaho—Politics and government. I. Title.
   E99.S63W66 2004
   323.1197'9430796—dc22
2004001012

Portions of this book appeared in the article "Negotiating Boundaries of Territory and 'Civilization': The Coeur d'Alene Indian Reservation Agreement Councils, 1873–1889," Pacific Northwest Quarterly 94 (Winter 2002/2003).

Map used in chapter openings courtesy of David Rumsey Map Collection, www.davidrumsey.com.

To the memory of my grandparents
B. F. and Orda Glodowski, Austin and Imogene Woodworth

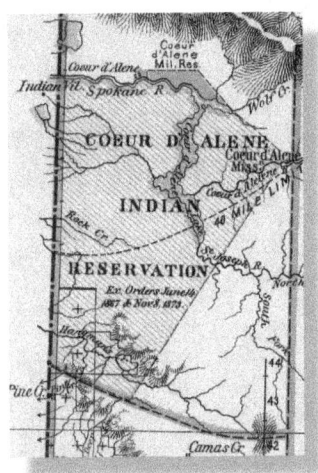

Contents

Acknowledgments / ix

Introduction / 1

1. The Nineteenth-Century Schitsu'umsh Landscape, 1800–1840 / 7

2. Crosses of Steel: Jesuit Missionary Foundings, 1840–1855 / 23

3. Isaac I. Stevens's Abandoned Treaty, 1853–1858 / 43

4. Territorial Defense: Participation in the Northern Plateau War of 1858 / 57

5. The Challenge of Nontreaty Status and the 1867 Reservation / 71

6. Presidential Intervention: The Creation of the 1873 Reservation / 85

7. Colville Agency and the Initial Assault on Reservation Boundaries, 1878–1886 / 105

8. The Agreement of 1887 / 123

9. Andrew Seltice, Assimilation Policy, and the Agreement of 1889 / 143

Epilogue / 167

Notes / 173

Bibliography / 209

Index / 223

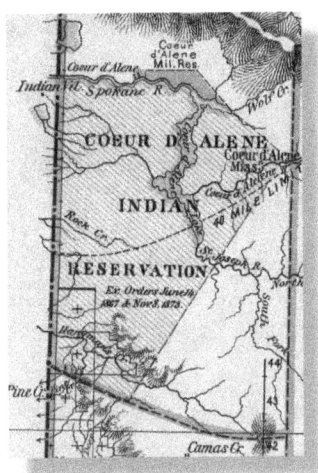

Acknowledgments

THIS BOOK COULD NOT HAVE BEEN COMPLETED without the help of many individuals. I owe a great debt to my colleagues and mentors at Washington State University, where the research for this book was initiated. Orlan Svingen always gave generously of his time. It was while working as his research assistant that I first became interested in this topic, and his mentoring provided the supportive intellectual environment necessary to pursue the subject. David Stratton has been a constant source of inspiration and support. His careful reading of early drafts of the manuscript improved it immensely. Susan Armitage and Paul Hirt contributed important insight and constructive advice. The anonymous readers of this book also improved it substantially. Any remaining inaccuracies of fact and interpretation, however, are mine alone.

During the course of my research, I have been aided by many archives and library staff members. Joyce Justice at the National Archives–Pacific Northwest Region deserves special mention. Without her perseverance this story would be much less complete. Kindra Serr, GIS technician at the Geographical Information Systems Center at Idaho State University, completed the maps for the project.

I received financial support for my research from the Margaret Pettyjohn Foundation and the P.E.O. Graduate Scholar Award. This aid helped make completion of this project possible.

My colleagues at Idaho State University expressed interest in this project and indulged me when I wanted to talk about it. Thanks also to my students in Native American and American West for their engaging dialogue and stimulating questions.

The staff at University Press of Colorado has been amazing. Special thanks to Sandy Crooms, for her patience and humor, and to Laura Furney and Cheryl Carnahan, for their expertise.

My parents, Gerald and Mary Ellen Woodworth, have been with me through this project, from start to finish, providing physical and intellectual nourishment. To John, thank you for believing and for being there. To Matthew, thanks for showing me the important things in life.

Mapping Identity

Introduction

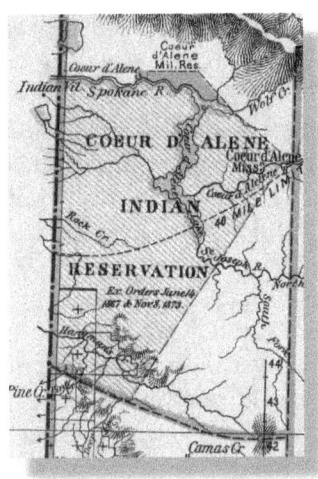

> And so he takes the heart / and he throws the heart, and of course . . . naturally . . . here is where the Coeur d'Alenes come from.
>
> —Excerpt from "Coyote and the Gobbler Monster"[1]

Many Native peoples in the Pacific Northwest share the mythology of the "Coyote cycle," but the specifics of the stories vary from tribe to tribe. These oral traditions contain the essential teachings of the Schitsu'umsh (pronounced Schēts·ü·ümsh), or Coeur d'Alene Indians.[2] Novelist and Coeur d'Alene tribal member Janet Campbell Hale remembered the Coyote stories from her childhood on the Coeur d'Alene Indian Reservation. Hale and her sisters would repeatedly ask her father and uncle to tell them the tales. "Because telling Coyote stories could cause the weather to change drastically," Hale wrote in her memoir, "and they didn't want to take a chance on its changing for the worse," the tribal elders would only tell the stories when "the temperature hit forty degrees below zero."[3] The oral tradition of the Schitsu'umsh forms part of a cultural and historical record that ties the tribe to its land in northern Idaho, where the tribe has lived for "many thousands of years."[4] The modern Coeur d'Alene Indian Reservation, located in northern Idaho and adjoining Lake Coeur d'Alene, occupies a small portion of the aboriginal territory of the tribe.[5]

This study is based predominantly on the records of the Bureau of Indian Affairs, the Office of the Interior Secretary, the War Department, and the Jesuit Archives of the Rocky Mountain Missions. It is an examination of the interactions between the Schitsu'umsh and non-Indians between 1805 and 1902 but does not purport to be a tribal history. The story presented here relies on a reexamination of Jesuit sources and federal documents and builds on a growing body of literature that presents an increasingly complex picture of federal policy, Native identity, and the creation of Indian reservations in the western United States. The choices, actions, words, and writings of the individuals highlighted within the Coeur d'Alene sphere of interaction—Chief Andrew Seltice, Jesuit Father Joseph Joset, General George Wright, topographical engineer John Mullan, Indian Agents Sidney Waters* and John Simms, resident farmer James O'Neill, interpreter Stephen Liberty, Commissioner Benjamin Simpson—suggest that the reservation era did not simply represent the end of a tidy process of U.S. expansion and conquest.[6] Schitsu'umsh leaders petitioned the federal government for tribal recognition, participated in the process of reservation making, redefined the term *Coeur d'Alene*, instituted agricultural policy, negotiated directly with railroad companies, made repeated demands of the Office of the Indian Commissioner, adopted non-Indians into the tribe, and maintained a police force. Women do not figure prominently in the records of government agencies and Jesuit missions; indeed, they are rarely mentioned. Yet women's voices can still be heard in these documents, if only in the silent spaces and omissions.[7]

Interaction between the Schitsu'umsh and non-Indian outsiders created two new entities in what became known as Coeur d'Alene country: the Coeur d'Alene Indian Tribe and the Coeur d'Alene Indian Reservation. Relations with explorers, fur traders, and missionaries created the interactive Coeur d'Alene identity. As James Merrell has argued, landscapes of contact—the nineteenth-century West in this case—were just as new to Native peoples as they were to Euro-Americans. It is not surprising, then, that in navigating this new world, Native people created identities for themselves that they used to interact with outsiders.[8] In the Schitsu'umsh example, this identity was simultaneously imposed by outsiders and edited, reformulated, and influenced by tribal people. I am not referring here to a clear demarcation or categorization of Indian identity but rather to a shifting construct used by outsiders to apply generally to the tribe and used by tribal leaders to enhance the tribe's ability to negotiate with outsiders. The non-Indian "mental map" of Coeur d'Alene identity was altered, reordered, and utilized by tribal leaders but was certainly not appropriated by all tribal people.[9]

The Coeur d'Alene Indian Reservation represents the other construct created during this time. The reservation boundary emerged in the wake of federal policy aimed at solving the "problem" of the Interior Northwest's "nontreaty bands," the group of tribal people who did not participate in Washington territorial governor Isaac I. Stevens's 1850s treaty negotiations. The reservation—

---

*Sidney Waters often appears as "Sydney" in the government documents.

both as an abstract idea and as a delineation of territorial boundaries—took form through a series of presidential executive orders and agreement negotiations between 1867 and 1889. The geographic ideology underlying the creation of the reservation, however, began long before the boundaries were outlined. When Meriwether Lewis and William Clark entered the region in 1805, they set in motion the process by which non-Indians mapped and conceived of the Schitsu'umsh people and their land. Eighty years later these mental maps influenced territorial negotiations with the Coeur d'Alenes.

The territorial demarcation of the reservation influenced the cultural landscapes of both the Schitsu'umsh and local whites. The literal and figurative mapping of the reservation created more headaches for the Indian Office than it solved. As the reservation boundary emerged, non-Indians protested it, encroached upon it, and ignored it. In response to the imposition of reservation boundaries, Chief Andrew Seltice presided over the consolidation of tribal farms and residences in the southwest corner of the reservation—a fertile area of rolling, grassy hills known as the Palouse. A division between river people and farm people, between Catholic and non-Catholic, between old ways and the new ensued. Reservation boundaries also altered the lives of area whites, who now had to ask permission from the Indian commissioner to procure wood, fish, camp, or otherwise use reservation resources. Indeed, the Indian agent's primary job in relation to the Coeur d'Alene Tribe during the early reservation period was to keep non-Indians off the reservation. Boundaries remained fluid, and trade between tribal members and non-Indians continued; but throughout the 1880s, whites became increasingly resentful of the tribe's resource wealth. Ironically, the creation of the reservation during the early 1870s led to resentment among whites that contributed to its partial dismantling in 1889.

Territorial negotiations and reservation boundary marking solidified the new "Coeur d'Alene Indians" identity. In close consultation with the Jesuit mission, the modernizing faction of the Schitsu'umsh gained political control and instituted a number of initiatives aimed at defining the Coeur d'Alenes as "civilized." This development combined with federal policy to create a new social order. For the federal government to negotiate with the tribe, it first had to determine who the tribal members were. Federal negotiators came to rely on the definition of Coeur d'Alene identity as sedentary, agricultural, and assimilated—even though many tribal members did not fit this description and lived fluid lives, crossing in and out of the reservation and in and out of what whites defined as Coeur d'Alene and non–Coeur d'Alene identity. Tribal members who resisted modernization and assimilation into the twentieth century disappeared from the written record represented in federal documents. Reservation policy highlighted identity divisions by giving resources—money in cash or kind—to Coeur d'Alenes who fit the government's definition, as influenced by Seltice and the Jesuit mission, of a "Coeur d'Alene Indian."[10] Thus, interaction

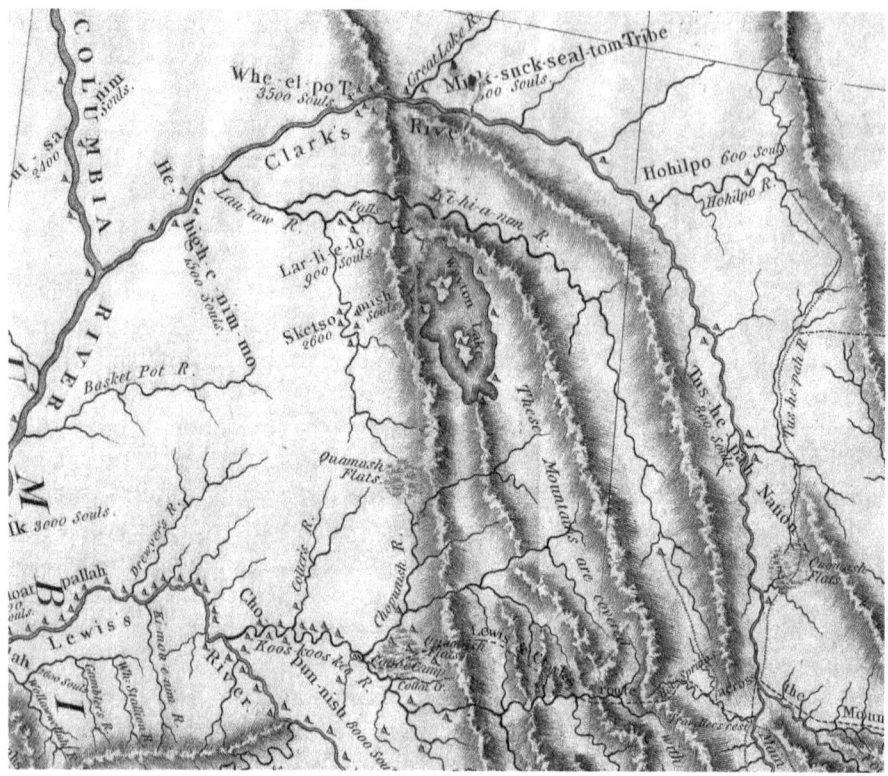

Map 1. Close-up of "Map of Lewis and Clark's Track Across the Western Portion of North America, 1814." Lake Coeur d'Alene appears as "Wayton Lake," and the Schitsu'umsh are described as "Sketsomish, 2600 souls." Courtesy, David Rumsey Map Collection, www.davidrumsey.com.

and reservation policy reshaped not only the boundaries of Schitsu'umsh territory but also the social and cultural landscapes.

As the process of mapping the reservation helped redefine Coeur d'Alene identity, nineteenth-century maps served as a history of non-Indian perceptions of identity and place in Coeur d'Alene country. Maps are visual constructs of ideas about geography, place, and power. Beginning with the Lewis and Clark Expedition, non-Indians defined, categorized, and appropriated Schitsu'umsh resources and identity on paper, long before real negotiations began. Maps preceded settlement and therefore influenced non-Indian perceptions of the people and places of the Interior Northwest. Nineteenth-century maps provided a visual accompaniment to a Euro-American narrative of "discovery," exploration, and settlement. Technological advances in cartography, the spread of public education with geography as a major subject, and a growing emphasis on atlas production combined in the early 1800s to create expanded demand for national maps.[11] The mapping of territory had become a mark of Euro-American progress—once a region was mapped, it was one step closer to "civilization." Mapmaking in the nineteenth-century United States was influenced by the nationalism inherent in European cartography during the same period.[12] As Americans moved westward, they created their own visual abstractions of Manifest Destiny. Private atlases proliferated, as did government-sponsored maps of frontier regions. These maps contained problems in scale and projection but revealed much about nineteenth-century notions of place and power.[13] In 1869 Congress authorized the U.S. Geological Survey of the Territories, which was replaced in 1879 by the U.S. Geological Survey. Thus, the mapping of reservations served not only to demarcate territory and to institute federal Indian policy but also to visually conquer geographic areas.[14]

The history of nineteenth-century interactions in Coeur d'Alene country attests to the multifaceted nature of contact and conquest in the Pacific Northwest. In this story the Indians are the first "homesteaders"; missionaries supply tribal people with firearms, later used to defeat a U.S. military force; tribal people protect white landowners' property and stock during an Indian "uprising"; Irish immigrants are classified as Indians; everyone, whites included, wants *on* the reservation; and the chief controls a police force feared by whites and Indians alike. Whites create mental maps of the land and the tribal people who live there, mental maps Indian leaders use to protect tribal resources. In the end, the careful assimilation policy advanced by Coeur d'Alene leaders redefined cultural boundaries in the same way reservation policy imposed territorial ones.

O N E

THE NINETEENTH-CENTURY SCHITSU'UMSH LANDSCAPE, 1800–1840

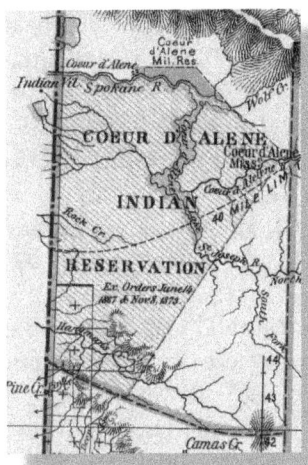

> This was the plan and purpose of nature before the coming of the white man. The majority of the Coeur d'Alenes were living in a paradise, in a land of their own, with no greed, no uncertainty, no depressions, no divorce and no government bureaus.
> —CHIEF JOSEPH SELTICE, SAGA OF THE COEUR D'ALENE INDIANS[1]

THE GREAT COLUMBIA RIVER OF THE U.S. PACIFIC NORTHWEST WINDS DOWN from British Columbia into Washington, forming the southern boundary of Washington and the northern boundary of Oregon. The Columbia's largest tributary, the Snake, slices through the deepest river gorge in North America—Hell's Canyon, with an average depth of 6,600 feet—before joining its mother river near Pasco, Washington. As it courses through Idaho, the Snake ties the noncoastal state to the Pacific Northwest. By the time the Columbia empties into the Pacific Ocean near Astoria, Oregon, more than 250,000 miles have been drained by its waters in the region American poet William Cullen Bryant described in 1814—the year the Lewis and Clark map (Map 1) appeared—as "the continuous woods / Where rolls the Oregon."[2]

Unaware of the vast arid stretches drained by the Columbia, Bryant viewed Oregon Country as a primeval forest. Eighteenth-century explorers also mistook the 1,270-mile river, surmising that the dense fog blanketing the shores of the north Pacific hid the Northwest Passage. Few early-nineteenth-century Americans could realistically conceive of the distant shores of the Pacific Ocean. The region known as Oregon Country encompassed a vast expanse of territory, including the present-day states of Washington, Oregon, Idaho, and part of Montana. England and the United States squabbled over ownership of the region, as both laid claim to it based on eighteenth-century exploration.³ When President Thomas Jefferson purchased Louisiana from France in 1803, the size of the United States doubled, and interest in the region beyond Louisiana increased. In an attempt to uncover a possible "Northwest Passage" that would link the Missouri River to the Columbia River, Jefferson commissioned Meriwether Lewis and William Clark to lead a scientific expedition to the Pacific Ocean.

Although the Corps of Discovery finally put to rest the question regarding the fabled Northwest Passage, the expedition recorded geographic, natural, and cultural information from St. Charles, Missouri, to Astoria, Oregon. Widely read at the time, the Lewis and Clark Expedition journals and maps formed the basis of the public's perception of Oregon until large-scale overland migration began to take place in the 1840s.⁴

Whatever the beliefs of American and British diplomats, public officials, and private citizens, the Columbia River region was a familiar landscape to the thousands of Native people who considered it home. Neither a river of perpetual forest nor a quick route to the riches of Asia, the Columbia provided the region's diverse inhabitants with a lifeline of fish and abundant vegetation. Native Pacific Northwesterners varied significantly in their relationship to the landscape. Peoples living in coastal areas benefited from mild, wet winters, varied plant species, dense forests, and access to the fruits of the sea. Groups in the arid and mountainous interiors relied on the Columbia River and its tributaries, principally the Snake, for fish but traveled widely throughout their territories in search of edible plants and wild game. Large numbers of these interior peoples lived in the Columbia Basin—an area bordered on the northeast by the Rocky Mountains, on the south by the Blue Mountains, and on the west by the Cascade Mountains. Here Salish- and Sahaptin-speaking groups coexisted with the Columbia and the basin's marked seasonal changes, characterized by an average temperature variation between summer and winter of 45 degrees Fahrenheit.⁵ Basin tribes met regularly at The Dalles, Oregon—the "best salmon fishery on the Columbia River"—to conduct trade, arrange marriages, indulge in horse racing and games, and share in communal meals.⁶ Petroglyphs and pictographs etched on basalt cliffs lining the Columbia River attest to the countless generations who convened on the river's banks.

The Schitsu'umsh (Coeur d'Alene) people traditionally inhabited and utilized an area of 4 to 5 million acres of land centered on the Spokane River drainage system and Lake Coeur d'Alene, in the far eastern section of the Columbia Basin.⁷ The tribe's homeland extended west to the open grasslands of the Palouse, east to the Bitterroot Mountains, south to the Clearwater River's headwaters, and north to the forests held by the Kalispel, or Pend Oreille, tribe. The Palouse and Nez Perce peoples occupied the territories to the south and southwest, and the Spokanes inhabited the region directly to the west. The Schitsu'umsh neighbor to the east, the Flathead people, lived on the other side of the formidable Bitterroot Mountains, now in Montana.⁸ The tribe possessed no tradition of ancestral migration. According to oral history, the Schitsu'umsh have inhabited eastern Washington and northern Idaho "since time immemorial."⁹

Estimates of eighteenth- and early-nineteenth-century Coeur d'Alene population numbers remain controversial. In 1904 anthropologist James A. Teit reasoned that based on the number of winter camps and villages he located, the pre-smallpox Coeur d'Alene population ranged from 3,000 to 4,000 persons. Modern analysis of the impact of virgin soil epidemics on Native populations, which had neither immune nor genetic resistance, suggests these early population figures are underestimated. Four decades ago schoolchildren were taught that "before Columbus" approximately 1 million people lived in North America. A better understanding of the destructiveness of Eurasian pathogens on American indigenous populations, careful analysis of reports of early explorers, and archaeological evidence now imply a predisease population in North America of between 2 and 18 million, with a population in the American West of about 1.155 million.¹⁰ Eurasian diseases—including smallpox, measles, influenza, and typhus—reduced some Native populations in the Western Hemisphere by as much as 95 percent. Before the introduction of Eurasian diseases and the late-nineteenth-century demarcation of tribal identity—the clear separation of the Coeur d'Alene groups from the Spokane groups, for example—Schitsu'umsh numbers may have corresponded to tribal estimates of 5,000.¹¹

Although language and economic patterns associated the Coeur d'Alenes with other Salish speakers of the Columbia Plateau, the geographic features of their homeland set them apart. The Coeur d'Alene people used tribal waterways—Lake Coeur d'Alene, the St. Joseph (or St. Joe) River, the Coeur d'Alene River, the Spokane River, the St. Maries River, and Hangman's (now Latah) Creek—to anchor their tribal villages. These important rivers provided transportation and a variety of fish, including several salmon species. The tribe ventured into the surrounding countryside in search of food and big game, but permanent structures along Lake Coeur d'Alene and its tributaries formed full-time communities. The Coeur d'Alene Mountains separating the tribe from the Flathead people in present-day Montana created an impenetrable barrier in the winter. During much of the year, the Coeur d'Alenes were forced to meet their subsistence needs within their own territory; fish, game, and roots provided the essentials of their diet. Eighteenth- and early-nineteenth-century Coeur d'Alene life, as revealed in written accounts based on oral testimony, evolved with the changing seasons. Representing decades of tribal transition, tribal members gave their recollections to James A. Teit in 1904, to linguist and folklorist Gladys A. Reichard in 1927 and 1929, to anthropologist Verne F. Ray between 1930 and 1934, and to ethnologist Stuart A. Chalfant in 1951. These oral accounts reveal a pattern of seasonal activities based on five seasons: spring, summer, autumn, late fall, and winter.¹²

The arrival of spring signaled an end to the careful rationing of winter stores of dried meat and roots. As the weather changed, Coeur d'Alene members used canoes to journey from winter villages on area waterways to root-digging grounds located in the southern reaches of their territory. They gathered the roots of several plant species, but the bulbous, starchy camas root constituted a particularly significant part of the diet. Favored Coeur d'Alene camas campsites included the low meadows surrounding present-day Tensed, Clarkia, Potlatch, and Moscow, Idaho. Fields of the bluish-purple camas blossom also provided the backdrop for intertribal trade, since some grounds served as camps for more than one tribe. At the camas field near Moscow, for example, Coeur d'Alene and Palouse root diggers socialized while they worked. Individual Coeur d'Alene groups each had favorite areas, and although they shared the sites among themselves, bands returned to a specific location each year.[13] Using wooden sticks with handles of elk antler, tribal women dug the camas roots and placed them in large baskets. Some of the men fished in local streams and traveled south and west to intercept the spring salmon run. Favorite salmon fishing sites included Kettle Falls, Spokane Falls, and Latah Creek. In the spring tribal members consumed much of the catch on-site, since the winter months usually exhausted the stored food supply.[14] While at the camas camps Schitsu'umsh lived in portable circular structures made of poles and covered with mats or skins.[15]

Summer was the season of leisure and abundance. Wild raspberries, blackberries, huckleberries, gooseberries, blueberries, currants, chokecherries, and strawberries provided easy pickings. Deer, bear, elk, and mountain grouse supplemented the diet. Schitsu'umsh elder Stanislaus Aripa told ethnologist Stuart Chalfant in 1951 that he remembered summer as a casual, relaxing time in which groups moved freely throughout the region and pursued activities such as horse racing and trading. During the warmest months, Aripa recalled, Coeur d'Alene men would "loaf along," hunting only enough meat "to get by on."[16] Coeur d'Alene women, however, worked hard throughout the summer to gather fruit and prepare food for the summer camp. As in other interior Salish tribes, Coeur d'Alene women exercised considerable authority in the allocation of tribal resources. Women bore the responsibility for gathering nonanimal products; drying and preserving meat, fruit, and roots for storage; tanning hides for clothing; sewing winter clothes with bear bone needles; preparing communal meals; and distributing food surpluses.[17]

Economic activity increased in late summer and early fall to provide for winter stores. Coeur d'Alene women preserved the camas and other roots gathered in July and August by cooking the tubers in earthen pits lined with rocks, layered with grasses and bark, and heated by fire. Food preparers stoked the fires on top of the pits for up to two days. The subterranean ovens yielded softened roots that the cooks crushed, shaped into cakes, and dried for easy storage. Fall hunts in the Clearwater and Bitterroot ranges provided the winter supply of game—elk, deer, brown and black bear. Joseph Seltice, son of Andrew Seltice (1819–1902) and chief of the Coeur d'Alene tribe from 1934 to 1949, wrote in his history that the elk populations of the Clearwater Mountains "could easily supply the entire Tribe with winter meat." The Clearwater River's Little North Fork, just south of Coeur d'Alene country, teemed with salmon during the fall run. "The salmon could be hooked out of the river," Seltice recounted, "nearly as fast as you could throw them on the bank." Salmon halved and dried in the sun, along with jerked meat, joined the camas cakes in the winter stores.[18]

The turning colors of leaves signaled the reconstitution of winter villages, located along tribal waterways. An intensely territorial people, the Schitsu'umsh returned to the same villages year after year. The tribe practiced a bilateral kinship system in which extended families recognized both the paternal and maternal sides of the family. Extended families wintered together. If the husband died, custom required that his brother take care of the widow and her children. Villages were connected by geography, blood ties, and marriage. Both men and women participated in the marriage selection process, but the bride usually lived with her husband's family. Since either spouse could dissolve the marriage with relative ease, village family systems remained flexible, their populations fluid.[19]

During both winter and summer, tribal members lived in conical dwellings supported by pine poles and covered with tule mats and bark. The lodges housed up to three families and were erected and owned by the women in the family. During the winter months the bands also used longhouses, communal structures from 15 to 24 feet wide and as long as 90 feet. The longhouses provided the community with a place to meet to conduct business or play games. They could also accommodate as many as six individual families. "Menstruation lodges" were also constructed, at a distance from the main village area, to house women during the ceremonial separation from the community required during their monthly cycles.[20] Unlike other tribes in the Columbia Basin, the Coeur d'Alenes utilized their winter lodges periodically throughout the year. Not all members of an extended family journeyed to the camas, fishing, or hunting grounds, so structures remained standing, and winter villages hosted a permanent population. Suggestive of the tribe's territorial orientation, the Coeur d'Alenes employed elevated storage platforms and circular defensive stockades of posts. The repetitive appearance of phrases such as "There was village" and "There were houses, many houses" in Coeur d'Alene storytelling further attests to the tribe's careful attention to territory.[21]

Anthropologist Verne F. Ray, working with tribal contacts in 1934, determined the existence of at least thirty-four permanent and semipermanent Coeur d'Alene villages along the Spokane, Coeur d'Alene, and St. Joseph rivers and on Hayden Lake and Lake Coeur d'Alene. Anthropologist Rodney Frey found that the villages were linked to at least three tribal groupings, or "bands": one located in the Hayden Lake and northern Coeur d'Alene Lake region, one along the Coeur d'Alene River, and one along the St. Joe. An additional band could have been centered in the Liberty Lake region, near present-day Spokane. The largest villages numbered 100 or more persons and were located at present-day Cataldo, Idaho; south of Lake Coeur d'Alene on the banks of the St. Joseph River; on the north shore of Hayden Lake; and at the present site of Coeur d'Alene, Idaho, on the northern shores of Lake Coeur d'Alene. Fishing provided fresh food throughout the winter months. Most of the villages remained occupied until the 1870s; some retained a permanent population as late as 1900. With approximately 125 permanent residents and a seasonal population of around 300, the tribal presence on the north shore of Lake Coeur d'Alene represented the most populous nineteenth-century village and was part of the approximately sixteen families or villages that comprised the Lake Coeur d'Alene band. The other main bands included the Coeur d'Alene River families—located throughout eleven village sites along the Coeur d'Alene River near what would become the Cataldo Mission (Old Mission) site—and the St. Joe River villages, six villages along the St. Joe in the vicinity of what would become the town of St. Maries, Idaho.[22]

These habitations remained economically and politically autonomous until changes in the mid-nineteenth century instigated a more formal organization. A village-appointed headman and council presided over local affairs. Headmen enlisted prominent individuals to serve as "head chief" during times of crisis or when specific circumstances called for an authority figure to speak for all the villages. The chiefs and village subchiefs served in advisory positions, and their authority rested on tribal consensus and band council meetings. Still, chiefs commanded considerable respect, as suggested by their prominent place in Schitsu'umsh oral tradition. Many Coeur d'Alene stories indicated the locations of tribal homes by reference to the residence of the local chief.[23] Heredity did not determine the chieftainship, and all male tribal members were eligible. Women did not hold the position of chief but could voice their opinions during public meetings. The village residence of the head chief, in keeping with the loose nature of Coeur d'Alene political organization, shifted with the current leader's desires. No permanent "seat" or main village existed. When Vincent became principal chief by "majority" consensus during the mid-1840s, he remained at his home on the shores of Hayden Lake, despite the previous chief's location at Coeur d'Alene village.[24]

Power also resided with the spiritual leaders of the tribe, the shamans, who maintained tribal ceremonies and conducted hunting and fishing rituals. Both men and women could hold the essential position of shaman. As Rodney Frey stated in his analysis of Schitsu'umsh authority, "[I]f the role of the chiefs was ultimately to help regulate the social and economic relations between the people and the landscape (by influencing the proper behavior of people), the paramount role of the shaman was to help regulate the spiritual relations between the people and the landscape."[25] The fact that women held this significant position, with its responsibility for the rituals associated with both life and death, indicates that in precontact society some women possessed spiritual authority at least equal to that of men, although there were more male than female shamans.[26]

Nineteenth-century Coeur d'Alene tribal members lived in an era of changing political, social, and cultural landscapes, as well as seasonal ones. Flexible political organization enabled the Coeur d'Alene people to absorb and embrace transition, but the tribe's strong territoriality maintained the geographic isolation of the Coeur d'Alene homeland. Until the presence of nonaboriginal intruders directly impacted events in Coeur d'Alene country, the tribe successfully managed changes resulting from the indirect influence of outsiders. Still, the introduction of horses into the Coeur d'Alene region in the eighteenth century altered subsistence patterns and social relationships. The movement of British, American, and French-Indian métis traders into surrounding territories offered the tribe access to firearms, which transformed hunting practices and strained intertribal relationships. The fur traders' presence also made the Coeur d'Alenes more wary of dealings with outsiders.[27]

Horses first appeared on the Columbia Plateau in the early eighteenth century, having made the trade migration from the aboriginal peoples of the Southwest, who procured the animals from Spanish colonizers. The climate of northern Mexico proved ideal for horse breeding, and by the eighteenth century wild herds roamed across the future southwestern United States. Amerindian peoples in the Southwest and on the southern Plains perfected the breeding and use of the horse, trading and raiding until the animals reached the Interior Pacific Northwest. The horse was introduced to Schitsu'umsh neighbors the Palouse as early as 1730.[28] The Nez Perce, the Schitsu'umsh neighbor to the south, may have first acquired horses from the Shoshonis. Together with neighboring tribes, the Schitsu'umsh embraced horsemanship and created an Inland Northwest "horse culture."[29]

The introduction of the horse brought economic and political change. Use of the horse facilitated travel within Coeur d'Alene country, and the new animals gradually replaced the canoe as the most popular mode of assisted transport. Families abandoned traditional water routes to the root-digging grounds in favor of treeless open stretches suitable for horse travel. Ease of mobility stretched the limits of the tribal homeland and changed former hunting patterns. Horses enabled the Coeur d'Alenes to join the Spokane, Nez Perce, Kalispel, and Kootenai tribes in crossing the Rocky Mountains into Flathead territory for an annual buffalo hunt. The western tribes gathered in the early fall near present-day Cataldo to prepare for the journey. They met up with eastern groups on the other side of the Rockies at St. Ignatius, Montana. That the western tribes congregated at a site on Coeur d'Alene land attests to the importance of the tribe's participation in the hunts. Entire households traveled to the buffalo grounds, sometimes as far east as the Dakotas. Coeur d'Alene families, with extra packhorses laden with meat and hides, returned to their homeland in early spring. The years in which these annual treks began remain uncertain, although the Seltice family history dates them as early as 1740. The buffalo hunting excursions were an integral part of society by the early nineteenth century. Tribal memoirs suggest their continued practice until the mid-1870s, when professional hide hunters began to systematically destroy the buffalo herds of the Interior West.[30]

The buffalo hunt expedited contact between the Coeur d'Alenes and the Amerindian peoples of the Great Plains, a circumstance that led to the adoption of several Plains cultural characteristics. Coeur d'Alene tribal members began using the hide-covered tepees and animal skin pack bags common to Plains tribes, items well suited to horse travel. Tribes on the eastern side of the Rocky Mountains referred to the Coeur d'Alenes as the "Bow and Arrow People." The Plains peoples traded buffalo meat, hides, feathers, and headdresses for Coeur d'Alene camas cakes, bows and arrows, pemmican, and salmon oil.[31] Schitsu'umsh participation in the buffalo hunts yielded a new level of prosperity and changed the traditional subsistence behavior of many tribal people, yet the tribe continued to rely on the procurement of vegetal foods—particularly camas root. As a result, the shift in power from women to men that occurred among some Plains tribes with the advent of the "horse culture" did not take place within the Schitsu'umsh. Some historians have found that the Plains' reliance on buffalo meat replaced the importance of nonflesh foods. Women in these groups lost power because they no longer controlled the procurement and distribution of food. Among Plateau groups, including the Coeur d'Alene, the buffalo hunts complemented traditional subsistence, and women maintained their important role within the food cycle.[32]

Geographic mobility accorded the Schitsu'umsh new opportunities for trade and increased contact with non-Indian peoples. The tribe's participation in the buffalo hunts corresponded with the emergence of expanded trade possibilities in the Interior Pacific Northwest. Although not intended as a strictly trade-oriented journey, Meriwether Lewis and William Clark's famed expedition flirted with the boundaries of Schitsu'umsh country and left trade possibilities in its wake. The Corps of Discovery traded with area tribes—including the Nez Perce, Palouse, and Yakima—for provisions and horses, ushering in a new era of contact with the U.S. government. With an eye to future trade, Lewis and Clark made extensive journal entries detailing the homeland and characteristics of the Northwest tribes with whom they had contact.

Expedition members had no formal contact with the Schitsu'umsh, but their campsites brought them into close proximity with the tribe, and their journals mention at least one chance meeting with Schitsu'umsh people. During the trip to the Pacific Ocean in 1805, Lewis and Clark crossed the Bitterroot Range and then camped with Nez Perce bands on the Clearwater River, adjacent to present-day Orofino, Idaho. Nez Perce chief Twisted Hair gave the starving explorers dried salmon, berries, and assistance in mapping the remainder of their journey. The captains sojourned on the Clearwater for several weeks during September and October, preparing canoes for the ensuing voyage to the Pacific. The Coeur d'Alenes, whose fall hunting and fishing excursions took them to the Clearwater, knew of these strangers' presence in the vicinity.[33]

During their 1806 return trip, Lewis and Clark spent nearly a month camped on the north bank of the Clearwater River, near present-day Kamiah, Idaho, while they waited for the snows to recede on the Continental Divide. The nearness of Camp Chopunnish to Coeur d'Alene country, as well as the duration of the explorers' stay, suggests that they had ample opportunity to learn of the Coeur d'Alene people. On May 6, while en route to the camp of Nez Perce tribal member Twisted Hair, Lewis and Clark encountered "three men, of a nation called Skeetsomish, who reside at the falls of a large river, emptying itself into the north side of the Columbia."[34] Information about the rivers of the Schitsu'umsh proved essential in mapping the region: "This river takes its rise from a large lake in the mountains, at no great distance from the falls where these Natives live. We shall designate this river, hereafter, by the name of Clark's river, as we do not know its Indian appellation, and we are the first whites who have ever visited its principal branches."[35] "In dress and appearance these Skeetsomish were not to be distinguished from the Choppunish," the journal noted, "but their language is entirely different, a circumstance which we did not learn till their departure, when it was too late to procure from them a vocabulary."[36]

The expedition journals thus mapped an identity for the Schitsu'umsh that was separate from other peoples and was intrinsically tied to the waters of the region. Expedition sketches of Coeur d'Alene country, drawn by Clark using information procured from the "Skeetsomish" and the Nez Perce, showed Wayton Lake (now Lake Coeur d'Alene) and tribal villages near the lake and the Spokane River. Clark identified six "Sket-so-mish"[37] villages in the area surrounding Wayton Lake and adjoining Spokane Falls. The journals estimated the number of Coeur d'Alene lodges at 120 and tribal population at 2,000, but Lewis and Clark apparently did not know of the tribe's villages near Hayden Lake or along the Coeur d'Alene River.[38] The journals indicated that Wayton Lake possessed two islands, was ten days around, and was seven days from the Chopunnish (Nez Perce).[39]

These notations formed the basis for the earliest Euro-American mapping of the Schitsu'umsh landscape. In the years after the Corps of Discovery completed its work, Samuel Lewis copied William Clark's original drawings for publication, which were engraved by Samuel Harrison. The Lewis and Clark maps appeared in the *History of the Expedition Under the Command of Captains Lewis and Clark* in 1814; the text was completed by Meriwether Lewis, William Clark,

Nicholas Biddle, and Paul Allen. The book's frontispiece map is a rendering of the entire length of the expedition's route. It includes population figures and village locations for the Native groups Lewis and Clark encountered or heard about from other tribal people. The map's representation of Schitsu'umsh country shows seven villages surrounding Wayton Lake, two villages at the site of Spokane Falls, and five villages along a river. The map indicates that the "Sketso-mish" numbered 2,600 souls, despite Clark's journal entry population figure of 2,000. This first Euro-American mapping of the Schitsu'umsh firmly established the group's identity as a lake people and identified the Schitsu'umsh homeland as rich in water and resources.[40]

The explorations of Lewis and Clark generated not only maps but a generation of traders who knew of the trans–Missouri River West because of personal involvement with the expedition or through publications of the corps. John Colter, a member of the Lewis and Clark Expedition, parted with the group during the return journey, according to Clark, after receiving a "very advantagious [sic]" offer to join two traders from Illinois who were traveling west in search of fur-bearing animals. After expedition members wished him "every suckcess [sic]," Colter became the first white man to explore present-day Yellowstone National Park and the area surrounding Jackson Hole, Wyoming. Colter went to work for a trading firm on the Big Horn River in central Montana, where his trapping excursions brought him into contact with the Blackfeet and Flathead peoples. Since Colter left no specific record of his journeys and contacts, his possible associations with other area tribes remain a mystery. His involvement, however, in Flathead battles with the Blackfeet intimates an extended relationship with the former tribe that would have placed the trader in the path of the Schitsu'umsh during their annual buffalo hunt. Following dissemination of the information gathered by Lewis and Clark, the opportunity to meet independent traders like Colter greatly increased in the Intermountain and Pacific West.[41]

Even before Lewis and Clark completed their exploration, international fur trading enterprises had pierced the borders of the Inland Northwest. Formed through a partnership of Montreal traders in 1783, the North West Company sent traders westward in the early 1800s to locate untapped fur populations and enlarge existing trade networks. Nor'wester David Thompson explored the vast regions of British Columbia, northern Idaho, and Montana between 1809 and 1811, descending the Columbia River to its mouth in 1811. Thompson founded two fur trading posts near the Schitsu'umsh homeland: Kullyspell House in 1809 and Spokane House in 1810. The forts served as satellites for a British global trading system. Post operators sent furs procured from Native trappers at the forts to corporate headquarters, where they were conveyed overland through Canada to Montreal or shipped overseas. Ammunition, whiskey, tea, blankets, cooking pots, and knives served as bartering tools to entice Indian people to participate in the post trading system.

In addition to economic functions, the posts served social and military purposes. Spokane House boasted a ballroom where Native women danced with post employees. The administration of the self-sufficient posts—farms, blacksmiths, sawmills—brought diverse peoples to the Inland Northwest. Many North West Company employees were descended from French or had mixed French and Indian ancestry. The Nor'westers whom the Coeur d'Alenes met were often representatives from various Algonquian tribes—peoples who for many years had traded and intermarried with French and English traders in the Great Lakes region. Although economic cooperation between post employees and Natives made the fur trade possible, relations did not always remain peaceful. When Native resistance to trading practices or to white presence in the region threatened to mount, the posts functioned as safe havens for outsiders.[42]

Interactions between fur traders and the Schitsu'umsh shaped the physical and mental landscapes of the region. Nineteenth-century explorers and fur traders instituted new trade routes, popularized the name *Coeur d'Alene*, and mapped the area. The Schitsu'umsh acquired a reputation for shrewd trading practices, fierce territoriality, and hostility toward non-Indians. No fur trading posts were erected within the borders of the Schitsu'umsh homeland, leading contemporaries and historians alike to assume that the tribe disallowed the building of such establishments on its soil. One historian has argued that the tribe kept David Thompson from conducting trade on its land, leading the explorer to establish his trading post in Spokane territory in 1810.[43] Ross Cox, traveling in 1812 with an overland American trading party sponsored by John Jacob Astor, recorded in his journal that the Schitsu'umsh displayed an unfriendly attitude toward traders. Known as the "Astorians," the group represented Astor's attempt to establish a fur empire in the Pacific Northwest and to compete in the interior with the North West Company. The Astorians established Fort Spokane in 1812 to rival Thompson's Spokane House, but they remained unable to position a trading center within the boundaries of "the Pointed Hearts," even after sending their "hardiest" negotiators. Cox thought the tribe was "more savage" than surrounding peoples and noted their inclination to eat raw game.[44] The tribe may have actively courted the "savage" reputation to keep outsiders at bay.

The tribe's reputation during the fur trade fueled the evolution of the term *Coeur d'Alene* and created a new identity for the group. The first recorded instance of the term *Pointed Hearts*, a loose English translation of Coeur d'Alene, appears in Albert Thompson's 1809 journal entries as a reference to Schitsu'umsh traders. The term can also be translated as "Heart of Awl," or "Pointed Heart." Thompson may have absorbed the term from French Canadian traders familiar with the Schitsu'umsh, but the name stuck and spread throughout the fur trading community, as evidenced by Cox's use of "Pointed Hearts." By the 1820s the Hudson's Bay Company, which absorbed the North West Company in 1821, was using the French form, "Coeur d'Alene," to refer to the three interrelated bands of Native people living on or around "Coeur d'Alene Lake."⁴⁵ Rumor spread among traders that the name originated from a confrontation between a Schitsu'umsh chief and a local trader. According to the legend, the French Canadian trapper became so exasperated with the chief's inflexible and stingy bargaining habits that he accused the tribal member of having "a heart like an awl's point."⁴⁶ No matter its specific origins, the name resulted from Schitsu'umsh contact with outsiders and in that context represents the tribe's resistance to outside interference.

The Schitsu'umsh ability to maintain distance between themselves and traders translated into few marriages between tribal women and outsiders, a common occurrence in most post locations. "The Coeur d'Alenes had more respect for their women [than other tribes]," Joseph Seltice wrote, "and never let them be taken in such a way."⁴⁷ Still, the Schitsu'umsh participated in the fur trade and in so doing etched new patterns of migration and trade on the landscape. Thompson, who also referred to the tribe as the "Skeetshoo Indians," noted on several occasions that they brought goods to Kullyspell House to trade. On September 9, 1809, Thompson noted that "at 2 PM, thank God, we arrived all well at the Saleesh River [now Clark's Fork River]; here we were met by fifty four Saleesh Indians, Twenty Three Skeetshoo; and four Kootenae Indians, in all eighty men, and their families; they made us an acceptable present of dried Salmon and other Fish, with Berries, and the meat of an Antelope."⁴⁸ On October 6, 1809, Thompson recorded the arrival of "forty four Skeetshoo Indians," who "traded near two hundred pounds weight of Furrs, and three Horses."⁴⁹

The "Coeur d'Alene" identity as a shrewd, territorial people—one created by both nonwhites and Native participants in the fur trade—was graphically reproduced on maps. In addition to being a fur trader, David Thompson was a map maker. Indeed, one reason Thompson left the prestigious Hudson's Bay Company for its rival, the North West Company, was to pursue his exploratory and mapping activities.⁵⁰ Thompson's surveys of what is now northern Idaho and his application of place names permanently influenced the cartography and mapping of the region. Thompson's "discoveries" were absorbed by cartographers, particularly Aaron Arrowsmith, who produced British maps between 1811 and 1814. Arrowsmith's 1811 map was a reproduction of several earlier editions; the Interior Northwest had remained unchanged since 1795. Schitsu'umsh country appeared at the confluence of two rivers; none of the modern tribal names appeared. References to the "Long Hair Nation" and the "Blue Mud Nation" are the only tribal identifications. A lake, possibly Lake Coeur d'Alene, is shown with a line extending to what is now the Snake and Columbia river system; the line is marked with the notation "the Indians say they sleep 8 Nights in descending this River to the Sea."⁵¹

The publication of the same map in 1814 revealed dramatic revision. The entire Interior Pacific Northwest had been filled in, including extensive detail concerning tribal people, land forms, and waterways. "Pointed Hearts Lake" appears, with one unnamed river leading into it on the east and one unnamed river leading from it on the west (now Coeur d'Alene River and Spokane River, respectively); the map also includes a "Pointed Hearts Knoll." The "Spogan" nation, now the Spokane, appears, as does the Choppunnish (Nez Perce) nation. The Schitsu'umsh are represented as the "Sin-nith-koo-mah-na" Indians; their placement on the map indicates their occupation of the lands adjoining Pointed Hearts Lake.[52]

As trade and geographic knowledge of the Interior Pacific Northwest increased, so did the penetration of new businesses. As the nineteenth century advanced, emergent "mountain" trade networks in the Rockies sandwiched the Schitsu'umsh between the old corporate posts on the west and new, competing trade interests on the east. Descended from the independent tradition of trader-explorers like John Colter, American mountain trading firms entered Flathead and Nez Perce territories in the early 1830s. Offering goods in return for beaver and other small animal pelts, two companies—the American Fur Trading Company and the Rocky Mountain Fur Trading Company—vied furiously for Native participation. The mountain fur trade utilized a "rendezvous system" rather than the more formal "post system" favored by corporations like the North West Company and its successor, the Hudson's Bay Company. Instead of using a permanent self-sufficient post as a distribution center for goods and pelts, the rendezvous system employed individual trappers who met at prearranged gatherings in the summer to trade skins for goods. The rendezvous meetings became notorious for raucous behavior and were often attended by Indian and non-Indian traders alike. The Coeur d'Alenes sold pelts of beaver, muskrat, otter, and mink to temporary mountain company posts in Flathead country and to individual brigade members during their trips to and from the buffalo hunting grounds.[53]

The fur trade interfered with the balance of power on the Plateau and the Plains and shifted relations among Indian nations. Schitsu'umsh participation in the buffalo hunts and the fur trade drew them into conflict with other tribes, particularly the Blackfeet of Montana. The Blackfeet resented the presence of western tribes in buffalo country and warred with their neighbors, the Flatheads, over hunting territories after the fur trade entered the region. The new trade routes carved into the landscape were fiercely guarded by all trading groups. The Schitsu'umsh fought with the Flatheads in battles against the Blackfeet, and at times the Blackfeet crossed over the mountains into Schitsu'umsh territory to challenge the tribe's warriors. Many western participants in the buffalo hunt—including the Shoshone-Bannock, Kutenai, and Nez Perce—joined together in territorial skirmishes with the Blackfeet.[54]

The last of the battles involving the Schitsu'umsh, according to the oral account of Father Brown, a Blackfeet descendant who served at DeSmet Mission in the 1950s, occurred on Grizzly Mountain sometime prior to the arrival of Christian missionaries in the region. Blackfeet interest in the post trade, for which the tribe was geographically disadvantaged, resulted in peace with the Schitsu'umsh. The Blackfeet had discovered that their warring tendencies kept them from full participation in the trade. Trade routes crossed intertribal boundaries, from which the distrusted Blackfeet were barred. Tribal tradition maintains that the eastern tribe sent women into Coeur d'Alene country to intermarry, resulting in blood ties that allowed a peaceful relationship to evolve and stimulated cooperation between hunting and trading parties. Coeur d'Alene legend includes a story about Magdeline, the sixteen-year-old daughter of a Blackfeet warrior who was sent by her father to cross the Bitterroot Mountains and marry a Coeur d'Alene man. Traveling alone and avoiding ferocious wolves and a tenacious grizzly, Magdeline successfully crossed the mountains and cemented peaceful relations.[55]

The Schitsu'umsh also experienced conflict with Northwest tribes, including their closest neighbors, the Spokanes and the Nez Perce. Tribal participation in the fur trade added value to prized hunting locations just as area fur-bearing populations diminished. Spokane tribal member Ignace Camille told Stuart Chalfant in 1951 that he remembered that his grandfather had discussed a peace pact effected between the Coeur d'Alenes and the Spokanes. Instigated sometime during the eighteenth century and negotiated at the confluence of the Little Spokane and Spokane rivers, the agreement ended a controversy over choice hunting and fishing areas.[56] Violent disagreements with the Nez Perce, the Coeur d'Alenes' powerful neighbor to the south, ignited sporadically throughout the centuries. Although intermarriage with the Nez Perce was not unknown, relations between the tribes were often strained. Conflict with their southern neighbor over territory and long-term rivalries intensified as the Coeur d'Alenes exercised greater mobility.[57]

Wars with surrounding tribes necessitated Coeur d'Alene access to firearms and contributed to the development of a more powerful tribal chieftainship. To acquire guns the Coeur d'Alenes continued to participate in the fur trade, even as that involvement contributed to the development of conflict with other tribes—thus creating a circle of interdependent relationships. Because of their relative isolation, the Coeur d'Alenes were one of the last Columbia Plateau groups to obtain firearms. The Kalispel, Colville, and Okanogan tribes all used ammunition prior to the Schitsu'umsh. Widespread use of firearms among the latter group did not occur until the 1830s, and many tribal members continued to use bows and arrows until the mid-nineteenth century.[58]

In turn, intertribal warfare and intricate dealings with fur traders demanded a higher degree of tribal organization. Although tribal succession during the pre-Jesuit period remains cloudy, evidence points to a centralization of political authority. When Vincent, also known as Bassa, became chief during the 1840s, the position acquired new significance as a permanent voice for Coeur d'Alene tribal matters. Rather than an intermittent, emergency-oriented position, Vincent's chieftainship was a full-time post. Indeed, Vincent's predecessor, Stellam, or Twisted Earth, had a son who refused to occupy the position because he "favored the life of freedom over the life of command."[59] Exposure to Plains tribes' more formal political organization during annual trips to the east contributed to Coeur d'Alene acceptance of a tribal chief. The migration of extended families to buffalo country and long-term absences from home demanded new survival skills—many of which the Coeur d'Alenes borrowed from Plains cultures. While engaged in the buffalo hunts, the tribe traveled in military fashion, used a specialized task system including scouts, and camped in a protective circular formation. Inevitably, strong leaders emerged during administration of the bison hunting parties.[60]

In addition to goods, trade introduced disease and farming techniques to Native peoples in the Columbia Basin. The Schitsu'umsh kept trading posts out of their country, but they could not do the same with the alien diseases carried by outsiders. The sicknesses crippled all Columbia Plateau tribes. Smallpox, measles, fever, and dysentery ravaged the Schitsu'umsh, traveling swiftly from village to village and wiping out entire families. The extent of illness inhibited the tribe's ability to care for the sick, further contributing to the spread of disease. Epidemics had reduced the Coeur d'Alene population to about 500 by 1850.[61] At the same time European pathogens ravaged the Schitsu'umsh population, the tribe instituted new agricultural practices. German botanist Charles A. Geyer, who visited the Plateau region during 1842–1844, noted that the Schitsu'umsh were successfully cultivating English white potatoes along the Coeur d'Alene River. He surmised that they had procured the potato from Hudson's Bay Company traders, probably at Fort Spokane, at least a decade earlier.[62] Potato cultivation may have increased the economic authority of women, who were likely responsible for planting and harvesting.

The Schitsu'umsh tradition of prophecy enabled tribal members to cope with the changes wrought by travel, trade, warfare, and disease. Prophetic visions played an important role in the people's daily lives. Adolescent tribal members pursued visions to aid them in decisions of adulthood. The visionary tradition of Circling Raven, who served as chief perhaps as early as 1760, gave the tribe hope in the midst of transition and death.[63] When ravens circled Coeur d'Alene encampments, Circling Raven interpreted their messages or warnings to the tribe. The chief's prophecies included the coming of "the Black Robe," a figure who would offer the tribe salvation from its enemies and from the suffering of life. The prophecy, foretold in about 1740, became part of Coeur d'Alene oral tradition as it passed down through the generations. In the 1830s Circling Raven's son, Stellam, who was in his nineties, continued the traditional search for the Black Robe.[64]

From Circling Raven to Twisted Earth, the Schi̱tsu'umsh landscape continued to provide the sustenance that many generations had enjoyed. The tribe's relationship to the landscape also underwent change. During a 100-year period (1740–1840) the Schi̱tsu'umsh people embraced the horse and its accompanying culture, participated in the fur trade while keeping trading posts off their lands, engaged in intertribal warfare, and dealt with the onslaught of crippling diseases. In their dealings with outsiders, they participated in the creation of a new identity as "Coeur d'Alenes," people with shrewd trading practices. Their responses to change mapped new patterns on the landscape: the Schi̱tsu'umsh adopted Plains hunting practices, acquired firearms, utilized new fur trading routes, and protected their homeland by recognizing the authority of a single tribal leader. Still, the Schi̱tsu'umsh continued their aboriginal subsistence practices and maintained their villages along Lake Coeur d'Alene and the Coeur d'Alene, St. Joe, and Spokane rivers. With the fulfillment of prophecy at mid-century, however, the tribe would undergo a more dramatic social, economic, and political transformation.

TWO

CROSSES OF STEEL:
JESUIT MISSIONARY FOUNDINGS,
1840–1855

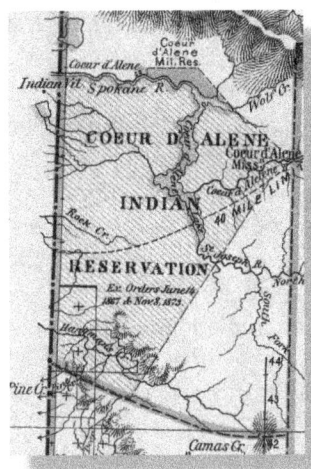

> My father looked for you for a long time. Many times he searched the entire Bitterroot Valley, and many times he went beyond the divide. Finally at an old age, he asked me to continue the search for the Black Robe. It has been fully a hundred years since my father first sang the prophecy songs of the "coming of the Black Robe."
> —CHIEF STELLAM (TWISTED EARTH), 1842[1]

IN SEPTEMBER 1841 THE FIRST WAGONS TO CROSS WHAT IS NOW western Montana entered the Bitterroot Valley of the Flathead Indian people, the Coeur d'Alenes' closest eastern neighbor and host of the annual buffalo hunts. The pack train carried four Jesuit missionaries under the direction of Father Peter John De Smet, a Belgian priest recently appointed superior of the Jesuits' new Rocky Mountain missionary effort. Weary from a journey that had begun months earlier in St. Louis, Missouri, the Jesuits arrived with wagons filled with Bibles, musical instruments, and a desire to bring Catholic Christianity to the "poor savages" of Oregon country. The appearance of this missionary ensemble heralded a new era of Indian-outsider relations in the Inland Pacific Northwest.

For the Schitsu'umsh, the arrival of Jesuit missionaries would ultimately mean a conversion to the farming life, a religious divide between those who practiced traditional spirituality and those who chose to become full adherents in the Catholic mission, and a decline in authority for some Schitsu'umsh—including women and those who did not follow the mission's teachings. The conversion to agriculture was never complete; neither was the dichotomy between those who practiced Catholicism and those who did not. Particularly during the first three decades of the mission, Schitsu'umsh farmers continued to hunt and fish, and Catholic Schitsu'umsh maintained their traditional spiritual practices.

More dramatic was the shift in tribal views regarding protection of the homeland. Prior to the arrival of Jesuit missionaries, the tribe had jealously guarded its territory by maintaining its isolation and consolidating tribal authority. The Jesuit vision of tidy Coeur d'Alene farms and orderly Catholic villages introduced the Schitsu'umsh leadership to the assimilation model for preserving tribal land and provided tribal leaders with a legalistic perspective useful in their dealings with non-Indians. U.S. law, the Jesuits explained, required that written promises be upheld by both sides. Tribal leaders eventually saw this as a way to preserve territory and tribal sovereignty. The Jesuits, of course, viewed assimilation not as a "tool" but as a desired end. The introduction of the notion of assimilation during the 1840s provided the means by which the tribe would, decades later, institute an assimilation policy that highlighted and created tribal divisions.

The Jesuit priests who came to Schitsu'umsh country brought the benefit of extensive European learning. These men were members of the educated upper classes in Europe, and although they spoke a number of European languages, they did not all speak English fluently. As members of the European elite, they had as little in common with ordinary American citizens living in frontier conditions as they did with their Native "charges." Nicolas Point studied in France, Switzerland, Spain, and the United States before founding St. Charles College in Louisiana. Joseph Joset possessed a strong academic background and taught at the College of Fribourg, Switzerland, prior to his appointment in the Rocky Mountain Mission. Father Nicholas Congiato, appointed superior of the Oregon and California missions in 1854, had served as vice president of the College of Nobles, Naples, Italy; vice president of the College of Fribourg; and president of a Jesuit college in Bardstown, Kentucky, before working in the Northwest missions. Other Jesuits who served in the Oregon missions had, among them, taught at four European institutions of higher learning and studied at eleven others, including the University of Paris. Their academic expertise ranged from theology to mathematics.[2]

The Jesuits also carried a tradition of institutional patriarchy. The Jesuits' rigid hierarchy rested with a superior general, elected for life, who served in Rome and reported directly to the pope. Provincial superiors and superiors of local residences reported up through the ranks. Founded by Ignatius Loyola in 1540, the Institution of the Society of Jesus "joined to the mystique of the monk the parallel mystique of the Renaissance knight."[3] Like other Catholic priesthood orders, the Jesuits maintained vows of celibacy and welcomed only men into their ranks. The rigidity of the Jesuit leadership structure and its complex decision-making hierarchy contrasted sharply with the Schitsu'umsh tradition of consensus building.[4]

The advance of Jesuit missionaries into Oregon country stemmed from the resurrection of the Jesuit Order by the pope in 1814. The Jesuit Order had been suppressed in 1773, and the study houses, universities, and libraries of the then 23,000 Jesuits were taken over by Catholic bishops or national governments or were allowed to fall into disrepair and disuse. The restored order was smaller, with fewer resources, and many Jesuits had immigrated to the United States to avoid the Italian and French revolutions. In 1830 Jesuit missions in the United States received formal authorization under the direction of the newly created Missouri Vice Province. Eighty Jesuit priests served in the Missouri Vice Province in 1841. In spite of the small number working in U.S. missions, Protestant competition for Oregon souls enabled De Smet to put his plans for a "mountain" mission in motion.[5] As stated by Jesuit priest and anthropologist Ted Fortier, the "Jesuits' goal in the Rockies was the crowning glory of their previous endeavors."[6]

The Jesuits were late arrivals on the religious frontier in the Pacific Northwest. Missionary activity in the region exploded after four Northwestern tribal members (three Nez Perce and one Flathead) arrived in St. Louis in 1831, seeking William Clark—famous among tribes since the Lewis and Clark Expedition and now superintendent of Indian Affairs. Since it had no adequate interpreter, the intent of the St. Louis Indian delegation remains unclear, but religious groups perceived it as a call for Christian baptism and teaching. Two other delegations—one in 1835 and one in 1839—also reached St. Louis and were perceived as requests for Christian religion. Protestant organizations responded by quickly establishing mission sites in the Pacific Northwest. Jason Lee founded a Methodist mission in the Willamette Valley in 1834. In 1836 the American Board of Commissioners for Foreign Missions sponsored the missionary efforts of Marcus and Narcissa Whitman and Henry and Eliza Spalding. The Whitmans located among the Cayuse people on the Walla Walla River. The Spaldings, believing they were finally answering "the call" of the St. Louis delegation, settled at Lapwai with the Nez Perce tribe, thirty-five miles south of Coeur d'Alene country. In 1838 the American Board of Commissioners added the Spokane tribe to its system of Protestant missions with the establishment of a site north of the Spokane River, approximately forty miles west of Lake Coeur d'Alene.[7]

The Protestant presence did nothing to dampen the resolve of the Jesuit fathers, for they believed their work with the tribes of the Rocky Mountains and the Pacific plateaus carried special spiritual significance. In the Jesuit view, the 1831 St. Louis delegation approached Clark with a request not only for Christian religion but for *Roman Catholic* Christian teaching. According to Jesuit histories, delegation members asked specifically for the "Black Robes" and the "book"—clear references to the attire worn by members of the Jesuit order and the texts of that learned society. Communicating only with hand signs, the delegation representatives may have been seeking salvation of a different sort—white medicine to combat new diseases or weapons to fight the persistent Blackfeet threat, for example. Regardless of its purpose, the journey led to the demise of the four Nez Perce and Flathead tribal members. Trail-weakened, two of the travelers died in St. Louis. The remaining delegation members started for home but failed to return to their villages, struck down by disease and enemy ambushes along the way.[8]

The Indian superintendency's inability to fully communicate with tribal delegations limited communication between missionary activity and the groups who had supposedly requested spiritual guidance. Tribes in the Northwest sought the guidance of missionaries but not for the reasons the men with the Bibles believed. The devastation of European diseases coupled with increased intertribal warfare in the first half of the nineteenth century caused Northwest tribal peoples to look beyond their boundaries for answers. Competition for buffalo hunting grounds between the Flatheads and western tribes—the Coeur d'Alene, Palouse, Spokane, Nez Perce, Kalispel, and Columbia peoples—led to war with the Blackfeet and the deaths of male warriors. Believing the Black Robes possessed "strong medicine" that could aid the tribe against its foes, the Flathead people welcomed Father De Smet and his colleagues with loads of buffalo meat. The Jesuits named their newly formed mission St. Mary of the Rocky Mountains.[9]

De Smet's dream of establishing successful Jesuit missions in the Interior Pacific Northwest followed the Paraguay reduction plan of the seventeenth and eighteenth centuries. Jesuit missions to the Guarani Indians of Paraguay used a central location, or "reduction," to attract Native peoples from different tribal groups and to convince bands within tribes to join together. The Jesuits introduced agriculture and livestock to encourage self-sufficiency within reductions, but tribal people continued to practice aspects of their subsistence culture, such as gathering plants and hunting game. During this process the missionaries introduced Christian teaching and baptism. The Paraguay reductions proved most successful in regions isolated from contact with other influences, such as European settlement, and eventually Jesuit law forbade foreigners to enter the reductions. At the pinnacle of their success in the 1730s, the Paraguayan reductions included thirty-one independent settlements with a total population of more than 140,000. The successes and failures of the Paraguay missions became part of the Jesuit archives, passed down among Jesuit scholars as a model for proselytizing activity.[10]

At campfires along the route from St. Louis to Montana, the Jesuit fathers studied Luigi A. Muratori's work *A Relation of the Missions of Paraguay*. De Smet thought of Muratori's treatise as the vade mecum, a reference manual for the establishment of missions in the Pacific Northwest. Muratori's information served as the basis for the design of the Rocky Mountain Mission, which was to be a "New Paraguay." Father Nicolas Point, De Smet's assistant and an artist, created graphite and ink renderings of the Jesuits' vision. His work provided graphic evidence of the Jesuits' goals, as well as a documentary of Native life in the missions. His drawing of the "Plan du Village des Coeurs-d'alenes," probably completed in 1842 as a blueprint for the mission, showed neat rows of houses and fields facing a cross-shaped mission. Point's work mapped the ordered, pastoral missionary village envisioned by the missionaries. The location of the church reminded reduction residents of the centrality of God in the mission effort. The tidiness of the reduction program encompassed more than the planning of each individual town, since the Paraguay experiment relied on the creation of a "chain" of semi-independent reductions. Isolated from outside influences, a rudimentary system of communication, trade, and protection reinforced the links in the mission chain.[11]

In anticipation of the establishment of a series of Northwest reductions, De Smet attempted to contact other regional tribes. In early 1842 the pioneering priest traveled to Fort Vancouver to meet with Catholic missionary vanguards Francis Blanchet and Modeste Demers. After discussing the future of the non-Jesuit Catholic effort in the Pacific Northwest and obtaining supplies for his fledgling Salish mission, De Smet returned to Montana, stopping along the way to meet with various tribal members en route to spring and summer gathering places. While passing through the Spokane Valley, west of the Coeur d'Alene homeland, De Smet encountered three Coeur d'Alene scouts. The men—No Hand, Polatkin, and Stellam—escorted the Black Robe to Coeur d'Alene chief Twisted Earth's lodge at the headwaters of the Spokane River. There, on the site of the largest nineteenth-century Coeur d'Alene village, the chief and the priest held a meeting. Because the two did not speak a common language, the details of this encounter remain clouded in tradition. Coeur d'Alene tribal oral tradition maintains that Twisted Earth, an elderly man of 104 years, spoke of the Coeur d'Alene Black Robe prophecy. "My Father looked for you for a long time," the legendary Twisted Earth told De Smet. "It has been fully [one] hundred years since my father first sang the prophecy songs of the 'coming of the Black Robe.' . . . Today that prophecy has been fulfilled." In response, De Smet spoke to the small gathering about "salvation" and promised to send Jesuit missionaries to the Coeur d'Alenes.[12]

The Coeur d'Alenes represented a promising opportunity to De Smet. The main requirements of the reduction model—isolation, potential for agrarian self-sufficiency, limited contact with outsiders—certainly fit the Schitsu'umsh tribe. The group had been notoriously wary of non-Indians, participating in the fur trade but resisting the erection of a post within tribal boundaries. In 1840 the Coeur d'Alenes had come into contact with few white settlers; the settlement influx did not occur in the Interior Pacific Northwest until the 1870s. The Coeur d'Alene homeland encompassed extensive waterways, timber resources, and expansive valleys of fertile land. Tribal members already obtained much of their subsistence from locations close to their permanent villages. And the Schitsu'umsh homeland was located in the center of the rectangular area encompassing the proposed Rocky Mountain reductions.[13]

Following his meeting with Chief Twisted Earth, De Smet journeyed to St. Mary's and instructed Nicolas Point and Charles Huet to start a mission among the Schitsu'umsh. Obligations in St. Louis prevented De Smet from ministering to the tribe himself. Point and Huet, accompanied by several Coeur d'Alene guides, crossed over the mountains in October 1842, descending into the Coeur d'Alene Valley on the first Friday of November—a Catholic day of devotion. In honor of the day's holiness, the Jesuits christened the site "Mission of the Sacred Heart." Of his first glimpse of Coeur d'Alene country, Point wrote in his journal: "What profound misery reigned among these people! What poor huts of straw and bark!" Point located the mission on the banks of the St. Joe River, a site "from which we could behold all the beauties and advantages of this area," and under the jurisdiction of a chief named Gabriel.[14]

While Point and Huet surveyed their new mission site, tribal members summoned the chief of the "Grand Lake," or Lake Coeur d'Alene. At this time, apparently, the chieftain located at the lake village exercised dominance over the other subchiefs. When "grand chief" Twisted Earth, whom Point called "Stellam," arrived, he evidenced jealousy toward the mission's location. "For several reasons he was jealous of the chief whose territory we had just visited," Point observed of Twisted Earth, "but most of all because the conduct of the latter was a living reproach to his own, which was anything but ordered." Despite the priest's low opinion of the chief, Point agreed to spend the winter with Twisted Earth, since "the territory of Gabriel would not immediately furnish subsistence to all of us." One month after consecrating the mission, Point celebrated the first Friday of December, during which he reported that each Coeur d'Alene individual approached a symbol of Jesus erected upon a tree and stated, "Jesus, I give you my heart." From that time on, Point wrote, gambling ceased, and the "noisy invocations of the manitous gave way to the cult of true prayer." Point exaggerated the mission's success, for either his own reassurance or that of his superiors, but at least some Schitsu'umsh clearly wanted Point to believe in their acceptance. Indeed, Jesuit records report that the Coeur d'Alene Mission enjoyed a 100 percent conversion rate.[15]

From the beginning, enough Coeur d'Alene tribal people supported the small Jesuit mission to justify its existence. Vastly outnumbered even by the disease-reduced Schitsu'umsh population of 500, the Jesuits would not have been able to maintain their residency if a majority of the tribe had opposed their presence. The existence of the Black Robe prophecy has been advanced to explain tribal receptiveness, but it is not clear when the prophecy account actually emerged.[16] The Joseph Seltice family history emphasizes the significance of the Black Robe prophecy, but that account must be evaluated in light of its strong pro-Catholic position. Certainly, some Schitsu'umsh people welcomed Jesuit missionary activity for reasons other than the power of prophecy. The Coeur d'Alenes, because of their trade and hunting relationship with the Salish people, knew of the Jesuit work among the Flatheads. The Jesuits represented a source of the white man's respected "killing power." Many tribal members believed the Jesuit fathers possessed a potent medicine that brought success in war and in the hunt. Flathead success in skirmishes and horse stealing against the Blackfeet following the advent of St. Mary's Mission seemed to ratify this view. Flathead accomplishments captured the attention of surrounding tribes, particularly as De Smet attributed Salish victories to the power of the Christian deity. The Columbia people of present-day central Washington, participants in the buffalo hunt, hoped the Jesuit fathers would instill peace among the feared Blackfeet. By 1846 even members of the Blackfeet tribe had come to believe the Black Robe religion carried a forceful spiritual element onto the battlefield.[17]

The nature of Catholicism also contributed to its acceptability. Unlike the Protestant missionary settlements among the Cayuse and Nez Perce peoples, the Jesuit fathers introduced Catholic ritual, songs, devotional chants, sacred calendar days and colors, and the use of water and incense to transcend the material realm. These elements, coupled with "victory medicine," appealed to the Coeur d'Alene tribal sense of purpose and view of spirituality.[18] As Jesuit priest and anthropologist Ted Fortier has argued, the Schitsu'umsh and the Jesuits shared a worldview in which certain individuals—shamans or priests—possessed unique spiritual gifts, including the art of healing.[19] For the Schitsu'umsh, the Jesuits represented a *new* source of medicine power, not a replacement for the old. Although the Jesuits acknowledged that Schitsu'umsh medicine possessed real power, they viewed it as "Satanic" and an affront to the "Divine Majesty." Jesuit theology insisted that power was divine only if it "came directly from God through angels, saints, or sacraments."[20] But many, if not most, Coeur d'Alene tribal members viewed Jesuit religion in the context of their traditional activities, such as hunting, trade, and territorial war. Indeed, in the prophecy story Circling Raven experiences his vision of the Black Robes while en route from a buffalo hunt and shortly after a confrontation with members of the Blackfeet tribe.

The Jesuit-Schitsu'umsh relationship evolved in a symbiotic manner. During the early missionary period, the Jesuits' vulnerability required that they refrain from the harsh tactics they would employ later in the century. Still, the mission rejected specific traditional religious practices like medicine bundles; forced a new, more rigid marriage contract; forbade polygamy and gambling; and burned ceremonial materials and dance regalia. Tribal members accommodated the Jesuits in some ways—particularly by adopting agriculture and the ceremonies associated with Catholicism—but quietly and invisibly rejected the priests' imposition into social and cultural practices. Resistance came in small gestures—maintaining medicine bundles or employing traditional dances—but accommodation often came in areas under direct control of the mission, such as church-sanctioned marriage.

The Schitsu'umsh slowly abandoned their traditional marriage practice—which had been characterized by mutual consent and relative ease of divorce—and adopted the Christian model of monogamous, contract union. The new Catholic contracts disadvantaged women, who could no longer easily extricate themselves from an abusive or despairing marriage. Under Catholic law, men held most of the rights in the marriage contract. Wives were to "obey," husbands to "provide" and "protect." In this model women also lost authority in the area of family and tribal economics. Where they had once tended the children in an extended community of other women and relatives, controlled the family lodging, and gathered a significant percentage of the community's dietary requirements, the new teachings reduced their influence to child rearing and limited the significance of the extended family. Catholic marriage and notions of European property ownership eroded the traditional female position in Schitsu'umsh society, but finding the Schitsu'umsh women's voice is difficult. The patriarchal Jesuits largely ignored women, government documents exclude women's influence, and the erosion of women's traditional authority is tied to the controversial role of the Catholic Church in the lives of the Coeur d'Alene people—many of whom remain devout Catholics to this day.[21]

The Jesuit introduction of European agriculture, farm implements, weapons, centralized political hierarchy, Catholic marriage, and western European concepts of property ownership contributed to the formation of a pre-government society based on the interplay of traditional Schitsu'umsh practices and Catholic culture. This transitory world—from about 1840 to 1855—was characterized by a continuation of relative isolation, the side-by-side coexistence of agriculture and migratory subsistence patterns, increased territoriality, and solidification of the Coeur d'Alene leadership structure. The process by which the Jesuits built mission churches on Coeur d'Alene lands illustrated the isolation of the tribe and the evolution of tribal acceptance.

Point spent the first winter with the most populous Coeur d'Alene band, located on the north shore of Lake Coeur d'Alene. The Black Robe celebrated Christmas Mass in 1842 with the Schitsu'umsh, evidenced by his watercolor drawing showing an evergreen-festooned altar in a small log cabin with a mat floor. Alternately sketching, painting, and preaching, Point planned his Coeur d'Alene "reduction" during the winter he spent with Stellam's people. With the arrival of spring, Point returned to the St. Joe River site he had chosen several months earlier, five miles from the present-day town of St. Maries. Brother Huet constructed a low-lying log hut packed with moss to serve as a chapel. By 1844, the Jesuits reported, 100 Coeur d'Alene families resided at the missionary village.[22]

Despite growing residency at the mission, these early years were marked by tribal ambivalence. Nicolas Point was considered a difficult man even by his Jesuit peers. Chief Twisted Earth disliked Point's patronizing manner and righteous views, and he taunted the priest by demanding, according to Point, "all the powder and tobacco we had" in return for the chief's protection. Traditional medicine men distrusted the Jesuit priest, and some tribal members remained distant, even antagonistic. Jesuit rejection of polygamy and gambling angered and alienated some tribal people. Women, who had held the powerful position of shaman, lost that vehicle of authority as the Jesuits worked to discredit traditional medicine. Anthropologist Rodney Frey found that the tribe's oral history of the early missionary period reflected division and subtle resistance. Some families secretly stashed their medicine bundles; many "went underground" with their spiritual practices. Stellam's group emerged as an opponent of the mission and a thorn in Point's side, whose biographer states that the missionary became obsessed by a personal vendetta against the subchief.[23] Problems with the St. Joe River site compounded Point's frustration. Annual spring runoff flooded the site, leaving mission buildings and fields under several feet of water. Lake Coeur d'Alene's waters backed up onto mission grounds, and mud made roads impassable and spring planting impossible. Capitalizing on the prevalence of standing water, mosquitos swarmed the site throughout the summer months, forcing Huet to take to his bed with "fever."[24]

The Jesuits capitulated to nature in 1846 when they moved the mission twenty miles northeast to a high knoll overlooking the Coeur d'Alene River.[25] De Smet dispatched Father Joseph Joset, a new arrival to the Rocky Mountain Mission, to assist with the relocation. The new site solidified the relationship between the Coeur d'Alene people and the Jesuits. Joset's arrival signified the beginning of a period known by Jesuit historians as the "golden age" of the Sacred Heart Mission. Concurrently, Nicolas Point, disenchanted with his stay among the Coeur d'Alenes and burdened with health problems, left the mission to await his requested transfer to the Brazilian missions. Point's emphasis on the ordered reduction did not afford him the luxury of flexibility in dealing with uncooperative weather, environment, or "neophytes." Joset, on the other hand, served as a stabilizing influence for the mission's new surroundings. Appointed general superior of the Rocky Mountain missions in 1845, Joset came to Sacred Heart Mission to make it his administrative headquarters. Perhaps because of his greater flexibility or his personality, most tribal members approved of Joset. With Point's departure and the new mission site, the opposition of the "Stellam faction" weakened. Indeed, Chief Stellam, or Twisted Earth, declared repentance and pledged allegiance to Catholicism after the mission's relocation. The construction of the Cataldo Church provided the cornerstone for this gilded period of cooperation between the Coeur d'Alene people and the Black Robes.[26]

Despite the required denunciation of polygamy and gambling, Jesuit histories report that during these early years between 75 and 100 percent of the Coeur d'Alene people accepted the Catholic faith. Whether the 75 percent denotes the number of Schitsu'umsh who converted after being introduced to

Catholicism or an actual percentage of the entire tribe's population remains unclear. At any rate, the Jesuit fathers believed the mission needed a church befitting its faithful. Located 240 miles from St. Mary's Mission in Flathead country, the isolation of Sacred Heart Mission made construction of a large edifice particularly difficult. Beginning in summer of 1846 several Schi̱tsu'umsh men, under the direction of Joset, began cutting lumber for a church using a hand-operated sawmill.

In 1848 Anthony Ravalli joined the Jesuit employ at Sacred Heart Mission. A talented architect, Ravalli produced plans for a large Roman Doric church, 90 feet long and 25 feet high. Coeur d'Alene tribal members carried the entire responsibility for preparation of building materials and construction of the church. Remarkably, workers dug over "3,000 square feet" of foundation stones from a nearby hillside, transporting them with a block-wheeled cart for half a mile to the building site. Large frame timbers traveled by hand cart for over a mile, and tribal members gathered clay for mortar and fiber for rope. By 1848 the foundation cornerstone had taken its place, and by July 1853 the massive project had advanced to completion. Ravalli carved wooden statues to adorn the walls, and Francis Huybrechts, a Jesuit brother, created seventeen bas-relief panels for the walls and ceiling. The finished structure boasted six heavy columns in the Greek Revival style, capped with a facade created according to the architectural principle developed by Pythagoras and known as the "Golden Section."[27]

Approximately 320 Coeur d'Alene people accomplished the work and did so without pay. How much coercion the Jesuits exercised in harnessing this labor is not clear. All the missionaries could afford to offer, Joset later wrote, "was once a day, a portion of mush; and a very poor thing it was: wheat crushed at the horsemill of the mission and boiled with water." Joset later expressed astonishment at the church's successful completion. "Two things, I must confess," he wrote, "pass my comprehension: first the daring of R. F. Ravalli, to undertake such a thing with such means and such hands: these [I]ndians had never even witnessed the raising of the smallest frame. Second," Joset continued, "the success without anybody being hurt."[28]

To the clerics, the completion of Cataldo Church appeared nothing less than a miracle, a sign of God's approval of Jesuit work among the Coeur d'Alenes. Indeed, the church quickly became a symbol of Catholic missionary work throughout the Interior Northwest and "the St. Peter's Basilica for tribes of the interior," as Jesuit historian Wilfred Schoenberg has called it. Representing the only permanent non-Indian settlement in the vicinity, the church and mission acquired para-political status as a source of law, order, supplies, and moral guidance. Perhaps more remarkable than their political and religious influence, the Jesuits' ability to obtain the Schi̱tsu'umsh Tribe's approval and aid in the construction contrast starkly with contemporaneous mission relations in surrounding areas.[29]

The Marcus and Narcissa Whitman effort at Waiilatpu became the site of the ultimate Native disaffection during these years. Never very successful in claiming converts, the mission became a major stopping-off point along the Oregon Trail. Wagon trains en route to the Willamette Valley stopped there to rest their animals and procure desperately needed supplies. Waiilatpu provided more than supplies to those illness, destitution, or inclement weather kept from finishing their journey. In 1844 the Whitmans adopted seven children, orphaned on the trail west; in 1846 six families and eight single men wintered at the mission; in 1847 Whitman allowed fifty-four emigrants to take up winter residency. Narcissa Whitman spent most of her time cooking and caring for overland emigrants, not "civilizing" the Cayuse. As historian Patricia Nelson Limerick has written, Marcus Whitman not only allowed the mission to be used as a settlers' way station, he welcomed the opportunity to help those who yearned to occupy and cultivate Indian land. The Cayuse, who resented the imposition of agriculture and property ownership upon their culture, became increasingly incensed with the presence of white "invaders" on mission lands. A measles epidemic swept the mission in 1847, killing many tribal members—who possessed no natural immunities to the disease—and sparing most whites. This unhappy set of circumstances created an environment ripe for cultural conflict. In November 1847 a small band of angry Cayuse men murdered Marcus and Narcissa Whitman and twelve other white mission residents.[30]

Although less extreme than the violent encounter at the Whitman Mission, American board missionaries Elkanah and Mary Walker and Cushing and Myra Eells experienced cultural difficulties of their own among the Spokane Indians. At their mission—Tshimakain—the Walkers and the Eells labored for nine years without converting any Spokane people. Difficulties between the tribe and their "teachers" ranged from disagreements over the fate of stray dogs in camp, which Walker commanded the Indians to destroy, to the missionaries' inability to learn the Native language. De Smet reported that the Walkers even resorted to baptizing their own young children to attract converts, a practice the Calvinist missionaries did not believe necessary for the salvation of infants. Upon learning the fate of their American board colleagues at Waiilatpu, the missionaries packed up their families and deserted Tshimakain, telling the Spokane people they would return. To the board, however, Eells described the future as "dark & uncertain." Indeed, the Walkers and the Eells did not again take up residency among the Spokane.[31]

The American board missions were not the only ones experiencing difficulty. St. Mary's Mission in Montana struggled for existence during this period, largely because the Salish people resented Jesuit activity among their bitter enemies, the Blackfeet. De Smet held a "peace camp" during which he believed an end to bloodshed between the Blackfeet and the Salish had been accomplished. War between the tribes continued, however, to the extent that the resident priests feared for their own safety. When baptism failed to have miraculous consequences or failures on the battlefield ensued despite the Black Robes' prayers, the Salish people began to question Jesuit power. Flathead disaffection with Jesuit teachings and direct confrontations with the resident priests led Joset to close the mission in 1850.[32]

The problems at St. Mary's Mission differed from those at Tshimakain and Waiilatpu because, unlike the Protestant missionaries, the Black Robes did not come to the tribes with families and the appearance of economic self-interest. Point and Huet possessed so few provisions during the early years that they subsisted in much the same manner as the Coeur d'Alenes. Joset used Coeur d'Alene methods to provide for his subsistence and thus won tribal members' respect. "Father Joset lived among the Indians," the Seltice family history states, "and he lived on what the Indians lived on: dried meat, dried fish and smulkin for dessert in the winter days." When tribal members brought Joset fish, the missionary reportedly refused to take the food, telling them "I have been catching my own fish . . . [and] will continue to get my own supply of fish."[33]

Since the missionaries relied on traditional subsistence patterns for their own survival, they did not force immediate changes in annual migrations to root and hunting grounds. These differences were evident in the layout of Protestant and Jesuit missions. The appearance of Tshimakain, for example, contrasted sharply with that of the Rocky Mountain Jesuit missions. Botanist Charles A. Geyer's 1843 drawing of Tshimakain—rendered during his botanical explorations of the area between 1842 and 1844—shows neat log cabins, fenced gardens, and well-tended pastures. No Indian residence, communal garden, or church appears; only the missionary couples' two log structures are apparent.[34] Tshimakain looked like a Euro-American homestead, whereas the reduction model of Sacred Heart Mission and the other Rocky Mountain missions followed a pattern very different from other non-Indian settlement. During the early years of the mission the priests encouraged fishing and hunting and allowed for the observance of traditional hunting rituals. Archaeological digs conducted at Cataldo reveal a continuity of traditional implement usage—pestles, hand stones, hammer stones—suggesting previous economic practices were maintained at the mission.[35]

The Jesuits initially used tribal subsistence patterns as a teaching opportunity, and hunting successes and failures were viewed in spiritual terms. Point accompanied the Coeur d'Alenes on their hunting and fishing expeditions from November 1842 to February 1843. The variety and abundance of wild game and fish in Coeur d'Alene country astounded the missionary. Point gave an inventory of the "most common" animals, including "the deer, the elk, the mountain lion, the carcajou, the white sheep, the bighorn, the goat, the wolf, the fox, the wildcat, the polecat, the hare, the otter, the weasel, the badger, the mink, the marten, the fisher, the beaver, the muskrat, a large variety of mouse-colored rats, squirrels, field mice . . . [and] four or five varieties of bear." Although he did not give specific fish species, Point noted that "fish are abundant in lakes, rivers, and small streams" in Coeur d'Alene country.[36]

Seemingly in awe of the process and the plenty of the catch, Point gave detailed descriptions of fishing on the "banks of the Spokane River, at the place where Lake Coeur d'Alene teems with a prodigious number of fish." Coeur d'Alene fishermen created a barrier in the stream flow using wicker screens anchored in the water by poles. Volunteering to erect the poles represented a "way to gain popularity" because of the near-freezing temperature of the mountain-fed river's water. The catch, Point wrote, "is usually so abundant that canoes are filled and emptied within a space of a few hours." When the number occasionally proved disappointing, Point turned to his religion for an explanation for this "cessation of temporal help." "As for the results of your hunting and fishing," the priest told tribal members, "if they have not been what they used to be, or more abundant still, blame no one but yourself." If the Schitsu'umsh continued to practice their old ways, the shortage would continue. Point instructed tribal members to search their "hearts and lodges" for remnants of the past and to surrender any "superstitious" objects to be burned at the church.[37]

If a scarcity of fish indicated God's displeasure, successful hunting outings were attributed to the grace of God. During Point's first winter with the Coeur d'Alenes, perfect deer hunting conditions prevailed in the region—large numbers of game, heavy snows causing the animals to move to lower elevations in search of food, and wet, confining snow in the valleys. On one occasion tribal hunters killed 600 snow-bound deer, approximately 6 animals per hunter, and did so with a minimum of powder and arrows since many of the trapped deer were killed by a quick twist of the antlers. Comparing this unusually abundant outcome to the Bible's miracle of St. Peter and the fishes, Point wrote, "so here did the hand of God manifest itself in a manner perfectly suited" to the Schitsu'umsh, whom, he noted, "could imagine nothing superior to good fishing and, above all, good hunting." In spite of Point's religious interpretation of the hunt, he allowed the hunters to observe traditional postkill rituals. The missionary attended the customary feast following the hunt, held at a chief's lodge, during which the hunters distributed the meat. The hunter responsible for the kill had the right to take the hide and half of the animal; his nearest neighbors took the head and the remainder of the carcass; the legs belonged to the community. Before allocating the meat, the chiefs said a prayer and ate the animals' hearts. Noting that this practice "is only a symbol of friendship, to which members of the feast attach no superstitious significance," Point supported the custom.[38]

This approach to teaching—to embrace subsistence patterns and use failures and successes as examples of God's reward or punishment—carried great risk. If the Coeur d'Alene people accepted the Jesuit interpretation of God's generosity or lack thereof, the Jesuit cause could be endangered by a sudden change in hunting and fishing outcomes. The Coeur d'Alenes, however, having long experience with their homeland's natural cycles, welcomed Jesuit prayers for the hunt but probably gave little credence to threats of scarcity. Periods of declining animal populations came and went, and generations of Coeur d'Alene people grew up with an oral tradition that viewed sparse hunting seasons as a natural course of events.[39]

Knowledge of scarcity cycles contributed to Coeur d'Alene willingness to accept another Jesuit teaching—agriculture. To the Jesuit missionaries of Sacred Heart, the introduction of agriculture played an essential role in Christianizing the tribe. Tilling the soil provided a way for the Coeur d'Alene people to escape perceived idleness and secure possession of their lands. Point viewed agriculture as an integral part of his ordered reduction among the Coeur d'Alenes, and his plans for Coeur d'Alene Mission show precisely cultivated fields arranged along militaristic lines. "Seeing these poor creatures inhabiting a country whose capacity to produce a hundredfold required only the sweat of their brows," Point admonished, "it was not difficult for me to assign the real reason for their misery." The obvious answer for Point resided in the need to teach tribal members "to enjoy work through help, encouragement, and recompense." Similarly, Joset identified "Native idleness" as the "greatest obstacle" in converting the Coeur d'Alene tribe. "They must be made industrious," the priest wrote, "and the obvious means to it is the farm."[40]

The practical aspects of agriculture attracted tribal members, who knew that despite the righteousness of the supposed "new" work ethic expounded by the Jesuits, hunting and gathering required tremendous effort for unpredictable gains. Indeed, the Coeur d'Alenes were already familiar with the white potato cultivation they had acquired from Fort Spokane traders. Since agriculture did not require a full year's commitment, its practice could supplement, rather than replace, subsistence economics. During the early mission years, families that lived at the mission embraced a form of subsistence agriculture—producing vegetable gardens, a few bushels of potatoes, oats for milk cows, and enough acres of wheat to provide a yearly flour supply. Tribal members cultivated the mission farm and their own small plots. These individuals became some of the first farmers in the Interior Pacific Northwest.

In the beginning, acreages remained necessarily small, since missionaries and tribal members plowed, seeded, and weeded by hand. Initially, the mission farm produced only enough for the mission and the five or six families that lived near it, but by the 1870s the mission farm amounted to more than 100 acres, and tribal members were extending cultivation and grazing activities into the Coeur d'Alene Valley.[41] The mission acquired several teams of oxen during the 1850s, which tribal members shared to pull their handmade plows. The oxen allowed Schitsu'umsh families to cultivate three acres or more. To mill their grain, farmers spread the new wheat on buffalo hides within a corral. Wild horses were herded into the corral and driven around its confines, thus forcing the wheat kernels from their husks. Schitsu'umsh family members ground their own grain, with stone mallets in stone kegs, or took the grain to Sacred Heart Mission. Some farmers constructed their own mule-powered mill on the mission grounds. As with the distribution of fish and game, tribal members shared the tasks associated with cultivation, but each family kept its own farm's yield.[42]

Joset made numerous references to Coeur d'Alene tribal enthusiasm for the plow in his history of Sacred Heart Mission. "From the start these [I]ndians showed a great preference," Joset declared, "for the producer of the farm." He noted that the tribal people particularly liked bread, which they called *senkolo*. To encourage the younger generation to learn agricultural practices, elders told their children they could "eat plenty of senkolo" while working with the fathers at the mission.[43]

Despite Joset's enthusiastic notations, the extent to which tribal members voluntarily embraced agriculture during the early mission years reveals itself in the way the farmers perceived those who chose *not* to farm. Joseph Seltice wrote that "not all the Indians were of this working type." Seltice characterized those who chose not to farm as lazy: "So much work, stooping all day! But, oh that bread! We can easily beg a couple of sacks of wheat from them in the winter, so why bother?" Seltice's words indicated the growing division between those, initially the minority, who accepted Jesuit teachings and those who did not. Written nearly a half century after the establishment of the mission, however, Seltice's work betrayed the Jesuits' strong influence and a clear pro-mission bias. The Seltice family history emphasized the acculturation of Jesuit teachings and undermined division, but its role as a piece of propaganda highlights the fact that not all Schitsu'umsh were happy farmers and church-going Catholics. Still, as the mission educated increasingly greater numbers of Schitsu'umsh children, the minority of Schitsu'umsh farming Catholics gradually increased. Nonfarming, non-Catholic tribal members either acquiesced or became separated from the "mission Indians." Many young tribal members schooled at the mission left with aspirations of owning their own farms and providing for their families through a combination of hunting and cultivation, even if they abhorred the sometimes severe methods of the Jesuits. According to both the Seltice family history and the Jesuit record, the practical lure of agriculture prevailed, and by the mid-1850s many Coeur d'Alenes had abandoned temporary winter lodges for "good log cabins with rock fireplaces."[44]

Farming, Catholicism, and assimilation would become tribal policy by the 1870s. A continuance of complementary hunting and gathering remained essential, however, since abundance depended on both means. Indeed, when supplies at the mission school became diminished in winter, Joset let the boys leave school to pursue the hunt. Joset defended this decision to his superiors by explaining that "at camp there is no want of occupation or of companions, they have food in abundance, which is rarely the case at the Mission." Although the advent of agriculture meant that at least some Schitsu'umsh spent more time within territorial boundaries, the ability to procure additional subsistence within those boundaries ironically attained greater significance. Farming became a man's occupation, but vegetable gardens usually fell under the purview of Schisu'umsh women.[45]

The priests clearly recognized that the tribe expected the mission to act as a supplier of firearms, since the Jesuits pursued this activity in spite of negative white sentiment and territorial laws. During the crisis following the deaths of Marcus and Narcissa Whitman, Sacred Heart missionaries vowed to protect the Coeur d'Alenes and ordered additional munitions. When the news of the uprising at Waiilatpu reached the white settlements in the Willamette Valley, nervous inhabitants demanded that the U.S. Army locate and punish the Cayuse offenders. Although the Cayuse did attempt to form a loose Indian confederacy in the region, the effort failed, and even most Cayuse people opposed an open war.

Peter Skene Ogden, a Hudson's Bay Company trapper who had extensive experience in Indian relations, successfully ransomed the surviving hostages at the Whitman mission. Still, many whites believed a general Indian war could erupt at any time, in part because of sensational rumors of Roman Catholic missionary responsibility for the Cayuse attack. American settlers responded with particular sensitivity to these assertions because the United States, after years of diplomatic struggle with Great Britain, had just recently gained control of Oregon country. Whereas the slain Marcus Whitman became erroneously known as the "savior of Oregon"—supposedly for bringing enough American settlers to Oregon to create a legitimate claim of majority occupancy—Catholic missionaries appeared un-American at best and as agents of the English Hudson's Bay Company at worst. Buoyed by these assertions, the new Oregon Territorial Legislature passed legislation forbidding the transfer of arms to Indian tribes in the Pacific Northwest and sent volunteer soldiers into Walla Walla Valley and beyond to capture the Cayuse attackers. The volunteers failed to locate their Indian prey, but they sufficiently offended the Palouse tribe—by confiscating their livestock—that the Palouse fought back.[46]

At Sacred Heart, Joset feared for his own safety as a Catholic missionary and for the safety of the Coeur d'Alenes, whose lack of involvement, Joset knew, would not be obvious to volunteers who lumped all interior tribes together. The proximity of the Spalding Mission at Lapwai, moreover, concerned the Jesuit fathers, since Henry Spalding was largely responsible for the rumors of Catholic involvement in the Whitman massacre. Joset traveled to Oregon City to protest the law against arms supply, arguing that not all interior tribes were hostile to whites and that some, like the Flathead, needed ammunition for protection against other tribes, such as the Blackfeet. When his pleas met a prejudicial reception, Joset ordered delivery of 1,080 pounds of powder, 1,500 pounds of balls, 300 pounds of buckshot, and 36 guns to Sacred Heart Mission.[47]

The threat of hostilities in the region, coupled with the convergence of territory and subsistence, contributed to the creation of a more centralized Coeur d'Alene political arrangement. When the Jesuit fathers arrived in Coeur d'Alene country, tribal members resided in several different bands and recognized numerous chiefs and subchiefs—some with local jurisdiction, others with powers associated only with certain activities, such as war or the hunt. Point's 1842 drawing entitled "Chiefs of the Coeur d'Alene When Sacred Heart, the Second Rocky Mountain Mission, Was Founded" shows fourteen leaders in circular order, representative of the tribe's nonhierarchical political organization. The chiefs in Point's drawing include Etienne, Ignace, Gabriel, Nichel, Pierre Ignace, Paulin, Louis Joseph, Paul, Placide, Isidore, Augustin, and Damas. Point listed their Christian rather than their tribal names. Point included two women's names and portraits—Marthe and Louise—somewhat outside the circle but connected to two of the chiefs. The appearance of women in the leadership structure is particularly striking, since the Jesuits do not refer to female political leaders after 1842. "Louise" may refer to Louise Siuwheemtuk who, according to the Seltice history, "was one of the first to receive baptism from Father DeSmet" and later "was a great help to the Black Robes in their struggle to christianize the Coeur d'Alenes." She "forsook all tribal honors and prestige, and she devoted herself entirely to the service of the Mission." The fact that she possessed "honors and prestige" within the tribe prior to her mission activities suggests that women held important positions of authority in pre-Christian Schitsu'umsh society. The Jesuits, at least in the case of Louise Siuwheemtuk, converted her traditional authority into Christian service under the control of the mission fathers.[48]

Coeur d'Alene participation in the buffalo hunt and involvement in war with the Blackfeet during the early nineteenth century started the trend toward a centralized leadership with limited tribal command. Jesuit teachings and adaptation of agricultural practices accelerated this shift in power—from a group of local and independent leaders to one leader with authority recognized by the mission and Catholic-agricultural Schitsu'umsh. Jesuit emphasis on the mission church as the center of the reduction community hid tribal divisions. Each band sent its children to the same school, although, as school reports indicate, not all families sent their children to the Jesuit school.[49] As the Jesuits worked to break down tribal bands, the mission Schitsu'umsh became increasingly comfortable with the role of a single chief, although local chiefs retained provincial power.

The traditional flexibility of Coeur d'Alene political life allowed for the necessary evolution of authority after the Cayuse scare. No hostilites had occurred in Coeur d'Alene country, but the Jesuit fathers and the tribe prepared for that possibility. Bassa, also known by his Anglicized name Vincent, became chief by majority vote in 1844. His chieftainship served a transitional role, as his "first command was preparedness." Vincent tied the role of head chief to protection of the tribe from outsiders. "He warned that the white man would be coming in great numbers," the Seltice family history states, "with violent intentions towards whatever the Indians were living on." The solidification of the head chief created the political apparatus through which the Coeur d'Alenes would confront outsiders throughout the second half of the nineteenth century.[50]

Ten years after his election as chief, Vincent's proclamation regarding the coming of white men came to fruition in the form of Isaac I. Stevens. Newly appointed governor of Washington Territory, territorial superintendent of Indian affairs, and director of the government's northern transcontinental railroad survey, Stevens came to bear significant responsibility for changes that threatened the Coeur d'Alene sphere. A man of unbridled ambition, Stevens viewed Washington Territory in linear terms of white settlement and "progress," leaving little room for the endurance of Native land and culture.

Passing through Coeur d'Alene country in 1854 while conducting the railroad survey, Stevens stopped at Sacred Heart Mission and met with the Jesuit missionaries. "Underestimated by all the authorities," Stevens later wrote, the Coeur d'Alene people "have some seventy lodges and number about five hundred inhabitants." Much impressed by the Cataldo Mission Church, Stevens gave the Coeur d'Alenes credit for the erection of a structure that "would do credit to anyone." Characteristically, Stevens attributed Coeur d'Alene "advances" to the Jesuit fathers, not realizing the extent of tribal initiative or of the interactive environment. "[The Indians] are much indebted to the good fathers for making considerable progress in agriculture," the new superintendent reported, and "they have abandoned polygamy, have been taught the rudiments of Christianity and are greatly improved in their morals and in the comforts of life." Stevens complimented the tribe's agricultural endeavors—reporting that tribal members cultivated about 200 acres, maintained a prairie for grazing of about 3,000 acres, and owned one "hundred pigs, 8 yokes of Oxen, twenty cows and a liberal proportion of horses, mules and young animals." The governor promised to provide agricultural assistance—seeds and implements—and gave regards from the "Great Father" in Washington. Meanwhile, Stevens the railroad developer looked ahead to white settlement, noting "I have no question that all the country from the Falls of the Coeur d'Alene to the Lower end of the Pend d'Oreille Lake, and from the Mission for some distance above the Lake, a region of three or four thousand square miles is adapted to grazing and culture." The arrival of the territory's new leader signaled an end to the mission era in Coeur d'Alene country, for another player—the U.S. government—now joined a field of intricate relationships.[51]

Between 1840 and 1855, cooperation and begrudging tolerance between the Coeur d'Alene tribe and the Jesuit fathers of Sacred Heart Mission resulted in the creation of a new transitory world of interaction in Schitsu'umsh country. The early missionary period introduced Roman Catholicism, wheat cultivation, Christian marriage, and a consistent source of firearms to tribal people, who, in turn, embraced each addition within a Schitsu'umsh framework. The Schitsu'umsh political structure became more pronounced, the identity of the Coeur d'Alenes as Catholic Christians was mapped, the assimilation model of resistance began to emerge, and references to Schitsu'umsh women disappeared from Jesuit accounts. The Jesuits gained converts and the hope of a "New Paraguay" among the Native peoples of the Pacific Northwest. Although the appearance in Coeur d'Alene country of Washington territorial governor Isaac I. Stevens heralded unprecedented changes, neither the European Jesuit fathers nor the Coeur d'Alene people could foresee the dramatic transformations that would engulf the tribe and shatter the region's fragile peace. Still, the effects of interaction—increased territoriality, the use of agriculture to stabilize a subsistence economy, and a centralized political structure—laid the groundwork for the tribe's calculated response to outsider encroachment.

THREE

ISAAC I. STEVENS'S ABANDONED TREATY, 1853–1858

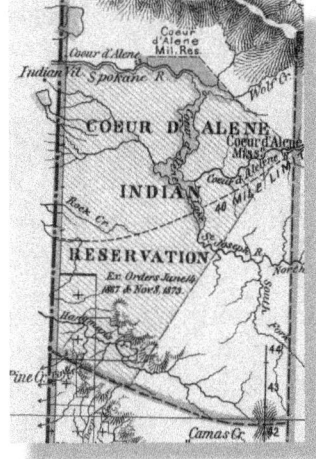

The territory between Lewis [the Snake] and Spokane Rivers is our garden; it is there our women dig the roots on which we live; if the soldiers come into these parts, the women will not dare to go and we will be famined.
—CHIEFS OF THE COEUR D'ALENE, SPOKANE, AND COLVILLE TRIBES, 1854[1]

The Indian title to land East of the Cascade Mountains should at once be extinguished.
—ISAAC I. STEVENS, 1853[2]

DURING THE 1850S THE COEUR D'ALENE PEOPLE, together with their neighbors in the Interior Pacific Northwest, experienced U.S. government territorial policy for the first time. Between 1845 and 1848 the vast areas of Texas, Oregon, New Mexico, and California became part of the United States.[3] Psychological and physical components accompanied territorial acquisition. Although not every American took part, a fever for advancing territory afflicted so many individuals that New York newspaper editor John L. O'Sullivan coined the term *Manifest Destiny* to describe the phenomenon. Americans also embraced the physical aspect of expansion. Many people, disgruntled with economic opportunities in the cities or on the arid plains, packed a covered wagon and headed for the country's newest territories. The Oregon Trail—a journey beginning at Independence, Missouri, and ending in the fertile Willamette Valley—proved one of the most popular westward routes. Between 1840 and 1860, 53,062 individuals arrived in Oregon Territory via the Oregon Trail; during the same interval, 253,397 American overland emigrants descended on the West Coast.[4] Oregon's territorial land laws encouraged homesteaders. The Oregon Donation Land Law of 1850 gave 320 acres of land to each male settler over age eighteen who had arrived prior to 1850; if married, the settler's wife received 320 acres in her own name. Those arriving after 1850 received 160 acres each, with the same provision for their wives.[5]

In theory, the United States recognized existing Indian title to the Oregon land affected by the Donation Land Law. The United States had recognized Indian title to land in the Northwest Ordinance of 1787, which created the territorial system in the United States; and the U.S. Supreme Court recognized Indian sovereignty in the Marshall Court ruling *Worcester v. Georgia*.[6] Since Native people held sovereign right to Oregon country, the United States was obligated to negotiate for its release before disposing of it through the Oregon legislation. Indeed, Congress made provision during 1850 for negotiation of treaties with the tribes of Oregon Territory.

In reality, however, the new territorial law awarded settlers land that had never been released by Native people. The Oregon Donation Land Act honored retroactive land claims, dating from the 1840s. Moreover, the legislation was in full effect long before Congress had fulfilled its treaty obligations to the Indian people of Oregon Territory. In his 1858 annual report, Commissioner of Indian Affairs Charles E. Mix described the legal and bureaucratic problems created by Oregon Territory's land policy. "When a territorial government was first provided for Oregon . . . strong inducements were held out to our people to emigrate and settle there," the commissioner declared, "without the usual arrangements being made, in advance, for the extinguishment of the title of the Indians who occupied and claimed the lands."[7]

Burgeoning populations on the Pacific Coast, coupled with the recognition that the Pacific Northwest could provide raw materials for eastern industry, suggested the need for a transcontinental railroad system. Isaac I. Stevens, an enthusiastic supporter of western expansion and transcontinental railroads, embodied the forces of Manifest Destiny in Washington Territory. His appointment as governor of Washington Territory placed the United States and the Native American peoples of the Pacific Northwest on a collision course. Stevens's vision for expansion in the West led him to seek the governorship of the young territory, which came with simultaneous appointments as territorial superintendent of Indian affairs and director of the northern railroad survey. Territorial governorships often meant isolation, tedium, and danger, but Stevens eagerly sought the position to propel his dream of a northern transcontinental railroad and his political fortunes.[8]

Stevens set out for Washington Territory in May 1853. During the six-month journey to the territorial capital of Olympia, Stevens met with northwestern tribal peoples, conducted the northern transcontinental railroad survey, and contributed to the non-Indian mapping of Native identity in the region. On May 10, 1853, Stevens informed Washington that he expected to encounter six tribes, with a combined population of 2,000, east of the Cascade Mountains. Following a route from Fort Benton to Fort Colville by way of Stevens Pass (now Lookout Pass) and Sacred Heart Mission, Stevens discovered that at least twice as many different Native tribes as his original estimate—over 6,000 persons—

occupied the interior region. Stevens was much impressed with these peoples, particularly the Coeur d'Alenes. "I was most struck with the comparative civilized condition," he wrote, "of the Indians, at the Cour d'Elaine [sic] mission." His December report described "large fields of wheat and potatoes," the "splendid" nature of the mission church, and the "indefatigable labor of the Fathers and Laymen of the mission." A sketch produced by John Mix Stanley, the northern survey's chief artist, portrayed Sacred Heart Mission facing the Coeur d'Alene River. Small buildings, tepees, and trees surrounded the famous church. The drawing evinced a pastoral quality reflective of Stevens's image of the site as a "civilized" haven.[9]

One of the earliest "Chinook" jargon dictionaries upheld Stevens's favorable view of the interior tribes. Published in Portland while Stevens was conducting the northern railroad survey, the dictionary listed "honesty, civility and generosity" as the main attributes of the Coeur d'Alene Tribe. The homeland of the "Pointed Hearts," the reference noted, "is more open than that of their neighbors, and well adapted for husbandry." Regardless of whether he was familiar with the Chinook dictionary, Stevens's convictions regarding the interior tribes motivated the politician to remove them to reservations. "The Indian title to land East of the Cascade Mountains should at once be extinguished," Stevens informed the commissioner of Indian affairs in December 1853. Concerned about the "number of settlement already commenced in the Indian Country," the governor justified removal of the tribes by emphasizing their cohesive political organization, adaptation of agriculture, and missionary involvement.[10]

The territorial leader cited the settlement of "half breeds and retired servants of the Hudson Bay Company" as evidence of the white advance, despite the fact that ten years earlier such an example implied English, not American, occupancy. In truth, very little white settlement existed at this time in the interior; most of Washington Territory's few thousand inhabitants were clustered near Olympia and in valleys adjacent to Puget Sound. Washington's settlers, moreover, struggled with a reputation as "the crudest elements of the frontier." Still, the expansionist governor claimed the existence of a "flourishing line of settlement in the Colville and Wallah Wallah [sic] vallies [sic]." These immigrants, he claimed, were "on excellent terms with the Indians." The main areas of non-Indian activity centered on the Whitman Mission site—which overland travelers continued to use as a way station—and on isolated streams in the Colville Valley of northern Washington Territory, where discouraged California prospectors chased gold rumors. Few emigrant families, however, maintained permanent homesteads in Washington's interior in 1853. Those familiar with the Whitman massacre would certainly have disagreed with Stevens's characterization of peaceful coexistence.[11]

While passing through eastern Washington, Stevens attached an American political and economic perspective to the tribal chieftains and villages he encountered. "All of [the interior tribes] have chiefs, who, are well-disposed towards the whites," Stevens contended, "and some of whom have great authority, not only with their own people, but, with the surrounding tribes." Using the Coeur d'Alene people as a model, Stevens declared that "all the [interior] tribes have made some progress in agriculture" and raise livestock. Yet as seen in Chapter 2, although the Coeur d'Alene mission economy appeared agricultural to a quick passerby, the Jesuits did not discourage seasonal hunting and gathering. Indeed, the mission farm and individual farms supported only a small portion of the Schitsu'umsh population. Ignoring the many hunting parties Stevens met during his trip to Olympia, the new governor overstated the sedentary lifestyle of eastern Washington tribes. Failing to distinguish between Protestant and Jesuit missionary efforts, Stevens declared that the missions to the Kalispel, Coeur d'Alene, Colville, Yakima, and Walla Walla were "calculated" to lead to white American settlement and "should be encouraged." European Jesuit missionaries did not, however, view themselves as vanguards for the pioneers or see in their mission the seeds of American expansionism.[12]

From the outset of his experience in Washington Territory, Stevens underestimated the territoriality and complexity of interior tribes, particularly the Coeur d'Alenes; and he misinterpreted the relationship between the Sacred Heart missionaries and the Indian people they served. The image Stevens presented to Washington, D.C., thus conflicted with the realities of interaction in interior Washington Territory. The traits Stevens used to justify tribal land reduction and removal—political cohesiveness, agricultural adaptation, missionary activity—contributed to inland tribal groups' ability to protect themselves against white encroachment. The Coeur d'Alene Tribe—Stevens's model of guided civilization—maintained its traditional territoriality throughout the nineteenth century, even as tribal members adapted a dual economy based on both hunting and gathering and agriculture. Moreover, the institution of a single Schitsu'umsh tribal chieftainship heightened the group's ability to organize and protect itself against outside intrusion. The governor's miscalculations resulted in unanswered tribal dissatisfaction and, ultimately, in violent confrontation.

Characterized by his biographer as "a regular go-ahead man," Washington Territory's new leader had no time for mental reservations. At Stevens's behest Congress ratified a bill creating a surveyor general for the territory early in the governor's term and granted treaty-making appropriations in 1854. Conditions in the region contributed to the governor's sense of urgency. Groups of settlers on the Oregon Trail sometimes experienced violence at the hands of disaffected Indian peoples, although more often the well-armed settlers inflicted the violence. Regardless of its source, unrest on the popular trail prompted Stevens to quickly eradicate Indian title to traditional land holdings. The Ward massacre, one of the few major Indian-inflicted tragedies, occurred in August 1854 along the Snake River in eastern Oregon Territory (present-day southern Idaho). Eighteen wagon train members perished as Shoshone Indians struck back after the small group of settlers fired at a Shoshone attempting to steal a horse.[13]

Although the Coeur d'Alenes escaped the onslaught of settlers traversing the Oregon Trail, Stevens's other major motivation for holding councils with eastern Washington tribes directly impacted the Coeur d'Alene people. Stevens feared the ongoing skirmishes between the Blackfeet tribe and the buffalo-pursuing tribes of the Interior Northwest threatened settlement of the region by creating dangerous conditions for explorers, surveyors, miners, and potential homesteaders. Stevens's interest in constructing a military road from the head of navigation on the Missouri River at Fort Benton to the Columbia River Valley at Walla Walla magnified these concerns. Still interested in a proposed northern transcontinental railroad route but mindful of the territory's immediate transportation needs, Stevens enlisted topographical engineer John Mullan to build the wagon road. Congressional approval for the project came in 1854. Stevens intended the Mullan trail to serve both as an alternative to the Oregon Trail and as a forerunner of the northern transcontinental railroad route. Once completed, the Mullan Road would, in the governor's view, attract settlement to Washington Territory, whose population stubbornly lagged behind that of neighboring Oregon.[14]

In mapping the region and traversing the Continental Divide, Mullan became more than a road builder. His relationship with area tribes provided the territorial government with valuable information and served as a link between the tribes and government agents. Mullan soon discovered that regional intertribal hostilities threatened the proposed road and white settlement. In response to Mullan's concerns, Stevens allowed the engineer to remain at Fort Benton until peace could be forced on the Blackfeet and their enemies, including the Coeur d'Alenes. Stevens wrote Colonel B. E. Bonneville of the Columbia Barracks in early 1854:

> In consequence of the delicacy of our Indian relations in the Eastern portion of the Territory and the efficient manner with which they are sustained by Lieut. Mullan—the Blackfeet East of the Rocky mountains, and the Flatheads, Pend d'Oreilles, Coeur d'Alene and other Indians west of the mountains being only restrained from hostilities by his presence and that of a small party at Fort Benton—I find it necessary as the Executive of the Territory and as Supt. [sic] of Indian Affairs to be determined by the action of Congress and the instructions of the Department to retain [Mullan] and that party at that point, till some definite action can be taken hereafter.

Such action included removing quarreling tribes to separate reservations, away from each other and off the path of white settlement.[15]

Stevens further developed his plan for eastern Washington tribal removal to reservations in a June 1854 report to Commissioner of Indian Affairs George

Manypenny. While conducting the road survey, Stevens wrote, Mullan found that Washington Territory Indians were forced to endure "the stealing of horses, and the loss of men from the war parties of the Blackfeet." These tribal peoples, the governor insisted, had "faith that the government will ultimately protect them." Stevens emphasized that no other group of Indian people was more deserving of paternalistic "protection." The Flatheads, Kalispels, Coeur d'Alenes, Spokanes, and Nez Perce had complied with Fort Benton's request for peace along the buffalo trail, whereas the Blackfeet had not. James Doty, who had accompanied Stevens on his initial voyage to Olympia and now served as Mullan's assistant, reported that during the winter of 1854, "never were so many Blackfeet war parties" present on the trails leading across the mountains. Still, Doty assured Stevens that "a single white can go in safety throughout their country and will be treated with hospitality." Unconvinced of whites' safety, Stevens assured his superiors that intertribal peace would result from treaty councils and the creation of reservations, and the interior "country must soon and rapidly be settled."[16]

Stevens's faith in Manifest Destiny resonated throughout his 1854 address to the territorial legislature. Outlining the accomplishments of Washington's first year, Stevens congratulated his fellow territorial leaders in language characteristic of the control he believed Manifest Destiny held over the "wilderness" and its occupants. "Just one year has rolled away since the proclamation was issued giving vitality to our organic act," Stevens declared, "and calling into existence a new component part of that great confederacy to whose extent nature has been unable to assign any limits." The address revealed Stevens's dream for Washington Territory, a vision excluding the region's Native peoples. "The emigrant looks forward to [Washington Territory] as his home," the governor optimistically stated; "princely merchants as the highway of the trade of nations; statesmen and patriots as a grand element of national strength and national security."[17]

Contemporary U.S. Indian policy supported Stevens's goal of advancing settlement by eliminating Indian land claims in Washington Territory. Prior to 1850, federal officials advocated a policy of forced removal and isolation, the creation of an Indian frontier line beyond which "civilization" ended and Indian people lived peaceably. Advocated by Andrew Jackson's presidency and the 1830 Removal Bill, the effects of Manifest Destiny revealed the policy's ever-present weaknesses. Tribes did not necessarily experience peace once isolated from whites, since long-standing conflicts existed between tribes and often between groups forced to live together in "Indian Country." The growth of the non-Indian American populace and its tendency to move westward in search of arable land made Indian removal obsolete. With U.S. acquisition of the continent's far corner—Oregon—and the subsequent territorial status of Washington and Oregon, the concept of a permanent "Indian frontier" faded. Indeed, the Pacific Northwest played host to the interaction of Native peoples and Euro-outsiders for fifty years prior to Stevens's arrival, as evidenced by Schitsu'umsh relations with traders and missionaries. Thus, the concept of Indian reservations, or islands of land set aside exclusively for use by tribal people, gained credibility in the western United States. With the Treaty of Fort Laramie in 1851, the federal government opened western land to settlement by allocating tribal peoples land designated by official boundaries and promising annuities and protection from white trespassers in return for surrendered territory. Implicit in the new reservation policy was an emphasis on education and assimilation. Treaties usually provided for schools and the appointment of a reservation "Farmer" to oversee the advancement of agriculture.[18]

Washington Territory's councils with the tribes east of the Cascade Mountains commenced with the 1855 Walla Walla Council. In preparation for the meeting, Stevens appointed career frontiersman Andrew J. Bolon as special Indian agent for the territory's eastern district. Bolon's instructions required him to "tour" the country, determine Native views toward whites, and "cautiously prepare the way for the negotiations which it is expected will be authorized by Congress." Stevens advised Bolon against making specific promises regarding federal purchase of Indian lands. "It will be sufficient to say to them that the Governor has recommended to the Great Father at Washington to pay them for whites settling in their country," Stevens suggested, "and that as soon as his will is known some good men will be sent to buy their lands and pay for them." To Bolon fell the responsibility of identifying alliances between tribes and locating chiefs with sufficient authority to sign treaties. Whereas Bolon's orders required him to threaten uncooperative tribes with dispersal of their lands without pay, he also needed to procure tribal support for the councils from the most influential groups and leaders. Stevens wanted tribes to remain uncertain about the status of their territories because he wished tribal leaders to be anxious to treat with the United States, and he did not want to promise payment for more land than absolutely necessary.[19]

The delicate nature of this task—which required persuasive reassurance combined with shrewd aloofness—challenged Agent Bolon. A man recognized for qualities such as strength and courage, Bolon lacked tact and exhibited disdain for Indian people. The agent gained the confidence of a few Indian leaders but antagonized many others. Bolon's relationship with the Catholic Oblate missionaries to the Yakima tribe cast a shadow over the impending treaty councils. Offended by the way Bolon conducted his affairs, Oblate fathers Charles Pandosy and Louis d'Herbomez requested the agent's dismissal as a federal official. Although Stevens sent a special investigator to look into the matter—James Doty—he suspected the priests of jealous maneuvering against secular intrusion. Old anti-Catholic resentments, born of suspicion of Catholic involvement in the Whitman massacre, surfaced within the territorial government, and Doty dropped his investigation of Bolon without an inquiry.[20]

With Bolon's difficulties and the open hostility of tribal leaders looming, Stevens began the Walla Walla Council in May 1855. Accompanied by Joel Palmer, Oregon's superintendent of Indian affairs, Stevens met intermittently for two weeks with members of the Nez Perce, Cayuse, Palouse, Umatilla, Walla Walla, and Yakima Tribes. The Northern Plateau tribes—including the Coeur d'Alenes—did not participate in the treaty conference, since Bolon had insufficient time to prepare all the central tribes. Deeming negotiations with the large Yakima and Nez Perce Tribes of utmost importance, Stevens determined that a separate conference would have to be held with the northern tribes. Approximately 5,000 tribal people convened for the meetings. The negotiations revealed Stevens's paternalistic attitude—he referred to tribal chieftains as "children" of the "Great Father" in Washington—as well as his Eurocentric inability to understand the spiritual relationship tribal people maintained with the land.[21]

In spite of tribal dissent, Stevens pushed his treaties, eventually obtaining signatures from chiefs he believed were representative of their tribes. In what became a source of great historical controversy, U.S. government officials often mistakenly attributed authority to tribal leaders to complete treaty negotiations. Use of the limited Chinook jargon also confused negotiations. In many cases the remainder of the tribe discovered such errors too late to reverse the action. This unfortunate trend played out at Walla Walla as Kamiakin, a Yakima chief, signed a treaty involving the Yakima Nation and several other tribal groups. At first solidly opposed to treaty negotiation, Kamiakin acquiesced in a gesture U.S. officials misinterpreted as leadership. The powerful chief, Stevens chose to believe, possessed authority for all Yakima and Palouse peoples, as well as several other Columbia River tribes. Although more centrally organized than many coastal tribes in Washington Territory, interior tribal leadership structure did not lend itself to hierarchical categorization. Federal negotiators "lumped several groups together under the leadership of Kamiakin," historians of the Palouse tribe have noted, "for the convenience of government officials, not the Indians."[22]

Three separate treaties—one each with the Nez Perce and Yakima peoples and a combined agreement with the Walla Walla, Cayuse, and Umatilla Tribes—emerged from the Walla Walla Council. The five tribal groups involved yielded approximately 60,000 square miles of land to the United States. The agreements stipulated that smaller tribes, like the Palouse, relocate to reservations set aside for larger tribal groups. This arrangement failed to consider existing intertribal rivalries and disagreements between bands belonging to the same tribe. Nevertheless, Stevens left Walla Walla for negotiations with the Flathead and Blackfeet Tribes in June, convinced that his arbitrations there had been a success.[23]

Meanwhile, nonparticipating Schitsu'umsh and Flathead observers, along with Sacred Heart Mission architect Anthony Ravalli and Jesuit missionary Joseph Menetrey, suspected otherwise. They recognized warning signs the white Americans either failed to see or chose to ignore. Many of the tribesmen at the council refused to accept gifts of tobacco—a traditional exchange of goodwill—and several left the negotiations early, disgusted by the process. To Stevens, the negotiation of treaties with two of Washington's most powerful tribes—the Yakimas and Nez Perces—signaled victory and the peaceful "removal" of the Indian problem in eastern Washington Territory. Jesuit and Indian onlookers, aware of conspiratorial talk within closed tepees, viewed the reluctant signing as a compromise designed to temporarily ward off federal interference. Father Joseph Joset, writing in a manuscript dated 1874, declared that the chiefs at Walla Walla "agreed to make a mock treaty, in order to gain time and prepare for war." The impressions U.S. officials at Walla Walla left on both Coeur d'Alene tribal members and Sacred Heart missionaries planted the seeds of imminent distrust.[24]

Stevens and his party arrived at Sacred Heart Mission ten days after breaking camp at Walla Walla. As Stevens informed Commissioner Manypenny, the route enabled the governor to inspect the "entire length of the Coeur d'Alene country." At the root grounds near present-day Moscow, Idaho, Stevens observed approximately 250 Coeur d'Alene people engaged in summer activities. Worried about reaching Fort Benton in time to complete councils with the Blackfeet and Flathead Tribes before the fall hunt, Stevens delayed talks with the Spokane, Colville, Okanogan, Lower Kalispel, and Coeur d'Alene peoples. The governor sent an advance party ahead to inform the Northern Plateau tribes of the change and to make arrangements for fall meetings. Stevens rejoined his men at the mission and explained to Father Ravalli and several Coeur d'Alene chiefs that he would return in mid-September for fall councils. Stevens invited the Coeur d'Alenes to send a delegation to witness negotiations at Hell Gate and Fort Benton, but tribal leaders declined. Disillusioned with events at Walla Walla, wary of their Blackfeet enemies, and comfortable in the knowledge that Stevens approved of the mission and the tribe's agricultural efforts, the Coeur d'Alenes distanced themselves from his negotiations, trusting that autumn would bring an opportunity to secure the future of their ancestral lands.[25]

If the Coeur d'Alene leadership and the Jesuit fathers viewed tribal religious and agricultural involvement as insurance against unjust treaties, Stevens perceived Coeur d'Alene "advances" as attributes in adjusting to reservation life and rapid assimilation. Following his visit at Sacred Heart, Stevens noted that "the Fathers at the Mission, show the most excellent disposition" and emphasized to Commissioner Manypenny that they "simply desire the Indians to be placed where they will do the best." Stevens failed to mention that the Jesuits thought the Indians would continue to "do the best" in their ancestral location.[26]

In October Stevens negotiated treaties with the far eastern tribes and instituted a fragile peace agreement among Blackfeet, Flathead, and Nez Perce members regarding buffalo hunting grounds east of the Rockies. The Flathead Treaty, effected by an impatient Stevens, transferred to the United States most of present-day western Montana—land traditionally held by the Flathead, Kootenay, and Kalispel Tribes.[27] The Schitsu'umsh, along with their buffalo hunting neighbors, would have been pleased with Blackfeet hunting concessions, but events in eastern Washington during Stevens's absence monopolized their attention. The discovery of gold on the Upper Columbia River drainage, near Fort Colville, during summer of 1855 precipitated a mining rush on the Interior Pacific Northwest. Because Fort Colville, the Hudson's Bay Company's chief inland post, had been the site of extensive trade between Hudson's Bay Company operatives and local tribal people since 1825, news of the discovery spread quickly to distant mining towns and tribal villages alike. Thousands of pan-bearing hopefuls poured into eastern Washington Territory, spurred on by the western Washington press and a "stagnant" business economy around the Puget Sound.[28]

The influx of outsiders angered local tribal people, particularly as it came in the shadow of the ill-received Walla Walla Council. The Stevens's treaty tribes expected that the governor would, as promised, keep intruders out of the region until reservations could be established and other provisions met, leaving an adjustment period of about four years. The presence and sometimes ruthless behavior of the miners suggested to tribal leaders that Stevens had broken his promises. Indeed, following the conclusion of the Walla Walla Council, regional newspapers like the *Olympia Pioneer and Democrat* featured articles on Washington Territory's newly "opened" spaces. Conversely, Stevens interpreted the mining rush as one more reason to quickly eliminate remaining Indian land title in the area. From Fort Benton Stevens dispatched Colonel H. R. Cooske to determine a time and place to negotiate with the Lower Kalispel and Coeur d'Alenes and to instruct Agent Bolon to do the same among the Spokane, Colville, and Okanogan tribes. "A gold fever has broken out in the region occupied by these Indians," Stevens wrote—giving no consideration to encroachment on the tribes with whom he had met at Walla Walla—"which only makes it the more imperative to lose no time in effecting treaties and placing the Indians on reservations."[29]

When trespassing miners stole horses and raped the daughter of Yakima chief Kamiakin, Qualchan, a young Yakima warrior and nephew of Kamiakin, pursued and murdered the offender near Snoqualmie Pass and then attacked a group of miners on the Yakima River, killing five. On his way to gather supplies for the ensuing Spokane Council when he heard of the hostilities, Agent Bolon altered his route and headed into Yakima country. Although controversy exists regarding Bolon's position among the tribes—Salish peoples like the Coeur d'Alenes apparently did not clash with Bolon—it seems clear that the agent's brash manner had angered many Yakima people. The civil servant unwittingly entered a volatile and complex climate of distrust and animosity. The Yakima people—with the exception of Qualchan and a few other warriors—peacefully withstood the onslaught of miners, but resentment mounted. Kamiakin did not condone the killings but issued warnings to all "Bostons" who crossed the Cascades. Competition between Qualchan and other young warriors created an unstable environment. Bolon heeded the warnings and turned back on the outskirts of Yakima country but joined a seemingly friendly group of Yakima riders. One of the young tribesmen, Moshell, murdered Bolon in an attempt to bolster his reputation in relation to Qualchan.[30]

News of Bolon's murder precipitated what became known among whites as the "Yakima War." Rumors spread quickly through the tense countryside. Many believed the Indians had formed a "confederacy" with which they planned to wage full-blown war throughout the territory. Area settlers and government officials, aware of Kamiakin's stance among the Yakima people, assumed that the chief was responsible for the hostilities. As with negotiations at the Walla Walla Council, whites ascribed more authority to Kamiakin than he actually possessed. Special Indian Agent J. Ross Browne claimed that Kamiakin "projected a war of extermination against the whole race of Americans within the country" and "spared no inducements to effect a coalition with the Nez Perces, Cayuses, Walla Wallas, and other tribes." When Brevet Major Granville Haller and one company of soldiers from Fort Dalles marched into Yakima country to pursue those responsible for Bolon's death, all opportunity for peaceful resolution evaporated. After two days of skirmishes with Yakima warriors, Haller retreated, inciting the regional press and sending a courier at breakneck speed to Governor Stevens, making his way back from Fort Benton.[31]

An exhausted courier intercepted Stevens with the news that "the Yakimas were in open war, that Maj. Heller [sic] had been defeated and obliged to return to the Dalles, and that there was but little doubt that the Cayuses, Walla Walla and Umatillas were hostile."[32] Stevens decided to push over the mountains to Sacred Heart Mission and hold a council to ensure the peaceful intentions of the Spokane, Coeur d'Alene, and Nez Perce Tribes. In the meantime, Nez Perce riders had informed the Coeur d'Alenes that one of Stevens's Indian scouts, Joseph Stellam—son of a Coeur d'Alene chief—had been killed by Americans in the Yakima fighting. Stellam's faction was gathered on the Coeur d'Alene prairie, southwest of the mission, and responded to the news by raiding Stevens's advance wagon column, which carried flannel shirts and other desirable items provided by the Indian Office. The wagons were freighted by other Coeur d'Alene members, under the employ of Indian Agent Bolon, and were driven off their charge by an angry Stellam and several other warriors. No killings took place, but the tribe divided over the incident. Jesuit histories characterize this episode as part of the progression of the Coeur d'Alene leadership from the old ways to the new agrarian, Catholic ways. Stellam "was an old rascal who was gradually being supplanted" by the Jesuits, whereas Andrew Seltice, a young Catholic subchief, "was especially embarrassed by the outburst."[33] Under the influence of

Father Joset, the wagons were recovered and moved to Antoine Plante's cabin to be held in safekeeping until the conference. One revolver, a pound of gunshot powder, and fifteen pounds of shot were not recovered.[34]

After crossing the Rocky Mountains in three feet of snow, Stevens reached Sacred Heart on November 24, 1855. He found tribal members "much excited" about developing events and "on a balance for peace or for war, and a chance word might turn them either way." The governor tried to calm "the spirits of the Coeur d'Alenes," who "talked well" but remained "somewhat uncertain" regarding the war.[35]

Stevens held the Spokane Council near Plante's ferry on the Spokane River during December 3, 4, and 5. Coeur d'Alene, Spokane, and Okanogan tribal leaders, Jesuit Fathers Joset and Ravalli, Hudson's Bay Company representative Angus McDonald, and area settlers attended the conference. The chiefs made clear to the governor the point at which the Yakima War would become a Northern Plateau war. Although Stevens reported to Manypenny that the chiefs "were apparently soothed and satisfied and they pledged themselves to protect all white men in their country and take no part in the war," Joset later wrote that the tribes gave Stevens an ultimatum upon which rested the region's peace.[36] "Many speeches were exchanged," Joset wrote, "but all the chiefs were agreed in one point: they begged that the troops should not come across Lewis [now the Snake] River." In reference to their economic and spiritual dependence on their land, Spokane and Coeur d'Alene chiefs described "the territory between Lewis and Spokane Rivers" as "our garden," where "our women dig the roots on which we live." Stevens "evaded the question," Joset suspected, because he could not promise that troops would stay south of the Snake River. The territorial leader decided not to attempt to negotiate treaties—over the objections of tribal leaders—believing the Indians' "minds [were] ever poisoned by all the artful stories and tricks of the hostile tribes." Instead, Stevens and the tribal leaders agreed that a council would be held in the spring.[37]

The Yakima War played out in a series of skirmishes between young Yakima, Walla Walla, Cayuse, and Palouse warriors—often without tribal sanction—and U.S. Army volunteers. Tribal involvement varied enormously and did not represent an organized coalition of tribes. Whereas tribal people endured internal generational disagreement and uncertainty regarding the war, local settlers—perhaps acting out of greed for Indian land—demonstrated eagerness to serve as volunteers. Volunteer units frequently played a role in protecting isolated western settlements in antebellum America. Often holding preconceived notions of Indian atrocities and frontier justice, volunteer regiments exhibited a ruthless disregard for the rights of tribal people and the possibility of peaceful coexistence.[38]

Governor Stevens and the armed confrontations of 1855–1856 in Washington Territory contributed to the evolution of the volunteer "Indian fighter" and revealed a schism between army officers and regulars on one side and volunteers and civil servants on the other. The widening fault line between the two groups resulted in an inconsistent Indian policy and a loss of trust among tribal authorities precisely when dependable leadership could have prevented bloody hostilities. The void in U.S. authority gave pro-war factions within tribes the confidence to drive whites from tribal land. It also put pressure on missionaries, such as Joseph Joset at Sacred Heart, to provide peaceful alternatives.

Following his conference with the Spokane and Coeur d'Alene peoples in 1855, Stevens organized the region's miners into a volunteer company known as the "Spokane Invincibles." Oregon volunteer units, organized by territorial governor Joel Palmer, joined Stevens and his militias in fighting the "hostiles." When Oregon volunteers seized and murdered Walla Walla tribal leader Peopeomoxmox, General John E. Wool, commander of the army's Pacific Department, objected to the militia's tactics. "I have great hopes that I shall be able to bring the Indians in [eastern Washington Territory] to terms," Wool wrote in a frigid letter to the capital at Olympia, "notwithstanding the volunteers killed the chief, Pee-pee-mox-mox, scalped him, cut off his ears and hands, as reported by volunteers, and sent them to their friends in Oregon." This occurred, Wool continued, after the chief had met the volunteers "under a flag of truce." "Such conduct," Wool sarcastically admonished, "may have caused feelings difficult to overcome." Stevens, in turn, accused Wool of failing to protect territorial citizens and government by providing inadequate numbers of army regulars. Peopeomoxmox died, Stevens argued, "while endeavoring to lead [the volunteers] into an ambush." Noting that his volunteer force numbered only twenty-five, Stevens charged that General Wool "neglected and refused" to send relief even though the commander knew the militia faced "imminent danger." Stevens did not elaborate on the source of the threat to himself and his volunteers, and Wool remained unconvinced.[39]

When Wool mounted a regular army offensive in spring of 1856 under the command of Colonel George Wright, he did so to secure peace east of the Cascades rather than to pursue war. Convinced that peace could only be achieved through a show of U.S. military force, Stevens fielded a volunteer regiment in defiance of Wool's regulars. The two groups increasingly worked at odds with one another. Unable to locate the hostile parties, Wright concluded that the Indians had backed down. The volunteer army, however, engaged in combat even with peaceable tribal groups. In July volunteers encountered a Cayuse camp in the Grande Ronde Valley. Perceiving the villagers' intentions—if not their actions—as combative, militia members raided the camp, stealing horses and burning lodges. Sixty Cayuse people, mostly women and children, perished during the brutal onslaught.

Stevens viewed the Grande Ronde massacre as the decisive victory of the "war" and declared peace at hand. With an embarrassingly ineffective peace council held by Stevens at Walla Walla in September 1856, the Yakima War staggered to an inconclusive end. Stevens attempted to hold a hastily arranged council with some Northern Plateau tribes following the resumption of peace, but most tribal leaders had already departed for the fall round of fishing and hunting. Fearing involvement in the Yakima conflict, the Northern Plateau tribal leaders still in the region shunned the possibility of meeting with Stevens at this time. Coeur d'Alene leaders, isolated from Fort Walla Walla and occupied by autumn activities, may not have been aware of Stevens's careless attempt to convene a fall council.[40]

To ensure continued peace, Wool, who blamed selfish acts of white settlers for much of the violence, promptly closed the Interior Northwest from further settlement. Although Governor Stevens decried Wool's action as illegal, the expanded presence of the army in the region maintained the integrity of Wool's orders. Fort Walla Walla, near the Whitman Mission site, and Fort Simcoe in Yakima territory were commissioned in response to the Yakima War. By 1858 Lieutenant Colonel Edward Steptoe, Fort Walla Walla's commanding officer, had garrisoned his new post with four companies.[41] The Yakima War and military occupation of the Interior Northwest changed the region forever. The Native groups who had lived there for centuries would be forced to either fight or accommodate the newcomers, as—despite Wool's moratorium—the newcomers were clearly on the horizon and could not be turned back.

With the end of the Yakima War, a fragile peace settled on the Interior Northwest. Still, unresolved problems seethed under the surface. Some Yakima and Palouse bands did not accept peace and tried to rally Native support among the Spokanes, Columbias, Colvilles, and Schitsu'umsh. These warring factions found an increasingly receptive audience among disaffected people from tribes without treaties. Adding to the frustration of the nontreaty Coeur d'Alenes and their neighbors, in 1857 Isaac I. Stevens won election as Washington's territorial delegate, ending his tenure as governor and superintendent of Indian affairs. His departure from the territory ensured that he would not hold the promised treaty council with the Schitsu'umsh and other Northern Plateau peoples. Indeed, these tribes were never Stevens's priority; he focused on treaties with tribes he considered more powerful, such as the Nez Perce and the Yakima. Dismissed by Stevens as a small, isolated, and civilized tribe under Jesuit jurisdiction, the Schitsu'umsh felt the governor and the United States had acted in bad faith. Stevens's mental map of the Coeur d'Alenes thus contributed to his neglect of Schitsu'umsh treaty negotiations. His failure to negotiate with the Schitsu'umsh and other nontreaty tribes delayed formal federal recognition of land claims and left these groups exceedingly vulnerable to non-Indian encroachment.

F O U R

Territorial Defense: Participation in the Northern Plateau War of 1858

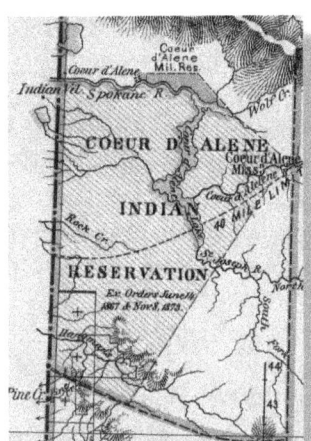

A terrible enemy did come, just as the circling raven foretold, and made war and there was much bloodshed and grief. The enemy was victorious and the way of life of a people was stamped out.

—Janet Campbell Hale, *Bloodlines: Odyssey of a Native Daughter*[1]

Isaac I. Stevens's broken promise of treaty negotiations with the Schi̱tsu'umsh and other Northern Plateau tribes bred distrust of the governor and of the government he represented. Concerned more about tribes he perceived as possessing real power, Stevens dismissed Coeur d'Alene influence as inconsequential. The presence of Sacred Heart Mission acted as a para-political force capable, in Stevens's view, of keeping peace between Indian people and intruders. Stevens overestimated Jesuit political influence with tribal members and underestimated Schi̱tsu'umsh resolve to protect territorial integrity. The legacy of the governor's neglect endured, even as Stevens left Washington to serve as the territory's delegate. Stevens's 1855 treaties remained unratified, largely because of Indian-white hostilities, the agreements the governor failed to negotiate left the Coeur d'Alenes and other nontreaty tribes susceptible to invasion, and his ultimate object—non-Indian agricultural settlement—stagnated as potential homesteaders perceived the Interior Pacific Northwest as an uncertain and dangerous place.

Despite General John E. Wool's closure of the interior and the increased presence of federal troops, conflicts between Indian people and non-Indians mounted. Wool's one exception to the ban on white encroachment—"the miners engaged in collecting gold at the Colville mines"—negated the effects of the commander's orders. Ironically, Wool set a precedent favoring extractive economic considerations over the rights of tribal people. The mandate to mining interests inundated the Colville Valley with prospectors. Discovery of gold deposits on the Fraser River in British Columbia further contributed to traffic moving through the Interior Northwest. Cattle and pack trains snaked through eastern Washington Territory to supply burgeoning mining camps. Governor Stevens's disapproval of Wool's territorial policies, moreover, led to the commander's replacement by Newman S. Clarke in May 1857. General Clarke's pro-settlement views made the resumption of hostilities in the interior more likely.[2]

Amid growing Indian disaffection with the miners and their suppliers, territorial officials issued only superficial warnings to outsiders. Before leaving office Stevens instructed William Craig, Indian agent for the Nez Perce, "to advise the miners of the conditions of the country and to caution them as to their deportment toward the Indians."[3] Apparently, not all visitors heeded such advice, for Palouse tribal members killed two prospectors near the Palouse River during spring of 1858. Coincidentally, a petition signed in November 1857 by forty miners seeking the assignment of U.S. troops to the Colville Valley reached commander Lieutenant Colonel Edward J. Steptoe at Fort Walla Walla on the heels of news of the miners' deaths. In addition, Antoine Plante's home at the Spokane ferry crossing was burned during this period. Although no proof existed, the former Hudson's Bay Company employee blamed area Natives for the arson. Intimations of Indian attacks coupled with the miners' request for protection convinced Steptoe to mount a northern expedition.[4]

As Steptoe readied three companies of dragoons at Fort Walla Walla, a small council of Coeur d'Alene, Palouse, Cayuse, Spokane, and Nez Perce leaders convened. Yakima chief Kamiakin and Tilcoax, a "refugee" among the Palouse tribe since the Cayuse uprising following the Whitman massacre, informed the participants of the deaths on the Palouse River and of conflicts between Native people and miners in the Colville Valley. Coeur d'Alene chiefs voiced concerns that either a retaliatory or an investigatory U.S. Army advance into their territory would occur during spring of 1858. Throughout the winter of 1857–1858, Father Joseph Joset recalled, "a great preoccupation prevailed among the Coeur d'Alene" regarding the possible deployment of troops. Considering the prospect an "idle tale," Joset discounted Coeur d'Alene concerns. "Indeed I could imagine no cause for such a movement of the army," Joset wrote, "except perhaps it should be to go to Colvile [sic], where I knew that since the introduction of whisky, there were some difficulties between the whites and the Indians." Joset recounted in his version of the events of 1858 that he believed Stevens respected the conditions set forth by the Northern Plateau tribes during the Spokane Council held in 1855. At that meeting the interior tribes had informed the governor that they would remain at peace unless troops occupied their territories without prior consent. The tribes identified the Snake River as the southern demarcation for this protected area. Despite his conviction that the army would not enter that region, Joset became alarmed when a Northern Plateau tribesman told him that if troops came, "the people will be awfully mad."[5]

Concerned that the mere presence of American soldiers in Indian Country would incite violence, Joset attempted to warn federal authorities. In April 1858 Joset embarked on a six-day journey from Sacred Heart Mission to Fort Walla Walla. As he approached Paradise Valley a messenger sent by Coeur d'Alene head chief Vincent Xwipep halted his progress. Vincent, camped with most of the Coeur d'Alene people at the seasonal root-gathering place near present-day Moscow, used scouts to track and protect Joset. When Vincent arrived at the missionary's camp, he convinced Joset to turn back. The priest's Coeur d'Alene guides were endangering their lives, Vincent explained, by undertaking the journey to Walla Walla. "The Paluses [sic] are trying every means to excite our young people to war against the Whites," the chief told Joset, adding that if Joset traveled through the Palouse "they will kill thy [Coeur d'Alene] companions, while hunting for the horses; they will noise about that [the Coeur d'Alene guides] have been killed by Americans, and there will be no controlling the people." Unfamiliar with the notoriously treacherous route and unable to locate non-Indian guides, Joset returned to Sacred Heart. Once at the mission Joset relayed his concerns to Nicholas Congiato, Rocky Mountain Missions superior, but the letter arrived "too late" to keep Steptoe from advancing into the region with his troops.[6]

Talk of war split the Coeur d'Alene leadership into opposing factions. Vincent and other tribal elders favored caution and desired that hostilities be prevented. Coeur d'Alene involvement in a war against whites, Vincent suspected, would result in tribal suffering regardless of the cause. A younger generation of Coeur d'Alene warriors, led by Milkapsi, pushed for tribal participation in a defensive confrontation to protect aboriginal territory. Influenced by Palouse leader Tilcoax and believing conflict with whites was inevitable, these young tribesmen represented a minority within the community. Throughout spring of 1858, peaceable influences prevailed. The Coeur d'Alene people agreed to pursue war only if military units forcibly entered their territory.[7]

Unmindful of the tribal councils anxiously forecasting his movements, Steptoe left Fort Walla Walla on May 6, 1858, with 159 poorly armed men composing Companies C, E, and H. The soldiers marched without sabers, carrying only muzzle-loading muskets with an inferior range of less than fifty yards. An oversight by the party's pack master resulted in a shortage of ammunition. Steptoe lightened his load by leaving boxes of ammunition in camp, and he dressed in casual civilian clothing, as though he were out for a Sunday ride.[8]

In contrast to Steptoe's men, interior tribes were well armed with superior Hudson's Bay Company trade muskets, highly prized for their long-range capability. In addition to a flourishing trade network established with the Hudson's

Bay Company, interior tribes procured firearms from other sources. The Coeur d'Alenes, as they had during the 1847 Cayuse War, often acquired their weapons through the Jesuit mission. Indeed, Father Joset's concern regarding the hostile climate in 1858 prompted the missionaries to destroy the weapons and ammunition housed at Sacred Heart Mission. When tribal members discovered the destruction, Joset later recounted, "they were very angry," and "some even proposed to plunder the Mission's house." The clerics could not destroy ammunition already held by Native people, however, and still other arms sources existed. U.S. federal charges that Jesuits supplied Indians with arms had led American troops to ransack and destroy the Oblate mission among the Yakimas in 1845 and had influenced Oregon Territory to call for the expulsion of Jesuit missionaries in 1848.[9]

Government documents suggest that representatives from the Church of Jesus Christ of Latter-day Saints (Mormons) helped procure weaponry for the interior tribesmen. After experiencing religious discrimination in Ohio, Missouri, and Illinois, these religious people migrated to the Great Basin surrounding Salt Lake (present-day Utah) between 1845 and 1848. There they established agricultural communities based on the Mormon doctrine of discipline and cooperation. Still, the Mormons continued to endure religious persecution for their practice of polygamy and other beliefs. In 1857 Brigham Young, then leader of the State of Deseret's theocracy, called upon his followers to resist U.S. attempts to establish territorial government in Utah. Mormon settlers braced themselves for a confrontation with federal troops. As tensions mounted, a group of Latter-day Saints and possibly local tribal people in southern Utah attacked a wagon train headed from Arkansas to California, killing perhaps as many as 120 men, women, and children, in what became known as the Mountain Meadows Massacre.[10]

Although a bloodless accord between Young and federal officials ended the "Mormon War" in 1858, the Latter-day Saints attempted to create allies among Native peoples in the Interior Northwest. Church representatives offered aid to the Yakima people during an 1854 council, and the commanding officers of the Walla Walla volunteers reported finding muskets and balls "bearing the Mormon brand" following altercations with interior tribes in 1855. Contemporary anti-Mormon sentiment casts doubt on the accuracy of federal accounts regarding Latter-day Saint arms supply. Nevertheless, because church theology embraced Native Americans as the descendants of the Old Testament's lost tribes of Israel, the Mormons attempted to forge cooperative relationships with western tribal peoples.[11]

Regardless of where they procured their weapons, the interior tribes of the Northwest prepared for the possible arrival of the army just as Colonel Steptoe, instead of taking the Colville Road, chose instead to lead his troops in a puzzling, winding northeastern course toward Schitsu'umsh lands. Scarcity of water north of the Snake River made this route an odd and dangerous choice, one Steptoe would not have pursued unless he planned to confront the parties held responsible for alleged raids and killings. "There appears to be so much excitement amongst the Palouse and Spokane Indians," Steptoe wrote in his April 17, 1858, report to the secretary of war, "to make an expedition to the north advisable if not necessary."[12]

While traveling south of the Snake, Steptoe encountered a small band of perhaps thirty Palouse tribal members. Rather than pursue the group at this time, Steptoe advanced toward the river crossing at Almota Creek. The Palouses, believing themselves trapped south of the Snake, traversed the waterway twelve miles above the safer, more common crossing controlled by Nez Perce member Tammutsa, or "Chief Timothy." Makeshift rafts presented no match for the runoff-drenched river, and a young Palouse woman and her two small children drowned. Coeur d'Alene sources indicate that Steptoe *did* pursue the Palouses and that his men "laughed and shot at the Indians fleeing across the river." The incident strengthened Native resistance against military encroachment. Coeur d'Alene tribal tradition maintains that the heart-broken husband and father returned to the spot annually to mourn the loss.[13]

At the confluence of Almota Creek and the Snake River, Steptoe enlisted Timothy's aid in fording the swollen water. When expedition guide John McBane refused to continue north of the pivotal waterway, the colonel accepted Timothy's offer to serve as scout. Once the troops crossed the Snake—the demarcation line tribal leaders had identified in 1855—the interior tribes regarded them as hostile.[14] Continuing his advance northward, Steptoe caught the attention of Coeur d'Alene, Spokane, Palouse, Yakima, Kalispel, Colville, and Columbia warriors scattered throughout the spring camas camps. Scouts crisscrossed Steptoe's path, reporting the army's progress to their leaders riding ahead. When Steptoe pierced the boundary of Schitsu'umsh territory above the Palouse River, a Palouse scout reported that army guide Timothy had a message for Chief Tilcoax: "[Tilcoax], very soon thy wives, thy horses, thy goods shall be ours." Father Joset later indicated that Tilcoax and Timothy were engaged in a feud, the origins of which the priest remained unaware. Timothy's taunting messages, however, suggest his involvement in ushering Steptoe's troops northward may have had roots in intertribal rivalry instead of in loyalty to the United States. Coeur d'Alene warriors, overhearing the exchange between the Palouse scout and Tilcoax, reportedly misinterpreted the comments as directed toward the Coeur d'Alene people as a whole.[15] Joset described the excitement among young warriors already prepared to fight. "Think of the effect of it upon the young," the missionary lamented, "who thought the[y] saw in the movements of the troops a confirmation of that word: they were pursued, without any provocation on their part." Tilcoax, Joset declared, "had just what he wanted, he who before and after this, did his utmost to raise enemies [sic] to the Whites."[16]

Historical controversy exists regarding whether Steptoe was actually in Spokane or Coeur d'Alene tribal territory. The Seltice family history states that "this part of the Palouse country belonged entirely to the Coeur d'Alene Indians. Deboos [a Coeur d'Alene tribal member] lived the farthest into the Palouse country at Colfax, and some four families of Coeur d'Alene Indians lived from Spangle to Potlatch. Coeur d'Alenes don't agree with 'historians' who claimed that this was the country of the Spokanes."[17] Following the Steptoe campaign, U.S. Army officials asked Father De Smet to write a detailed account of Coeur d'Alene tribal territory. "The Spokane prairie," De Smet wrote, "is claimed by the Coeur d'Alene Indians. Using Lake Coeur d'Alene as a 'central point,' their country may extend 50 miles to every point of the compass."[18]

As Steptoe continued his advance north of the Palouse River, Chief Vincent approached the column and demanded an explanation for the trespass. Steptoe, who did not seem to know the difference between the Spokane and Coeur d'Alene peoples and failed to recognize that he was encroaching on Coeur d'Alene territory, informed the chief that he had no business with the peaceable tribe and was on his way to Colville. Vincent pointed to the threatening appearance of the howitzers and to the colonel's peculiar route, well east of the usual Walla Walla–Colville Road. Chief Vincent and several Spokane leaders refused to give Steptoe canoes and assistance in crossing the Spokane River. Thus denied crucial aid in an unfamiliar land, the colonel apparently decided to spend the night and return to Fort Walla Walla the next day. Although Vincent distrusted Steptoe's intentions, he returned to the Coeur d'Alene camp and attempted to calm the young warriors. Joset finally arrived in the evening, but Vincent told the priest he "had no rest the whole day" from trying to keep peace. Joset also endeavored to reassure the tribesmen, but "they kept the all night [sic] yelling their war songs." Meanwhile, Steptoe formulated the return trip to Fort Walla Walla and sent a messenger to request a detachment to protect the Snake River crossing. The Indian courier, assuming Steptoe's force would face annihilation before ever reaching the Snake, failed to deliver the communication.[19]

Steptoe turned back the following morning, May 17, with Father Joset following at breakneck speed. The missionary caught up with Steptoe and improvised a meeting between the commander and Indian leaders. Most of the chieftains, with the exception of Vincent, refused to attend. The conference was briefly interrupted by an argument between Coeur d'Alene warrior Melkapsi and another tribal leader, but the council ended with a handshake and "mutual satisfaction." Joset returned to camp—a distance of fifteen miles—arriving just in time to hear shots at the rear of Steptoe's column.[20]

Confusion among Coeur d'Alene and Palouse tribesmen resulted in the first firing. Father Joset blamed Coeur d'Alene warrior Paschal Stellam, who shot at Steptoe's men out of frustration and anger when tribal elders reprimanded his friend Melkapsi for disrupting the peace process. Seltice family tradition places the responsibility with Yakima tribesman Qualchan, who led raids against miners at the outset of the Yakima War, and five Palouse riders. Whoever fired the initial shots, Coeur d'Alene warriors quickly became involved in the fighting. When the soldiers cut down three prominent Coeur d'Alene warriors—James Nehlukteltshiye, Zachary Natatkem, and Victor Smena—approximately 1,000 Indian warriors mobilized against the small army contingent. Perhaps as many as 200 Coeur d'Alenes took part in the battle, along with nearly 200 Yakimas, 150 Spokanes, and varying numbers of Palouse and other tribesmen. Steptoe's troops "labored under the great disadvantage of having to defend the pack train while in motion," the commander later reported, "and in a rolling country peculiarly favorable to the Indian mode of warfare."[21] Attempting to protect the flank of the column while under continuous fire from Yakima and Coeur d'Alene guns, the officers commanding Companies E and C—Lieutenant William Gaston and Captain Oliver Taylor, respectively—were killed. Company C dragoons engaged in hand-to-hand combat over the downed Taylor before transporting the mortally wounded captain behind the lines.[22]

By late afternoon Steptoe found himself and his miserably outfitted force stranded on a 150-foot hill near present-day Rosalia, Washington. Outnumbered, surrounded, isolated from reinforcements, and perilously short of ammunition, Steptoe pondered the almost certain demise of his troops. At about 10:00 P.M. he attempted a silent escape through Indian lines. "Leaving the disabled animals and such as were not in condition to travel so far and so fast" and burying the two howitzers at the crest of the hill, Steptoe's haggard column disappeared into the darkness. Remarkably, no Indian warriors pursued the group, and Steptoe, finding that Fort Walla Walla forces had not secured the river crossing, again relied on the aid of friendly Nez Perce Indians to cross the Snake. Once south of the river, the colonel limped into Fort Walla Walla and historical infamy.[23]

Non-Indian accounts of the incident labeled Steptoe a hero and a tactical genius. Even Joset attributed the feat to Steptoe's abilities as a commander. One army contemporary wrote that the flight demonstrated "evidence of endurance that has few examples in history."[24] Some accounts gave the credit to guide Chief Timothy or other Nez Perce members, who supposedly located a gap in Indian lines for the colonel to slip through. Coeur d'Alene versions differ on both points. The Seltice family history maintains that the Coeur d'Alenes arranged Steptoe's escape by sending a message to the commander—signed by Father Joset—in the names of Vincent, Seltice, and Peter Wildshoe. "There is an opening made for you down the slope that hits the creek," the note purportedly read, "so you can make a get away." As the desperate troops made their way through enemy lines, Schitsu'umsh warriors beat their drums to "cover their retreat." Joset did not mention the Steptoe note and could hardly have signed it because he was not on the battlefield.[25]

A recent history argues that the most likely explanation is that "the Coeur d'Alenes, hoping to seize the lion's share of abandoned military equipment, ushered the troops through the Indian line."[26] Schitsu'umsh accounts of burying two of Steptoe's wounded soldiers, abandoned during the escape because of their wounds, implies that the Coeur d'Alene warriors witnessed and allowed Steptoe's retreat. Following Steptoe's route, the Coeur d'Alenes found a mortally wounded sergeant, W. C. Williams, lying in the grass. When the suffering man asked the Schitsu'umsh warriors to shoot him, they declined, but a tribal woman stayed with him until he died. Coeur d'Alenes also located Victor C. De Moy, an immigrant soldier so severely wounded he used his last ammunition to kill himself. According to the Seltice family history, the Indians gave each soldier "a lonely and sorrowful burial and placed a cross over their graves." When army officers returned to the Steptoe battlefield, Coeur d'Alene informants revealed the location of those graves, and a Coeur d'Alene source escorted officials to the site where a tribal member had found the corpse of Lieutenant Gaston and buried him in a shallow grave.[27]

The nature of interior tribal warfare contributed to Steptoe's escape, mainly because the tribes did not organize themselves into a solid, united front. Each group fought independent of the others. Given the loose organization of these fighting units, gaps may have existed in the lines surrounding Steptoe's troops. Indeed, some Spokane participants had temporarily left the battlefield to procure fresh horses, perhaps leaving an opening in the line.[28] Moreover, tribal leaders fought for specific objectives, not for total war. From the Schitsu'umsh perspective, Steptoe had already been soundly defeated as he awaited his fate on the small hillside; complete annihilation was not necessary. To offer a cornered enemy escape represented a greater source of power than sheer destruction. Despite his daring flight, Steptoe's expedition embodied a stark failure for army regulars in the Interior Pacific Northwest. The colonel's force sustained seven dead, six critically wounded, seven wounded, and one missing. Although the Indians endured greater casualties—nine killed and approximately forty-five wounded—the stakes were high for Fort Walla Walla. Hopes for white settlement dimmed with the humiliation of an army commander. Steptoe's defeat frightened all whites in the region; Joset commented that even Sacred Heart Mission "was none too safe."[29]

Indeed, when Joset returned to Sacred Heart following the Steptoe debacle, he found that several travelers were trapped at the mission. Four white men had stopped at the mission looking for food and had entered a hazardous environment. "A widow squaw," Joset explained, "whose only son Zachary had been killed [in the battle with Steptoe], by her wailings was exciting the men to vengeance." Joset hid two of the whites in a mission house while the others took refuge in the nearby woods. Joset then convinced tribal member Bonaventure Zemplsenxul to guide the men "over the mountains." Joset provided the group with provisions, and the Coeur d'Alene guide took them by canoe at night to the trail leading over the Bitterroot Mountains. Joset later received a letter of gratitude from the party.[30]

With the future of Fort Walla Walla and Interior Northwest settlement at risk, General Newman S. Clarke followed a twofold course. The general pursued peace with tribal people but prepared for war. In a June 1858 letter to Father Joset, Clarke requested that the priest remain among the Indians "that they may be brought to a sense of their wrongs towards the United States and the destruction awaiting them, if they do not by submission avert the war." Clarke's peace proposal required hostile tribes to put down their arms, return government property including Steptoe's buried howitzers, and surrender the tribal individuals responsible for inciting war. Joset and Superior Father Nicholas Congiato traveled among the tribes for several weeks. The priests exercised little influence, however, with tribes such as the Palouse, who rejected Clarke's demand of unconditional surrender. The Spokanes were willing to negotiate but refused to turn over neighboring tribal individuals. Actually, the conditions of Clarke's peace could not be met. Some of the plunder had been sold—Coeur d'Alene tribal members had bartered U.S.-branded horses, along with other Steptoe battlefield items, to Fort Colville traders. Tribal chieftains' limited authority hindered their ability to force the surrender of individuals. Finally, unconditional surrender contradicted traditional peacemaking customs, which often included an exchange of gifts to indicate the sincerity of both sides.[31]

Half of the Coeur d'Alene warriors involved in the Steptoe battle returned home for the summer round of camping while the rest, about 100 tribesmen, stayed with the Yakima warriors and prepared for future military engagements. Coeur d'Alene chief Vincent responded to the peace proposal by describing the terms as "somewhat harsh" and "hard to enforce . . . [since] one hundred Coeur d'Alenes have already put down their arms, and they won't take them up again unless they are forced to." Tradition dictated that the families of fallen warriors make the decision for war or peace. "Among the Coeur d'Alene, the Chief Vincent, with nearly fifty men stood to their promises and remained at the Mission," Joset remembered, "but the others, at the sollicitation [sic] of the relatives of the three killed ones, resumed the war path."[32]

His peace proposal defied, General Clarke dispatched all available troops from posts as distant as California to the Interior Northwest. Captain Erasmus D. Keyes, commander of four companies, traveled from San Francisco to The Dalles on June 21 and spent the next month vigorously training his men. In August Keyes and his soldiers marched 177 miles to Fort Walla Walla, where they met Colonel George Wright, in charge of the retaliation against the Northern Plateau tribes. On August 25 and 26 Wright and 900 men, armed with Springfield rifles boasting a range of 1,000 yards, crossed the Snake River. Thirty-three "friendly" Nez Perce accompanied the expedition as scouts and interpreters.

John Mullan, whose work on the Fort Benton–Walla Walla military road had ceased with the outbreak of hostilities, served as topographical engineer.

Wright inflicted Steptoe's vengeance in two engagements. The Battle of Four Lakes began on September 1, ten miles west of Spokane Falls. Approximately 500 Indian people—including 100 Coeur d'Alenes—engaged Wright. Quickly respectful of the long-range capacity of the Springfield rifles, the defenders kept their distance and eventually retreated after setting fire to the prairie. Coeur d'Alene tribal members maintained that only a Spokane and a Yakima lost their lives during this encounter, but contemporary army accounts place the number of Native casualties closer to 60. The Indian custom of dismounting while sighting and firing may partially account for this discrepancy, since troops could have mistaken riderless horses as an indication of the Native dead and wounded. Actual casualty numbers, as Captain Keyes observed, could not be ascertained because the Indians always carried their dead and wounded off the battlefield. Wright's forces came away unscathed.[33]

Beaten back and angered by the audacity of the "trespassers," the Indian forces—172 Yakima, 150 Spokane, and 50 Palouse in addition to the Coeur d'Alene tribesmen—regrouped. When Wright's soldiers began to move toward the Spokane River on September 5, the Indians set fire to the native grasses and began firing on the troops amid the confusion of the smoke. "A strong wind was blowing in our faces," Keyes wrote in his memoir, "and the flames were shooting high and constantly extending." The Indians pursued the army, in what became known as the Battle of Spokane Plains, for fourteen miles—over "hills and ravines, woods, rocks and bare level ground." When the regulars reached the Spokane River, the Indians retreated, unable to "press the troops any further." Despite the shower of bullets and the deadly splintering of the pine stands from which the army drove the Indians, few casualties resulted. A shell-torn tree limb threw Kamiakin from his horse, severely wounding the Yakima chieftain. Army casualty reports listed one wounded. Coeur d'Alene witness Andrew Youmas counted three dead—one apparently from his own people—and four wounded for the Indian side. The Coeur d'Alene force lost one warrior.[34]

Even though the Indians withdrew as the army neared the Spokane River, the Spokane Valley engagements proved that Wright's extensively trained and carefully outfitted troops were unable to decisively defeat the Northern Plateau tribes. The Battle of Spokane Plains tested the soldiers' skill and endurance. Captain Keyes, who had ridden "eighty miles on the same pony of incredible endurance," returned to camp exhausted. "I kept my saddle till my tent was pitched," he later recounted, "then I dismounted, took a glass of wine, gave orders not to disturb me, and lay down on my back to rest." In tribute to the intensity of the Indian defense, Keyes did not "move a muscle" for a full half hour and "felt the whole time that if I did move one I should die." An experienced "Indian fighter" as well as Union officer during the Civil War, Keyes declared of Spokane Plains, "Never before, or since, was I so nearly finished by the toil of war."[35]

The Indians and the army had reached a stalemate. The tribesmen had temporarily retreated, but some groups repositioned themselves for further engagements. The army's spectacular show of force had failed to substantially reduce the enemy's number. In an unfamiliar land, facing the onset of winter, and unsure of the opponent's location, Wright was by no means assured of future victories. Still, the Coeur d'Alenes and their allies chose to discontinue the hostilities, largely because of factionalization and intertribal disagreement.[36]

The Battle of Spokane Plains magnified discord within the tenuous tribal ranks. As with other participating groups, the Coeur d'Alene contingent fractured as some warriors, influenced by Father Joset's peace efforts and aware that tribal chief Vincent did not support their involvement, deserted the loose confederacy and returned to the mission. Although Joset, finding the ex-warriors "too faithless," refused to negotiate directly with Wright on their behalf, the priest sent Coeur d'Alene member Sebastian Zulyatsot to present their peace proposal. On September 10 Zulyatsot arrived at Wright's camp. The peace messenger found that the colonel, in an effort to achieve an emotional victory in the wake of an uncertain military one, had captured and shot approximately 800 of the interior tribes' grazing horses. Army officers drove the animals into a high enclosure and spent two days destroying the "noble beasts." Captain Keyes, who had favored killing the animals, ultimately expressed dismay at the "sight" of the slaughter. "They were all sleek, glossy, and fat, and as I love a horse, I fancied I saw in their beautiful faces an appeal for mercy," Keyes intoned. As for the shooters, Keyes thought that "towards the last the soldiers appeared to exult in their bloody task."[37]

Arriving in the midst of the slaughter, Zulyatsot extended to Colonel Wright the Coeur d'Alenes' peace offer. Wright sent Zulyatsot back to the mission with a handwritten message to Joset and the promise that the army column would arrive at Sacred Heart Mission within three days. In the communication Wright exaggerated his military victories—saying "kind fortune has favored us thus far, beyond our most sanguine expectations"—as an effort to gain advantage over the peace process. Indeed, the horse slaughter, although brutal by modern standards, was successful in achieving Wright's objective—the Indians were made aware of U.S. military might with minimal loss of life. The commander gave assurances that peaceful Coeur d'Alene individuals had "nothing to fear," but he added that "nothing but an unqualified submission to my will can now avail [the hostiles]."[38]

True to his word, Wright arrived at Sacred Heart Mission on September 13. Along the way his soldiers staged a "victory" march through Coeur d'Alene lands, killing beef cattle and setting fire to barns and stacked hay. The troops consumed only the hind quarters of the cattle, further angering their owners—

families that had remained neutral during the conflict. The Coeur d'Alene people viewed Wright's actions as duplicitous, since he professed peace but allowed the troops to display "their heroism by seeing who could destroy the most property of the innocent." The slaughter of livestock and barn burnings left an indelible impression on the Coeur d'Alenes, who already found it difficult to trust a government that had failed to deliver promised treaty negotiations.[39]

Despite their misgivings, ninety-five Coeur d'Alene families gathered at the mission to negotiate peace with Wright. The women hauled wood for Wright's camp while the men pastured 500 cavalry horses. After several days of talks the Coeur d'Alenes agreed to a seven-part peace treaty. Complex factors influenced their acceptance of the demands. The tribesmen felt their military showing was sufficient to draw federal attention to the interior Coeur d'Alene presence and win respect for tribal territory. In addition, Coeur d'Alene leaders thought acceptance of peace would facilitate long-awaited treaty negotiations, which the tribesmen hoped would sanction territorial boundaries. Indeed, Article Six of the treaty dictated "that when the foregoing articles shall have been fully complied with, a permanent treaty of peace and friendship shall be made."[40]

Chief Vincent and four other tribal leaders signed the document, pledging the return of army property and the surrender of individuals responsible for starting the attack on Steptoe, who would be returned to the tribe—contingent on "good conduct"—at the end of six months. The peace treaty also guaranteed whites "unmolested" travel through Coeur d'Alene country. For his part, Wright promised that "no war shall be made upon the Coeur d'Alene nation in the future."[41] As Jesuit historian Robert Burns has argued, Wright did not possess authority to negotiate "treaties." The negotiations were viewed as "preliminary," printed as part of a congressional report detailing the hostilities and regarded as simple peace agreements. They were not formally ratified by the U.S. Senate.[42]

Wright's entourage rode out of the mission grounds on September 18, crossing the Coeur d'Alene River with the assistance of tribal members and their birch canoes. At the end of the month Wright held separate peace councils with Spokane and Palouse leaders. Father Joset induced at least 100 Spokane members to attend the peacemaking. Coeur d'Alene warriors Melkapsi and Andrew Seltice signed the Coeur d'Alene treaty at the Spokane Council, for they had refused to attend the earlier mission conference. Their names, although not on the original treaty, were inserted in published version.[43]

After the Spokanes had agreed to peace, Yakima and Palouse leaders—"emboldened" by the two existing peace agreements—approached the colonel. Wright's meeting with these groups, however, resulted in retribution rather than peace. Yakima chief Owhi, riding alone, approached the army camp and asked for peace. Wright, sensing an opportunity to capture Owhi's elusive son, Qualchan, put the elder chief in chains and dispatched a messenger to the younger chief. Owhi would be hanged if Qualchan failed to turn himself in to Wright within four days. Before the messenger could complete his task, however, the younger Yakima chief, apparently unaware of his father's capture, rode in to Wright's camp. Two warriors and his wife, who carried a ceremoniously decorated sword symbolizing peace, accompanied the young chief. Wright seized Qualchan and within fifteen minutes of his arrival directed the troops to hang the young warrior. Six Palouse tribesmen met their deaths in a similar manner near the banks of Latah Creek, thereafter known by tribal people as Hangman's Creek (now the creek is again referred to as Latah). Captain Keyes, who gave a gruesome account of Qualchan's death in his memoir, called this site the "Camp of Death."[44]

Wright dealt with Palouse and Yakima leaders more harshly than he did with Coeur d'Alene participants because he judged the former responsible for the hostilities. The Jesuit priest Joset influenced Wright's views of tribal involvement, to the advantage of the Coeur d'Alene people. Colonel Wright thanked Joset for "zealous and persevering efforts in bringing about this [Coeur d'Alene] accommodation, which has terminated so successfully." Regarding tribal members, the commander expressed "the great pleasure I have felt in seeing them come with all their people, promptly, and willingly, and acknowledging their errors, and putting their trust in us in all things." Sacred Heart Mission also made a favorable impression on Wright's officers. Father Joset's "self-denial" made such an impact on Captain Keyes during the Coeur d'Alene conference that he subsequently joined the Roman Catholic faith.[45]

Joset's involvement in the 1858 peace councils indicated the complex role thrust upon the mission by the encroachment of miners, settlers, and federal officials on interior tribal lands. During the 1858 hostilities, Sacred Heart functioned both as a safe haven for frightened whites and as a peacemaking ground. Although Isaac I. Stevens no longer served as territorial governor and superintendent of Indian affairs, his legacy became the Northern Plateau War. Governor Stevens's underestimation of the Coeur d'Alene Tribe and of its territorial protectiveness created fertile ground for conflict. Denied promised treaty negotiations and faced with invasion by federal military forces, some Coeur d'Alene people resorted to armed defense of their territory. The resulting peace treaty with Wright marked the first agreement concluded between the U.S. government and the tribe. The Coeur d'Alene people accepted peaceful resolution, but they remained confident that tribal warriors had shown a respectful forcefulness in protecting the integrity of their territory. The war also altered tribal politics. After the war tribal leaders, relying on the promises made in the Wright document, turned to peaceful means of resistance—characterized by a structured assimilation policy. This also meant a shift in political leadership, now firmly allied with the Jesuits. Anxious to return to seasonal activities in the wake of peace, tribal members readied their winter houses in a landscape altered by treaties, gold, and warfare.

F I V E

The Challenge of Nontreaty Status and the 1867 Reservation

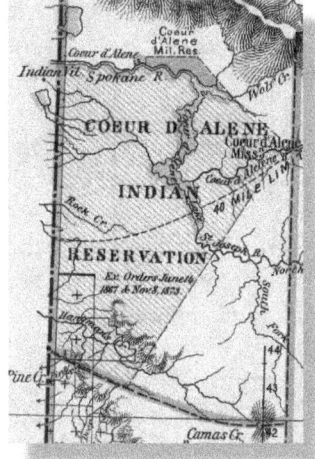

> I fear that the location of our road, and the swarms of miners and emigrants that must pass here year after year, will so militate against the best interests of the [Sacred Heart] mission that its present site will have to be changed or abandoned. This, for [the fathers] and the Indians, is to be regretted; but I can only regard it as the inevitable result of opening and settling the country.
> —John Mullan, February 14, 1863[1]

THE 1858 PEACE AGREEMENTS OPENED A NEW PHASE OF RELATIONS between non-Indians and Native American peoples in the Interior Pacific Northwest. If Colonel George Wright's battlefield victory seemed inconclusive to tribal people, the peace agreements of 1858 represented an unqualified success for territorial and federal entities. The defeat of the Northern Plateau tribes stimulated non-Indian interest in the region. The outbreak of the Civil War in the eastern United States intensified the flow of settlers both in and out of the Pacific Northwest. The Union and Confederate armies drew military personnel from western forts, but the war encouraged settlers from border and war-torn states to try their luck farming, ranching, or mining in the relatively peaceful trans-Mississippi West.

Following Appomattox in 1865, federal attention returned to the West and to relations with Indian peoples there. In victory the Union pursued a northern vision of western development that sought to curb local and state control. Post–Civil War Republican politicians maintained strong ties to corporate industry and encouraged its expansion into the western territories. As president, Ulysses S. Grant pursued an aggressive Indian agenda—known as "Grant's peace policy"—aimed at "civilizing" the nation's tribal people and emphasizing a cooperative relationship among government, religious missionaries, and western industry.[2] The infancy of an extractive economy, the creation of sizable enclaves of white settlement, and the intensified struggle of nontreaty Indian tribes to keep their lands influenced Schi̱tsu'umsh and U.S. government interaction between 1859 and 1870. By the end of the 1860s the federal government had mapped a reservation for the Coeur d'Alenes. Within the struggle, Andrew Seltice emerged as a dynamic Coeur d'Alene tribal leader whose political savvy and anti-encroachment tactics succeeded, for a time, in preserving the tribe's hold on its traditional land base.

In the wake of the military defeat of the Northern Plateau warriors, the federal government's attention returned to the issue of mapping reservations for the nontreaty tribes. Twenty years of Oregon Trail traffic had crowded the Willamette Valley, forcing homesteaders to retrace their steps in search of available land. Pressure to settle the Interior Northwest mounted as the wave of emigration began moving east instead of west. Despite the 1858 peace treaties, Brigadier General William S. Harney, who replaced General Newman S. Clarke as commander of the Department of Oregon, doubted that the Northern Plateau tribes had been completely subdued. Harney requested that the San Francisco troops stationed in Oregon and Washington territories remain throughout the winter of 1858–1859. General Wright, offended at the suggestion that the western Washington tribes had not been completely defeated, quickly assured Harney "that we have nothing to apprehend." Then he declared, the "*Nez Perces, Spokanes, Coeur d'Alenes, Pelouses* [sic]*, Walla Wallas,* and other tribes residing on both banks of the Columbia and its tributaries, are now regarded as entirely friendly." Wright opposed the establishment of additional permanent posts, recommending instead that annual expeditions "be made through Indian country, north, east, and south of Fort Walla Walla" to maintain peace. Conscious that Washington Territory's settlement rate still lagged behind Oregon's, Wright and other Department of Oregon officials made public peace declarations to embolden would-be settlers. To prove that the interior was safe for settlers, Harney reopened the Walla Walla Valley—previously closed because of the war—in October 1858.[3]

Meanwhile, Isaac I. Stevens, now functioning in his role as Washington's congressional delegate, lobbied for approval of his 1855 treaties. Five years of intermittent hostilities made ratification of Stevens's treaties with the Walla Walla, Yakima, Cayuse, Umatilla, and Nez Perce peoples essential to the opening of interior Washington. Stevens's replacement in the territorial superintendency—James W. Nesmith, who served a joint Indian superintendency for Oregon and Washington—eagerly supported congressional approval of the 1855 agreements. The Senate ratified Stevens's nine treaties in March 1859.[4] With the treaty tribes confined to reservations, homesteaders, miners, railroaders, and timber barons confidently entered the Inland Northwest. The nontreaty Coeur d'Alene, Spokane, Lower Kalispel, Lakes, Colville, San Poel, Methow, and Okanogan Tribes faced the onslaught of newcomers without federal recognition or protection of their home territories.[5]

In an effort to seal peaceful relations between the United States and the Plateau nontreaty tribes, General Harney appointed Father Peter John De Smet as an army chaplain. Harney knew of De Smet's favorable reputation among the Roman Catholic Plateau peoples, particularly the Coeur d'Alenes, and hoped the Jesuit priest could influence even non-Catholics to remain at peace. De Smet wintered with the tribes during 1858–1859, counseling them "both as an agent of the government and in his clerical capacity, as to the advantages accruing to them by preserving peaceable and friendly relations with the whites at all times." De Smet used Sacred Heart Mission as a base of operations, as did other whites in the area including topographical engineer John Mullan. If Father Joset's role in the 1858 peace process contributed to the mission's para-political reputation, De Smet's stay there in his official capacity as army chaplain confirmed it. Ultimately, De Smet spent eighty-seven days at the Coeur d'Alene facility. Severe weather and biting cold emphasized the site's isolation and prompted De Smet to refer to those months as "the long and dreary winter."[6]

Three months with the Coeur d'Alene people convinced De Smet that tribal warriors had been pulled into the battles of 1858 when their territory was invaded by the army. No long-range offensive plan of attack against the military had ever existed among the Coeur d'Alenes. The real inciter of the bloodshed, De Smet concluded, was Palouse tribesman Tilcoax. "From all I can learn," he reported to General Harney's aide, Captain Alfred Pleasonton, "[Tilcoax] . . . has been the prime mover in all the late wars against Colonel Steptoe and Colonel Wright." Father De Smet further absolved the Coeur d'Alenes in November 1858 by using his influence to win the release, four months early, of the Coeur d'Alene hostages taken by Wright during the peace council.[7] Despite the treaty stipulation that the hostages remain at Walla Walla for six months, De Smet successfully secured their homecoming because, according to one Jesuit account, "they had been a source of edification to the troops there by reason of their Christian character and prayerfulness." De Smet also had a personal interest in freeing the Schitsu'umsh hostages; their capture and the tribe's participation in the 1858 hostilities reflected poorly on Sacred Heart Mission's spiritual influence. By helping clear the tribe's name, De Smet maintained Sacred Heart's stature as a symbol of order in the "wilderness." De Smet's public relations effort proved successful, for the early release of tribal members Milkapsi and Stellam contributed to a growing postwar perception of the Coeur d'Alene tribe as Christian, hard-working, and "civilized."[8]

Following the long winter at Sacred Heart Mission, De Smet recommended to Captain Pleasonton that a delegation of interior tribes travel to Fort Vancouver, on the Columbia River in western Washington Territory, to meet with General Harney and "renew the treaty of peace." Harney seized the opportunity to put the previous year's hostilities to rest and enthusiastically represented the idea as his own in correspondence with his superiors. Despite the demands of spring subsistence activities, De Smet managed to recruit chiefs from the Coeur d'Alene, Kalispel, Flathead, Colville, and Spokane Tribes to attend the meeting. At the suggestion of Sacred Heart missionary Gregory Gazzoli, Coeur d'Alene tribal members elected delegates. The tribe chose to send Andrew Seltice instead of Chief Vincent, indicating tribal resentment of Vincent's crusade against Coeur d'Alene involvement in the battles with Steptoe and Wright. Vincent's approach had impaired his authority, whereas Seltice's participation in the battles and resistance to Wright's conditions for peace had earned him respect. Seltice's role in the Fort Vancouver delegation marked the first of many instances in which the chief met with federal government or military officials on behalf of the Coeur d'Alene tribe. Tribal members voted to send Bonaventure to accompany Seltice, and the presence of two Coeur d'Alene delegates when no other Northern Plateau tribe sent more than one further enhanced the Schitsu'umsh group's image.[9]

Seltice's newfound authority represented a shift in power, from the lake and river people to the agricultural mission Schitsu'umsh. Among the first tribal converts to Catholicism, Seltice and his extended family were devout Catholics and close allies of the Jesuit mission. Seltice was about forty years old, and his appearance was already distinguished and dignified. He wore his hair shoulder length (later he wore it short) and dressed in white clothing. Considered wealthy by his peers, Seltice owned horses and herded cattle in the Spokane Valley, near what is now Liberty Lake. There he built a log home and barns and held annual gatherings for tribal members. His father, Moses Seltice, farmed near present-day Post Falls, Idaho. Seltice's father was a modest farmer; the younger Seltice accumulated his wealth during his lifetime. Seltice had twenty-three children. All historical accounts of Andrew Seltice credit him with intelligence and shrewd negotiating skills. Seltice's charismatic leadership and his connections to the Jesuit mission dominated tribal affairs for the next four decades.[10]

In May 1859 Father De Smet accompanied the seven representative chieftains to Fort Vancouver. As a recent De Smet biographer noted, the Jesuit priest and General Harney pursued different goals for the delegation's three-week stay in western Washington Territory. De Smet focused on impressing the delegates with the technology and superiority of "civilization." The priest led the group on tours of Portland, Oregon; Vancouver, Washington Territory; and other cities in the vicinity. De Smet spotlighted industrial establishments, steam engines, printing presses, forges, and manufacturing enterprises. The Jesuit also emphasized the need for conformity in a civilized world by taking the tribesmen through the grime-laden walls of Portland's prison.[11]

Harney's priority—the official council with the chiefs—occurred on May 28, 1859. "These chiefs have all declared to me the friendly desires which now animate them towards our people," a pleased Harney wrote regarding the meeting, "and they assure me that their own several tribes are all anxiously awaiting their return to confirm the peace and good will they are hereafter determined to preserve and maintain." For his part, Harney reiterated the peace pledges of Wright's 1858 treaties. To convince American civilians and Jesuit benefactors of the council's success, the Jesuit missionaries manipulated released versions of the chiefs' formal portrait to make it appear that all tribal representatives wore Euro-American–style clothing. Original copies of the photo reveal the prevalence of braids, beads, and other traditional tribal adornments.[12]

De Smet's official reports of his winter with the Coeur d'Alenes revealed both the extent of the tribe's homeland and the character of the Sacred Heart Mission's grounds in 1859. "Taking Coeur-d'Alene Lake as a central point," the missionary wrote, "their [Coeur d'Alene] country may extend fifty miles to every point of the compass." This circumference, according to De Smet's report, contained Lake Coeur d'Alene, the St. Joseph and Coeur d'Alene rivers and valleys, numerous smaller lakes, and multitudes of pine stands. These waterways abounded "wonderfully in mountain trout and other fish," and the forests were "well stocked with deer, with black and brown bears, and with a variety of fur-bearing animals." Other area tribes respected Coeur d'Alene territorial boundaries. The Spokane prairie's "abundant" grasses and roots provided all the local tribes with subsistence, for example, but the Coeur d'Alenes claimed the thirty-square-mile Spokane River drainage area. Regarding the region's potential to attract white settlement, De Smet indicated that the tribal heartland—Lake Coeur d'Alene and the river valleys of its drainage—was unsuitable for homesteading. As residents of Sacred Heart Mission had long known, the St. Joe and Coeur d'Alene river valleys experienced frequent spring flooding, and the priest could identify "no arable land" along Lake Coeur d'Alene. He was mistaken, but he may have downplayed the fertility of the land to dissuade settlement. The army chaplain also predicted that "the long winters and deep snows must retard the settlement of this country."[13]

Still, De Smet acknowledged the probability of non-Indian settlement in the open, fertile spaces of the Interior Northwest, particularly in the wake of the 1858 peace treaties and the Senate ratification of Stevens's 1855 treaties. De Smet suggested that the federal government negotiate with the nontreaty tribes for the creation of reservations to reduce their susceptiblility to invasion and violent confrontation. "Should all the remnants of Indians be gathered in this upper region" on one large reserve, the missionary reasoned, "one single military post might suffice to protect them against all encroachments and infringements of evil-disposed whites on Indians, and of Indians on the rights of whites." Perhaps influenced by the cohesiveness of the legendary Jesuit reductions in Paraguay, De Smet objected to "the way the reserves are laid out in Washington and Oregon Territories, far and wide apart, surrounded and accessible on all sides by whites" and "lead[ing] to the speedy destruction of the poor Indians." De Smet emphasized the federal government's responsibility to provide protection and aid to the Native peoples of the Interior Northwest, thus defining a new partnership between the Jesuit missionaries and federal officials. "Providence has intrusted and placed these weak tribes under the care and protection of a powerful government, whose noble end has always been to protect and advance them," De Smet declared, whereas the Jesuits' work as missionaries had been impaired by a lack of "adequate means." With the government as provider, the Jesuit missionaries were free to pursue their work as spiritual guides and purveyors of "civilization."[14]

Indeed, De Smet's 1859 correspondence also chronicled the maturation of Sacred Heart Mission. Nearly twenty years after its inception, the mission housed—in addition to its Italian Renaissance–style church—eight log houses, a barn, a stable, a flour mill, a blacksmith shop, a carpenter shop, and several bakeries. De Smet noted that two cultivated fields produced high yields—80 to 120 bushels of wheat per acre—even with primitive equipment. The priest's ink and sepia illustration of Sacred Heart Mission identified twenty-three separate buildings and natural features.[15]

Despite Father De Smet's recommendations regarding treaty reservations for the Coeur d'Alenes and their neighbors, circumstances diverted federal and territorial attention away from the problems facing nontreaty interior tribes. In June 1859 De Smet resigned as army chaplain and returned to administrative missionary work in St. Louis. With De Smet's departure the nontreaty groups' desire to negotiate title to their lands, particularly the Coeur d'Alene and Spokane Tribes, was temporarily forgotten. Adding to the void, the secession of the southern states and the outbreak of the Civil War in the eastern United States in 1861 drained manpower and resources from western military forts and territorial governments. Isaac I. Stevens, serving in the army during 1862, became one of the Union's 16,000 casualties during the Battle of Chantilly in Virginia. The intensity of fighting kept Congress too busy with wartime allocations to consider appropriations for negotiating with the Northern Plateau tribes.[16]

Territorial officials left Washington Territory for battlefields in the East, but an onslaught of prospectors and homesteaders maintained the flow of traffic into the region. Topographical engineer John Mullan resumed work on the military road from Fort Benton to Fort Walla Walla in accordance with the 1858 peace treaties, and his crew managed to finish the 624-mile project by 1862. As early as November 1860 Mullan reported that a large military party had successfully traveled over the route. Mullan wrote in his report to the secretary of war, "As you are aware, during the summer of 1859 and 1860 the Missouri River was proved to be navigable within one hundred miles of the Rocky Mountains, and during the present season a military detachment of three hundred recruits, under Major Blake, ascended in steamers as high as Fort Benton, where, taking land transportation, they moved safely and in good season to Fort Walla Walla." Dense forest and flooding forced Mullan to spend several seasons at Sacred Heart

Mission. Initially, the road circled the southern portion of Lake Coeur d'Alene and then cut through the St. Joseph River valley. Mullan's men struggled for a week clearing thick underbrush between the St. Joe and Sacred Heart Mission. Flooding on the St. Joe convinced Mullan that he had chosen the wrong course, and additional government appropriations allowed the topographical crew to reroute the lake portion in 1861. The new route skirted the northern part of the lake and extended from the Coeur d'Alene tribal winter village, on the lake's north shore, to the Sacred Heart Mission.[17]

During his time at the mission Mullan developed a friendship with the Jesuit fathers. Indeed, Mullan possessed ties to Jesuit missionaries through a relative, Father Elden Mullan, who served as the first American assistant to the father general. When Joset threatened to abandon Sacred Heart during the 1858 war, Mullan lobbied to keep it open—perhaps with an eye to the completion of his road. Joset later gave the lieutenant credit for continuing the mission and thus providing "the salvation of these poor Savages."[18]

Merely a clearing through the trees in some places, the Mullan Road promised rough and unpredictable travel. Still, the route's ability to increase regional traffic ranked second only to the Oregon Trail. Mullan's extensive topographical reports and maps also generated interest in the region and contributed yet another non-Indian map of Coeur d'Alene country. All of Mullan's maps of the region—the maps of the military road and of Colonel Wright's campaign—feature the "Coeur D'Alene Mission" as a stopping-off place but do not include a feature for "Coeur d'Alene Indians." On the official "Map of Military Road From Fort Walla Walla on the Columbia to Fort Benton on the Missouri," the Crow, Gros-Ventres, Blackfeet, Bannock, Flathead, Snake, Colville, and Yakima Indians all prominently marked but not the Coeur d'Alene. In omitting the Schitsu'umsh, Mullan mapped an identity for the tribe as inconsequential and therefore an insignificant barrier to non-Indian settlement.[19]

The Mullan Road's significance increased as mineral finds occurred during the 1860s and 1870s throughout the Interior Northwest. Residents of Walla Walla Valley discovered gold on Oro Fino Creek, a tributary of the Clearwater River, in 1860. This find, coupled with others in the Boise Basin in 1862, created a swell of mining communities. Much of the mining traffic came from California and western Washington via the Columbia River and Mullan Road. Over 10,000 prospectors used the Columbia as passage to the mines in 1861, more than 24,000 reportedly used it in 1862, and in 1864 approximately 36,000 miners traveled the route.[20]

Exploding mining populations in remote areas of eastern Washington Territory prompted the creation of Idaho Territory in 1863. Political as well as spatial considerations inspired the new entity's conception. Washington's territorial legislature in Olympia represented the Unionist and Republican ideals of western Washington residents. Largely composed of Democrats sympathetic to the southern cause, eastern Washington's large mining communities threatened Olympia's Republican majority. Introduced by Washington's delegate to Congress, the bill to create a separate territory for the mining towns found support with President Lincoln and the Radical Republican Congress. The creation of additional western states offered the Republicans a defense against the return of southern Democratic representatives in the event of a Union victory. But the political need to embrace widely scattered mining communities resulted in an awkward territorial boundary. Extending from near the 117-degree longitudinal line east to the Rocky Mountains and south to the Snake River Plain, the perimeter included all of present-day Idaho and part of western Montana. The territorial statute recognized Indian title to land and required that tribal rights to territory be extinguished prior to settlement. The territorial boundary line split Coeur d'Alene territory and mapped an "Idaho" identity for the Schitsu'umsh tribe.[21]

The Coeur d'Alene people perceived Mullan's military road and the new territorial boundary as undesirable encroachments, but the Peace Treaty of 1858 stipulated that whites be allowed "unmolested travel" through their country. The missionaries' friendly relationship with Mullan contributed to a decline in Jesuit authority with tribal members who opposed the road and marked the beginning of an internal schism that only grew worse as non-Indian pressure increased. The Jesuits had opposed war in 1858 and now seemed to welcome this new encroachment. In 1863, when Father Joset—concerned about mining traffic and the implications of Idaho Territory—proposed that the Coeur d'Alene people consolidate in the Palouse Valley, away from the lake and the mission, he met fierce tribal resistance. Coeur d'Alene families resided throughout Coeur d'Alene country—in the Spokane Valley, along the St. Joseph and Coeur d'Alene rivers, on Lake Coeur d'Alene, on Hayden Lake, on Liberty Lake, and in the Palouse Valley.[22]

Father Joset attempted to convince all the Coeur d'Alenes to move to the most fertile part of their country to keep it out of non-Indian control, but tribal members resisted for fear of losing remaining landholdings. "Building our houses, building our barns, building rail fences to keep stock off our fields and gardens," Spokane Valley resident Andrew Seltice declared, "we planned a permanent home for our children for all time right here." Giving up part of their aboriginal territory, Seltice continued, would "be good news for the packers who just travel around with no obligations and not even a farm to look after!"[23] Seltice was a Catholic and a mission supporter, but he feared moving would send the message that the tribe no longer needed the river and lake territory. Since Seltice later reversed his position after assuming the role of chief, this early resistance is telling. When Seltice reversed course in the 1870s, he did so with the understanding that he was sending important messages to whites about tribal land use.

Addressing Joset as "White-head," Peter Wildshoe, another Coeur d'Alene leader, also protested Joset's suggestion that the tribe relocate: "We can't be obligated to move again and again. Some people will take everything you have if you relax and give in. But we are not giving an inch! If this is what you call 'civilization,' then why can't we go east where all the whites are. We would just pick out some land and tell them to move aside, because 'We want your best land!'"[24]

Coeur d'Alene tribal leaders closely monitored rumors about the American war in the East. In 1863 Father Joset informed the tribe that the tide had shifted to the North. "When the war is over," the priest declared, "President Abraham Lincoln will want the entire Northwest settled by whites." Tribal uncertainty regarding the outcome of the Civil War, particularly since it came in the wake of the 1858 war, prompted changes in Coeur d'Alene leadership. In August 1865 Vincent recognized the support for Andrew Seltice and relinquished his right as head chief in favor of the younger man. "Because he is always working hard," Vincent said of Seltice, "he is highly gifted with many more possessions than I have." "Because of this," the elder chieftain continued, "he can afford to be generous, not just to a few, but to all his tribesmen." Seltice, along with his brothers-in-law Peter Wildshoe and Tecomtee, had been consolidating his power since the end of the war in 1858. His annual feasts, held at his home in the Spokane Valley, attracted 500 people and earned him the respect of the tribe. Seltice accepted the chieftainship on the grounds that it was "the wish of the entire tribe," and committed himself to "a life-long obligation . . . [of] directing the people toward spiritual goals, towards prudence, and not seeking worldly pay for one's time."[25]

A wealthy farmer and rancher, Seltice came to the position of head chief seasoned in relations with white outsiders. As a participant in the 1858 Northern Plateau War and the 1859 Vancouver delegation, Seltice considered the preservation of Coeur d'Alene tribal land and the advance of the tribe's agricultural economy the most significant challenges of his chieftainship. Seltice's stature within the non-Indian community and his close connection to the Jesuit mission meant outsiders would view his chieftainship as inclusive. Despite the fact that subchiefs continued to exercise local authority, Seltice's position came to represent the entire tribe. At the same time, outsiders recognized the Sacred Heart Mission as the only source of non-Indian authority in the Coeur d'Alene region. The Jesuit fathers stood to benefit from a strong Catholic chief and supported Seltice's rise to power. The integration of political and religious authority, as represented by the chief's participation in Holy Day celebrations, illustrates the connection between Catholic partriarchy and consolidation of the chieftainship. One of his first duties as chief, the Seltice history recounts, was to coordinate the tribe's observance of the Catholic Holy day Feast of the Assumption of the Blessed Virgin Mary.[26]

The emergence of the "Soldiers of the Sacred Heart," a militia composed of mounted, well-armed Catholic Schitsu'umsh warriors, best illustrates the connection between Chief Seltice's authority and the Jesuit mission. Under the chief's direction, the forty or so soldiers maintained order in the Coeur d'Alene region by upholding the Catholic law of the mission and tribal leadership. Seltice and the mission fathers used the group to break up horse racing events, to limit alcohol consumption, and, among other things, to prohibit adulterous behavior. The Seltice history recounts one episode in which Father Caruana ordered Seltice to send the Soldiers of the Sacred Heart into Colville country to "bring back a Coeur d'Alene named Mool-le-men-kin, who was living there with another man's wife." Seltice objected that the Coeur d'Alenes did not "have any business" in that country, but Caruana insisted they were "under oath to the Sacred Heart." Seltice acquiesced, and fifteen Coeur d'Alene soldiers rode to Colville where they broke into a large lodge and attempted to take Mool-le-men-kin by force. The Colvilles objected, and the soldiers backed down when they realized the episode could turn bloody.[27]

The soldiers were more willing to engage in violence in their own territory. Punishments for offenders included whippings and confinement in the tribal jail, known as the "skookum house." Scattered references to this para-military force in federal documents between 1870 and 1900 attest to the group's often brutal power, which the Colville Indian Agency accepted without question.[28]

As Seltice prepared to fight for Coeur d'Alene lands, the end of the Civil War in 1865 returned national attention to the West and relations with Native peoples. The defeat of slavery and the wartime success of northern capitalism combined to create a generation of powerful industrialists and entrepreneurs who looked westward to the completion of transcontinental railroads and the emergence of mining, agricultural, and timber empires. Union officers, now more numerous than ever, crossed the Mississippi to operate military posts and protect settlers. Freed from the burdens of war, homesteaders took advantage of, in contemporary American poet Walt Whitman's words, "the open air in the far west."[29]

Land laws passed during 1862 aided the western capitalist and settler alike. The cornerstone of the Republican land program, the Homestead Act, awarded 160 acres of the public domain to anyone willing to pay a small filing fee, make improvements, and reside on the property for five years. The Pacific Railroad Act created the apparatus through which Congress awarded land grants to transcontinental railroads connecting the Pacific Coast to eastern population centers. Railroad legislation complemented the Homestead Act by providing markets for western farmers. In 1864 the Northern Pacific Railroad, the route favored by the late Isaac I. Stevens and tremendously significant for settlement in the Pacific Northwest, received the largest of the railroad grants: twenty sections of land for each mile of track constructed in states and forty sections of land per mile laid in territories. The Northern Pacific's land grant came to about 40 million acres. Railroads received their lands in a checkerboard pattern that allowed the federal government to retain control of alternating sections along the track. Finally, the Morrill Act provided states with land grants for the development of public institutions devoted to higher education of the common people.[30]

Native American occupation of aboriginal lands represented a national obstacle to the postbellum Republican agenda for industrial development and land distribution in the trans-Mississippi West. At the regional level, Indian claims created the potential for armed conflict as miners, timber barons, and homesteaders showed up to stake their Manifest Destiny. Sacred Heart Mission served as a buffer between the boisterous mining camps in northern Idaho Territory and the Coeur d'Alene Indians, but Idaho's early territorial governors attempted to define a reservation for the tribe to avoid confrontations between Indian people and outsiders. When Governor Caleb Lyon moved the territorial capital from Lewiston to Boise in 1864, he limited the territorial government's ability to influence events in the northern region. Idaho's Second Territorial Legislature created Kootenai County to provide local government for northern Idaho, but its stipulation that fifty "qualified" citizens had to petition to formally organize was not met until 1881.[31]

To keep miner-Indian contact to a minimum, Lyon recommended a treaty with the Coeur d'Alene Indians, giving the tribe a reservation centered on and administered by the Jesuit mission. Lyon's treaties with the tribes of southern Idaho, however, proved so unpopular that the *Idaho Statesman* declared that the governor needed a military escort to avoid violence or death. In this charged atmosphere Lyon fled the territory, taking $46,418 from the treasury and his hopes for negotiations with nontreaty tribes with him. Still, Lyon's recommendation set a precedent for consideration of a Coeur d'Alene Reservation within Idaho territorial boundaries.[32]

In 1866 territorial governor David W. Ballard inherited northern Idaho's problems, which had escalated during Lyon's ill-fated term. Residents of Lewiston, still angry about the territorial capital's defection to Boise, threatened secession. The prevalence of saloons, disregard for personal property rights, and the virtual nonexistence of sanitation in Idaho Territory's mining "tent towns" resulted in an intoxicated, frustrated, and violent population. Citizens' vigilante groups formed in Lewiston, Idaho City, Payette, Boise, and Salmon. Vigilantes in what is now Montana but was then Idaho Territory hanged twenty-four men in just a few weeks' span in 1864.[33] Mining camps in Coeur d'Alene country expanded without the benefit of government or law. Sacred Heart Mission and the tribal police provided the only semblance of authority in the region. In 1865 prospector Charles Wilson found himself forced to seek sanctuary with the Jesuit fathers. Wilson had led 600 men to the Coeur d'Alene River's north fork with the promise of prolific mineral finds. When the gold failed to materialize, Wilson's companions threatened to kill him. Wilson found refuge at the mission, and a lay brother smuggled him to safety during the night.[34]

Governor Ballard lacked treasury funds and was unable to procure federal help because southern sympathizers in the territorial legislature refused to institute the loyalty oath required by the Radical Republican Congress. He thus explored creative options for keeping the territory intact. A reservation for the Coeur d'Alene Tribe provided the means to cement the panhandle to territorial government in Boise. More important, keeping the tribe in northern Idaho rather than removing it to a reservation outside the territory meant retaining the de facto governing influence of Sacred Heart Mission. In 1866 Ballard, in his dual office as governor and superintendent of Indian affairs, received permission from the Bureau of Indian Affairs to investigate tribal land claims in the territory and to recommend reservations. Without consulting the Coeur d'Alene leadership, Ballard settled on a reservation

> commencing at the head of the Latah, about 6 miles above the crossing on the Lewiston trail, a road to the Spokane Bridge; thence running north-northeasternly to the St. Joseph River, the site of the old Coeur d'Alene Mission; thence west to the boundary line of Washington and Idaho Territories; thence south to a point due west of the place of beginning; thence east to the place of beginning.[35]

On June 14, 1867, President Andrew Johnson issued an executive order creating a reservation for the Coeur d'Alene Indians with Ballard's boundaries. The General Land Office did not inform the Coeur d'Alene people of their new reservation, and no plans to force tribal members to live within its confines surfaced within the Department of the Interior. Because Idaho Territory's statute required that Indian land titles be extinguished, this reservation was not in keeping with the law. Until the Land Office conducted surveys of Idaho Territory's public lands and negotiated with the Coeur d'Alenes for release of their aboriginal territory, the 1867 reservation existed only on paper.[36]

Ballard's recommendation for a Coeur d'Alene reservation reflected the economic goals of the Idaho Republican Party. Reservation boundaries avoided Mullan Road, the northern transcontinental railroad route surveyed by Stevens, areas of mineral activity, and the Sacred Heart Mission. These important landmarks of white settlement remained under territorial jurisdiction. Failure to place the reservation in close proximity to the Jesuit fathers revealed the mission's new status. No longer exclusively associated with the Coeur d'Alene tribe, by the 1860s the site had evolved into a widely recognized way station, trading center, and operations base. The 250,000-acre reservation also mirrored Father Joset's values. It encompassed part of the area the Coeur d'Alenes referred to as "Palouse Valley" or "Paradise Valley," where Joset had recommended that the tribe relocate in 1863. Reservation boundaries included only the southern tip of Lake Coeur d'Alene and the mouth of the St. Joseph River. Because of their potential mineral wealth and transportation opportunities, all other Coeur d'Alene waterways—except Hangman's Creek—remained outside the reservation.[37]

The 1867 executive-ordered reservation represented an early attempt by territorial officials to map the identity of the Coeur d'Alenes as a sedentary reservation people and to procure valued resources for non-Indian use. Although the tribe remained unaware of the edict for several years, its members would certainly have rejected the reservation boundaries. In 1863 the Coeur d'Alene people had refused to abandon village sites on the Coeur d'Alene and St. Joseph rivers and on Lake Coeur d'Alene in defiance of Father Joset's earnest recommendation that the group consolidate within Hangman's (Latah) Valley. Coeur d'Alene leaders dodged this early threat to tribal lands, not because non-Indian intentions changed but because no surveys existed of the region in question. The validity of the reservation was in question, moreover, because Indian title had not been quieted.

But the lack of clear federal intent regarding the Schitsu'umsh people and their landholdings left them vulnerable to the designs of resource-hungry outsiders. Thirteen years after territorial governor Isaac I. Stevens promised tribal officials a treaty, nine years after General George Wright separately pledged a "permanent treaty of peace and friendship," and eight years after Father Peter John De Smet in his capacity as army chaplain formally recommended the creation of reservations for the Northern Plateau peoples, the Coeur d'Alene Tribe still retained its nontreaty status. Forced to face the opening of the Interior Northwest without federal protection against white encroachment, Chief Andrew Seltice instituted an intratribal defense strategy designed to preserve Coeur d'Alene lands and waterways.

SIX

Presidential Intervention: The Creation of the 1873 Reservation

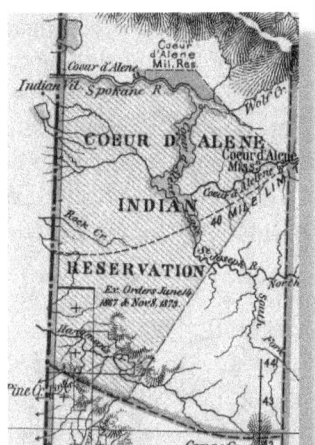

> It would be expensive, troublesome, dishonorable, and wicked to drive these people away from their homes where they have lived from time immemorial, to give place to cunning men who have supplanted them and procured the action of the Government against them.
> —John P.C. Shanks, special Indian commissioner, August 14, 1873[1]

AT THE BEGINNING OF THE 1870S, THE COEUR D'ALENE PEOPLE pursued their farming and traditional subsistence activities unhindered by the boundaries of their 1867 executive-ordered reservation. A political effort on behalf of Idaho territorial officials, the reservation existed only on maps; no surveys of northern Idaho had been conducted, and the Indian land titles guaranteed by the creation of Idaho Territory remained in place. Tribal members continued to occupy the land and waterways of their ancestors, living in villages on the Coeur d'Alene, St. Joseph, and Spokane rivers; in all the river valleys; on the Spokane Prairie; and on the shores of Lake Coeur d'Alene, Liberty Lake, and Hayden Lake. Tribal leaders and the priests of Sacred Heart Mission, however, recognized the mounting external pressures that could drive them from their homeland. The legalistic Jesuit fathers pushed for negotiation of the often promised formal treaty, which would give the Coeur d'Alenes monetary compensation for land surrendered and secure for the tribe an acceptable reservation—one that provided ample ground for the expansion of agricultural enterprises.

Chief Andrew Seltice adopted the Jesuits' judicial approach in his crusade to preserve Schitsu'umsh land and farms. At the same time, he embraced non-Indian views of Schitsu'umsh farming and religious practices and worked to enhance a growing outsider perception that the tribe was "civilized" and a "better class of Indians." The view that the Schitsu'umsh were more "civilized" than other peoples of the Interior Northwest had first emerged during the peace treaty process at the end of the 1858 war, when Father Joseph Joset had successfully labored to represent the Coeur d'Alenes as Christianized and generally peaceable.[2] In promoting Schitsu'umsh "progress," Seltice shifted his focus away from traditional village sites to fenced and "improved" lands and advanced a strategy of agricultural consolidation in the Palouse region of the Coeur d'Alene homeland.

The Schitsu'umsh fearfully witnessed the beginnings of non-Indian homesteading in their country during the late 1860s and the 1870s. Unlike the transient prospectors, these determined families arrived intending to stay. By 1872 regional enclaves of non-Indian settlement dotted Palouse country to the south. Most of the new homesteads surrounded present-day Colfax, Washington, but nuclei of settlement also appeared at Lower Union Flat, Upper Union Flat, Paradise Valley, Palouse City, and Pine Creek. Residents of the last three locations found themselves within twenty miles of Coeur d'Alene tribal farms and villages. Walla Walla newspaper editors remarked on the exodus to the Palouse, noting that the area seemed a favorite with stock growers. Indeed, most early non-Indian settlement focused on livestock rather than cultivation. These newcomers desired the region's prolific bunchgrass as much as the rich soil. In 1871 Palouse ranchers drove more than 5,000 head of cattle to the Snake River for transport to markets.[3]

None of the region's government agencies possessed the leadership, authority, or political will necessary to offer support to the Schitsu'umsh, even as their lands were invaded by non-Indians. Idaho Territory struggled with so many internal problems that it could rarely boast a treasury or a resident governor. David Ballard, who had recommended the 1867 reservation boundaries, was succeeded in the governorship in 1871 by Thomas M. Bowen, who stayed just long enough to determine that he could not make his fortune in the Idaho mines. Bowen's replacement, Thomas W. Bennett, remained in office for four years but was absent for twenty-three months of his term. In 1875 charges of illegal ballot counting, embezzlement, and excessive absence drove Bennett from office. The infamous cycle continued with Bennett's successor, David P. Thompson, who remained in office only four months.[4]

Similar difficulties plagued the federal agencies designed to help meet the challenges of non-Indian and tribal interaction in the Interior Northwest. Both the Colville Agency in northeast Washington Territory, assigned the administrative duties of the nontreaty tribes, and the Washington Superintendency of Indian Affairs struggled with disorganization and corruption throughout the territorial phase.[5] In April 1867 newly appointed Washington superintendent Thomas J. McKenny wrote to Commissioner of Indian Affairs Lewis V. Bogy to complain of corrupt Indian agents. McKenny identified agency physicians who had no knowledge of medicine, agents who attended political conventions using agency funds, and agency personnel engaged in illegal gambling and horse racing with tribal people. "In fact the Indian Department so far at least as this Superintendency is concerned," McKenny declared, "has been made a mere political machine."[6]

William Park Winans's tenure as Indian agent at Colville Agency during the early 1870s reveals the disservice accorded Indian people by the political nature of appointments in the Washington superintendency. A well-known trader who often sold whiskey to Indian people, Winans's appointment met immediate opposition. Colville District farmer-in-charge George W. Harvey called a council of Washington Territory's nontreaty tribes and the Coeur d'Alene Indians in May 1870 to discuss his suspicions regarding Agent Winans and the expansion of non-Indian settlement in the region. Over 1,000 tribal people from the Kalispel, Spokane, Coeur d'Alene, Lakes, Colville, Okanogan, San Poil, Methow, and Columbia tribes attended the meeting at Rock Creek on the Walla Walla Trail. Harvey used the forum to propel his own career in the Indian Service by promising to protect Indian land if the tribes would support him as Indian agent. Harvey accused Winans of promoting white settlement and of driving the tribes "like sheep to the mountain tops." Chiefs from all the tribes present, except the Moses band of Columbia Indians, signed a petition supporting Harvey and opposing white encroachment.[7]

Winans retained his position as agent, but the petition prompted Commissioner of Indian Affairs Francis Walker to request that the Interior Department consider setting aside a reservation for the nontreaty tribes. On April 9, 1872, President Ulysses S. Grant met the commissioner's request by issuing an executive order creating a reservation for nontreaty tribes on the Columbia Plateau. Despite the fact that the Coeur d'Alene people already possessed an executive-ordered reservation dating from 1867, albeit a questionable one, the new decree made provision for them and listed their number at 700. Bounded on the west by the Columbia River, on the south by the Little Spokane River, on the east by the dividing line between Washington and Idaho territories, and on the north by the Pend Oreille River, this reservation encompassed the old Hudson's Bay Company post known as Fort Colville, the U.S. Army's Fort Colville, and the Colville Indian Agency.[8]

Although the boundaries made sense from an administrative perspective—Colville Agency would be located on the reservation—Winans vehemently opposed the executive order. As Farmer Harvey suspected, Winans was not pursuing tribal people's best interests. Instead, the agent pocketed cash from white settlers eager to keep their potential Homestead Act claims from becoming Indian reservation land. Winans embarked on a furious letter-writing campaign to "save" white settlers' farms in the Colville vicinity. His correspondence with Superintendent McKenny and Washington Territorial Delegate Selucious Garfield resulted in a change of policy less than three months after the first executive order. On July 2, 1872, President Grant issued another decree, this time restoring the boundaries of the April reservation to the public domain and creating a new reservation bounded on the north by the forty-ninth parallel, on the south and east by the Columbia River, and on the west by the Okanogan River. Located west of the Columbia in a northern, arid, infertile region with a short growing season, this reserve failed to meet the nontreaty tribes' agricultural and subsistence requirements. For the Coeur d'Alene people, the new Colville Reservation represented a particularly disturbing scenario. If they were forced to relocate, the West Columbia reserve would isolate them from their aboriginal territory, traditional waterways, root-digging grounds, cultivated fields, and Sacred Heart Mission.[9]

In response to the sudden appearance of homesteaders and to rumors that the Coeur d'Alenes would be forced to move to the Colville Reservation, Head Chief Andrew Seltice embarked on a two-front defense against white encroachment. Denied assistance from territorial and federal agencies, the tribal leader created an internal anti-invasion policy. Between 1870 and 1875, Seltice changed his mind about consolidation and moved his agricultural operations from the Spokane Valley to a region characterized by rolling hills and fertile soil known by the tribe as Ni'Lukhwalqw.[10]

Long used as a traditional camas-digging site and located southwest of Lake Coeur d'Alene near Hangman's Creek, Ni'Lukhwalqw occupied a pocket between dense evergreen stands to the north and east and the undulating grasses of the Palouse to the south and west. The area offered abundant timber, farmland, and water and had already become a target for non-Indian homesteaders. Coeur d'Alene women had stumbled upon crude cabins in the area while on a camas-digging trip. When they heard of the invasion, tribal leaders reacted by advocating removal to the location. Seltice and the mission fathers emphatically urged *all* tribal members, regardless of whether they were associated with the mission, to relocate. In cultivating the Paradise Valley region, as Joset had recommended several years earlier, Seltice intended to create a buffer against white settlement. "If you are there first," Father Joset pleaded, "no one can order you off your land that you have already settled."[11] The move did not signify the surrender of other aboriginal territory or a systematic abandonment of tribal waterways. In an effort to put as much tribal land under cultivation as possible, the chief encouraged tribal members to practice full-time agriculture but initially did not dissuade members from participating in traditional subsistence activities.[12]

Although Seltice did not forbid continuation of traditional subsistence activity, the consolidation isolated tribal members who chose not to relocate and created significant religious, economic, and geographic divisions in Coeur d'Alene country. The relocation also influenced gender roles. Within the traditional seasonal pattern of land use, women had procured a significant amount of the tribe's food, particularly camas; had prepared, preserved, and distributed food; and owned the food-processing tools. Within the families that participated in large-scale cash crop agriculture, women lost these traditional avenues of authority. Men now controlled the harvest of food and the tools of food production. Women continued to participate, especially through raising vegetable gardens and processing food, but their gathering role and its concomitant power disappeared in the tidy fields of hay, oats, and grain. Part of the Jesuit mission effort, moreover, was to introduce Native women to Catholic standards of female behavior, including obedience to husband and God and devotion to church, home, and children. Joset complained, prior to the agricultural consolidation, that the relative power of women inhibited the Jesuits' proselytizing efforts: "How difficult to establish Christian subordination. How often a passionate woman would fill the camp or the whole tribe with disorders: when angry she always could drive the man away, for she could always tell him I don't need thee."[13]

The Jesuit mission possessed a compelling interest in the Palouse relocation. It had the potential to consolidate the Schitsu'umsh population in one place—much more in keeping with the reduction model than the current scattered population—and thus would allow the Jesuits to more easily "establish Christian subordination." Jesuit sources indicate that between 40 and 100 people lived at the mission on Coeur d'Alene River, whereas total tribal population was around 500.[14] In an undated manuscript entitled "History Manuscript of Sacred Heart [Old] Mission," Joset gave this justification for Palouse relocation: "The boys at the mission house contracted habits quite different from savage life: the old savage fare would not do for them: but they could not be always boys they grew up to manhood they married and of course they should think about their own household: they wanted to start their own farms and they received encouragement."[15]

The Seltice history recounts that by 1875 a sizable number of tribal members had relocated to the Palouse. During this time Seltice also cracked down on horse racing and whiskey consumption. By 1876 the Hangman's (Latah) Creek consolidation had become mission policy, and Jesuit Father Alexander Diomedi "ordered" remaining families to move.[16] Still, a number of families refused to relocate on the grounds that they did not want to give up traditional subsistence patterns or village sites:

> If we moved to the Palouse country, how could the game, berries and fish ever be replaced out in that country? Ground squirrels are all you have there.
> Should we give up this paradise, for hard work, trouble and hunger? We only have just one life here; why should anyone try to ruin this life? We will oppose anyone who tries to make us move. Give us a moderate and a regular life, and we will live longer.[17]

Tribal informants told Rodney Frey that some families continued to reside in the lake and river regions well into the twentieth century and that tribal waters continued to form the soul of the tribal landscape.[18] Photographs from the early twentieth century support Frey's informants. An unidentified tourist took a photograph of a Schitsu'umsh encampment along the St. Joe River after the turn of the century. A tepee sits in a clearing near the water while telephone wires pass overhead, processed logs float in the river, and the hill above the camp shows obvious signs of logging.[19]

The reports filed by agents at the Colville Agency also provide evidence that many Schitsu'umsh maintained their traditional seasonal practices. "The Indians are very much scattered at present," Agent John Simms noted in his October 1874 report. "[N]early all are in the mountains hunting; they go a great distance from here, even beyond the Rocky Mountains in some instances."[20] Even the Seltice family account admits that "there were some Coeur d'Alenes who did not come together in unity with the others, who did not attend the Christian services. Such were the Timothy's [sic] who lived at the head of navigation on the St. Joe and were considered by some to be outlaws."[21]

The actual number of surplus-producing farms instituted on the Coeur d'Alene Reservation during the early reservation period is difficult to ascertain, since officials at Colville only visited the reservation a few times throughout the year and reported on only the most obvious activity. Agents at Colville often relied on the Jesuits for their information, and they regularly exaggerated Coeur d'Alene farming success. The Jesuit mission and the tribal leadership had their own political reasons for exaggerating tribal agricultural advances. What is clear is that the number of farms in production throughout the 1870s and 1880s could not have supported the entire Schitsu'umsh population. When James O'Neill visited the reservation in 1879, four years after Seltice reported that many tribal people had relocated to the Palouse, he found about fifty-four operating farms, "nearly all inclosed, and running from 5 acres to nearly 100 in cultivation, and nearly all having either a small dwelling or [a] barn of logs." O'Neill also noted that at DeSmet "they have laid out a small villlage, streets and alleys, &c." Although the agent was impressed with these accomplishments, his report verified that an economic hierarchy had formed. The "larger farmers have each good farm implements," he explained, and they aspire to "build larger and better" houses near DeSmet. Nonagricultural peoples possessed neither implements nor big houses.[22]

Although most tribal members continued, out of necessity, to hunt and gather in familiar places, the tribe's leadership and the Jesuit mission mapped an agrarian identity for the group. The significant but unclear number of people who did not practice any kind of agriculture—not even a garden plot or a small field of hay—were left politically, economically, and geographically isolated from tribal leadership. The mission's view that these peoples were less "progressive" and less "civilized" added a cultural distancing to their geographic isolation. In economic terms, the river and lake people did not share in the growing wealth associated with tribal and mission farms. Moreover, Seltice's tactical need to present the tribe as Catholic, modernized, and progressive meant the leader and the mission identified the Coeur d'Alenes as people who farmed in the Palouse, attended Mass, lived in log cabins, and wore Euro-American clothing. The Seltice tribal history distinguishes between "progressive" and "lazy" people. Joseph Seltice, Andrew Seltice's son, explained:

> There were some of the Coeur d'Alene that I refer to as the "lazy ones," who were never involved in these big fall hunts. They were too lazy to hunt, and too lazy to work and build a log cabin for their families. They kept on living in the old bark tepees; and whenever the bark rotted away, there was always more bark around to replace it. If they did go hunting, they didn't pack a buckskin tepee, but just used a frame of rough poles covered with coarse grass to shelter their families. There were three or four such families that did not come together for Church days or for any other tribal gatherings. They were always looked down upon by the rest of the Tribe.[23]

Tribal members whose behavior did not fit the "progressive" standard were separated from the tribe as tribal identity became associated with Catholicism, sedentary housing, and agriculture.

As the second part of his two-pronged defense, Seltice and the mission fathers actively pursued allies within the Indian Office, regional military posts, and local government. The chief began by petitioning Interior Department officials for federal recognition of tribal land claims. An English speaker but not comfortable with the written language, the chief relied on Sacred Heart missionaries to write the petitions. The Jesuits, drawing on a tradition of analytical education, contributed legal wording to the documents and formulated judicial arguments on the tribe's behalf. Although the Jesuits influenced the wording of the documents, the sense of the petitions reflected the tribal leaders' values. Essential to this effort was the need for the Coeur d'Alenes to appear capable of participating in non-Indian diplomatic and legalistic processes—to appear, in other words, as Christian, hard-working, "civilized," and lawful individuals.

Seltice sent his first plea to the Interior Department during winter of 1871, requesting title to aboriginal territory and emphasizing tribal occupation of Hangman's Valley. After receiving no response other than "vague reports," Coeur d'Alene leaders again petitioned the Interior secretary on November 18, 1872. This time they requested specific title to the mission church, the St. Joseph River valley, and the Coeur d'Alene River valley. The 1872 petition explained that the Coeur d'Alenes had failed to refer specifically to the mission and valleys in the first document "because in our ignorance we thought it a matter of course." The valleys, Seltice and nine other chiefs contended, "have been from old [the] habitual residence of most of us" and would not provide ideal conditions for white settlers, "being every spring under water." The few high areas spared spring inundation, the petitioners noted, had been "fenced in and cultivated" by tribal people. In a passage illustrative of Seltice's political savvy and understanding of farming and subsistence requirements, the petitioners rationalized that the request "would appear too much, and it would be so if all or most of it were fit for farming." Since most valley land was "either rocky, or too dry, too cold, or swampy," the Coeur d'Alene people valued these regions for their ability to provide traditional subsistence.[24]

The politically astute document employed the language of assimilation and betrayed the strong influence of the Jesuit fathers. "With the word of God we took labor too; we began tilling the ground and we like it; though perhaps slowly we are continually *progressing*," the document explained, "but our unaided industry is not as yet up to the white man's. . . . [F]or a while yet we need have some hunting and fishing." After expressing regret at their participation in the 1858 hostilities, the chieftains maintained that the peace treaty with Colonel Wright, which mandated unmolested non-Indian travel in Coeur d'Alene country, thus recognized tribal title to the same. Not only had the Coeur d'Alenes kept their peace treaty promises, they had not disturbed the "many white men" who "came and settled on what we thought our own land." Unlike other, less progressive tribes, the Coeur d'Alenes had rejected aid of tools, clothing, and food—desiring only title to traditional lands, the maintenance of Catholic priests and nuns to teach their children, and the ability "to depend on our own hands." The petition closed with the request that the interior secretary send an agent to "come and visit the land, see what we ask for, and what we have done already." Signed and transcribed at Sacred Heart Mission, the petition carried the marks of ten tribal leaders—headed by Andrew Seltice—and the signatures of three Jesuit priests: G. Gazzoli, J. Joset, and D. M. Cataldo.[25]

Seltice's petition drive occurred during an era of Indian policy known as President Ulysses S. Grant's "peace policy." Aspects of this strategy included the appointment of Christian church nominees as agents and the use of religious organizations to teach Indian people on reservations "the arts of civilization and self-support." The policy reflected a postbellum evangelical reform movement prevalent in both Congress and the Indian Office. Seemingly incompatible with the Republican economic agenda, religious reformers provided the means to peaceably remove the Indian obstacle from the path of western extractive industry. Evangelical tactics had limits, however, and the Grant administration advocated severe punishment—with the War Department's help—in dealing with tribes that refused to cooperate with the president's "civilizing" methods.[26]

Seltice's emphasis on agriculture and a Christian way of life appealed to evangelical reformers in the Indian Office and Congress. Few government personnel could fault the 1872 statement by Coeur d'Alene petitioners that "uncertainty tends to paralyze our people: when certain of a home they will work with a new energy."²⁷ By emphasizing a tribal interpretation of the 1858 peace settlement with Colonel George Wright, the leaders also sought the support of military officials. In June 1872 George Sanford, captain 1st Cavalry, reported to the assistant adjutant general at the Department of the Columbia that his inspection of Coeur d'Alene country and the home of Chief Seltice afforded "the most creditable exhibition of industry that I have ever seen among Indians." Impressed with improvements in the Hangman's Creek area, Sanford reported that "these Indians have a great number of horses and cattle, they have ploughed up a great deal of ground, built fences and cabins and are farming in earnest." Sanford found the Coeur d'Alenes "anxious to know my business" and adamant about their title to their lands, particularly those surrounding Lake Coeur d'Alene's tributaries, which they informed Sanford General Wright had promised them fourteen years previous. "The Indians are strongly attached to the [Hangman's] valley," Sanford reported, "and refuse to let any white man come into it to settle." Sanford met with Sacred Heart missionary Father Cataldo, who told the officer the Coeur d'Alene people were "all anxious to become farmers and give up their wandering life."²⁸

Sanford's routine inspection of the Native people between Forts Lapwai and Colville prompted Brigadier General Edward R.S. Canby of the Department of the Columbia to request the Interior Department to issue assurances to the nontreaty tribes "as to the permanency of their present home." Canby blamed Indian Office officials for acting "without authority" and "unnecessarily" alarming the Coeur d'Alene and Spokane Indians regarding their possible relocation to the Colville reserve. The superintendent of Washington Territory informed Canby "that no instructions had been given for the removal of any Indians to the new reservation west of the Columbia River." The Coeur d'Alene people, Canby upheld, by virtue of the "special provision" provided them by the 1867 executive order, should not be forced to move to the West Colville Reservation. The lack of military presence between Forts Lapwai and Colville made it desirable for the Department of the Columbia to keep the peaceable Coeur d'Alenes and their Jesuit mission in place. "The progress that these indians are making is exceedingly satisfactory," Canby concluded, "and I regret that they have been disturbed by any apprehensions as to the permanency of their location." Major General J. M. Schofield, the commanding officer of the Pacific Division in San Francisco, forwarded Canby's concerns to Secretary of War William Belknap, who passed them on to Secretary of Interior Columbus Delano.²⁹

Sanford's report prompted another military inspection of Fort Colville, this one conducted by Assistant Inspector General E. H. Ludington on August 11, 1872. Ludington's findings supported Sanford's report. Colville Agency tribes remained adamantly opposed to the West Colville reservation. Ludington reported that although none of the tribes had made specific threats, "the Chiefs of the Spokanes and Coeur d'Alenes say that they had better be killed where they are than to starve on the reservation, and that they cannot move." Again, Seltice emphasized to Ludington that the Coeur d'Alene people had been given "perpetual possession of Hangman Valley" by their 1858 agreement with General Wright. Tribal leaders also informed the inspector of their neighborly conduct toward non-Indian squatters on Coeur d'Alene land. Belknap forwarded Ludington's report to the Interior secretary and Indian commissioner within days of the Sanford report, asking for information regarding the state of affairs at Colville Agency.[30]

Delano took note of the military's recommendations, for during the Grant administration the army had launched a campaign to take over Indian affairs. Hostility between tribal people and the army posts on the Great Plains made a mockery of Grant's peace policy and led military commanders such as General Schofield to argue against the cost and inefficiency of splitting responsibility for Indian affairs between the War and Interior departments. Supporters of military control pointed out that preexisting army forts could be used as Indian agencies. The intensity of the humanitarian Christian reform movement and fear of a large peacetime standing army in the western United States ultimately dictated that Indian affairs remain under civilian control. Still, Belknap's interest in affairs at Colville Agency represented a challenge to the Interior Department's authority, forcing Secretary Delano to counter with policy originating within the Indian Office.[31]

News from local officials at Fort Colville further contributed to the pressure on the Interior Department to address the dilemma of the Coeur d'Alene Tribe and other nontreaty tribes in the Interior Northwest. John A. Simms, appointed July 8, 1872, as Agent William Park Winans's replacement at Colville, held a council with the Plateau tribes in November 1872. Having just experienced an excellent fall round of fishing, the chiefs of the Colville, Coeur d'Alene, Spokane, and Kalispel Tribes reaffirmed their rightful occupation of aboriginal territories and again rejected the West Colville Reservation boundaries. The United States and Great Britain "did us a great wrong" in creating the dividing line between their countries, Spokane Chief Garry asserted, "and now it is not right for the President to make a reserve for us without our consent." Chief Seltice supported Garry, saying, "We have not sold our country and shall not leave it." In his November 1872 report to Superintendent of Indian Affairs Robert H. Milroy, Simms declared that only the appointment of a special commission to treat with the interior peoples would "satisfactorily" end tribal rumblings concerning the West Colville Reservation. Simms urged that the matter receive prompt attention, since rumors of the extension of the Northern Pacific Railroad into eastern Washington were contributing to both non-Indian settlement and Indian wariness.[32]

County commissioner and attorney Charles Ewing echoed Agent Simms's concerns. Chief Seltice decided to weight his petitions with the testament of a local non-Indian settler, and in June 1873 Ewing wrote to Secretary Delano on behalf of the tribe. Ewing requested that a commissioner of "personal integrity, friendship and devotedness to the Indians" be sent to negotiate for a reservation large enough for the Coeur d'Alenes and "their Indian friends who wish to settle among them." The 1867 reservation, Ewing asserted, even if it had been surveyed, was too small for the tribe's needs. When offered guarantees "that they will never be disturbed" on their land, Ewing stated, the Coeur d'Alene people "will be the happiest and most devoted wards or citizens of this Republic." The Coeur d'Alenes requested that John B. Monteith, agent for the Nez Perce Indians, not be among the commissioners dispatched for the "big talk." The Coeur d'Alene Catholic leadership believed Monteith, a Protestant, lacked "sufficient official dignity" and did not consider him a friend. Ewing recommended the speedy dispatch of a Catholic-slanted commission to formulate an agreement with the Coeur d'Alene tribe.[33]

Criticism of the West Colville Reservation flew at the Indian Office from all directions. Finally, in July 1873 Secretary Delano appointed John P.C. Shanks, Thomas W. Bennett, and Henry W. Reed to investigate complaints lodged by the nontreaty tribes, to hold councils, and to formulate recommendations. Treaty making with all Indian tribes had terminated in 1871 with passage of the Indian Appropriations Act; thus, the Shanks commission possessed the power to negotiate "agreements" instead of "treaties." Touted as one of the Grant administration's Indian policy reforms, abolition of the treaty system did not mean the end of tribal land cessions or of the creation of reservations. After 1871, reservations resulted from presidential executive orders or agreements. Unlike treaties, agreements required approval by both the House and the Senate.[34]

Although not a member of the Shanks commission, Monteith possessed separate orders dating from March 8, 1873, directing him to visit the Coeur d'Alene people and determine the conditions necessary for the tribe to accept the boundaries of the 1867 executive-ordered reservation.[35] Shanks, a congressional representative from Indiana, and Bennett, territorial governor of Idaho, stopped at the Nez Perce Indian Agency en route to their councils with the nontreaty tribes and offered to escort Monteith to Coeur d'Alene country. Aware of the tribe's sentiments toward him and thankful for the company, Monteith agreed to accompany the commissioners.[36]

Agent Monteith and the special commissioners arrived at the outskirts of Coeur d'Alene territory on July 23, 1873, and held a council with tribal leaders on July 25, 26, and 27 at Hangman's Creek. When asked what country they claimed, Monteith recorded in his notes that Coeur d'Alene tribal leaders replied, "We start at the head of the Palouse and run across to Steptoe Butte, from that point to Antoine Plants [sic] ferry on the Spokan [sic] River then to the foot of Pend D'Oreille lake thence up lake to the sumit [sic] of Bitter-root Mountains then along sumit of mountains to place of beginning." Coeur d'Alene representatives insisted that their acceptance of any reservation hinged on the inclusion of their vast country's heartland: the rivers and valleys surrounding Lake Coeur d'Alene.[37]

Several days of discussions among Monteith, Shanks, Bennett, and Chief Seltice gave way to a written agreement amending the 1867 reservation's boundaries. The new boundaries included the Coeur d'Alene River valley, part of the St. Joseph River valley, Lake Coeur d'Alene, the Coeur d'Alene River from Sacred Heart Mission to Lake Coeur d'Alene, part of the St. Joseph and St. Maries rivers, the southern bank of the Spokane River until it crossed into Washington Territory, and a large portion of Hangman's Valley.[38] The reservation abutted Sacred Heart Mission but did not include mission lands. Coeur d'Alene leaders agreed to relinquish the mission lands, perhaps with the Jesuit priests' assurances that the farms would remain under tribal control.[39]

Encompassing approximately 590,000 acres, the new boundaries more than doubled the size of the 1867 reservation. This unusual increase in reservation size stemmed in part from the carefully cultivated image of the Coeur d'Alenes as "civilized" and thus worthy of resource wealth. Nez Perce Agent Monteith defended the boundaries by pointing out that the old reservation excluded the farms in the Coeur d'Alene River valley, in Hangman's Valley, and in the vicinity of the mission. Inclusion of the southern part of the Spokane River, Monteith's notes explained, allowed the Indian Office to place mills at Upper Spokane Falls at less expense than building a steam mill. In return for the surrender of all aboriginal territory outside reservation boundaries—an area of approximately 4 million acres—the agreement granted the Coeur d'Alene people implements and tools, including wagons, plows, harnesses, reapers, and mowers; buildings, including a sawmill, grist mill, schoolhouse, and blacksmith shop; and professional reservation officials, including a blacksmith, carpenter, and physician. The agreement also included monetary compensation of $170,000, a sizable sum for the day, payable in 5 percent bonds.[40]

Although the commissioners and Coeur d'Alene tribal leaders initially expressed satisfaction with the agreement, events following the Hangman's council suggested that Shanks never intended for the agreement to receive congressional approval. Ironically, Monteith had been more instrumental in the negotiations with the Coeur d'Alenes than commission members had, and perhaps Shanks experienced bureaucratic jealousy. Regardless of his motivation, Shanks effectively killed the Hangman's Creek agreement during his next council. After concluding the meeting with the Coeur d'Alenes, he hurried to Colville Agency to hold talks with the remaining nontreaty tribes. Members from the Colville, Lakes, San Poil, Okanogan, Spokane, and Kalispel Tribes gathered on August 12 at the old Hudson's Bay trading post to listen to Shanks and Colville

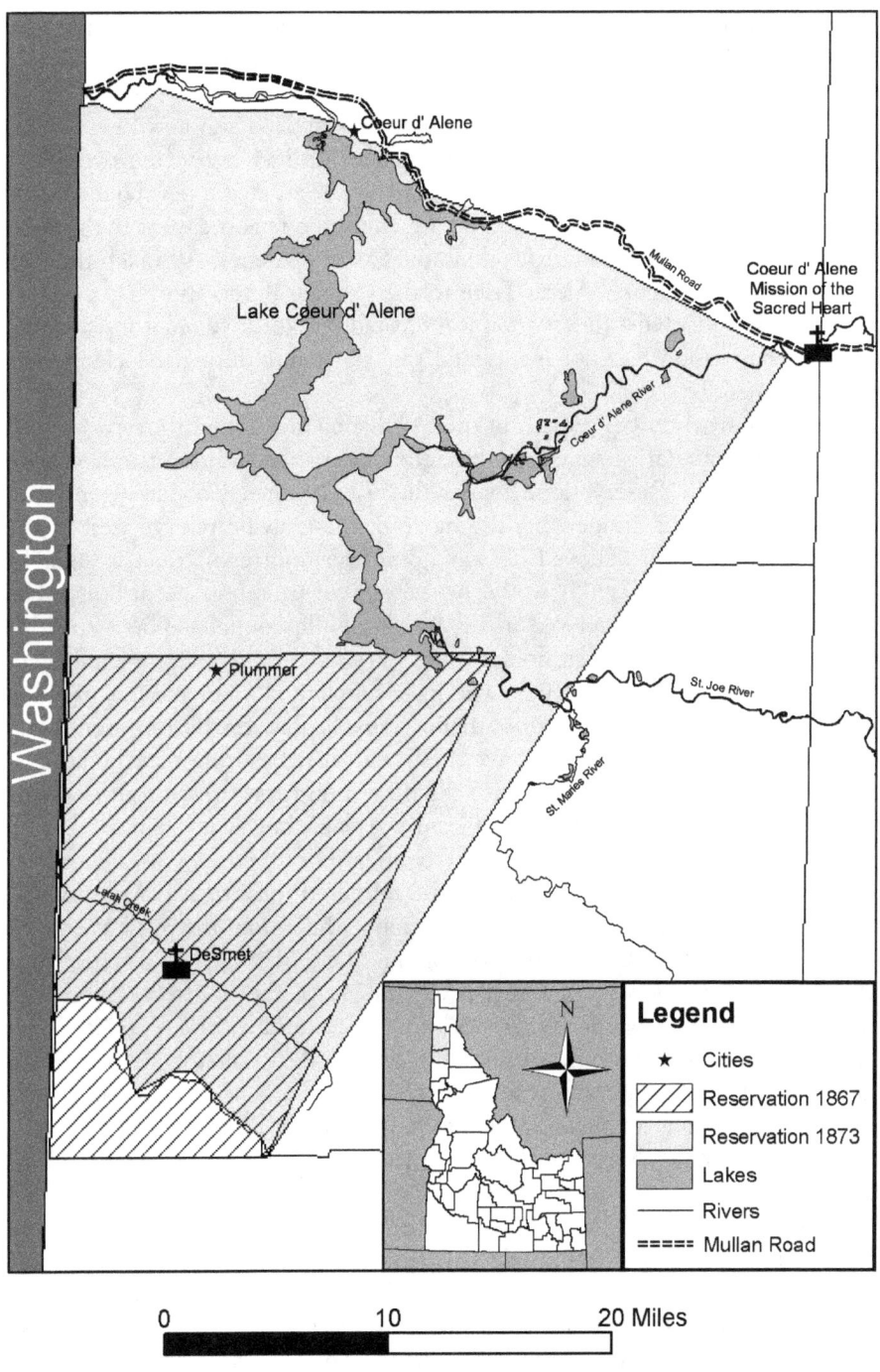

Map 2—The 1867 and 1873 Reservations

Agent John Simms. The Coeur d'Alenes did not attend the council, nor were they expected to, since they had just concluded a council with the commission. Strangely, despite the absence of Coeur d'Alene representatives and the newly negotiated Hangman's Creek document, Shanks applied the new negotiations to the Coeur d'Alene Tribe as if the agreement he had conducted two weeks earlier did not exist. When Shanks, for example, negotiated a new boundary for the Colville Reservation, extending it to include the region east of the Columbia River, he made provision to include the Coeur d'Alenes. Although the idea of removing the Coeur d'Alene Tribe to the Colville Reservation had surfaced when the West Colville Reservation was created by executive order in 1872, the Shanks commission had not mentioned that possibility during the Hangman's Creek council.[41]

The nontreaty tribes present at the Colville council found the new Colville Reservation boundaries agreeable—none of these tribes wanted to relocate to the West Colville Reservation. Shanks distrusted former Colville Agent Park Winans's motives in influencing the move of the Colville reserve west of the Columbia River and believed he was doing the nontreaty tribes a favor by erasing Winans's legacy. "It would be expensive, troublesome, dishonorable, and wicked," Shanks declared in his post–Colville council report, "to drive these people away from their homes where they have lived from time immemorial, to give place to cunning men who have supplanted them and procured the action of the Government against them." Inexplicably, Shanks apparently did not consider it dishonorable to drive the Coeur d'Alenes from their homes and force them to take up residence with the other nontreaty tribes on the Colville Reservation. For the benefit of the Coeur d'Alenes, however, Shanks included a sliver of Hangman's Valley within the boundaries of the new Colville reservation. Still, without the tribe's consent, he relegated the Coeur d'Alene people to a reservation that, if enforced, would remove them from the nucleus of their territory. When he returned to Washington, D.C., Shanks filed a report with the other commissioners that suggested that *all* of the nontreaty tribes had participated in the Colville conference. Equally disturbing, Shanks relayed that "these Indian tribes propose surrendering their title to all the country south and east" of the Colville reservation. Certainly, the Coeur d'Alene people did not intend to give up their aboriginal title to Idaho lands to move onto a reservation completely removed from both their waterways and Sacred Heart Mission.[42]

Fortunately for the Coeur d'Alenes, the agreement concluded between the tribe and the commissioners in July 1873 reached Washington prior to Shanks's report on the Colville council. President Grant, concerned about the prevalence of whiskey in the mining camps near Sacred Heart Mission and the possibility of violence if whites encroached on the boundaries agreed upon by the Coeur d'Alene leadership, chose to act unilaterally. He accepted the reservation boundaries agreed upon by Coeur d'Alene leaders, Indian Agent John Monteith, and the Shanks commission. On November 8, 1873, Grant issued an executive order setting apart and withdrawing from sale the area stipulated by the July agreement. The president, who maintained strong ties to the transcontinental railroad companies, had a political interest in keeping peace in northern Idaho—one of the areas transected by the Northern Pacific. By November 14 the commissioner of the General Land Office had been notified to prepare the paperwork for the creation of the reservation, and the U.S. Indian inspector at Olympia, Washington Territory, had been directed to inform the tribe. The 1873 executive order created a reservation centered on Coeur d'Alene waterways but did not give tribal people compensation for lands outside reservation boundaries. Monetary compensation for released territory and any other provisions could be provided only through negotiation of an agreement. The president withdrew the lands as an emergency measure designed to keep out trespassers and avoid confrontation within the proposed boundaries. Grant apparently believed the Hangman's Creek agreement would receive congressional approval, thus giving the Coeur d'Alene people the stipulated payments for surrendered territory.[43]

Meanwhile, on November 17, 1873—nine days after Grant created the new Coeur d'Alene reservation—the special commission composed of Shanks, Bennett, and Reed formally rejected the Hangman's Creek accord in favor of the Colville agreement. The commissioners vaguely noted that they "only joined Mr. Monteith [in the negotiations with the Coeur d'Alenes] as there seemed to be a necessity for it at the time." Four months later, however, "after an investigation of the whole subject," the Shanks commission advised "that the agreement entered into with the Coeur d'Alenes be not confirmed, but that the reservation recommended by the commission for the nine tribes, including the Coeur d'Alenes, be adopted." In accordance with the commission's wishes, in January 1874 Secretary of Interior Columbus Delano withdrew from congressional consideration the Hangman's Creek agreement. Delano then forwarded the commission's Colville agreement to the Senate Committee on Indian Affairs. Indian Agent John Simms's 1873 census of white inhabitants residing within the proposed Colville Reservation boundaries accompanied the commission's findings. Showing a total of 159 families, or 318 inhabitants, with at least $164,700 in taxable property, Simms's tally doomed the Colville agreement, which died in committee. Thus, neither of the Shanks commission's two accords—Hangman's Creek with the Coeur d'Alenes and Colville with the other nontreaty tribes—received congressional approval. The Shanks commission's failures meant that for the nontreaty tribes, with the exception of the Coeur d'Alenes, circumstances remained the same as before. The disputed boundaries of the West Colville Reservation remained intact. By virtue of Grant's intervention, however, the Coeur d'Alene people emerged from the Shanks debacle with an executive-ordered reservation of almost 600,000 acres located within the heart of Coeur d'Alene country, encompassing all of Lake Coeur d'Alene and portions of other tribal waterways.⁴⁴

When informed of the creation of the 1873 reservation, Coeur d'Alene tribal leaders recognized the boundaries they had agreed upon during negotiations with the Shanks commission. Still, tribal leaders expressed dissatisfaction that they had not received the implements, buildings, agency personnel, and monetary payments promised them by the commission. To tribal leaders, who cared little for the distinction between executive orders and agreements, U.S. officials seemed to be honoring only half of the bargain. Chief Andrew Seltice thus refused to surrender any traditional tribal territory outside the reservation until the tribe received compensation, and the Coeur d'Alene people made no effort to move within the confines of the new reservation (even some tribal farms were situated outside the borders of the reservation). Coeur d'Alene families still frequented their traditional seasonal camps without regard to territorial restrictions. Seltice, however, along with other tribal leaders such as Peter Wildshoe, continued to consolidate farm operations in Hangman's Valley, and a large number of tribal people followed their lead. Yet although they used oxen teams to move their households to the Palouse, even Seltice and Wildshoe continued to graze their livestock—about 1,600 horses and cattle apiece—in the Spokane Valley.⁴⁵

By 1877 tribal members who chose not to break ground in Hangman's Valley and the Palouse area experienced not only political isolation but also increasing difficulties with miners and homesteaders. Regardless of whether they maintained permanent residences within or outside the 1873 reservation boundaries, these families found that without the protection of tribal consolidation, they could not defend themselves against encroachment. The General Land Office had not yet surveyed the 1873 reservation, leaving the Coeur d'Alenes vulnerable to trespassing even on land set aside for their use. Tribal families with livestock often discovered that they had lost animals during the night to drunken miners passing through the area. Non-Indian settlers harassed tribal people, such as the elderly widow Wham-shen-mel who farmed about three acres with her young son near present-day Potlatch, Idaho. The small family raised enough wheat for themselves and relied on fishing in a nearby creek for most of their food. Reluctant to relocate, Wham-shen-mel resisted as long as she could, even when whites offered to pay her $200 for her property. With Seltice's encouragement and aid, the woman eventually abandoned her split-cedar cabin, loaded what belongings she could behind a horse, and rode to her new location with her son dragging behind on a makeshift harness. She did not receive the promised payment for her farm.⁴⁶

The increased flow of liquor, moreover, led to violent confrontations between tribal people living on the outskirts of Coeur d'Alene country and non-Indian prospectors and travelers. Tribal member Quinmosee controlled the Spokane River crossing and charged non-Indians a fee—often whiskey—to ferry them across on one of his rafts or in canoes. Eventually, Quinmosee became a belligerent alcoholic who once dumped his passengers in the middle of the river after discovering that they could not pay. On several occasions his behavior forced Seltice to intervene to prevent minor hostilities. Seltice worked continually to persuade Coeur d'Alene people displaced by white settlement to move to Hangman's Valley and begin cultivating farms. The chief provided his own livestock and implements and organized cooperative support for those forced to leave their ancient homes.[47]

The Jesuits completed their move to Hangman's Valley by 1877. Although it was difficult for the fathers to abandon the beautiful old mission church, now known as Cataldo Mission, the move breathed new life into the Coeur d'Alene proselytizing effort. By the early 1880s the new mission included a church, a rectory for the Jesuit fathers, and a boys' boarding school.[48] The Sisters of Providence of Mary Immaculate (Sisters of Charity) established a convent and a girls' boarding school at DeSmet in 1878.[49] As DeSmet evolved into a center of economic, political, and religious authority, families who remained on tribal lands outside Hangman's Valley became increasingly isolated from the tribe's power structure. With the boarding schools came the imposition of non-Native language, an assimilation tactic that further accentuated the growing divide between the DeSmet Schitsu'umsh and the river and lake people.

Talk of war among the nontreaty Nez Perce bands, who objected to the elimination of Wallowa country from their northeastern Oregon reservation, alarmed the Jesuit fathers who thought white encroachment might drive the Coeur d'Alenes to participate in the hostilities. With war on the horizon, the Jesuits tried to tighten control of the mission Indians and to persuade all remaining "wayward" Schitsu'umsh to move to the new mission area. When war came during spring of 1877, the Schitsu'umsh leadership was not drawn into the conflict. Coeur d'Alene leaders had little reason to enter the conflict on the side of the Nez Perce bands, as Nez Perce involvement in the Steptoe and Wright campaigns was viewed as betrayal. Seltice's focus became protection of Schitsu'umsh farms and a careful public relations campaign to ensure that area whites did not mistake Coeur d'Alenes for the "hostile" Nez Perce.[50] Moreover, the conflict altered the tone of Coeur d'Alene petitions and gave Jesuit missionaries and tribal leaders additional evidence for their argument that the tribe was "civilized" and assimilated.

After General Oliver O. Howard gave the nontreaty Nez Perce people a thirty-day ultimatum to leave their ancient home in the Wallowa Valley and relocate to a reservation on the Clearwater River, angry Nez Perce raiders murdered four notorious anti-Indian settlers. The tragic consequences drew an unwilling Indian people into what became known as the Nez Perce War. Chief Joseph helped lead a desperate group of 800 tribal people, mostly women and children, on a 1,700-mile search for refuge among friendly tribes. Exhausted by the relentless pursuit of General Howard and the toll of the four-month journey, Chief Joseph surrendered only forty miles south of the Canadian border.[51]

Initial Nez Perce military success terrified white settlers. Whites in the Pine Creek region, just south of the Coeur d'Alene farm consolidation, panicked when they realized they were sandwiched between the Schitsu'umsh on the north and the Nez Perce on the south. Wild rumors of murderous Indians fueled white paranoia.[52] When the rattled settlers fled, leaving their homesteads and cattle unattended, Andrew Seltice offered to provide protection and sent the Soldiers of the Sacred Heart to feed livestock and guard property. Throughout summer of 1877 the soldiers patrolled the area, maintained fences, and hunted down stray animals.[53]

Seltice also clamped down on the activities of suspicious tribal people, particularly if they camped on or crossed Coeur d'Alene land. The Schitsu'umsh camas grounds in Paradise Valley had been a summer gathering spot for local tribes since the early 1870s. Seltice initially welcomed the visitors, but after the Jesuits moved the mission to DeSmet, the large, raucous gatherings only nine miles from the mission site offended the fathers. The camp became a center for drinking and racing and attracted the wary eyes of local whites. When several Nez Perce warriors rode into the 1877 encampment with a stolen horse, boasting that they had killed a white man, Seltice quickly instituted damage control. Since information about the Nez Perce bands' conflict with the U.S. Army was scanty, peppered with rumor, and often incendiary, Seltice could not afford to have local non-Indians believe he was harboring hostile Nez Perce individuals.[54]

Seltice confiscated the stolen horse, returned it to the Pine Creek settlers with a member of the Soldiers of the Sacred Heart, and used his militia to investigate the murder charge. When the inquiry revealed that Nez Perce warriors had indeed killed a white man—John Ritchie, a homesteader who lived in the Hangman's Creek area—Seltice ordered Schitsu'umsh at the camas camp and those who lived nearest the Pine Creek settlement to join the rest of the tribe at the mission. He also used his militia to force other tribal people to vacate Schitsu'umsh lands, although the historical records do not indicate exactly how this was accomplished. The summer camp dispersed, Joseph Joset assured Indian Agent John Simms on July 4, because the Indians were "afraid both of the whites and of the Coeurs d'Alene [sic]." Joset also reported the camp's breakup to James Ewart, owner of the General Merchandise Company in Colfax, who transmitted the information to worried Colfax residents. In response to Seltice's peacekeeping efforts, the captain of the Palouse Rangers—called up to protect Colfax citizens—"guaranteed" Coeur d'Alene tribal members passage on regional trails closed to all other tribal parties.[55]

Andrew Seltice's actions during the Nez Perce conflict cemented the reputation of the Coeur d'Alene tribe. As a result of their terror of Indian "depradations," area whites created mental maps of Indian identity. The Coeur d'Alenes were peaceable and civilized; the Nez Perce were warlike and uncivilized. The Coeur d'Alenes were assimilated; their neighbors were not. An example of the mental map of identity imposed on Interior Northwest peoples appears in the correspondence Pine Creek residents generated during summer of 1877. In a letter addressed to the "Priests and Chiefs of the Coeur d'Alene Indians," Pine Creek residents expressed appreciation "for your kindness toward us during the present excitement and for the trouble and the pains you have taken in assuring that there was no danger." The Pine Creek settlers fled, they explained, not "for fear of you but for fear of *other* Indians." In return for tribal protection, ninety-nine Pine Creek homesteaders signed a petition pledging "to do anything in our power to promote the peace and happiness" of the Coeur d'Alenes. "In return for your kindness," the Pine Creek residents extolled, "we the undersigned citizens are willing to assist you in petitioning [the] Government to grant you a good title to your land, that you may lead a quiet and peacable [sic] life." Ironically, the Pine Creek petitioners were themselves trespassers on tribal territory.[56]

True to their word, on August 25, 1877, the non-Indian Palouse residents sent a petition to the commissioner of Indian affairs acknowledging "the loyalty of the Coeurs d'Alene Indians" throughout the Nez Perce crisis. Seltice's "influence is great among the Northern Indians," the petitioners declared, "and it has been used to maintain peaceful relations between the Whites and Indians." General Frank Wheaton, who received orders from General Howard to hold a Spokane council and determine the northern tribes' sentiments, agreed with the petitioners. Sacred Heart missionaries and a Coeur d'Alene deputation led by Seltice escorted Wheaton to the site. The conference—held at Lower Spokane Falls on August 15 and attended by chiefs of the Coeur d'Alene, Spokane, Kalispel, Palouse, and Colville Tribes—provided a forum for Seltice, who gave the first speech. According to Father Cataldo's notes of the event, Seltice described the aid he had given to area settlers and "exhorted all the Indians present to follow his example." If forced to enter the hostilities, Seltice declared "he would take part with the U.S. soldiers." The Jesuit priests present at the conference believed Seltice's carefully chosen words carried great weight with the Catholic Indians attending. At the close of the conference General Wheaton and staff officer Melville Wilkinson praised Seltice's leadership and reassured the chief of tribal land claims.[57]

It appeared that, in the wake of the Nez Perce debacle, the Coeur d'Alenes had achieved a new level of respect that could translate into solidification of their hold on the 1873 reservation and federal recognition of, and payment for, aboriginal land claims. Despite the reassurances, however, Seltice and the Jesuit fathers recognized the predicament of the nontreaty Nez Perce as an indication of nontreaty groups' precarious position. Throughout the following decade they would use the Coeur d'Alenes' "civilized" reputation, consolidation of tribal farms near Hangman's Creek, and the relocation of the mission to DeSmet to successfully make the case for federal agreement negotiations. In using the mental map of tribal identity provided by the Nez Perce conflict, however, Coeur d'Alenes who did not fit the "civilized" profile could not be included as members of the tribe, at least when dealing with outsiders. They were also more at risk from the trespassing that would occur in ensuing decades. An explosion of mining activity in the Coeur d'Alene region during the 1880s, coupled with the arrival of large numbers of homesteaders, would test the effectiveness of Seltice's assimilation policy. The consolidation at Hangman's Creek would be protected, but the tribe could not hold on to "unimproved," "nonagricultural," or "unfenced" lands. Coeur d'Alene Reservation boundaries would be reshaped to reflect tribal assimilation policy and non-Indian pressure for mineral wealth, timber, and waterways.

SEVEN
COLVILLE AGENCY AND THE INITIAL ASSAULT ON RESERVATION BOUNDARIES, 1878–1886

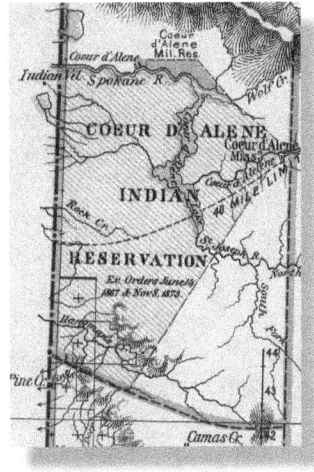

> Are we squirrels or the like animals, thus to drive us into a wilderness, where nothing can be raised to support people? Or are we fishes, that we should be made to live in the water? We say that we are men, as well as any whites are.
> —CHIEF ANDREW SELTICE, 1883[1]

A WIDESPREAD ASSAULT ON THE BOUNDARIES of the 1873 executive-ordered reservation began almost immediately after the Coeur d'Alenes consolidated within its confines. A gold rush on the North Fork of the Coeur d'Alene River forced tribal leaders to fight to keep invaders off reservation lands. Mining, railroad, steamship, and timber entrepreneurs pierced the borders of the reserve—sometimes with the permission of the Indian Office but often without it. The Colville Indian Agency, located in the northeast corner of Washington Territory at Chewelah and assigned the administrative duties of the Coeur d'Alene Reservation, failed to maintain an influential presence or to provide adequate protection against encroachment. Ironically, the tribe's economic success in Hangman's Valley and its proximity to DeSmet Mission allowed Colville Agency officials to ignore it, especially since the agency was overwhelmed by the needs of other groups under its jurisdiction—including Chief Joseph's Nez Perce. Why, Colville officials wondered, should the agency waste precious manpower and resources on a relatively prosperous people when other nontreaty tribal members, like those of the Spokane bands, were struggling to fend off starvation and alcoholism? Indeed, the Jesuit mission—having long functioned in the region as way station, peacemaker, and protector—stood unrivaled as a well-respected institution of stability. The new raid on Coeur d'Alene resources—land, timber, water—

strengthened Chief Seltice's antiencroachment campaign and challenged the Indian Office's obligation to protect reservation boundaries.

Chief Seltice's agricultural consolidation effort alienated some Schi̠tsu'umsh but enriched others. By the early 1880s the concentration of Coeur d'Alene farms and population in the Palouse exceeded that of surrounding white communities. Coeur d'Alene members operated more than 100 farms in Hangman's Valley. Cultivated land on those farms ranged from 70 to 650 acres, but the Coeur d'Alenes possessed much larger fenced acreages for grazing. They raised both wheat and oats, the surplus of which they sold to the nearby army post—Fort Sherman—and surrounding communities. To transport their crops to market, the Coeur d'Alenes used the extensive network of waterways on their reservation. Tribal members devised flat barges by attaching several canoes together and placing platforms on top of them. These improvised crafts provided transport for up to three tons of grain and could be floated on Lake Coeur d'Alene, the Coeur d'Alene River, and the St. Joseph River. In 1880 the Coeur d'Alenes erected a large granary and wool house for winter storage on the banks of Lake Coeur d'Alene. Because of such improvements, their agricultural operations exceeded in sophistication and acreage many of the surrounding 160-acre Homestead Act claims.[2]

Indeed, in 1880 Spokane Falls, the future metropolitan center nearest the Coeur d'Alene Reservation, was nothing more than a fledgling frontier community with a sawmill and a meager population of settlers banking on the arrival of the Northern Pacific Railroad.[3] Idaho Territory—created in 1863 after gold finds in the Clearwater and Boise basin regions—attracted thousands of non-Indian residents, remained sparsely populated, and as a result of its awkward boundaries, was geographically divided.[4] The Idaho population was centered in scattered mining camps, such as Idaho City, hundreds of miles from the northern panhandle. Although limited white settlement began moving into eastern Washington and northern Idaho in the early 1870s, concentrated non-Indian penetration started on Coeur d'Alene Lake's north shore when the U.S. Army built Fort Coeur d'Alene in 1878.[5]

General William T. Sherman chose the site in 1877 during an inspection tour of Northwest military forts. Intended to keep peace between settlers skittish because of the 1877 Nez Perce War and tribal people and to retain Mullan Road, Congress granted the post 1,000 acres of land at the point where Lake Coeur d'Alene drains into the Spokane River. With the staffing of the fort came young officers and their families, such as John Hickey and his daughter, Maggie Hickey Groves. Maggie Groves, six years old when her father arrived at the post, recounted to the *Coeur d'Alene Press* in 1958 that the Coeur d'Alene town site was initially little more than the soldiers and their families, living in tents, and a few Indian families occupying tepees along the banks of the Spokane River. Groves's remembrances point to continued Coeur d'Alene habitation of the old village site on the lake.[6]

Isolation continued to compound the administrative difficulties of the Colville Indian Agency, which was located approximately 120 miles from the Coeur d'Alene Reservation—a considerable distance considering the rough terrain and lack of passable roads. Moreover, Chewelah proved a poor site for a headquarters. Although the agency's managerial responsibilities extended to over 3,500 Indian people affiliated with the Spokane, Colville, and Coeur d'Alene Reservations, fewer than 100 tribal members lived within a 30-mile radius of the Indian agent. The Spokane and Colville Reservations were each at least 30 miles away. Moreover, the agency grounds housed no government buildings—consisting only of a one-story frame structure that served as both office and residence for the agent, a log house for the physician, and a "stable good enough for the few dilapidated animals belonging to the government."[7]

The Colville Agency first exercised direct influence on Coeur d'Alene Reservation affairs in early 1880 with the creation of an "agency farmer" position for the tribe. James O'Neill, who at the time served as farmer at the Colville Agency, received the new appointment. The duties of the position included protecting the reservation "from the encroachments of white settlers." O'Neill received an increase in salary to $1,000 per year.[8]

Despite the job's residency requirement, O'Neill remained at Chewelah, where neither farmer nor agent was in a position to influence events on the reserve. The omission of any mention of administrative difficulties in official inspection and agency reports between 1880 and 1885 created a figurative as well as a physical distance between the agency and the Coeur d'Alenes. Indian Service positions became more competitive as the bureaucracy swelled in response to an increasing number of reservations. The organization had long been plagued by corruption and an intricate spoils system that dictated the political appointment of Indian Agency personnel, but beginning in the 1880s the patronage system came under attack.[9] As a result of increased competition for jobs and greater emphasis on competency, agency personnel located at isolated posts such as Chewelah—far removed from the centers of power—resorted to giving a more attractive account of their performance than reality could support. For career professionals in the Indian Service, a stint as the agent of a little-known frontier post provided a step to better positions—if it appeared the enterprise was well managed.

O'Neill's reports indicate that he was sincere in performing his duties, but his efforts were continually hampered by the Indian Office's internal problems and the logistical issues confronting Colville Agency. O'Neill visited the Coeur d'Alenes "at convenient intervals," perhaps three or four times a year.[10] Unable to address specifics regarding daily conditions on the reserve, O'Neill's infrequent reports did not allow for a detailed account of reservation affairs. In fact, the agent at Colville generally related conditions at the Coeur d'Alene Reservation to the commissioner, thereby eliminating the need for O'Neill to conduct his own correspondence. Careless management characterized the Colville Agency during these years, attesting to its second-rate status as a frontier post. Moreover, Coeur d'Alene farming successes, although they gave the tribe economic stability, allowed the Colville Agency to overlook tribal complaints. Schi̱tsu'umsh who did not reside at the mission were ignored by the agency, which had a difficult enough time procuring information about the mission Indians. Thus, the fact that agency reports fail to mention Coeur d'Alene people who lived great distances from the mission is no indication that such people did not exist but rather constitutes further evidence of the incomplete record available to Colville agents. The reports filed by the agency, however, since they offered no indication of tribal divisions, bolstered the image of the Coeur d'Alenes as entirely Christian and agricultural.[11]

Characteristic of reports throughout the 1880s, O'Neill's annual report in August 1880 was dominated by a description of Coeur d'Alene tribal farms and the erection of new buildings. Tribal members enlarged old farms and broke ground for 60 new farms during summer of 1880. The report noted the considerable acreage of many of the farms—including those of tribal leaders Basil, who cultivated more than 100 acres, and Seltice, whose plots ranged in size from 40 to 650 acres. O'Neill estimated that the reservation housed about 160 farms, all "exceptionally fenced," and he spoke of the preserve's "fine meadows of Timothy [hay]." According to the report, the tribe had erected 30 new buildings with the aid of a portable sawmill they operated themselves. O'Neill concluded that the reservation existed in harmony with its white neighbors, who occupied bordering areas. "They [the Coeur d'Alene people] go on the principle of live and let live," O'Neill wrote, "and there is no difficulty or trouble between them."[12]

Early Indian Office field inspection reports—authorized by the appointment of inspectors in July 1873 for the purpose of reporting general conditions at agencies, schools, and reservations—enhanced the tranquil image of the Coeur d'Alene reservation. The Office of Indian Affairs (OIA) intended that field inspections provide a tool with which to regulate agency personnel and ensure tight organization within the Indian Office.[13] Field Inspector Robert A. Gardner's report of the Colville Agency in 1882 gave little attention to the Coeur d'Alene Reservation except to buttress the reports made by Farmer O'Neill. Gardner found O'Neill "a man of good moral character, experience in the management of Indians, Energy, and business capacity." The inspector described the Coeur d'Alene people as "practically self-supporting" despite a lack of "material assistance" from the government. Coeur d'Alene tribal members numbered approximately 425, lived in "comfortable houses," wore "citizens['] clothing," and, Gardner emphasized, "are universally conceded to be the best Indians in this part of the country." He ended his comments by describing the Coeur d'Alenes as a people ready to "receive their lands in severalty."[14]

Proponents touted "severalty," the granting of land to individual tribal members, as the ultimate answer to the "Indian problem." Lawmakers legitimized the ideal in 1887 with passage of the Dawes Severalty, or General Allotment, Act. Reservations were intended only as halfway houses that would allow tribal people to prepare themselves for the dissolution of traditional practices and the adoption of individualistic rather than communal values. Indian policy would no longer be needed because tribes would cease to exist as individuals became assimilated. Private property ownership provided the cornerstone of the reservation-to-assimilation construct. Communal tribal holdings—transformed to small, privately owned farms through severalty, or allotment—provided the economic means necessary to instill in Indian people the pride of ownership, responsible citizenship, and a rural Christian work ethic.[15] The act's language recognized all executive-ordered reservations as possessing the same legal standing as negotiated reserves, which gave further legitimacy to the Coeur d'Alenes' 1873 reservation.[16]

Although it was supported at the time by most Indians' rights organizations, this paternalistic panacea revealed more about the psyche of a nation struggling to maintain its self-image as an agrarian society than about realistic solutions to the problems confronting Native Americans. Supporters of allotment—known as "Friends of the Indian"—failed to consider the infertile location of many Indian reservations, the lack of agricultural tradition within most tribes, the capital necessary to transform reservations into thousands of small farms, and the rapidly advancing urbanization of the United States.[17]

Inspector Gardner, like several other government officials, believed the Coeur d'Alene people had reached a sufficiently high level of "civilization" that they could move directly to severalty, eliminating the need for future appropriations for the Coeur d'Alenes. Gardner thus did not recommend an increase in agency personnel. Instead he suggested that the government presence on the reserve be reduced by eliminating one of the interpreter positions. The inspector was aware, no doubt, that the tribe often relied on Jesuit missionaries to provide translation services. In a high-handed fashion characteristic of federal dealings with the Coeur d'Alenes, Gardner further advised that Baptiste Peow's band of Spokane Indians, who numbered approximately 150 and did not reside on a reservation, "move onto the Coeur d'Alene Reservation." Apparently disregarding the fate of the reserve should the Coeur d'Alenes receive allotments, the inspector explained that "good land" remained available and under-utilized. The Coeur d'Alenes would welcome the Spokanes, Gardner reasoned, since Baptiste's son was married to Chief Andrew Seltice's daughter and the Spokane band practiced Catholicism.[18]

By the 1880s the Spokanes represented, in the non-Indian mental map of Indian identity, the opposite of Coeur d'Alene civilization and industry. In the minds of local whites, the Spokane people lived in "scattered" bands; they did not practice agriculture; some were Catholic, some were Protestant, and some possessed no "white religion." Federal documents refer to the Spokanes as "very poor," "ignorant," "degraded," and "much addicted to intoxication and gambling."[19] Citizens of Spokane Falls repeatedly complained of "drunkenness and prostitution" among the Spokane Indians. In response to white complaints, the Colville Indian agent requested that the mayor of Spokane impose a curfew on "all Indians being within the city's confines after sunset who cannot give a good reason for their presence under penalty of a small fine or imprisonment."[20] Indeed, Washington territorial law dealt more harshly with Natives viewed as "disorderly," and citizens' militia groups formed to protect white property.[21] Placing the Spokanes on the Coeur d'Alene Reservation would remove them from contact with whites and expose them to "good Indian" behavior. The de facto fluidity of the Coeur d'Alene Reservation boundary, and the disassociation of more traditional Schitsu'umsh from the mission, also allowed for the non-Indian classification of some Coeur d'Alene people as members of "roaming Spokane bands." Certainly, individual Coeur d'Alene members, including Chief Seltice, had blood and marriage ties to the Spokanes.

Although the Spokane people did not move onto the reservation until late in the decade, Coeur d'Alene leaders and Jesuit missionaries supported the idea and the image it portrayed—not only was the tribe "civilized," but it was willing to share its wealth and good habits with less fortunate neighbors. "I have to say that the desire of Chief Seltis [sic] and other chiefs or headmen as expressed in Council," the commissioner wrote to Colville Agent Sidney Waters in 1883, "that the Spokane Indians who are hanging about the town of Spokane Falls, in idleness and beggary, should be settled with them upon their reservation . . . is highly commendable in them and meets with my hearty approval."[22] Seltice noted in a letter to the agency that the Spokanes "will not appreciate your trouble for them" but added, "if the Spokan [sic] come we are all glad. . . . [W]e want to make only one people." In his qualifications for Spokane removal to the Coeur d'Alene reserve, Seltice's views of assimilation and tribal identity emerged. The Coeur d'Alenes would not allow the newcomers to choose land all in one location, Seltice added, "because when they [the Spokanes] will be only in one place they will not leave their old habits of gambling, drinking and so on—but when they are mixt [sic] with us they will soon get over of [sic] their old habits."[23]

The generous consideration of the destitute Spokane bands enhanced the tribe's image as progressive and self-sufficient. Inspector Ward further solidified the independent reputation of the Coeur d'Alenes in his 1884 inspection report of the Colville Agency. "The Coeur d'Alene Indians," Ward wrote in the one sentence he devoted to the tribe, "are in good condition, raise considerable grain and many have good herds of cattle and horses, a few are quite wealthy, live in frame and log houses."[24] By late 1884 federal inspectors and

Colville Agency employees exhibited a decidedly casual attitude toward the tribe. Inspector Newell's report of December 12, 1884, failed to mention the tribe specifically and only commented on the performance of James O'Neill, the "resident" farmer. Newell's admission that O'Neill "deserves especial mention" for his thirty years of public service reveals little about the actual conditions on the reservation. Whereas the report vaguely praised O'Neill for providing "a most healthful moral influence," it offered no useful information or recommendations.[25]

In spite of the neglect of Colville Agency personnel and Indian Office inspectors, Coeur d'Alene farming methods approached new levels of development during the mid-1880s. Resident Farmer O'Neill's 1884 report praised the "progress they [the Coeur d'Alene people] are making and the great interest manifested by them in their farm work, in their fences, cultivation in improving the breed of their horses and cattle, and in fact all things to make their farming a success." The average fenced acreage on the reservation, O'Neill reported, was now 200 acres. The leading tribal farmers, however, possessed much larger enclosures, as tallied by the resident farmer: "Regis and his brother have about two miles square—Aeneas between 400 & 500 acres—Leo 250 acres—Peter and Sebastian and Charles Lewis have each about 1½ miles square." All of the farms, O'Neill noted, were "well cultivated" and carefully fenced. Several leaders—including Seltice, Regis, Basil, and Bartelmy—employed white farmhands and operated the latest farm machinery.[26]

The reports filed by O'Neill and the inspectors indicate the growing economic division on the Coeur d'Alene reserve. Tribal leaders such as Seltice and Regis continued to increase their wealth after consolidation. The distance of the Indian agency also meant the Coeur d'Alene farming economy functioned independent of government intervention. Even into the mid-1880s, however, not all tribal people farmed. Colville Agency's inability to police reservation boundaries affected those individuals the most directly. Despite growing problems with whites in hunting areas and fishing grounds, many continued to practice their annual subsistence rituals, traveling outside reservation boundaries to traditional locales. Sidney Waters's 1884 winter agency reports reveal that all of the tribes under Colville jurisdiction participated in this autumn rite. "Most of the bands are in the mountains on their annual fall hunt and there are none visiting the Agency," Waters recounted in November. Representatives from the tribes sent scouts back to communicate with the agency, suggesting a pattern of organization associated with the hunts that apparently met with the agent's approval. "From the reports brought in by their runners," Waters concluded, "they are meeting with much success, and at all points [are] very peaceable and quiet."[27] A month later Waters reported that the Indian people, "having returned from their Fall hunting expedition," were preparing their homes for winter occupancy.[28]

Agency reports are also significant for what they fail to reveal. The tribe's attempts between 1882 and 1883 to procure funds from the Indian Office to purchase a portable sawmill illustrate the government's use of reservation prosperity to ignore or deny the group's needs and problems and illuminates the relationship between agency neglect and non-Indian trespassing. Correspondence between Indian Agent John Simms and Commissioner Hiram Price during 1882 called into question the existence of the sawmill Farmer O'Neill referred to in his 1880 report of conditions on the Coeur d'Alene Reservation. O'Neill may have assumed the Coeur d'Alenes possessed a sawmill when in fact they had only a makeshift mule-operated contraption.[29] At any rate, Simms requested on behalf of the Coeur d'Alene tribe that a portable sawmill be erected on the reservation. Price at first denied the request, citing insufficient funds and the apparent prosperous condition of farming operations on the reserve—which suggested the tribe was capable of constructing a sawmill without assistance.[30] He retracted his earlier position in July 1882 by allowing Simms to contract with a private individual to cut limited lumber, not to exceed 500,000 feet and for the purpose of rebuilding one of the Coeur d'Alene school buildings recently destroyed by fire. The commissioner ordered that dead and fallen timber on the reservation should be used whenever possible instead of green trees and that lumber derived from live trees "must not under any circumstances be sold."[31]

Despite Price's consent to the hiring of a private contractor, Simms again requested that the Indian Office purchase a portable sawmill, owned by M. J. Sexton, for the Indians' use. Commissioner Price responded that the Indian Office did not have available the $2,000 necessary to purchase the sawmill and failed to understand "why the Government should furnish the Indians of your agency with a mill, when the fact is taken into consideration that they raised more than 100,000 bushels of wheat and oats in the past season, and are the possessors of many thousand head of horses and cattle." Then, exaggerating the "aid" the Indian Office had given the Coeur d'Alenes, Price withdrew the subject from further consideration. "With the aid they have already received from the Government, and the advance they have made in the habits of industry and civilization," he declared, "I see no reason why further aid should be extended them, except for educational purposes."[32] Although Inspector Gardner revealed in November 1882 that the Coeur d'Alenes remained "anxious and desirous that the Government assist them in the purchase of a portable stream saw mill" and recommended that the Colville Agency "be authorized to purchase" the machine for the tribe's use, the commissioner did not change his position.[33]

The commissioner's refusal to purchase a sawmill for the Coeur d'Alenes created administrative difficulties for Colville Agency. After Price gave permission for the Coeur d'Alenes to hire a private contractor to cut a limited amount of timber, several private contractors appeared on the reservation, and the Indian agent proved unable to enforce the commissioner's limitations. Since they had been denied the funds to purchase Sexton's portable sawmill, the Coeur d'Alenes had contracted with M. J. Sexton and Codd of nearby Colfax—a firm that welcomed the opportunity to saw lumber for the mission and the tribe. The Sexton firm erected a sawmill on the reservation in 1882. It furnished lumber to the Coeur d'Alenes at a reduced price of seven dollars per 1,000 feet. Even when the Colville agent reported the mill to the commissioner, Indian objections to its closure allowed Sexton to remain open for business.[34]

The missionary fathers, Indian Agent John Simms, and Chief Seltice also made an agreement with Zaccheus Lewis who rented a sawmill at Little Falls on the Spokane River, along the northern boundary of the reservation. Between May 1, 1883, and August 1, 1884, Lewis sawed and removed 400 pine trees—an average of 400,000 board feet—from the Coeur d'Alene Reservation. Chief Seltice intended to use the lumber for the Coeur d'Alenes living along the Spokane River, particularly Subchief Stellam who owned a ranch near there. By special agreement with Simms, Lewis paid the Coeur d'Alenes in lumber and flour, delivered on order by the owner of the mill, Frederick Post. A German immigrant, Post came to the area in 1871, as his name on Treaty Rock in Post Falls attests. He began building the sawmill, the first commercial operation of its kind in Kootenai County, on the upper falls of the Spokane River in 1876 but did not complete the job until 1880.[35]

When Agent Simms resigned his position in 1883, he ordered Lewis to stop cutting timber; but at the request of tribal members residing in the area, Lewis sawed the rest of the logs stipulated under his agreement with Simms. According to Lewis, Coeur d'Alene tribal members, communicating through an interpreter, informed him that they had received a permit from the new agent, Sidney Waters, to saw the timber.[36] When Special Agent Prosser reported the violations committed by Lewis and Post, Waters denied any involvement. In April 1885 Waters responded to Commissioner Price's request for a full account of the Lewis trespass. The agent explained that since October 1883, when Waters assumed the agency post, no trees had been cut by Lewis. Waters asserted that he had never met Lewis or Post and that "no permission has ever been given or any agreement ever been entered into with me granting them the privilege of cutting and removing timber from the Coeur d'Alene Indian Reserve." "I believe Lewis went on the reserve on his own responsibility," Waters surmised, "and afterwards being found there by the Indians made it all right with them by giving them some lumber and flour."[37] Waters also accused Post and Lewis of fraud, suggesting that with a mill located on the Spokane River, away from the road, the conspirators had taken the opportunity to cut timber and then claimed to have had an agreement with the agent to help "the poor Indians."[38]

Post responded to Waters's accusations by admitting that he had cut the timber, but he argued that the transaction was legal because he had obtained the consent of both the Coeur d'Alenes and the Indian agent. "I am an old man, not being educated in the English language," Post explained. "You say you are a stranger to me if you knew me you would not take [sic] to me in that language," he indignantly asserted, adding "I am not a man to commit trespass." The community of Post Falls, Idaho, which grew up around the sawmill, looked to Post as its founding father.[39]

Unfortunately, the absence of documents written from the Coeur d'Alene perspective precludes a conclusion regarding the events surrounding the Lewis timber trespass. Clearly, the Coeur d'Alene people found a way to procure needed lumber, and the commissioner's refusal to purchase a sawmill for them restricted the ability of the Colville Agency to regulate the cutting of timber on the reservation. Perhaps Agent John Simms, recognizing the discrepancy between the commissioner's ruling and the Coeur d'Alenes' need for lumber, became involved in an illegal agreement with Lewis. Simms's quiet departure from office in late 1883 suggests his involvement, either at the request of the Coeur d'Alenes or for his personal gain or both. Potential profits certainly motivated the private contractors, but the commissioner's obstinance made their presence possible.

Timber trespassers represented only one kind of threat to the integrity of reservation boundaries. Farmer O'Neill's admission in his 1884 report that "there is some disatisfaction [sic] in regard to the boundary line" minimized a problem that had been brewing since 1880. Homesteaders began to trickle into the fertile lower Coeur d'Alene River valley in the northeast corner of the reservation in the early 1880s.[40] Indeed, the director of the Bureau of Catholic Indian Missions, B. A. Brouillet, had found a problem with illegal trespassing while touring Pacific Coast Indian agencies in 1881. After communicating with the Coeur d'Alene people, Brouillet reported to Commissioner Price that the Indians "anticipated much trouble in the near future." Brouillet asked Price to commission a survey of the reservation since the boundaries were not clearly marked, emphasizing that "the longer such action is deferred the greater will be the encroachment by the whites."[41] No effort on the matter ensued, and in July 1882 Agent Simms asked Price for a survey because "nearly all the timber in that section [along the southeastern border] is on the reservation, and the uncertainty as to the actual boundaries leads to many acts of trespass." The commissioner responded by directing William Chandler, surveyor general, to make arrangements for the survey the following spring.[42]

Darius F. Baker, deputy surveyor, completed the work in April 1883. He chose not to follow the instructions outlined in the 1873 executive order, which specified that the northern reservation boundary should run from "the Coeur d'Alene Mission on the Coeur d'Alene River (but not to include the lands of said mission); thence in a westerly direction, in a direct line, to the point where the Spokane river heads in, or leaves the Coeur d'Alene Lakes."[43] As Baker's field notes reveal, the surveyor determined that to run the westerly line from the southwest corner of the mission, excluding the Jesuit farms and buildings, "would work a hardship on the Indians and would undoubtedly cause troubles, as they had always believed" the line began from the northeast corner of the mission holdings. Baker, realizing that to start from the southwest corner would leave tribal "gardens and improvements entirely off the Reservation," began instead at a point 67.30 chains, or just under a mile, north of the southwest corner of the mission.[44] Baker thus interpreted the order in favor of the tribe's—and the mission's—own map of what the reservation encompassed.

Affirmation of the reservation boundaries, however, did not solve the trespassing problem, as whites simply ignored the newly surveyed boundary. Chief Andrew Seltice complained of these unfortunate circumstances in October 1883. "Before the Surveyors had come to survey the Coeurs-d'-Alene reservation boundaries," Seltice wrote to Indian Agent Simms, "we were, as you know, rather uneasy about it. When at last they came and drew the boundary lines, we thought every trouble was over: but we scarcely had one day of rest." Just as the surveyor put away his chains, white settlers in the Coeur d'Alene River valley threatened tribal members with a petition to "open the very best portion of this reservation and send us to the other side of the St. Joseph river." Seltice dismissed the settlers' alleged lack of timber, explaining that the tribe had "always told them that they could have all the fire wood they wanted." The tribal leader saw something more sinister in the settlers' actions than the simple need for fuel and building material:

> Now what our friends the whites mean we do not know. Are we squirrels or the like animals, thus to drive us into a wilderness, where nothing can be raised to support people? Or are we fishes, that we should be made to live in the water? We say that we are men, as well as any whites are. From the land they would take us away, we get our food, our clothing and whatever we are in need of. For we till our land, raise crops, keep herds of cattle and thus provide for ourselves.[45]

Seltice hoped this direct reference to assimilation policy would convince the Indian Office to protect Coeur d'Alene territory; after all, the tribe could not farm without land.

In fall of 1883, just months after Baker completed his survey, the discovery of gold along the North Fork of the Coeur d'Alene River dramatically changed the face of the region and represented a severe challenge to the authority and ability of Colville Agency to control intruders. Vast numbers of prospectors infiltrated the area, most crossing through the reservation's northeastern corner. Gold fever, coupled with the arrival of the region's first transcontinental railroad, instantly made the Schi̱tsu'umsh tribal homeland desirable and accessible. Completed in 1883, the Northern Pacific route cut through Idaho Territory north of the Coeur d'Alene Reservation, but it entered Spokane Falls and stimulated interest in the Coeur d'Alene ore strikes. Following the North Fork gold discovery, the Northern Pacific issued circulars advertising the strike.[46]

Transcontinental rail service provided a national market for regional agriculture and offered access to the Coeur d'Alene mines. Newcomers came by way of Northern Pacific stations at Spokane Falls or Rathdrum, Idaho Territory, where they procured stagecoaches that took them to landings on Lake Coeur d'Alene. There they boarded the *Amelia Wheaton*, the lake's first steam-powered vessel. Built in 1880 at Fort Coeur d'Alene, the 85-foot stern-wheeler hauled mostly supplies for the post, but with the sudden population surge army commanders allowed the ship to transport fortune seekers to the mines. Soon, other steamboats began plying Lake Coeur d'Alene's waters. The *Coeur d'Alene*, a 120-foot stern-wheeler built by Portland investors, and the *General Sherman*, a small craft built for the local trading corporation King and Monaghan, both began service in 1884. Stage and steamboat operators lined their pockets as passengers paid a premium for their trip to the mines. In 1884 a prospector traveling from Spokane Falls to Eagle City could expect to pay fifteen dollars for the ride and an additional eleven cents per pound of freight.[47]

No other city benefited more from the gold rush than the previously struggling community of Spokane Falls. With its newfound fame as gateway to the Coeur d'Alene mines, the city became known simply as Spokane. Disclosure of Andrew Prichard's placer gold finds, on a North Fork tributary later known as Prichard's Creek, produced such excitement that Spokane businesses experienced immediate runs on supplies. By November 1883 nearly 1,000 people prepared to winter near the North Fork's first gold town, Eagle City. In Eagle City—composed of about twenty log cabins serving as hotels, saloons, mercantile establishments, and a recorder's office—goods were expensive and scarce. Thus, a steady stream of supplies flowed in from Spokane, finding their haphazard way across the Coeur d'Alene Reservation. Spokane businessmen became increasingly cheerful as Eagle City's population soared to 2,000 by summer of 1884. During 1884, over 5,000 prospectors arrived to try their luck on the North Fork.[48]

At the same time, ranchers living in eastern Washington discovered the wealth of summer forage available in the foothills of the Bitterroot Mountains. John and Alex McGregor, pioneer ranchers in Washington Territory, grazed a total of more than 1 million sheep during the 1880s and 1890s. Competition with cattle growers forced sheepherders to travel 150 miles or more to provide for their herds. Northern Washington's Okanogan highlands provided winter feed, whereas the Bitterroots became the favored summer feeding site. Sheepherders crossed Coeur d'Alene Reservation on their way to and from the Bitterroot pastures, helping themselves to timber, water, and forage along the way.[49]

The Colville Agency struggled to deal with the flow of traffic moving across Coeur d'Alene Reservation. As a result of distance and the conventional view that the Coeur d'Alenes could take care of themselves, the agency found it was not in a position to prevent widespread trespassing on the reserve. In March 1884 Agent Waters complained to Commissioner Price that the rush to the Coeur d'Alene mines had resulted in many forms of intrusion—that is, "the building of roads, bridges, etc. and the crossing of the reservation at different points by *thousands* of miners, the building of steamboats at different points to run upon Coeur d'Alene Lake within the borders of the reserve, with different landings upon the same."[50] The agent lamented that he was "powerless to prevent" the encroachment and asked for instructions.[51]

On April 23 Waters visited the Coeur d'Alene Reservation and confirmed his fears. Waters found non-Indians erecting a hotel and a restaurant at Rockford Landing on Lake Coeur d'Alene and others cutting timber at Farmington Landing for sale to the steamers. In an action that involved him in the political maneuverings of the traders and steamship operators on Lake Coeur d'Alene, Waters approached the steamboat *Coeur d'Alene*'s operators, demanded payment to Colville Agency for the countless cords of wood for fuel taken from the reservation, and ordered them to discontinue their practice of buying reservation timber.[52]

In response, Coeur d'Alene Steam Navigation Company, the Portland firm that owned the vessel, sent angry telegrams and letters to its Oregon congressman J. N. Dolph. The company accused Waters of conspiracy, arguing that the *Coeur d'Alene* was intentionally kept from docking to give a monopoly to its fiercest competitor, the *General Sherman*, owned by the trading firm King and Monaghan. Coeur d'Alene Steam Navigation Company's secretary described the *General Sherman* as "a craft of no value, and no use, in navigating the tributaries of the Lake," thus explaining why "our steamer . . . is doing all the business, which has excited their jealousy—hence their efforts to make us trouble." The Portland company's representatives had no intention of backing down, and they ordered their captain "to land whenever the necessity demands, to buy wood from the Indians whenever his vessel needs it . . . to go along quietly about his business which is accommodating the public."[53] In response to these allegations, Waters telegraphed Washington: "No discrimination made between any boats on Coeur d'Alene lake landing. All have same privileges only prohibition was to all of them against purchasing wood cut by trespassers on reserve. No difficulty in procuring wood at either end of route off reserve."[54] Regardless of the agent's declaration that wood could be procured off the reservation, the Coeur d'Alene Steam Navigation Company's persistence showed the challenge Waters faced in attempting to enforce his own regulations.

Upon his return from visiting the Coeur d'Alene Reservation, Waters reiterated his concerns that trespassing continued on the reserve. Despite the completion of the Baker survey in 1883, Waters nervously inquired whether the survey lines "were ever definitely located last fall." Apparently, the Indian Office had failed to notify him of the newly surveyed boundary line because the agent believed the atmosphere had been too smoky from forest fires to complete the work. "It is imperatively necessary that monuments be at once set," Waters urged, "as towns are being located and encroachments already commenced I think on the N.E. line of the Reserve."55

Indeed, unknown to Waters, five days earlier Idaho territorial delegate T. F. Singisen had requested that the interior secretary restore to the public domain "that portion of the Coeur d'Alene Indian Reservation in Idaho Territory, situated east of the Coeur d'Alene Lake, and located between the mouth of Wolf Lodge Creek on the Northeastern extremity of said reservation and the St. Joseph's River on the southeastern portion of said reservation." Singisen, apparently unaware of traditional Schitsu'umsh land use and of the comments Seltice made in 1883, contended that this area "is not now, nor ever has been occupied by the Indians." The territorial representative reasoned that "the present mining excitement" in the region made it imperative that the reservation be opened, since its presence near the mines caused a "fruitful source of trouble to the miners and settlers, as well as to the Government, without proving in the slightest degree beneficial or useful to the Indians."56 Not only did the northern boundary remain ambiguous, the Colville Agency did not even know of its location as surveyed. By the time Waters received a copy of the map and field notes of the survey in November 1884, the mining rush had been in full swing for a year, and innumerable encroachments had taken place.57

Commissioner Price's response to Waters's account of the "disturbed condition of affairs on the Coeur d'Alene Reservation" downplayed the significance of the trespassing. Price recommended that the miners be given right-of-way across the reservation, but they should not be allowed to "loiter or hang around" Indian homes. "In all probability," the commissioner predicted, "the rush will soon be over." His comments implied that the burden the mining rush caused the Coeur d'Alene people failed to compare with the needs of the prospectors, who "ought not to be put to the inconvenience and expense of going around the reservation when a much shorter route is open to them across the same." The commissioner also raised no objection to the trespassing steamboats. Noting that "several" vessels were already operating on Lake Coeur d'Alene, Price did "not see that any harm would result if more were added."58

On behalf of the Coeur d'Alenes, Andrew Seltice responded to the uncontrolled encroachments with a letter—transcribed by the Jesuit fathers—to Farmer O'Neill in August 1884. The tribal leader repudiated a rumor that the Indians charged white travelers a toll. "No one indian asked [for a toll], and no white paid it," Seltice explained. The rumor had originated from an isolated incident in which a Coeur d'Alene member "said a few words" to a white intruder carrying heavy loads across a bridge, breaking it down and making no repairs. Seltice defended the Coeur d'Alene individual Indian, using the example to express tribal views of the encroachment problem. "We think that the whites have nothing to complain [about]," Seltice admonished, since "the whites last year were requested to contribute to building the bridge but no one offered a cent or a day of work—Besides the bridges except one are private made by one or two Indians for their conveniance [sic]." Contrary to the commissioner's statements, the Coeur d'Alenes incurred great inconvenience as a result of the trespassers and came to believe, as Seltice stated, that the whites "have bad feelings towards us, because they envey [sic] our land, our efforts and may be our property too." The failure of white intruders to keep their promise to finance the construction of a road from the mission to Farmington in eastern Washington, and their reluctance to pay for damages to private property, augmented a growing distrust among Coeur d'Alene leaders. Whites, they concluded, "would like to see us gambling, drinking and to drive us in the woods and die, and happily and joyfully take possession of our fields already fenced, broken and plowed."[59]

Chief Seltice understood the Colville Agency's responsibilities and held Agent Waters accountable for the uncontrolled trespassing on the Coeur d'Alene Reservation. The Jesuit fathers as well as the Coeur d'Alene people thought the agency had neglected its duties to the reservation. When the Colville Agency finally provided on-site personnel for the reservation, it was in the form of a physician. Dr. John A. Sweeney received an appointment as Coeur d'Alene reservation resident doctor and "additional farmer" in March 1885. Sweeney's careful reports reveal that he held genuine concern for the tribe and suggest that he experienced profound frustration with the awkward bureaucracy within which he tried to function. Problems associated with the reservation's isolation from Colville Agency angered and worried the physician. Medicine ordered took months to arrive. Indeed, the doctor often had to wait until someone from DeSmet Mission made a trip to Spokane before he could procure supplies. Separated from his family and living in substandard housing, Sweeney blamed Agent Waters, who seemed to ignore the Coeur d'Alene people. Sweeney wrote the agent often, asking for supplies, medicines, and housing materials. "I have not received any communication from you for some time," Sweeney noted in a letter to Waters, adding, "I hope to have the pleasure of seeing you here soon, as there are many things in which I would like your advice."[60]

Chief Seltice also wanted a visit by Agent Waters. The chief befriended Dr. Sweeney and used him to convey his views to the agent. In June 1885 Sweeney recounted to Waters the chief's frustration: "He [Seltice] is always glad to see Maj. O'neil [sic], but as he is not the agent, that he does not feel as well satisfied as if you would come yourself, as you are the agent. He compares you as equivalent to $1.00 and Maj. O'neil as equivalent to $.75 and therefore would like to have the dollar, better than the seventy five cents."[61] In addition, Sweeney asked the agent on behalf of Seltice to give Subchief Stellam, "now living at Spokane bridge," documented proof of the reservation boundaries. Stellam was "continualy

[sic] annoyed by white people comming [sic] on the reserve for wood, and driving sheep on his lands."[62] No Colville Agency documentation suggests that Waters granted Sweeney's or Seltice's requests. Indeed, the commissioner suspended Waters from office in 1885, replacing him with Benjamin Moore. Waters protested his suspension, claiming he had done all he could "to lift [the Indians] up from their degradation and misery."[63]

Despite Commissioner Price's prophecy of a temporary problem, the encroachments of the early 1880s represented only the beginning of a pervasive onslaught of intruders. In addition to the presence of many new people and their use of resources, the miners and their supporting industries introduced a silent but deadly invader to the Coeur d'Alene people. Steamboats and mining traffic instigated a lively liquor trade that offered unprecedented access to the illegal spirits. The Trade and Intercourse Act of 1834 had banned the sale of liquor to Native people in "Indian Country"; additions to the act specified that alcohol could not be sold on Indian reservations. Although liquor had long been used by traders in the Interior Pacific Northwest, the Jesuit mission and the Coeur d'Alene leadership had been relatively successful in keeping the tribe isolated from the worst aspects of this illicit trade.[64]

The gold rush, however, brought unprecedented amounts of liquor to the reservation. The booze flowed on steamboats as rowdy mining parties made their way to new communities in the Coeur d'Alene district. In 1886 Inspector General H. M. Lazelle found that the vessel *Coeur d'Alene*, owned by the trading firm of C. B. King and Monaghan, had been in violation of federal liquor statutes probably since its introduction. Lazelle reported that while transporting mining, fishing, and sightseeing parties, King and Monaghan kept an "open bar" on the craft "at which drinks of various sorts of liquor, were very freely and frequently sold." When stopping at landings, steamer operators exercised the pretense of pulling "down the glass window in front of the bar for a moment, until the boat was again afloat, when the business of mixing and selling drinks was at once resumed and continued."[65]

The Justice Department agreed with Lazelle that "the entire lake of Coeur d'Alene, and about twenty-five miles of the river of Coeur d'Alene—from the mouth up, as far as the landing on that river, known as the "Old Mission"—lay wholly within the Coeur d'Alene Indian Reservation." Federal laws prohibiting the sale or consumption of alcohol on Indian reservations therefore applied to the *Coeur d'Alene* even while the ship was out on the lake, since the surface water was considered part of the reservation. Threatened with losing its license, the King and Monaghan firm turned its "barroom" into a "stateroom" and agreed to a bond forbidding liquor sales. Problems continued, however, especially since the new Colville agent, Benjamin Moore, was unwilling to stop the flow of alcohol. Moore, as required by his office, took affidavits from residents who swore that the traders sold liquor. Moore's friendship with James Monaghan, however, persuaded him to show the statements to the steamboat operator. Monaghan promptly intimidated the witnesses into keeping quiet. Thus, when later asked about the validity of their sworn statements, witnesses denied ever having seen the liquor sales.[66]

Throughout the North Fork gold rush, the Colville Agency either concealed problems or provided only temporary solutions. Indian agents John Simms and Sidney Waters both left office under suspicious circumstances during this period, and Agent Benjamin Moore actively participated in a cover-up of the illicit liquor trade on Coeur d'Alene reservation. Moore was replaced by Rickard D. Gwydir in 1886. A native of Kentucky and a Confederate Army veteran, Gwydir brought his wife, Mary, and their three children to Washington Territory. Gwydir admitted that "it has been customary to print annual reports with the brightest colors," but since he presumed that the commissioner "wants facts, not fancies," he pledged to "write without the coloring."[67] The commissioner had moved the agency to a location on what was then the Spokane Reservation, north of the Spokane River and one mile from the confluence with the Columbia, just prior to Gwydir's arrival. Noted for his straightforward manner, his habit of dressing in Kentucky frontier-style fringed leather, and his inclination to jump nude into snowbanks, Gwydir reported that the agency move provided scant improvement:

> A more unsuitable site could scarcely have been found. The only advantage it has over Chewelah is that it is on the [Spokane] reservation. The buildings consist of one double cottage, finished, which is occupied by the agent, clerk, farmer, interpreter, and, when I have one, laborer; one double cottage, unfinished, one office for agent, one warehouse finished, one barn and stable combined nearly finished, and one office for the doctor unfinished. There is no fencing or lumber to fence with. The agent who estimated for the buildings neglected to estimate for lining and papering part of the property; also forgot that it was necessary to have a cistern, out-houses, and fencing. The buildings are situated on a high sandy plateau, bearing a luxuriant growth of sage brush, and nearly 300 feet above the Spokane river, so as to be beyond irrigation from that stream; the spring, about 200 feet farther up the mountain, will, by building a reservoir, give sufficient water to supply the wants of the agency and agency stock, but not enough for irrigation.[68]

Gwydir's correspondence continued to be frank and, at times, sarcastic. He lasted only two years before packing up his family and leaving the agency for prospecting opportunities in the region.[69]

Operating largely independent of the agency, Coeur d'Alene tribal leaders struggled as miners and other whites crossed the reservation, felled tribal timber, and destroyed reservation bridges. Of great concern was the imposition of an illicit liquor trade that Chief Seltice and DeSmet missionaries had, until now, successfully fended off. Although the encroachments angered and inconvenienced tribal members, they drew attention to the tribe and helped instigate the authorization of new negotiations. As the decade wore to a close, Seltice's assimilation policy finally paid off with the creation of an agreement recognizing Schitsu'umsh land claims, providing payment for released territory, and confirming the boundaries of the 1873 reservation.

EIGHT

THE AGREEMENT OF 1887

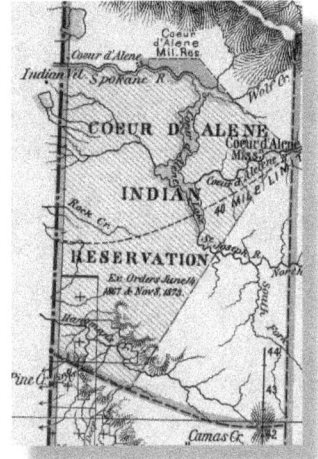

It is agreed that the Coeur d'Alene Reservation shall be held forever as Indian land as homes for the Coeur d'Alene Indians, now residing on said reservation, and the Spokane or other Indians who may be removed to said reservation under this agreement, and their posterity; and no part of said reservation shall ever be sold, occupied, open to white settlement, or otherwise disposed of without the consent of the Indians residing on said reservation.
—ARTICLE FIVE, NORTHWEST INDIAN COMMISSION AGREEMENT, 1887[1]

GOLD DISCOVERIES ALONG THE NORTH FORK OF THE COEUR D'ALENE RIVER brought thousands of outsiders to the Coeur d'Alene tribal homeland during the early 1880s. The upstart communities of Eagle City, Murray, Butte City, and Myrtle personified the fluid, highly speculative populations characteristic of boom-and-bust mining towns throughout the Interior West. With little regard for property rights or reservation boundaries, placer miners traipsed across Coeur d'Alene Indian Reservation at will. Mining suppliers and steamship operators invaded Indian land in search of timber or trading opportunities. Still, the North Fork's mining towns did not represent a permanent population. When the gold disappeared or simply failed to materialize, so did the prospectors. The Colville Indian Agency approached the onslaught as a temporary problem to be endured. Conversely, Coeur d'Alene leaders perceived the mining and timber encroachments of the early 1880s as evidence of things to come.

Discovery and development of silver and lead deposits during the second half of the decade on the South Fork of the Coeur d'Alene River confirmed tribal suspicions. Driven by the industrial nature of lead and silver mining, the new communities heralded the arrival of a permanent extractive market economy.[2] At the same time, the character of non-Indian homesteading on the Palouse changed from small and transient to large and permanent. Livestock operations gave way to large-scale farming enterprises, further entrenching an economy based on extractive industry. A supporting timber industry emerged to provide barns, farmhouses, storefronts, and the boardwalks of dusty mining towns. The emerging extractive economy monopolized natural resources, severely limiting traditional subsistence practices. The new resource brokers valued profit over the rights of Native people.

Alarmed by the apparent permanency of the region's new inhabitants, Chief Andrew Seltice renewed his petition campaign. Joined by other tribal leaders and the Jesuit fathers at DeSmet Mission, Seltice repeatedly asked federal officials to negotiate an agreement that would give the Coeur d'Alene tribe monetary compensation for aboriginal land located outside the 1873 reservation boundaries. The chief also sought federal aid in protecting the integrity of the 1873 reservation. Locked in a pattern of denial and incompetence, the Colville Agency failed to control the illicit extraction of reservation resources. Finally, an agreement negotiated in 1887 by the congressionally appointed Northwest Indian Commission rewarded the efforts of Chief Seltice and the DeSmet missionaries. As the agreement awaited approval, however, the forces of the extractive economy moved to undermine it.

Disappointed that the North Fork ran muddy green rather than gold, placer miners looked to the South Fork as a new source of potential wealth. Several individuals quickly found that although the southern tributary's streams produced little gold, the land along the banks of the river hid prodigious deposits of silver and lead, along with other industrial ores. The first lode discovery—the 1884 Tiger claim—introduced the vast riches of Canyon Creek, a tributary of the South Fork. Other claims on Canyon Creek quickly followed. Joined by the stakers of the Poorman, San Francisco, and Gem-of-the-Mountain claims, William R. Wallace and his son located the Ore-or-no-go in 1884. James Toner's 1885 stake of twenty acres, which he called "Hecla," affirmed Canyon Creek's status as an ore-producing center. During the same year Noah B. Kellogg and partner Phil O'Rourke located the Bunker Hill and Sullivan property, whose rich deposits eventually yielded more ore than any other single Coeur d'Alene mine. Situated ten miles west of Canyon Creek on Milo Creek, the Bunker Hill and Sullivan represented the South Fork's other great mining hub. By 1890 two dozen claims surrounded the original sites.[3]

The 1872 Mining Law governed subsurface mineral finds. It required prospectors to precisely stake their property and limited individual claims to 600 by 1,500 feet lengthwise along the ore-bearing vein.[4] Although the possibility of staking a lode claim attracted would-be prospectors, the discovery of subsurface minerals failed to incite the kind of frenetic activity associated with pan mining. Extraction of deep-occurring lead and silver ore required organized manpower and capital. Mine owners used a complex system of tunnels and shafts to remove the ore. Once at the surface, crushers reduced the size of the muck, or the raw ore. Mine workers then smelted the crushings to achieve a pure product. This intricate process involved several stages of development. After a mineral discovery, the claim's owners gathered capital and made improvements. When ready for production, the owners hired wage earners to man the mine. During the final stage the large-scale industrial mining operations produced profits for a small number of owners. The resulting extractive economy created a resident working class. The lives of wage-earning miners, who lived and worked in gloomy "company" towns, resembled those of eastern factory workers.[5]

The transition from individual placer mining to corporate mining on the South Fork took time. Unlike the haphazard settlements spawned by placer mining, the nature of subsurface mining created lasting communities with slower population growth. The population of the North Fork's settlements outnumbered the populations on Canyon and Milo creeks for much of the 1880s. Situated at the confluence of the South Fork and Canyon Creek, Wallace welcomed its first settlers in 1884, but two years later only 5 people lived there. Not until 1889 did the population approach 1,000. The towns of Burke and Gem, located on Canyon Creek, boasted only 1,050 inhabitants combined in 1888. The city of Wardner, located near the Bunker Hill and Sullivan claims, housed 1,500 residents by 1887. Whereas the South Fork did not experience the wild population fluctuations characteristic of the North Fork, the construction accompanying growth in cities like Mullan indicated permanence. Several miles east of Wallace, Mullan's meager populace of 150 boasted twenty log cabins, fifteen frame houses, two hotels, and a sawmill. As the mines began producing in the late 1880s and early 1890s, the permanent populations of the South Fork cities built upon the strong foundations laid during the early years of development.[6]

Despite its growth pattern, industrial mining represented an unprecedented threat to the original occupants of Coeur d'Alene country. Massive profits created an extractive culture dependent on the mining process. Motivated by the conversion of natural resources into profit, this culture balked at the land claims and resource needs of the Coeur d'Alene people. The mining claims occurred outside 1873 reservation boundaries, but they rested on lands the Coeur d'Alenes had not formally surrendered. The nature of subsurface mining, moreover, threatened the reservation's resources. The methods of extracting vein ore pervaded the natural environment in ways alien to placer mining. Miners blasted hillsides, burrowed through mountains, and diverted thousands of gallons of water to wash away unwanted earth and rock. After flushing the mountain sides, the once pure waters of the Coeur d'Alene River returned to their banks polluted by tailings and refuse. From there the river flowed into the Coeur d'Alene Reservation, eventually dumping heavy metal deposits into pristine Lake Coeur d'Alene.[7]

A system of western water rights known as *prior appropriation* allowed mine owners to divert and pollute the waters of Coeur d'Alene Reservation. Water rights in the eastern United States followed the English common-law tradition of *riparian rights*, which held that users had to own land adjacent to the water source. Riparian law prohibited rights holders from altering the source's course, appreciably reducing its volume, or polluting the share of those downstream. During the 1850s, however, miners in California rejected riparian rights, which they found insufficient for their needs. California courts agreed, thus installing a new system based on the exclusive rights of the first claimant. The first "appropriator" could use all the claimed water with no attention to the needs of those downstream. The new doctrine treated water as a commodity akin to land, minerals, and timber. Like other natural resources, water could then be sacrificed for the profits of western extractive industry. By the time prospecting began along the Coeur d'Alene River, prior appropriation had become a common pattern of water rights in arid regions and mining districts in the West.[8]

Commercial mining also created a demand for timber, which during the late 1880s in Coeur d'Alene country grew to importance as an extractive industry in its own right. The pioneering efforts of people like Frederick Post served as the foundation on which the region's new entrepreneurs built a booming lumber business. Construction in the mining towns along the South Fork demanded a local lumber supply. Local timber barons could transport their logs cheaply to markets as far west as Spokane Falls utilizing Coeur d'Alene waterways. By 1887 five independent sawmills served the mining towns of the South Fork, each cutting about 1 million board feet per year. In 1888 Kootenai County's lumber industry flaunted seven sawmills and five shingle mills, valued at approximately $146,000. Family owners William, John, and Jesse Fisher prided themselves on the capacity—20,000 feet per day—of the sawmill they erected at St. Maries in 1889. A fledgling community located along the St. Joseph River, St. Maries fell within 1873 reservation boundaries.[9]

The Colville Agency's inability to police commercial ventures along the South Fork led to unprecedented timber encroachment. Small amounts of timber left the reservation by illegal means prior to development of the South Fork mines, but these violations occurred largely with the knowledge of the Coeur d'Alene tribe. The Coeur d'Alenes allowed Post to cut reservation timber because tribal members needed the lumber. The Indian Office's refusal to grant the tribe a reservation sawmill forced Coeur d'Alene members to contract out for the processing of their own trees. Tribal members also permitted a few settlers in the Palouse to take the timber they needed from the reservation. The scope and character of timber trespassing, however, changed dramatically with the advent of the extractive economy.

The evolution of M. J. Sexton's mill, located at the head of Hangman's Creek, illustrates the progression of this new resource-based entrepreneurialism. Sexton supplied the lumber necessary for the construction of DeSmet Mission. When Coeur d'Alene tribal members requested that Sexton's service remain in effect after completion of mission construction, the Indian Office granted Sexton permission to operate his mill until 1888. Federal regulations, as described in Chapter Seven, governing Indian reservations limited the mill's production to dead and fallen logs cleared for cultivation, and they prohibited Sexton from selling any lumber beyond that not required for on-site use. With the birth of the South Fork's mining towns, however, Sexton gave in to the temptation of expanding markets. Between 1882 and 1892 he cut and sold 8,311,344 feet of lumber, far more than required by DeSmet Mission or tribal farms. Sexton continued production at the mill even after Colville Agency representatives asked him to remove his operations. General Land Office special agent A. F. Leach investigated the mill and determined "that the lumber had all been cut from green and growing trees, [Sexton] having taken the best marketable trees and leaving the small trees standing." None of the land Sexton logged had been cleared for cultivation. "As there are no whites upon the Reservation," Leach surmised, "all of the lumber cut and sold to whites was taken off of the Reservation, and I learn that the Indians sold quite a quantity of their lumber."[10]

Sexton also operated a mill at Plummer, on the Coeur d'Alene Reservation, during 1890 and 1891. At that site the mill operator cut and sold 2,563,707 feet of lumber—all taken from green trees in remote, noncultivated areas and sold outside the reservation. When confronted by Indian Office representatives, Sexton denied responsibility and refused to pay for stolen lumber. To avoid prosecution, Sexton closed the mission mill in 1892 and moved the Plummer mill to Harrison in 1891, where he continued operations outside the purview of the Colville Agency. Agency records indicate Sexton escaped having to make compensation for his lumber trespass, as did most other unlawful loggers on the Coeur d'Alene Reservation during this period.[11]

The illegal production taking place at Sexton's mill outraged settlers in counties adjoining Coeur d'Alene Reservation, not because they perceived the logging as wrong but because they wanted access to the timber themselves. Local newspapers in Farmington, Washington, became a mouthpiece for non-Indian homesteaders who decried Coeur d'Alene tribal control of reservation timber, farmland, minerals, and waterways. When Father Paschal Tosi of DeSmet Mission complained to the Colville Agency about the slanderous articles, the agent replied that "what the papers of Farmington may say does not trouble me in the least." The agent assured Tosi that the executive order of 1873, which set aside Coeur d'Alene Reservation "for the exclusive use of Indians (and not for whites)," remained in effect irrespective of the wishes of area settlers.[12]

Still, many non-Indian homesteaders sought Indian Office support in undermining tribal ownership of the Coeur d'Alene Reservation. Writing on behalf of the Central Organization of the Farmers Protective Association of Whitman County, John M. Reed, J. N. Batthis, and D. B. Conrad complained to the commissioner of Indian affairs in December 1885 that the location of Coeur d'Alene Reservation "cuts off a large portion of Whitman and Spokane Counties from timber." The Coeur d'Alene people forbade outsiders to take timber from their preserve, the committee asserted, leading to the "probability of a clash between the whites and the Indians." Whitman County residents blamed DeSmet Mission for exercising undue influence on the reservation. Among other accusations, Palouse squatters charged that mission fathers awarded special resource privileges to people with church ties. Those with an unfair advantage, the farmers protective committee asserted, included the Sexton sawmill—which the settlers believed used the mission only as a "pretense" for conducting a much larger, illegal business. The Coeur d'Alene Indians "are self-sustaining," committee members contended, "and should have their lands in severalty and the remaining portion not occupied by Indians should be opened for white settlement." The settlers viewed the presence of the Coeur d'Alene Reservation and the DeSmet Mission as repellant to non-Indian development of timber, mining, and agriculture. The Farmers Protective Association erroneously regarded the homestead claims of squatters as superior to the executive-ordered Coeur d'Alene Reservation.[13]

H. B. Cartmill, another local settler, joined the farmers protective committee in protesting Coeur d'Alene tribal title to reservation timber. White families fought bitter Palouse cold and virtual starvation, the farmer indignantly informed the Indian affairs commissioner, while the Coeur d'Alene tribe possessed "a vast forest," enough "to last this country for hundreds of years." Apparently unconvinced of tribal title to the reservation, Cartmill protested that "the little handful of Indians that are in possession of these forests think that we poor white people must pay them for every stick that we get off from their supposed lands."[14] Settlers like Cartmill, Reed, Batthis, and Conrad felt betrayed by the Coeur d'Alene Reservation boundaries, particularly after the establishment of the South Fork mines stimulated competition for resources. Never mind that the homestead locations chosen by the settlers, combined with their consumption habits, created resource shortages. In Cartmill's view, the whites remained innocent victims, cheated out of their right to timber by a small band of Indians and some enterprising Jesuit priests. That the Coeur d'Alenes presented themselves as successful farmers and ranchers only heightened the resentment of poor whites.[15]

Coeur d'Alene Reservation Resident Farmer James O'Neill conceded that a scarcity of timber in adjoining areas forced white settlers to travel between twenty and sixty miles in search of fuel. Noting that many whites "do suffer in cold weather for the want of a comfortable fire," O'Neill suggested that the Coeur d'Alenes "would be glad to cut the dead and fallen timber and sell to those wanting fuel or fencing as they have been doing for the steamboat during the last year or two." Colville Indian Agent Benjamin Moore concurred "that the Indians have more lumber than they can use in years" but strongly recommended that the settlers be forced to pay for reservation timber.[16] Commissioner of

Indian Affairs Atkins supported O'Neill's suggestion to allow the sale of dead and fallen timber. The commissioner, however, voiced concerns over regulation of timber sales. Atkins explained:

> The great difficulty in this dead and fallen timber question upon other reservations has been that the privilege granted to the Indians to cut and sell such timber, has been seriously abused through the influence of contractors for profit alone, thereby in a great measure frustrating the original intention of the Department, which when it granted the privilege, did so on the principle of actual necessities, and never for a moment contemplated that the matter would assume such proportions as it has done in certain cases.[17]

With the commissioner's reluctant consent, Farmer O'Neill and Chief Seltice negotiated an arrangement allowing tribal members to sell dead and fallen timber at fifty cents per two-horse load or one dollar per load if cut by tribal people. Upshaw used a May 18, 1882, circular from the Indian Office, regulating timber sales, and a U.S. Supreme Court case as the basis of his decision. Only Coeur d'Alene Indians could cut the dead and fallen timber, and no green trees could be cut.[18]

Meanwhile, the changing nature of agriculture in the lands bordering the Coeur d'Alene Reservation created even greater competition for resources. The Northwestern Improvement Company, a subsidiary of the Northern Pacific Railroad, sold more than $7 million in Palouse farmland between 1880 and 1890. Whitman County's population soared to 19,109 by 1890; Latah County boasted approximately 9,000 residents by the end of the decade. Prior to the early 1880s, most of the homestead operations in Latah and Whitman counties operated ranches or subsistence farms. During the mid-1880s, however, settlers on the Palouse discovered the fertile soils of the well-drained, sun-drenched rolling hillsides. With the completion of Northern Pacific Railroad feeder lines, like the one completed in 1884 between present-day Connell and Colfax, farmers moved away from livestock to cash crop production. Whitman County's 1884 cattle population—20,000—was half that of previous years. By the late 1880s, wheat and rye farmers received forty to fifty cents per bushel from Portland, Oregon, buyers. The establishment of the first Whitman County Agricultural Fair in 1887 signaled participation of area farmers in the new extractive economy. The Colfax *Commoner* announced that the purpose of the county fair was to showcase "what has already been accomplished in the line of stock breeding and scientific farming" and to "encourage work in the same direction in the future." Whitman's grain yields acquired legendary status by 1890, elevating it to the status of Washington's "banner agricultural county."[19]

Coeur d'Alene farmers practiced sophisticated cash crop agriculture long before most of their white neighbors. Chief Seltice's move to Hangman's Valley created a Coeur d'Alene agricultural empire, now threatened by mining, timber, and settlement. The tribal leader's foresight in establishing control of Paradise Valley, however, and his concerted assimilation policy impressed outsiders and made valuable allies in the tribal struggle for territorial integrity. Indian Office officials and community leaders joined Chief Seltice as he renewed his petition campaign for federal compensation of seized territory and for enforcement of reservation boundaries. On March 23, 1885, Seltice and others petitioned President Grover Cleveland, Secretary of the Interior Lucius Q.C. Lamar, and Commissioner of Indian Affairs John D.C. Atkins. The Coeur d'Alene petitioners argued "that their rights as Indians have up to this date, been very largely neglected by the proper authorities of the United States." Written by Louis Kaizemet, a young Coeur d'Alene student at DeSmet Mission, the document outlined the tribe's relations with the United States with remarkable precision. Kaizemet cited U.S. statutes in a comprehensive history of Northern Plateau Indian policy. Using updated language, the petition reiterated the Native boundaries tribal members had identified during the 1873 agreement negotiations:

> Beginning at a point on the Pelouze River, west [to] a high butte, now known as and called Steptoe Butte, thence extending north-westwardly to the Spokane River, at a point on its north bank formerly resided at by Antoine Plant, a half-breed Indian; thence extending to the lower end of the Pend d'Oreille Lake; thence eastwardly to the summit of the Coeur d'Alene Mountains separating the waters of the Flathead or Missoula River from those of the Coeur d'Alene and St. Josephs [sic] River; thence southerly along the summit of said Mountains to the most southern thereof, whence flow the waters of the Pelouze River; thence westwardly along the southern rim of the water-shed of the waters of the Pelouze River to the point of beginning.[20]

Chief Seltice, five subchiefs, and the additional forty-two Coeur d'Alene men who signed the petition further noted that all of the described aboriginal territory, except the portions currently occupied by the tribe on the reservation, "have been taken possession of by the whites, without remuneration or indemnity." The Coeur d'Alenes made it clear that they knew the value of this property—now "dotted by numerous and valuable wheat farms, with many forests of valuable timber," and containing the Coeur d'Alene mining district's gold, silver, and lead mines, "said to be extensive and rich." Much of the timber, the petitioners noted, had been cut and conveyed to local sawmills or floated downriver to Spokane. Coeur d'Alene lands also contained Fort Sherman, a military installation protecting reservation transportation networks. The Coeur d'Alenes used white dependency on these networks to argue the necessity for a fair agreement. The petition informed federal officials that the reservation encompassed the portion of the Northern Pacific Railroad from near Spokane to Lake Pend Oreille, as well as the steamboat routes on Lake Coeur d'Alene and the Coeur d'Alene River.[21]

Seltice and other tribal leaders used the Nez Perce conflict, now eight years old, to represent the Coeur d'Alenes as a different kind of Indian tribe—one that protected, rather than attacked, local whites:

> Your Petitioners are now, and for many years last past have been not only friendly to the whites but they remind you of the fact that when Joseph's Band of Nez Perces, in 1877 rose in rebellion against the United States resulting in the loss of many valuable lives of your people and in great cost to your government and when a large portion of the white male population in the Territories of Idaho and Washington with their wives and children fled from their homes and from the country, that it was your Petitioners who went to their rescue and protected them and their homes and their property at their own expense and at the risk of their lives until such a time as peace and confidence had been restored, and until the return to their homes of said white population[.][22]

Although pledging to maintain peaceful relations with their white neighbors, the Coeur d'Alenes recognized the value of the land taken from them and demanded specific redress. "Our people now need grist and saw mills and proper farming implements and machines," the tribal leaders declared, "to help to teach us and our children proper industrial pursuits." The petitioners attributed the success of the tribe's agricultural enterprises to the teachings of the Jesuit fathers rather than to the direction of Colville Agency officials. In the spirit that defined relations between the missionaries and the Coeur d'Alenes, the tribe sought federal confirmation of the land the Indian people had granted to DeSmet Mission—two square miles of farmland and one square mile of timber—when the mission moved from the Coeur d'Alene River to Hangman's Valley. The petition closed with a request for the government to send "a proper Commission of good and honest men" to conduct negotiations "by which your Petitioners may be properly and fully compensated for such portion of their lands not now reserved to them." The Coeur d'Alene chieftains also desired affirmation of the 1873 reservation boundaries and annual payments to be made in livestock, tools, mills, and mechanical instruction.[23]

John A. Sweeney, resident physician at Coeur d'Alene Reservation, submitted the petition to Colville Indian Agent Sidney Waters with a "warm" recommendation. Resident Farmer James O'Neill wrote a separate supporting letter. Unlike other Indian tribes, the farmer recounted, the Coeur d'Alenes worked hard "when it was considered by an Indian a disgrace *to* work and when it was almost impossible to procure the necessary implements to work with."[24] Now, the farmer declared, all the Coeur d'Alenes "are good farmers," with the older members cultivating upward of 300 fenced acres. The younger members struggled with a scarcity of means that, O'Neill believed, the fulfillment of petition requests would remedy. Waters immediately forwarded the petition to Commissioner Hiram Price, glowingly endorsing the Coeur d'Alene people and supporting their wishes. The "time has now arrived," Waters proclaimed, "when something must be done for these Indians." The executive-ordered reservation of 1873 "is looked upon with longing eyes by the whites," he explained, "who are fast settling up the country owned by these Indians." Even the settlers whose property the Coeur d'Alenes conscientiously watched over during the 1877 Nez Perce scare, the agent reported, "are ready to step in and possess themselves of their reservation."[25]

Indeed, Pine Creek– and Farmington-area settlers submitted their own petition to Congress in 1886. It came to the attention of Coeur d'Alene tribal members and DeSmet missionaries when it appeared in Coeur d'Alene City's newspaper, the *Coeur d'Alene Sun*. Entitled "Petition of Freeholders of Spokane and Whitman County, Wash. T., and Nez Perce County, Idaho," the document used the tribe's agricultural successes to argue for the allotment in severalty of Coeur d'Alene reservation. The Indians "have become intelligent, civilized and christianized," the petitioners intoned, and are "eminently qualified to assume all the privileges and responsibilities of citizenship." Tribal members, moreover, desired severalty, according to the timber-hungry settlers, but the Jesuit fathers at DeSmet had influenced them to cling to their reservation. The document referred not to the Coeur d'Alene Reservation but rather to the "DeSmet Mission with-hold." The petitioners thus turned the reservation into a special Jesuit privilege, a twist of phraseology designed to incite local Protestants.[26]

Predictably, the "freeholders" asserted that *they* be given access to the remaining DeSmet Mission with-hold after allotment. The writers justified this proposed land and timber grab with a wildly illogical argument: the Coeur d'Alenes numbered fewer than 500 and could not "utilize said immense area of land"; area settlers, who by their own volition had chosen a treeless plain, were "dependent upon the timber growing on" the Coeur d'Alene Reservation; and the "tribute" exacted by the Indians and "their religious guardians" for reservation timber was an unjust indecency, since "they have an abundance and to spare." The offending tribute was the charge required by the commissioner of Indian affairs for the sale of the reservation's dead and fallen timber. In stark contrast to Coeur d'Alene avowals of peace in the tribe's 1885 petition, the tricounty residents threatened the tribe and the Jesuit fathers. Coeur d'Alene selfishness "has created a deep-rooted and bitter feeling of animosity on the part of said inhabitants towards said Indians and their self-constituted guardians and advisers of said Catholic Church," the petitioners warned, "which is liable at any time to take the form of organized violence against said Indians and their religious guardians aforesaid."[27]

Months would pass before the homesteaders' petition reached the House and Senate in Washington, D.C., but Coeur d'Alene tribal members responded immediately to the settlers' accusations. An emergency tribal council convened on April 11, 1886, during which Coeur d'Alene leaders formulated a formal response to each of the non-Indian petitioners' points. The document, which appeared in the April 24 edition of the *Spokane Falls Review*, denied that area settlers encountered great difficulty in procuring reservation lumber, and asserted that rather than the small tribal population claimed by the "freeholders," that there "are seven hundred and fifty persons or thereabouts belonging to the tribe." Chief Seltice noted that if acquiring the timber presented such an inconvenience, "there would not be as many wagons crossing the reservation." "Each year," the chief recounted, "there are not less than five hundred loads of timber hauled." Furthermore, the tribesmen asserted that they had "never refused any person timber for fuel; but now as so much has been said, we now object to any person taking more."[28] The council members concluded:

> The persons that made said petition claim to be our friends of long acquaintance. If so, they must be well aware that their petition is untruthful and malicious. This is what I Seltise [sic] and the council think at this time, after again and again protesting against the slander thrown on our church and pastor, who never interfered with our land, so called taxes or any other temporal concern, but only taught us how to become good christians, and useful members of society. This we are obliged to say in justice to the innocense [sic] and self-denying spirit of our fathers so maliciously slandered.[29]

While tribal members met in council, the Jesuit fathers of DeSmet Mission launched a series of public relations countermoves. On April 6, 1886, an anonymous editorial, signed only "Traveler," appeared in the *Coeur d'Alene Sun*. Almost certainly the work of the Jesuits, the piece gave a brief history of Coeur d'Alene Reservation and highlighted the validity of the 1873 reservation boundaries. It also asserted that the area's "old settlers," who admired the Coeur d'Alene people for their pioneering advances in agriculture, would refuse to sign the petition. The Traveler differentiated between the region's first, subsistence-based homesteaders, who maintained cordial relations with the tribe, and the area's new industrialists, whose only concern involved extracting natural resources and advancing large farming operations. The editorialist also refuted charges that reservation land was underutilized. Because tribal usage differed from that of the extractive-oriented white settlers, large agricultural areas appeared unused. In actuality, the Coeur d'Alenes practiced an intricate crop rotation system by taking advantage of seasonal inundation and clearing fallow fields with precision burn techniques.[30]

In addition to writing newspaper editorials, the Jesuits of DeSmet Mission published a pamphlet entitled "The Coeur d'Alene Reservation: Some Facts Proving That the Petition for Its Opening Is Based and Built on Misrepresentations." The booklet, written by Lawrence Palladino, made many of the same points as those made by Jesuit editorials and Coeur d'Alene tribal council members. The Coeur d'Alene people possessed title to their reservation and to "another tract," Palladino emphasized, "which they formerly occupied, and which is now settled by whites, without any compensation having been made to the Indians for its loss." As for the homesteaders' claim that tribal people possessed more land than they needed or used, Palladino submitted that many individual, foreign, and nonresident U.S. landholders controlled much larger tracts. English Syndicate No. 3, with 3 million acres in Texas, and Holland Land Company, with 4.5 million acres in New Mexico, headed the Jesuit's list. Among resident landowners, Palladino aptly cited the transcontinental railroads, which among them possessed federal land grants in excess of 107 million acres. "Has not the day gone by for the rights of the Indians," Palladino thundered, "to be trampled upon by a few covetous landgrabbers? Will not Congress see justice done to the Redmen?" Students at St. Ignatius Mission in Montana privately printed the pamphlets and circulated them throughout northern Idaho Territory.[31]

The Jesuit fathers had also procured influential allies in Washington, D.C. Joseph Cataldo, superior general of the Rocky Mountain Missions, wrote to John Mullan in January 1886. Then serving as commissioner of the Bureau of Catholic Indian Missions and as an attorney specializing in territorial issues, Mullan had maintained the relationship he fostered with the Coeur d'Alene missionaries during the construction of Mullan Road. Cataldo asked for Mullan's support in pursuing agreements for the Spokane and Coeur d'Alene Tribes. The Spokane chief Louis Wildshoe[32] had come to Cataldo asking for help for "the miserable condition in which more than four hundred people of his tribe are since the coming of the whites into their territory." The Catholic Louis band of Spokane people remained estranged from their Protestant tribesmen, the Spokane Garry band. Cataldo believed removal of the Catholic Spokanes to the Coeur d'Alene reservation and removal of the Protestant band to the Lower Spokane reservation would eliminate problems for both tribes. The disenfranchised Spokane bands would finally possess a homeland, and the Coeur d'Alenes would receive compensation for surrendered territory through the necessary agreement.[33]

Mullan acquiesced, writing first to the Catholic Mission Bureau and then forwarding the report to the interior secretary's office. Themes of negligence and broken promises littered Mullan's correspondence. Governor Isaac I. Stevens had overlooked these tribes in 1855, Mullan contended, when he "failed to conclude any treaty negotiations with either the Colville, Spokane, or Coeur d'Alene Indians." As a result of this neglect, all three of the tribes lost traditional tribal territory to the unlawful encroachment of whites. When the Coeur d'Alenes finally received an executive-ordered reservation, Mullan continued, the government did not compensate them for their land outside reservation boundaries or provide appropriations for the administration of their reservation. In conclusion, Mullan recommended that a commission be appointed to negotiate "a proper and just treaty between [the tribes] and the United States, and by which an adequate compensation could be had for the value of the lands of which, in my opinion, they have been so wrongfully divested."[34]

Mullan's influence produced a Senate resolution on March 30, 1886, which requested that the commissioner of Indian affairs provide all correspondence relating to the Coeur d'Alene, Spokane, and Kalispel Tribes. After receiving the Indian Office record, the Senate concurred with Mullan. The federal record of the Coeur d'Alenes, after the 1858 peace treaty, showed the kind of "advancement" in civilization that by 1887 reformers in Congress and in the Indian Office hoped to see in all tribes. The Senate inserted funds for the creation of a commission to negotiate with tribes in Minnesota and the Northwest in the Indian Appropriations Act of May 15, 1886. The Northwest Indian Commission—consisting of John V. Wright, Jarred W. Daniels, and Harry W. Andrews—received orders from the Indian commissioner to meet with the Spokane and Coeur d'Alene peoples in relation to relocating the Upper and Middle Spokane bands on the Coeur d'Alene Reservation. The Indian Office refused to entertain the idea of an additional reservation for the Spokanes, but no one in Congress or the Indian office questioned the validity of the Coeur d'Alene Reservation. If the Spokanes lived with the Coeur d'Alene people, perhaps Coeur d'Alene prosperity would transform them into self-supporting farmers. The appropriations act also enabled the special commissioners to provide monetary compensation for surrendered territory and to allocate funds for reservation improvements—such as blacksmiths, sawmills, and schools.[35]

As soon as Mullan became aware of the appointment of the Northwest Indian Commission, he notified Father Cataldo in a "confidential" letter. Mullan advised the Jesuit superior of the upcoming negotiations with the Spokane and Coeur d'Alene peoples and offered myriad suggestions. "Let it be distinctly understood," Mullan wrote, "that . . . all the negotiations held between said commissioner and the Coeur d'Alenes, or the Spokanes, or the Pend d'Oreilles shall be in the presence of the Fathers." Mullan also recommended that the Indians "insist" that the reservation lands given to the missionaries "be confirmed." In negotiations with the Coeur d'Alene Tribe, Mullan continued, "let the treaty specially provide that their present reservation be absolutely confirmed to them for all times and that no change is to be made in regard thereto at any time hereafter without their knowledge and consent." Father Cataldo notified the fathers at DeSmet to prepare for the upcoming council.[36]

The three commissioners, after completing negotiations with tribes in northern Montana, traveled by train to the Pacific Northwest in February 1887. They arrived in Spokane in late February. The group held its first Northwest council, with the Upper and Middle Spokane bands, in early March. Father Cataldo attended the meeting, further exacerbating the religious differences between the Protestant leader Garry and the Catholic chief Wildshoe. The Spokanes at first demanded that they be granted a reservation centering on the Little Spokane

River, but the commissioners insisted that the terms of the appropriations act did not allow for the creation of new reservations. When tribal leaders persisted in their demand, the commissioners telegraphed Commissioner Lamar. Lamar replied that "the President directs me to inform you that [the] wish of the Indians for creation of [a] new reservation for their occupancy can not be complied with under law." The Spokanes finally accepted the rejection after Father Cataldo assured them of its authenticity. Wright and his fellow negotiators did not mention the possibility of placing Garry's group on the Lower Spokane Reservation.[37]

Ultimately, the Spokanes reluctantly agreed to relinquish all tribal land to the United States and to remove to the Coeur d'Alene Reservation. Although the Coeur d'Alene people had not yet been formally consulted, the commissioners informed the Spokanes that they would be allowed to choose their own plots from "a tract of land to be laid off and surveyed for the purpose." Tribal members who occupied improved property eligible for the Homestead Act were allowed to remain on their land. Moreover, Spokane tribal members who desired to remove to either the Colville or the Flathead Reservation could do so, with a pro rata share of the benefits provided by the agreement. In return for traditional territory, the agreement arranged for payment of $95,000 to the Spokane bands, primarily to help the tribal people begin farming in their new location.[38]

With the conclusion of the Spokane council, Wright, Daniels, and Andrews boarded wagons that took them to Farmington, Washington. While in Farmington the commissioners questioned local people on their opinion of the Coeur d'Alene Reservation. Wright and his companions learned that the tribe had a reputation for "self-reliance" and "shrewd" fiscal habits. Indeed, Coeur d'Alene trade with towns adjacent to the reservation amounted to more than $25,000 annually. From Farmington the group proceeded to the Coeur d'Alene Reservation, a distance of twelve miles. Chief Seltice—accompanied by Soldiers of the Sacred Heart, mounted and armed with Winchester rifles—met the commissioners at the reservation boundary and escorted them to DeSmet Mission. The ceremony associated with the tribal escort awed the visitors and demonstrated Seltice's desire to appear both assimilated and powerful. The firing of a salute announced the chief's presence, after which Seltice dismounted and welcomed the commissioners to the reservation. When the entourage arrived at DeSmet village, "[T]he entire male population and many women and children had assembled." All the tribal people "filed in front of the Commission, each one shaking hands with them and saying some kind words."[39]

The reservation's landscape and agricultural enterprise equally impressed the visitors. "The day was bright," the commissioners later reported, "and we had a fine opportunity of seeing the country, which is the finest in the West." The Coeur d'Alenes possessed "good productive farms, good houses, barns, gardens, horses, hogs, cattle, domestic fowls, wagons, agricultural implements of the latest pattern," the report extolled, "and indeed everything usually found on flourishing farms." Wright and his companions found the Coeur d'Alene people "industrious, thrifty, provident," and "ambitious to excel."[40] Before beginning the proceedings the commissioners visited the Jesuit school at DeSmet, where a twelve-year-old student, Paul Polatkin, had prepared a formal introduction. The text of the speech, framed under direction of the Jesuit fathers, emphasized the Coeur d'Alene work ethic. The commissioners' visit, Polatkin declared, would prove that the Coeur d'Alene people "earn their bread by the sweat of their brow." The students of DeSmet school, Polatkin continued, "are by no means idle, but try every day to add another grain of knowledge to our store."[41] The commissioners praised the students and expressed pleasure "at seeing that Indian boys were the equals of the white boys in capacity to receive an education."[42]

Whereas the commissioners were impressed with the boys' school, they were wowed by the girls' school, where Wright's comments betrayed the patriarchal views of the nineteenth-century Indian Office and of much of American society. Wright told the female pupils who had misspelled a few words on the chalkboard, "I think you knew how to spell them, and failed because of the natural timidity and modesty which is the glory of your sex. I had rather see a girl misspell an hundred words through modest embarrassment than see her spell a whole dictionary of words correctly, she lacking in that quality which so highly adorns woman and which renders her the object of our love and admiration." The commissioners were thrilled that "the children of the white and red races" mingled together in the same school, where they marched "in the same path, with the same hopes, the same aspirations, the same flag of red, white, and blue, the same country, and all striving to reach the same blue heaven above." Continuing his distillation of patriarchal, Christian, and pro-assimilation views, Wright assured the female students that it would be "on this reservation [that] the Indian problem will be solved at last":

> There have been times in the past when the Indian nights were without stars, and when the whole heavens above were dark with black and threatening clouds, but I feel glad to be able to say to you that it will be so no more. . . . Here it is demonstrated that the Indians can work, and are willing to work and make a living for themselves, their wives, and their children, and that Indian children can stand side by side with the children of the Anglo-Saxons and compete with them in the race for knowledge and learning. The stars are beginning to appear in your heaven and the clouds are rolling by; even now the silver lining appears, and the glorious light of reason, science, and religion will ere long include your race in its broad scope and shed its benign rays on your humble homes.[43]

The Northwest Indian Commission talks began March 25 at DeSmet Mission. Wright explained the commissioners' desire to relocate the Spokane bands on Coeur d'Alene Reservation, and Chief Seltice expressed pleasure at the federal appointees' presence. Harry W. Andrews read and interpreted the terms of a prewritten agreement in which the commissioners attempted to meet the demands of Chief Seltice, the mission clerics, and John Mullan. Although tribal members voiced approval of the agreement, they expressed concern regarding white encroachment and the survival of Coeur d'Alene Reservation. "When assurances were given them that they would be protected by the Government in their homes and reservation," Wright later recounted, "their gratitude knew no bounds, and it is the sincere belief of the Commissioners that Chief Saltice [sic] and every able-bodied man of his tribe could be relied on in any emergency in the defense of the flag and the country with as much certainty as any community in the Union." Seltice informed Wright that he would meet with tribal members during the evening and resume talks the following day.[44]

On March 26 Seltice and eighty-four other tribal members signed an agreement that revealed heavy Jesuit and Coeur d'Alene influence. The tribe formally surrendered title to all tribal lands outside the 1873 reservation boundaries, an area in excess of 4 million acres. The Coeur d'Alenes also consented to the transfer of the Spokane bands to the Coeur d'Alene Reservation. In return for their concessions, tribal members received $150,000, to be used for construction of a sawmill and a grist mill and for other reservation improvements. Recognizing that the Coeur d'Alenes possessed modern farm implements and better schools than many of their white neighbors, the commissioners provided that tribal funds could be allocated to individual members on a pro rata basis. The commissioners blamed Washington Territorial Governor Isaac I. Stevens for failing to negotiate a treaty with the tribe during 1855, when compensation for lands could have been made prior to the non-Indian invasion. At the insistence of Chief Seltice and the Jesuit fathers, the commissioners inserted Article Five, which assured the tribe that the preserve "shall be held forever as Indian land and as homes for the Coeur d'Alene Indians, now residing on said reservation." In their official report of the council, the commissioners claimed the clause "was unnecessary, inasmuch as no such thing would happen." The commissioners had acknowledged what they viewed as the infallibility of the 1873 executive order, but tribal members remained suspicious, and rightly so.[45]

Additionally, tribal leaders insisted on the insertion of two other articles. Article Twelve provided that Stephen E. Liberty, Joseph Peavy, Patrick Nixon, Julien Boutelier, and their families—all Catholic immigrants who had befriended the tribe—could remain on Coeur d'Alene Reservation. Unique circumstances had contributed to the development of a strong bond between these individuals and Chief Seltice. Their presence on the reservation represents the complexity of Coeur d'Alene identity in the late 1880s. Whereas some traditional Schitsu'umsh were isolated from the tribe's leadership, Seltice "adopted" non-Indians into the tribe. Seltice had met Liberty, a French-Canadian trapper, and

Following the 1887 negotiations, Coeur d'Alene and Spokane tribal leaders posed with Indian agent Rickard Gwydir for this studio portrait. Left to right, top row: Robert Flett, Colville Agency interpreter; R. D. Gwydir, Colville Indian agent; James Gibson, Colville Agency clerk. Middle row, left to right: Billy Mason, Spokane; Andrew Seltice, Coeur d'Alene chief; Spokane Garry, Upper Spokane chief; unidentified nephew of Andrew Seltice (child). Left to right, lower row: Nellie, daughter of Spokane Garry; Pier Bartholomew, Spokane subchief. Courtesy, Edwin Swergal Collection, Northwest Museum of Arts & Culture/Eastern Washington State Historical Society, Spokane, Washington, Negative no. L86-10.39.

Peavy, a French-Canadian blacksmith, during the 1870s while the chieftain still lived near what became known as Liberty Lake. Liberty learned the Coeur d'Alene language, married a French-Indian woman, and worked as an interpreter for the tribe. When Seltice moved his farming operations to the Hangman's Valley area, he invited Liberty's family to accompany him and operate its own farm on Coeur d'Alene Reservation. Peavy moved onto the reservation in 1877, when Seltice offered his family protection during the Nez Perce conflict. Boutelier, a wagon maker from Quebec, helped save Chief Seltice's life, the Boutelier story recounts, during the early 1880s when the tribal leader's horse-drawn sled broke through the snow and ice on a pond near the reservation. Out of gratitude, the story goes, Seltice offered Boutelier gold, which he refused, and then farmland on Coeur d'Alene Reservation, which he accepted. Patrick Nixon, an Irish immigrant, and his wife, Mary Francis, moved to Washington Territory in 1879.

The Irish family struggled for existence in a small cabin on the outskirts of Coeur d'Alene Reservation. After several years of near starvation, Chief Seltice took pity on the Nixons and offered them a home on the reservation.[46] The four families were incorporated into the tribe during a tribal council in 1885.[47]

The Bouteliers, Libertys, Peavys, and Nixons all possessed deep ties to Catholicism and to the Jesuit mission and became members of Seltice's inner circle. Stephen Liberty, a Canadian, had attended a Catholic seminary in Quebec before moving to the Pacific Northwest Territories. Julien Boutelier's wife, Mary Elizabeth Chamberlaine, spent much of her childhood in the convent of the Sisters of Notre Dame in Oregon City. The families' descendants continued the Catholic tradition and connection to DeSmet Mission: Julien Boutelier's daughter Pauline became Sister Joseph Mary of the Sisters of Charity of Providence and served at the DeSmet girls' school; Mary Liberty and Benjamin Nixon—the children of Stephen Liberty and Patrick Nixon, respectively—married, and their son, Bernard John, was ordained a Jesuit priest in 1942.[48]

When notified of the Coeur d'Alene "adoptions" of "French Catholics" by the Colville Indian agent, the commissioner of Indian affairs directed that all agents should be "vigilant" in excluding "all such persons" from the Northwest reservations. "It is against the policy of the Department," Acting Commissioner A. B. Upshaw informed Colville Agency, "to permit white men having Indian wives (especially those who have once left the reservation) to reside on Indian reservations." The commissioner worried that white settlers "not similarly circumstanced in regard to marriage" would file complaints with the Indian Office.[49] Article Twelve indicated that all the immigrants were married to Indian women, whereas only Boutelier's half-Iroqouis wife and Liberty's wife, Christine Barnabee, possessed Indian heritage—a deception designed either by Seltice or the Northwest Indian Commission to avoid potential disapproval in Congress or in the Indian Office. Protected by their association with Seltice and the mission, the four families remained on the reservation. Liberty later claimed Seltice had persuaded him and the others to move onto the reservation and that "under the recognized law and custom of the tribe, the Chief of the tribe had power to make and promulgate its laws and had power to determine who should constitute the members of the tribe."[50]

The insertion of the "Liberty Clause" in the Northwest Indian Commission agreement suggests that, in 1887 at least, Coeur d'Alene tribal members tolerated Seltice's generosity. The families, however, positioned themselves to profit from their association with the tribe, and by the end of the 1880s they had alienated many tribal members. The families made repeated requests for resource rights on the reservation.[51] The families took up good lands and then invited extended family members to join them on the reservation. Mary Elizabeth Boutelier's family moved onto the reserve, as did Stephen Liberty's brother, Joseph Edmond Liberty.[52]

After insisting on the adoption of his white allies, Seltice demanded that the mission fathers and sisters receive title to the lands the tribe had given them when the mission relocated to DeSmet in 1877. By the terms of Article Thirteen, the missionaries received one section—640 acres—for the girls' school, one section for the boys' school, and one section of timbered land. The DeSmet Mission would hold title to the 1,920 acres as long as the clerics continued to provide religious and educational services to the tribe. The article ensured the continued para-political presence of the Jesuit fathers on Coeur d'Alene Reservation.[53]

Unique in many ways, this remarkable document stood as an anachronism in 1880s Indian policy. Sixteen years after Congress formally ended treaty making with Indian tribes, the Northwest Indian Commission negotiated an agreement that was essentially a treaty in every way but the name. Indeed, both the Coeur d'Alene leadership and the commission believed they were conducting treaty negotiations; the tribe viewed the document as a long-awaited treaty, and the commissioners perceived their work as redress for the hardship of nontreaty status. In their postcouncil report the commissioners noted that prior to the 1887 negotiations, the Coeur d'Alene people "had no treaty relations with the Government and had no assurances of its fostering care."[54]

Moreover, the agreement with the Coeur d'Alenes transpired during the same political season that witnessed the end of federal Indian reservation policy. President Grover Cleveland signed the Dawes Severalty Act, or General Allotment Act, in February 1887. The culmination of reform efforts aimed at eliminating the need for Indian reservations, the Dawes Act authorized the president to divide existing reservations into 160-acre tracts and to allot them, one-quarter section at a time, to each individual member of the tribe. The allotments came not with a title but with a patent, which the federal government held in "trust" for the individual. At the end of twenty-five years, provided the patent holder met the qualifications of "citizenship," the allottee would receive clear title to the land. Reformers believed that once Indian people experienced pride of ownership, they would become self-sufficient and break free from their dependence on the federal government. Eventually, proponents of the Dawes Act hoped, the Indian Office would no longer be necessary because there would be no Indian tribes, only fully assimilated individuals. As Indian Commissioner Thomas J. Morgan stated in his 1889 annual report, "[T]he reservation system belongs to a 'vanishing state of things' and must soon cease to exist."[55]

The failure of the Northwest Indian Commission to address the Dawes Act during negotiations with the Coeur d'Alenes indicates that Wright and his companions assumed the tribe possessed exceptional title to its reservation. The late 1880s climate of allotment, assimilation, and the concomitant disintegration of Indian reservations makes the inclusion of Article Five—the limitless pledge that the Coeur d'Alene people would retain title to their reservation—amazing in its contradiction of current Indian policy. During negotiations with the Spokane bands, for example, the Northwest Indian Commission implied that tribal members would be given allotments once they relocated to Coeur d'Alene Reservation. Yet the commissioners chose not to raise the subject of severalty during negotiations with the Coeur d'Alenes, perhaps because the tribe had attained self-sufficiency on its own. Why allot these tribal people 160-acre plots when the average Coeur d'Alene enclosure exceeded a quarter section? The commissioners' failure to mention severalty in the context of the 1887 negotiations suggests that Coeur d'Alene political sagacity and agricultural enterprise immunized the tribe, at least temporarily, from the Dawes Act.[56]

As the Northwest Indian Commission departed from DeSmet Mission, it appeared to the Coeur d'Alene people that they had at last achieved a treaty and federal compensation for surrendered territory. The petitions of tribal leaders, the influence of the Jesuit missionaries, and the efforts of John Mullan had temporarily beaten back the forces of the extractive economy. Still, the agreement was subject to ratification by the House and Senate, and it had already attracted an army of enemies. The region's extractive entrepreneurs had been given a new weapon in the form of the Dawes Act. In addition, another threatening force for change—the push for Idaho statehood—emerged as the territory gained population. The combination of these circumstances launched the negotiation of another agreement before the end of the decade.

NINE

ANDREW SELTICE, ASSIMILATION POLICY, AND THE AGREEMENT OF 1889

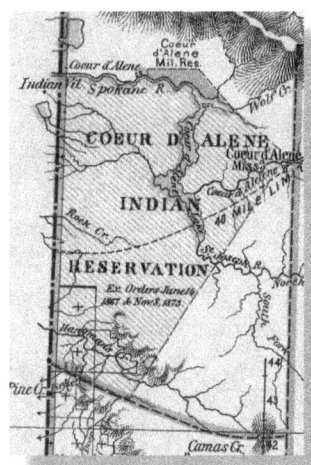

> We met and there was two kinds of talk; one was strong and one was weak. We come to-day to talk about the two understandings, yours and ours. I, as an Indian, like my land; am very anxious to have land; I do not care about money.
>
> —CHIEF ANDREW SELTICE, 1889[1]

EVEN AS THE NORTHWEST INDIAN COMMISSION AND THE COEUR D'ALENE LEADERship negotiated the 1887 agreement, proponents of an emergent extractive economy in northern Idaho Territory engaged in a campaign to discredit the validity of the 1873 reservation boundary. At the same time, internal changes in the Idaho Territorial Legislature lessened regional differences between northern and southern Idaho and paved the way for a united drive for statehood. Within the statehood movement, Idaho businessmen and farmers worked to ensure that Idaho would control its own natural resources. Passage of the Dawes Act in 1887 gave northern Idaho's extractive industrialists ammunition to lobby for additional Coeur d'Alene lands. The policy changes inherent in the Dawes Act, coupled with Idaho's statehood movement, stymied congressional approval of the 1887 agreement and provided the impetus for negotiation of yet another arrangement with the Coeur d'Alene Indian Tribe—this time for the cession of mineral and timberlands.

The 1889 negotiations took place within a charged atmosphere. Federal commissioners felt pressured by non-Indian supporters of an extractive economy and the commissioner's office to quickly produce a favorable agreement; Seltice's assimilation policy and the careful definition of the tribe as "civilized" meant it was the Christian, modernizing element that agreed to the new land cessions;

and tribal members long disassociated from the DeSmet consolidation suddenly had no choice but to move within reservation boundaries and give up their homes on the sites of original Schitsu'umsh villages.

The process by which the 1887 agreement was tabled and new negotiations were authorized resulted from the sudden power of an insistent, permanent, industrial population in Idaho. Prior to the arrival of the Northern Pacific Railroad in 1883 and the maturity of mining, timber, and agricultural enterprises in Idaho, the sprawling territory seemed doomed to perpetual second-class status. A string of corrupt, incapable, and mostly nonresident territorial governors and officials ensured that Idaho teetered on the brink of bankruptcy throughout its territorial years. Many northern Idahoans still resented the capital's location in Boise. Moreover, northern Idaho residents distrusted the prevalence of Mormon religious influence in southern Idaho. The southern territory's Mormon population tended to vote in a Democratic bloc, leading northern Idahoans to speculate that the Latter-day Saints used politics for religious ends. Secession of the territory's northern panhandle seemed more likely than statehood. The territorial legislature's passage of the Idaho Test Oath in 1885, however, partially mollified the northerners, for it required sworn testimony to determine a potential voter's religious affiliation. Seemingly harmless, the Test Oath was in fact an attempt to thwart Mormon suffrage, since Idaho law prohibited those who belonged to an organization that sanctioned polygamy from voting, holding office, or serving on a jury.[2]

The influx of people to Idaho's new extractive industries throughout the 1880s had, by the end of the decade, changed the demographic composition of the region and provided a catalyst for statehood. The 1880 federal census showed a population of 32,610 in Idaho Territory. Ten years later the resident count had boomed to 88,548, an increase of 171.5 percent. In 1890 Kootenai County, which embraced the Coeur d'Alene Reservation, boasted a population of 4,108. Latah County, created in 1888 and situated directly south of Kootenai County, reported 9,173 occupants in 1890. The new residents came to Idaho to participate in an extractive empire of agriculture, lumber, and mining. Many had already made their fortunes elsewhere; they sought investment opportunities, not 160-acre homesteads (although the homestead population continued to increase as well). Men like Amasa B. (Mace) Campbell and John A. Finch—who represented a Youngstown, Ohio, syndicate and capitalized the Hecla mine in 1891—came to Coeur d'Alene country as representatives of large investment firms Back East. They were interested in profit, not territorial rivalries, and they wanted the economic freedom statehood provided.[3]

Northern Idaho's railroad, timber, mining, and agriculture barons desired the resources of Coeur d'Alene Reservation as much as they did statehood. As the Northwest Indian Commission negotiated with the Coeur d'Alene Tribe in 1887, petitions and correspondence from area settlers and businesspeople demanding access to reservation land and resources trickled into the Indian Office. After completion of the 1887 agreement, the trickle became a flood. Commissioner John Atkins sent Colville Indian Agent Rickard Gwydir a sampling of such correspondence in July 1887. Atkins included a request from Nelson Martin of Spokane Falls for permits to maintain steamboat and lumber landings on the banks of the Coeur d'Alene River. Martin also intended to build a large warehouse on the river to store lumber and supplies awaiting "transport to Wardner mines." The commissioner curtly denied Martin's application, but it represented only one of many made by local residents. Indeed, Atkins was more worried about those who did *not* bother to apply for permits. In voicing his concern that the Colville Agency could not "sufficiently control" the reservation pirates, Atkins reminded Gwydir of one of the agent's recent letters to the Indian Office. "There are many whites who are waiting for the slightest opportunity to get on the Reserve," Gwydir had written, "and after they get a foot-hold, it will be hard to dislodge them."[4]

In response to Atkins's concerns, Agent Gwydir dispatched Coeur d'Alene Resident Farmer T. Holmes to "search for trespassers" in the lake vicinity of the reservation. Accompanied by Basile, a member of the Soldiers of the Sacred Heart (also known as the Coeur d'Alene Tribal Police by the late 1880s), Holmes searched the rough terrain between the Coeur d'Alene and St. Joe rivers and found extensive evidence of campsites, illegal construction, and staked mining claims. The inspector discovered that Nelson Martin *had* erected a warehouse on the reservation in spite of the Indian Office having denied his permit. When questioned, Martin responded that he had "*given* the building to Indian Edward and then *rented* it from him." Holmes reported that this sort of scheming should be disallowed and added that "it is the intention of the whites to cover every available place on the shores of the Lake." Local militias were forming in Rockford and the surrounding region to protect non-Indian encroachments from Chief Seltice's police force, Holmes continued, and precautions would have to be taken to prevent an outbreak of violence between the two groups.[5]

Representative of these aggressive new resource opportunists, the Washington and Idaho Railroad (W&IRR) secured its "foothold" on the reservation during the second half of the 1880s. When agents from the W&IRR approached Andrew Seltice with a proposed route through Coeur d'Alene Reservation, Seltice welcomed the idea, which was in keeping with the "civilized" and agricultural image the leader wished to portray. With the understanding that his sanction would mean tribal influence on the project, Seltice informed the interior secretary in 1886 of the tribe's willingness to allow the railroad to cross the reservation. "Our tribe, unlike most of the North Western Indian Tribes, are in great part Farmers, raising large quantities of Great crops," Seltice explained, "and this Rail Road will when finished afford us a market for the same in the Coeur d'Alene Mining Towns and the Towns of Washington Territory." In December

1886 Seltice and other tribal leaders held a council with company officials, during which they signed a formal agreement. In return for reservation access, railroad officials promised Coeur d'Alene tribal members free transportation for their freight, potentially giving Coeur d'Alene farmers an economic advantage in the region's agricultural market. Seltice also demanded that the tribe receive $2.50 per acre for unimproved land and $25.00 per acre for improved land along the path of construction.[6]

This agreement foreshadowed future negotiations, in that Seltice distinguished between "improved" agricultural lands and "unimproved" lands—a differentiation that reflected the chief's value system. Nonagricultural, unfenced land was, in the leader's view, simply not as valuable to the tribe. In addition, the railroad assured the Coeur d'Alenes that it would construct a warehouse and sidetrack near DeSmet Mission for the exclusive use of the Coeur d'Alene people. This agreement attests to the preeminent role market agriculture played in the tribe's economy by 1887. Tribal people who did not participate in this market economy had lost their authority within the tribe. The shift to the market economy also influenced gender roles. Women had traditionally provided a significant amount of subsistence through gathering, preparing, and storing food. Food had now become a market commodity—cultivated, processed, sold, and purchased by men.[7]

After completion of the agreement with the Coeur d'Alenes, Washington and Idaho Railroad officials became impatient with the formal process necessary to receive congressional approval for their right-of-way. In 1887 W&IRR executives started construction along a route north of Farmington, which the tribe had *not* approved. Angered by the breech of contract, Seltice promptly rescinded his consent for the road. Since the railroad had never secured Indian Office approval, Colville Agency officials halted its construction. By then, however, a cloud of controversy hovered over W&IRR officials. In May 1888 T. R. Tannatt, general agent for the Oregon Railway and Navigation Company (OR&N), accused Elijah Smith, president of the OR&N and principal in the W&IRR, of fraud and conspiracy. As soon as he received the formal consent of the Coeur d'Alene Tribe, Tannatt asserted, Smith "abandoned" the W&IRR office in Farmington and turned over all the company's maps, plats, and equipment to the OR&N. After the local board of directors resigned, Smith assigned the company's stock to New York investors. In effect, Tannatt continued, "the W.&I.R.R. Co. ceases to exist under charter stipulations, not having an office or Board of Directors in Washington Territory or elsewhere." The W&IRR agents, Tannatt believed, held their franchises only to prevent the Northern Pacific Railroad from building into Farmington. The agent concluded that the people of Farmington, as well as many Coeur d'Alene tribal people, still desired construction of the W&IRR.[8]

Contrary to Tannatt's statements, however, many tribal members opposed the road and resented Seltice's initial agreement with the company. The controversy highlighted tribal divisions and revealed the growing schism between Schi̱tsu'umsh who used the land in traditional ways and those who embraced market agriculture. The fight for right-of-way also made clear the growing factionalism within the tribe regarding the role of Stephen Liberty and the other whites Seltice had adopted. Gwydir reported in June 1887 that he "found the Indians very much opposed to any R.R. through the Reserve and very bitter in their feeling towards a man named Liberty who they say has been influencing Seltise [sic] against the interest of the Tribe."[9] A year later, in August 1888, Gwydir again reported on the sentiments of the tribe. In a recent visit he found that "fully two thirds of the Indians were opposed to the R.R. and that it was creating a very bitter feeling against Seltice."[10] Louis Lee, a licensed trader with trade relations with the tribe, issued a sworn statement that Seltice had "lost his influence with the Indians by reason of his conniving with the Railroad Company, and that they would have rebelled and deposed him but for the efforts and influence of the Indian Agent."[11] Special Inspector Robert Felt met with more than 100 tribal members in September and reported that all but "ten or thereabouts" opposed the road because it "ruined the trail from the Lake to the Old Mission their route along the Coeur d'Alene River, destroyed all their hay lands on that side of the river and that whiskey was being brought on the Reservation and given to the Indians." The majority of the group, Felt continued, thought "the chief men of the Indian tribe had been bought by the Railroad Company" and "if it were not stopped they desired a new chief."[12]

Finally, on October 1 the interior secretary dispatched Special Indian Inspector Frank C. Armstrong to ascertain once and for all the feelings of the tribe on the railroad matter.[13] Armstrong met with W&IRR officials, Father Joseph Cataldo, and eighty tribal members over age eighteen in late October. Weldon B. Heyburn, attorney for the W&IRR, eloquently defended the road and assured tribal members that they would receive free cargo passage and monetary compensation for their lands.[14] The proposed route commenced near Farmington and connected the eastern side of the reservation with the mining towns on the northwestern side. Ultimately, eighty-five tribal members consented, as their marks on the agreement show, to grant the right-of-way. As part of the new contract, Seltice stipulated that the railroad representatives help the tribe lobby for congressional ratification of its 1887 agreement with the United States.[15]

Although the October council allowed the W&IRR to begin construction, it did not end the controversy. Many tribal members voiced displeasure with the new agreement, and some sent testimonials to the commissioner of Indian affairs. Quin A Mo Say deposed that "he is a member of the Coeur d'Alene Tribe of Indians" but that he "was not notified to be present at the last meeting alleged to be held in the month of October, 1888, and if he had been present he should have opposed the right of way for said Railroad."[16] Mars Asellah Clis Clis

Tah maintained that although he had attended the October conference, he had not signed the consent form, and his name on the document was forged. The approximately ninety Indians present at the conference, Mars Asellah Clis Clis Tah continued, "did not consent thereto and went away from said conference angry and dissatisfied and expressed their dissatisfaction by unmistakable demonstration, and that their names were signed to the papers by Chief Saltees [sic]."[17] Pat Mulvern, another member of the Coeur d'Alene Tribe, testified that "there was no representation on behalf of the Indians" at the October conference, where "many Indians' consent was obtained by being hired by the company [the Washington & Idaho Railroad]." Mulvern also blamed Special Indian Inspector Armstrong for mismanagement of the conference. Armstrong had spoken in favor of the road, Mulvern reported, and had convinced uncertain tribal members when he argued that the agreement "was the best bill they could get" and that "the Road would go through anyhow."[18]

Non-Indians in the region also objected to the October conference. James N. Glover, a prominent Spokane Falls businessman and president of the First National Bank, telegrammed the interior secretary that the assent of the Coeur d'Alene Tribe had been "obtained by bribery and fraud."[19] M. M. Cowley, a non-Indian resident at "Cowley's bridge" in Spokane County, Washington Territory, testified before a Washington Territory notary in November. Cowley stated that his proximity to the reservation during the past sixteen years had given him occasion to interact regularly with the Schitsu'umsh. Cowley swore "that he has frequently heard many of said Indians say that they were opposed to allowing any railroad to cross their reservation" and that the Indians "living on said reservation in the vicinity of my residence have stated to me that they are still opposed to allowing any railroad to cross their reservation, and that they wished to have another Council . . . so that they could give expression of their wishes."[20] Cowley's reference to "in the vicinity of my residence" is strikingly important, as it indicates a geographical division between Schitsu'umsh in the Spokane River area and the mission Indians.

Although many tribal members, particularly more "traditional" people, opposed the encroachment of the line and accusations of bribery and fraud continued to haunt the project, the railroad began service in 1889. Construction of the track required massive amounts of timber, most of which came off the reservation and was illegally processed at the Sexton mill. By 1890 the Oregon Railway and Navigation Company had absorbed the new track, which it leased to the Union Pacific Railroad.[21]

The presence of a transcontinental spur line in Coeur d'Alene country served the interests of Schitsu'umsh farmers but also made the landscape more appealing to non-Indians. As requests to partition the reservation poured into the Indian Office, the Schitsu'umsh people remained bitterly divided. Tribal controversy surrounding Chief Seltice's dealings with the W&IRR, and intimations of tribal disapproval of Stephen Liberty's influence, signaled that by the late 1880s a number of Schitsu'umsh distrusted the Indian leader and his connections to the non-Indian world. These internal social fissures suggest that Seltice's authority was not as complete as it appeared on the surface. As a result of the Jesuit and Coeur d'Alene leadership's assimilation policy, the Schitsu'umsh were divided along religious, geographic, cultural, and economic lines. These divisions influenced tribal reactions to the challenges associated with Idaho's statehood movement, particularly in the tribe's response to aggressive efforts to partition Coeur d'Alene Reservation.

The political career of Fred T. Dubois illustrated the connection between the Idaho statehood movement and the crusade to open Coeur d'Alene Reservation. A Republican, anti-Mormon crusader, Dubois spent most of the 1880s as a United States marshal in Idaho Territory. He sought to undermine the power of the territory's Democratic Party by associating it with the Mormon Church. When anti-Mormon sentiment produced the Test Oath and spawned a Republican-friendly political environment, Dubois benefited. In 1886 he became the territory's congressional delegate and used his presence in Washington, D.C., to lobby for Idaho statehood. Concurrently, Dubois, who had forged strong ties with the mining industrialists of northern Idaho in his attempt to keep the panhandle from seceding, also campaigned for local control of Coeur d'Alene Reservation resources.[22]

The torrent of correspondence flowing into the Indian Office decrying Coeur d'Alene tribal control over its reservation resources contributed to congressional willingness to entertain Dubois's recommendations. In January 1888 the Senate blocked approval of the Northwest Indian Commission's 1887 agreement with the Coeur d'Alene Tribe. Instead, it issued a resolution aimed at uncovering the extent of resources under Coeur d'Alene ownership. Concerned about "allegations" that the tribe numbered "only about 476," occupied a reservation in excess of 480,000 acres, and possessed "Lake Coeur D'Alene, all the navigable waters of Coeur d'Alene River, and about 20 miles of the navigable part of Saint Joseph River," the Senate directed the interior secretary to report on the reservation's specifications. The senators expressed specific interest in mineral wealth and waterways. The resolution requested advice regarding the opening of the reservation "under the mineral laws of the United States" and on releasing "any of the navigable waters" from its limits. Although the document questioned the location of the 1873 reservation boundaries, it recognized tribal sovereignty over the resources encompassed by them. At issue, therefore, was the position of reservation lines, not the validity of Coeur d'Alene tribal claim to the reservation's land and resources.[23]

The interior secretary sent the resolution to the commissioner of Indian affairs, who submitted his findings to the Senate in February 1888. The Coeur d'Alene Reservation, Commissioner Atkins reported, "embraces an area of 598,500 acres, or 935 square miles," and "all the navigable waters of Lake Coeur d'Alene, except a very small fragment cut off by the north boundary." The Coeur d'Alene River traversed the reservation for twenty-five miles, all of which was navigable. The commissioner's information regarding the St. Joseph River, however, revealed only that it entered the reservation before emptying into Lake Coeur d'Alene; no data could be obtained regarding navigability. These traditional tribal waterways, the commissioner's report indicated, remained under tribal control by virtue of the 1873 executive order. Atkins used 1887 census reports to place Coeur d'Alene tribal population at 487.[24]

Because most Coeur d'Alene people farmed in the Hangman's Creek area, south of the reservation's lake and major rivers, the commissioner suggested that "changes could be made in the boundaries for the release of some or all of the navigable waters" of the reservation. Since the tribe had never agreed to release its aboriginal waterways, any transfer would have to be effected through negotiation of new agreements. As for the detachment of mineral lands, Atkins referred to recent inspection reports of the Coeur d'Alene Reservation. Inspector Gardner had found in 1886, for example, that the Wolf Lodge district, located in its northeast corner and rumored to contain vast mineral wealth, provided no service to the tribe beyond an occasional elk or deer. Both Atkins and Gardner regarded the Coeur d'Alene agricultural empire in the southwest corner of the reservation as evidence that the tribe did not need the remainder of the reservation. Their "mental map" of Coeur d'Alene identity placed all the Schitsu'umsh people in the Palouse region and failed to take into account the complexity of tribal usage and tribal divisions.[25]

The Indian Office's perspective of tribal land and resource usage corresponded to that of Congress. Passage of the 1887 Dawes Severalty Act upheld this narrow perception of resource utilization; land, water, timber, and minerals all represented individual sources of wealth. The Dawes Act granted land to individual Indians for agricultural purposes but did not consider traditional forms of land use worthy of allotments. Contrary to non-Indian notions of Coeur d'Alene identity, many Schitsu'umsh people continued to use their waterways and timberlands in innumerable cultural, economic, and practical ways. Tribal members utilized Lake Coeur d'Alene and its rivers to convey crops to market, to travel within the reservation, and to procure fish and waterfowl. In 1887, when Special Agent G. W. Gordon asked a general council about receiving lands in severalty, they unanimously rejected allotment. Tribal members indicated that they needed all of the reservation's resources, not just individual farms, to maintain the Coeur d'Alene economy and lifestyle.[26]

Outsiders misinterpreted the complexity of the Schitsu'umsh economy because they did not understand cyclical, traditional patterns of usage and because their identity map of the tribe allowed them to see only the agricultural holdings of the group in the Palouse region. After more than twenty years of leadership,

Seltice's chieftainship and the Jesuit mission were indistinguishable markers of the "Coeur d'Alene Tribe." Assimilation policy contributed to non-Indian perceptions by defining tribal identity. Seltice adopted non-Indians, like Stephen Liberty, and at the same time rejected the membership of unwanted Schitsu'umsh and Schitsu'umsh relatives. In 1885, for example, Seltice had rejected the membership of a man known as "Whilcomte" who, by Seltice's own admission, possessed "Coeur d'Alene blood in his body" and who may have been considered a member of the tribe decades earlier. Speaking through John Sweeney, additional farmer at Colville Agency, Seltice argued that Whilcomte, accused of murdering a white man, was "more calispel [sic] than anything else." Seltice did not want whites to associate a "bad man" with the Coeur d'Alenes because he was concerned the tribe would "receive a bad name because of the bad doings of indians of other tribes."[27]

Commissioner Atkins's report revealed the Indian Office's perception of Coeur d'Alene identity, but it also upheld tribal title to reservation land. The commissioner emphasized that any transfer of resources would have to take place with the "full and free consent of the Indians" and with "proper compensation." The tribe, he assured Congress, had released nothing within the boundaries of its reservation. The Coeur d'Alene people "have all the original Indian rights to the soil they occupy," Atkins asserted. "They claimed the country long before the lines of the reservation were defined by the executive order of 1873," the commissioner continued, "and the present reservation embraces only a portion of the lands to which they laid claim." Moreover, Atkins added, these aboriginal claims had been repeatedly recognized by the Indian Office and Congress, as in the congressional appropriation for the Northwest Indian Commission in 1887. Despite its reluctance to ratify the Northwest Indian Commission's agreement with the Coeur d'Alenes, Congress had recognized tribal title to reservation lands and resources merely by issuing instructions to the commission to negotiate with the tribe. Because of the validity of Coeur d'Alene land and resource claims, Atkins recommended that Congress should first curry favor with the tribe by ratifying the terms of the 1887 agreement before attempting to negotiate for the release of reservation property.[28]

The Indian commissioner's report sealed the fate of the 1887 agreement, which failed to achieve congressional approval during the Fiftieth Congress. The report confirmed the fears of resource opportunists within Congress, who learned that the reservation encompassed not only Lake Coeur d'Alene and its tributaries but wealthy mineral ledges as well. They refused to ratify an agreement that upheld the reservation's present boundaries. Instead, Delegate Dubois and his allies in the Fifty-first Congress ignored the advice of Commissioner Atkins and authorized additional negotiations with the Coeur d'Alene Tribe, under authority of the Indian Appropriations Act of March 1889, without first approving the 1887 agreement. Benjamin Simpson, John H. Shupe, and Napoleon

B. Humphrey received appointments in May as special commissioners to arrange for "the purchase and release by [the Coeur d'Alene] tribe of such portions of its reservation not agricultural."[29]

John Mullan, who continued to serve as legal counsel to the Coeur d'Alene Tribe and the DeSmet missionaries, informed Chief Seltice of congressional intent to renew negotiations. Seltice and other tribal leaders objected to the formation of the new negotiating body, as evidenced in a stern letter addressed to President Benjamin Harrison in April 1889. "We know that some few Whites around covet the small, little reservation left to us, and prevent that ratification [of the 1887 agreement]," the tribal leaders asserted, "but it seems to us very strange that the great government of Washington should covet a few hundred thousand acres of our land left to us after our giving to said government nearly four millions of acres of very rich and valuable lands and minerals." Seltice, Regis Captain, and Peter Wildshoe informed President Harrison that they could not be expected to conclude another settlement "before the ratification of the first agreement." The Coeur d'Alenes employed a nineteenth-century stereotype of Indian people to entreat the president to demand congressional approval of the 1887 agreement. "People call you the great Father and the good Father," the petitioners declared, "and we know that a good, great Father protects all his children, but especially the little ones; and are we not the smallest of all your children?" Although Seltice, Captain, and Wildshoe each affixed their marks to the document, Father Joseph Cataldo penned the letter and signed his name as a witness.[30]

Mullan delivered the letter to the president on May 28, 1889. Waving aside the objections of Coeur d'Alene leaders and Superior Father Cataldo, however, the Interior Department issued the commissioners their official orders in June. To facilitate negotiations that appeared difficult from the outset, Interior Secretary John W. Noble inserted a crucial loophole in the commissioners' instructions. Rather than prescribe Indian Commissioner John H. Oberly's agreement formula, which required the consent of "not less than three-fourths of all the adult male members of the tribe occupying the reservation," Noble determined that "if in open council it may be shown that the tribe is willing to be represented by its headmen and councillors, such headmen and councillors may sign the agreement on behalf of the tribe." Noble offered no suggestions regarding how the commissioners might ascertain the validity of tribal representatives. This broad interpretation of tribal representation, Noble asserted, "will save time and money and will accomplish the end desired by the law."[31] The interior secretary predicted that the commission would not be welcomed by the tribe and that it would encounter difficulty convincing the Coeur d'Alene people to release large portions of their reservation. Thus, Noble's ambiguous requirements ensured that the commission could obtain an agreement regardless of the actual number of tribal people in attendance at the negotiations.

Noble's loophole also allowed the commissioners to overlook the bitter tribal divisions that characterized the reservation and threatened Seltice's authority. During the late 1880s, anger over the chief's dealings with the Washington and Idaho Railroad and the tactics of his police force exacerbated long-standing geographic, economic, and religious differences. Tribal opposition to the W&IRR had defined and widened a rift between the chief and more "traditional" Coeur d'Alene tribal members. The antics of the Soldiers of the Sacred Heart, moreover, terrorized white and Indian reservation residents alike. The quasi-military force issued its own, often brutal brand of Catholic law. Federal documents and mission logs refer to whippings administered to offenders of Seltice's temperance policy, the forcible return of women to their husbands' homes, and the harassment of non-Indian establishments that occasionally sold liquor to tribal people. It was illegal to sell liquor on the reservation, but the tribal police threatened establishments located off the reservation in nearby non-Indian communities.[32] Seltice and his officers also maintained a jail, known by tribal members as the "skookum house."[33]

The Simpson commission's choice of interpreter for the negotiations, Stephen Liberty, further highlighted divisions on the reservation. As a consequence of his position with Seltice and the recognition of his tribal identity in the 1887 agreement, Liberty stood to benefit from the approval of the old agreement and the negotiation of any new agreement resulting in monetary compensation to individual tribal members. Many tribal people distrusted Liberty because of his influence and for his alleged role in convincing Seltice to agree to the Washington and Idaho Railroad right-of-way. Liberty's personal interests meant he could not perform as an unbiased interpreter for the proceedings. His appointment as interpreter, moreover, provided him with one more way to make money from his association with the tribe. It also meant nonmission Schitsu'umsh, if they knew about the proceedings at all, would associate the negotiations with Seltice and the mission.

The Simpson commission arrived at DeSmet Mission, after an organizational conference in Portland, on August 5, 1889, for a series of four difficult councils. In stark contrast to the ceremonial welcome given the Northwest Indian Commission in 1887, the Simpson group received a chilly reception. It was clear from the start that tribal leaders would not cooperate unless the 1887 agreement provisions were included in the new negotiations. It was also apparent that the territory the United States most wanted to buy—the so-called nonagricultural lands located in the northern part of the reservation—was the only territory the tribe would, if absolutely necessary, consider selling. The area met important criteria for both groups: it contained vast waterways, plentiful timber, and potentially wealthy ore deposits; and it did not contain the tribe's agricultural enterprises in the southwestern corner of the reservation. It did, however, encompass the tribe's traditional lake and river (Spokane and Coeur d'Alene) winter village sites, and it continued to provide sustenance for Schitsu'umsh who did not rely entirely on farming.

Hal Cole, Indian agent at Colville, met the Simpson commission and informed the entourage that the Coeur d'Alenes remained steadfast in their refusal to participate in negotiations until the 1887 agreement received congressional sanction. After Benjamin Simpson telegraphed Commissioner Thomas Morgan with the dilemma, he received permission to "insert a clause in the proposed treaty to the effect that it shall not be valid until [the] former treaty is ratified." At the opening council on August 14, Simpson assured Chief Seltice that the 1887 agreement would be approved *if* the tribe agreed to discuss the release of reservation land. "That treaty is a wall we can not see through," Seltice responded, adding, "[w]hen it is down we can see through and talk." Chief Seltice granted the commissioners permission to inspect the northern portion of the reservation, appointing a member of the tribal police to conduct the tour.[34]

Simpson and his companions spent nearly two weeks exploring the northern reaches of Coeur d'Alene Reservation. After navigating thirty miles of the Coeur d'Alene River and eight miles of Lake Coeur d'Alene, inspecting the "great mineral belt" of the Wolf Lodge area, and cataloging the timber stands of pine, cedar, and tamarack, the negotiators returned to DeSmet Mission. The next general council convened on August 27. The discussions resumed with Simpson's assurance that the land in question—timber and mining resources—provided no value to the Coeur d'Alenes, who were in his estimation now an agricultural people. "The time is come when you, like the whites, should depend upon the cultivation of the soil. . . . When we look on your broad acres now in cultivation," Simpson declared, "we are astonished and gratified." "We know," the commissioner continued, describing the ideological basis for federal Indian policy, "that the cultivation of the soil is the very foundation of civilization, prosperity, and wealth." What the commissioners did not say is why whites would want useless timber and mining lands when the civilized Natives had no use for them.[35]

When Seltice again raised the 1887 agreement as a roadblock to further negotiations, Simpson misrepresented congressional intent. "What was done by the last commission is like cooking a dinner, then setting it to one side to wait," Seltice proclaimed. "[Y]ou do not cook a dinner and lay it aside, then cook another dinner before you have eaten the first; it is that way with these treaties." Simpson attempted to console Seltice and then misstated the facts when he declared that "the treaty of two years ago has not been ratified for want of time; there is no objection to it, and it will be ratified when Congress meets." Seltice responded that whereas Congress "has much power" and "a great deal to do," the Coeur d'Alene people "don't amount to any more with them than a lot of coyotes, and anything we do they do not care about."[36] Simpson persisted. He reiterated that a new agreement would make provision for ratification of the 1887 agreement and that the commissioners remained keenly interested in purchasing a large part of the reservation. When Seltice inquired about the boundaries of the area the commissioners had in mind, Simpson read this description:

> Commencing at the northeast corner of the Coeur d'Alene Reservation, thence along the northern boundary line of the reservation to the northwest corner; thence south along the division line between Washington and Idaho Territories to a point 12 miles south of the said northwest corner; thence due east to the west margin of the Coeur d'Alene Lake; thence southerly along the west shore of said lake to a point due west of the point at the mouth of the Coeur d'Alene River; thence due east across said lake to said point; thence southerly along the east shore of said lake to a point 1 mile north of the St. Joseph River; thence on a parallel line with the north bank of said St. River, 1 mile distant from said bank, to the east line of said reservation; thence northerly along the east line of said reservation to the place of beginning.[37]

Simpson's proposed boundaries encompassed all the timber in the northern portion of the reservation, Coeur d'Alene River and its mouth, the Coeur d'Alene River valley, the Wolf Lodge mineral region, the agricultural land surrounding the Old Mission, and much of the eastern and western shores of Lake Coeur d'Alene—including the northern two-thirds of the lake. Simpson made it clear, however, that "if we buy this land you still have the St. Joseph River and the lower part of the lake and all the meadow and agricultural land along the St. Joseph River." By using the phrase "you still have," this sentence recognized Coeur d'Alene tribal ownership of the lake and portions of the rivers. Seltice balked at Simpson's proposals, stating "there is one great dissatisfaction" among the Coeur d'Alenes regarding the proposed boundary lines and the unratified agreement of 1887. With negotiations at an impasse, the commissioners agreed that the chief should meet privately with tribal representatives to discuss the issues at stake.[38]

Four days later, on August 31, the Simpson commission and the Coeur d'Alene leadership reconvened. Seltice informed the commissioners that at the tribal council "there was two kinds of talk," one "strong" and one "weak." The "strong" talk prevailed, and the tribe was now willing "to let some [land] go." The tribal leader gave a brief history of Coeur d'Alene land claims, beginning with General George Wright's peace treaty in 1859 and ending with the contract involving the Northwest Indian Commission. The 1887 commissioners had "said they would make a tie to our land that would never be untied," Seltice remembered, "and to-day I think this is still my mind as when we treated with them." Thus, with an eye to ratification of the 1887 agreement, Seltice offered to sell the land that "lays along the northern boundary of our reservation, and from eastern boundary of Coeur d'Alene River, and western boundary of Coeur d'Alene Lake, and south to mouth of Coeur d'Alene River."³⁹ In return, Seltice demanded $5.00 per acre and inclusion of the 1887 terms.

Several tribal farms fell within the boundaries of Seltice's proposed cession, and the leader demanded that those members be individually compensated for their improvements. The commissioners retorted that their instructions did not allow them to negotiate with individual tribal members. Moreover, the government representatives desired the forested land on the western side of the lake in addition to that which the tribe offered. The commission respected the needs of the tribe, Simpson acknowledged, but he urged that "the more land you let us have the more money you will get." Seltice stood by his initial offer. When Simpson argued that Congress would never approve such a high price for the land, Seltice replied, "When you make your report to Washington let them say whether it is too much." At the close of the proceedings the commissioners telegraphed the Indian Office to request that they be allowed to offer $500,000 for the cession.⁴⁰

The commissioners met in a "special arrangement" council with Chief Seltice and male tribal members for the fourth and final time on September 8. Second Chief Pierre Wheyilshoo (Peter Wildshoe) told the commissioners the Coeur d'Alenes were willing to sell a portion of the reservation west of Lake Coeur d'Alene, in addition to the area between the Coeur d'Alene River and Lake Coeur d'Alene. Simpson asked if the tribe would also cede acreage south of Coeur d'Alene River. Wheyilshoo responded that the commissioners could draw the line wherever they wanted. This curious reversal of position evinced no objection from Chief Seltice, which suggests that tribal members had agreed in advance to accept the federal government's terms. Why, after years of protectionary efforts, would the Coeur d'Alene leadership move in this direction? Above all, Seltice wanted to protect tribal agricultural enterprises located in the southwestern consolidation area. If this required the release of some "less desirable land," that was acceptable as long as ratification of the 1887 agreement afforded additional protection to remaining lands and resources. Tribal leaders believed they had no choice but to agree to sell reservation lands or Congress would not uphold the boundaries of their 1873 reservation. In fact, they had already won this battle, as the Dawes Severalty Act recognized tribal rights to executive-ordered reservations. Apparently unaware of the Dawes Act's stipulations, Seltice accepted a lesser evil to gain a congressionally sanctioned reservation. Wheyilshoo's rapid qualification of his offer—"Are you sure now that they will ratify that former treaty that was made? That is all we want now, the ratification of the former treaty"—made clear that approval of the former agreement was crucial to the decision at hand.⁴¹

Seltice and Wheyilshoo continued to insist eloquently that individual tribal members receive compensation for their farms, but they did not ask for additional funds for people living on unfenced land. Simpson reiterated that it would be impossible to compensate individual members; such claims would have to be paid out of the total dispersal. Negotiations faltered, and tempers flared. "Did you not say when you came," Subchief Basil (spelled Bazil in the negotiations) accused, "that Washington did not want you to buy farms?" Simpson again stated that he was authorized only to pay the $500,000; "we will pay that and urge the Government to settle as soon as [the agreement is] ratified." Simpson almost certainly meant that the commissioners would urge the interior secretary to move quickly in procuring the $500,000. Seltice's next statement suggests that he may have interpreted Simpson's words as assurance that tribal members would receive compensation from the federal government in addition to the $500,000. "It is not from you," Seltice remarked, "[that] we want the pay." A savvy politician, Seltice continually reminded the commissioners that he knew the money did not come from them, that they were representatives of an extremely wealthy government that *could* afford to pay, regardless of what the commissioners had been "authorized" to offer.[42]

The next few minutes of the fourth council represented a unique turning point in Coeur d'Alene relations with the federal government. Despite Seltice's continued resistance to the negotiation terms, he accepted the government's offer in an unusual statement—striking either for its abrupt transition or for its poor translation (reproduced here as it appeared in the council minutes): "Five hundred thousand dollars is a little sum; the ground is full of gold that is worth millions. We are in a hurry to get through thrashing; can you come to-morrow and get those here at the mission to sign the agreement, and then go and see the ones who are out harvesting?" Simpson agreed to return the next day with the documents, and the official portion of the negotiations ended.[43]

The marks of Chief Seltice and 143 other male tribal members appear on the agreement document, dated September 9, 1889. Some put their marks on the document at DeSmet Mission, whereas the commissioners hand-delivered it to others at work in their fields. Stephen Liberty, Louis Bartholemew, and M. S. Monteith witnessed the signings.[44] The signatories included the non-Indian men adopted by the tribe and their sons: S. Liberty (signed as both a tribal member and as the official interpreter), Edmond Liberty, John Pevey (Peavy), Adolph Bulter (Boutelier), Jerry Butler (Boutelier), Alfred Butler (Boutelier), and Patrick Nixon.[45]

The simple contract contained only four articles. First, the Coeur d'Alenes agreed to release to the United States a "portion of their Reservation" with these boundaries:

> Beginning at the North East corner of the said Reservation thence running along the Northern boundary line north 67 degrees 29 min. West to the head of the Spokane River to the North West boundary corner of the said Reservation, thence South along the Washington Territory line twelve miles, thence

due East to the West shore of the Coeur d'Alene Lake; thence Southerly along the West shore of said Lake to a point due West of the mouth of the Coeur d'alene [sic] River where it empties into the said Lake: thence in a due East line until it intersects with the Eastern boundary of said Reservation, thence Northerly along the said Eastern boundary line to the place of beginning.[46]

The second and third articles gave the tribe $500,000 for the release of the reservation territory. The commissioners arranged for the dispersal of the money on a per capita basis to male heads of households—an unusual move General Simpson justified with the argument that "the Coeur d'Alene Indians are far advanced in civilization, and from what is known of their habits and past life it would not be unreasonable to assume that they would make just as good use of their money if paid in this way."[47] The last section declared that "this Agreement shall not be binding upon either party" until the outstanding 1887 agreement received congressional approval. Thus, the new accord was subject to all the provisions of the previous document, including payment of $150,000 in 1887 for previously ceded tribal territory.[48]

In anticipation of the bill's passage, mining entrepreneurs and homesteaders staked claims in the northern portion of Coeur d'Alene Reservation. Eager settlers like James M. Ballard filed "possessory right" claims with the Kootenai County recorder's office. When Commissioner Morgan denounced Ballard's claim and declared that he possessed "no shadow of right on the reservation," the Colville Agency ordered Ballard's removal. Still, the Indian Office and the agency stood powerless as hundreds of preemptive squatters invaded the reservation. The War Department informed the Indian Office in October 1890 that more than 1,000 homesteaders had illegally entered tribal land. The agency farmer received instructions to remove all trespassers, but the encroachment continued. In March 1891 the 1889 agreement received congressional approval, which opened the northern portion—approximately 184,960 acres, or 289 square miles— to settlement under the public land laws then in effect in Idaho Territory.[49] The transfer symbolized the values of both federal negotiators and tribal leaders: it included the dense forests, alleged mining lands, and navigable waterways so desired by non-Indians but preserved the tribe's agricultural holdings in the Hangman's Creek area.

The payment schedule for the $650,000 paid to the tribe for the land transfer reflected the connection among power, identity, and money inherent in the 1889 negotiations. Joint ratification of the 1887 and 1889 agreements recognized Liberty and the other three Catholic families as members of the Coeur d'Alene Tribe. These four families received more than $35,000—over 7 percent—of the Coeur d'Alene agreement payment. As both a tribal member and an interpreter for the proceedings, Liberty personally received over $9,000. The Patrick Nixon family received more than $7,000. The four families used their

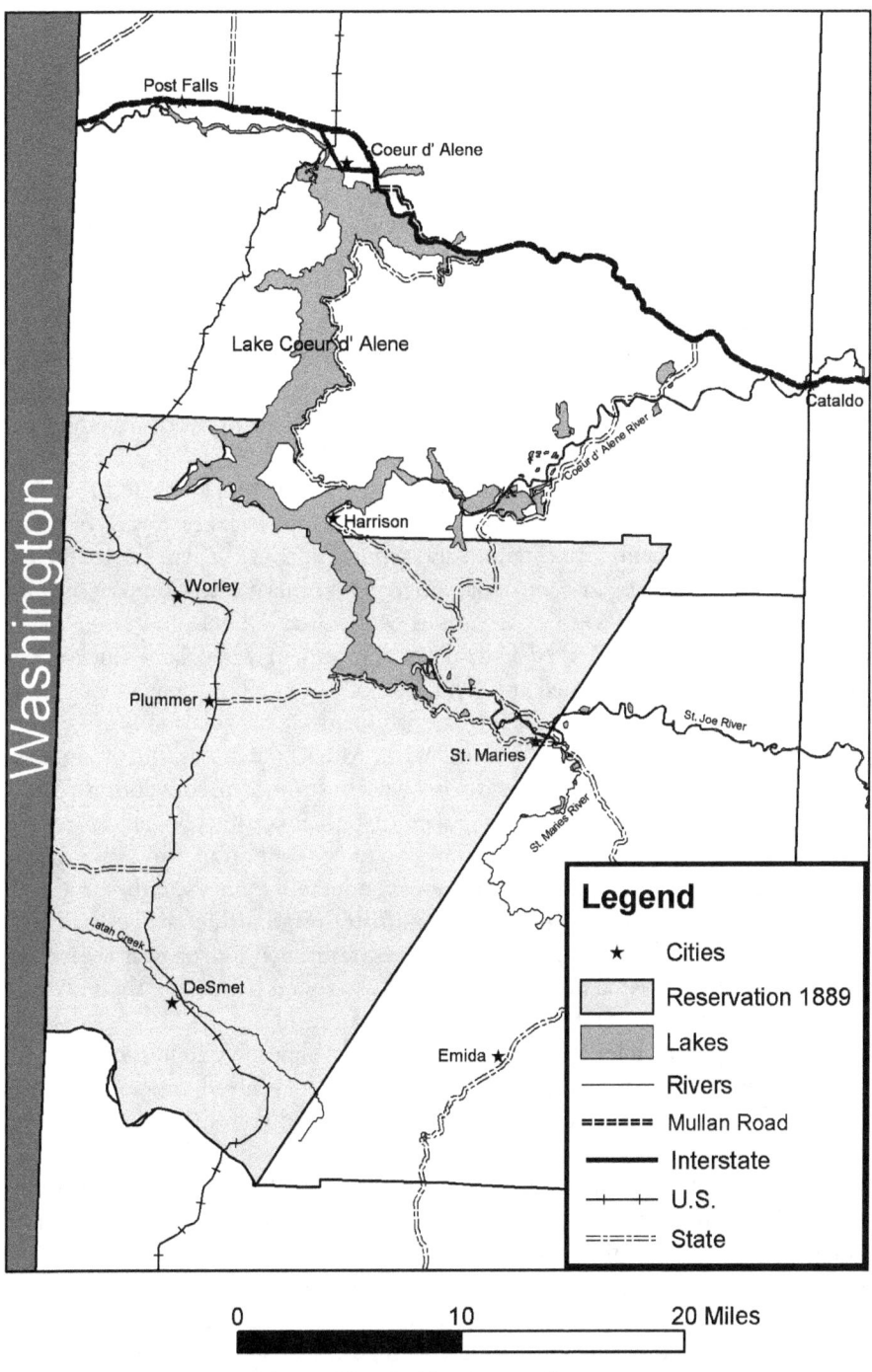

Map 3: The 1889 Reservation Cession

payments to purchase more land and consolidated their landholdings through marriage: one Nixon son married a Peavy daughter; another Nixon son married Stephen Liberty's daughter; and Rosilda Liberty married Adolph Boutelier (Butler). By the early 1900s Liberty's holdings included several thousand acres of farmland, some adjoining the reservation and some on the reservation.[50] The government posts created by the 1889 agreement also enriched the white adopted families. At the request of Stephen Liberty and Chief Seltice, Joseph Peavy was appointed blacksmith at the Coeur d'Alene Reservation in 1894. The position included a blacksmith shop, an annual salary of $900, and supervision of several staff carpenters.[51]

As the 1889 negotiations proceeded, the Idaho statehood movement gained momentum. Dubois, a member of the House Committee on Territories, introduced a bill to provide for Idaho statehood during the Fifty-first congressional session. Idaho statehood bills had been introduced previously, but prior to 1889 the Democrats—who at various times controlled both the House and the Senate—ignored the bids of the northwestern territories because it was believed they would elect Republican senators and representatives. When the 1888 election placed Republicans in control of Congress and the White House, resistance to admission of the far-western territories evaporated. Dubois and other Idaho statehood proponents received federal encouragement when lame-duck president Grover Cleveland signed the Omnibus Bill in 1889. An emergency measure meant to garner political favor, the law made it possible for Washington, Montana, North Dakota, and South Dakota to become states, but it snubbed Idaho. Undaunted, Idahoans held their own constitutional convention—without congressional endorsement—in hopes that their territory would be admitted on the coattails of its neighbors. The Idaho convention met in Boise during August 1889 as the Simpson commission conducted councils with the Coeur d'Alene tribe. The Idahoans put forth a constitution that the territory's citizens approved in November. Dubois submitted the constitution to Congress in December. Both houses debated and passed Idaho's statehood bill during the Fifty-first Congress, and the new state entered the Union on July 3, 1890.[52]

At the time of statehood, the agreement the Simpson commission had negotiated with the Coeur d'Alene Tribe had not yet received congressional approval. Thus, the 1873 executive order forbade the state from assuming control of resources within reservation boundaries. Since the Coeur d'Alene Tribe had not yet ceded its reservation resources, the state could not assume control of reservation waterways. As soon as Congress validated the 1889 document, state officials used it as justification to absorb the Simpson commission cession. The state was forced to honor Coeur d'Alene control of waterways within the remaining reservation area, however, as evidenced by the rent private entities paid to the Coeur d'Alene Tribe for use of the St. Joseph River and Lake Coeur d'Alene. In 1902 the St. Joe Boom Company received permission from the Indian Office to use the St. Joseph River for commercial purposes—but only after agreeing to pay the Coeur d'Alene Tribe $500 in rent per year, to comply with all Interior Department regulations, and to allow inspections by the local U.S. Army engineer officer. The fact that the Coeur d'Alene Tribe maintained control of the St. Joseph River indicates that the state of Idaho did not assume sovereignty of Coeur d'Alene Reservation waterways at the time of statehood.[53]

The transfer of property in 1889 capped a period of internal division within the tribe that began in the 1840s with the introduction of European-style farming and Catholic Christianity by Jesuit missionaries. By 1889 the pro-agriculture, modernizing elements within the tribe prevailed, at the expense of members who favored different cultural, economic, and spiritual ways. Ratification of the 1889 agreement dealt a final blow to tribal members living in river and lake regions; they had to move within reservation boundaries, take up sedentary farming, or face white encroachment and harassment without the protection of the tribal police, the Jesuit mission, or the Indian agent.

With the land transfer of 1889, the Interior Northwest's extractive industrialists triumphed. Schitsu'umsh forests, waterways, and rich mining lands were quickly settled and built up by non-Indians and eastern investors. These local resource brokers served a larger industrial system. At midcentury, America had been a rural nation of agriculturalists. By 1890 an industrial revolution had transformed work; increasing numbers of Americans earned their livelihood toiling for large manufacturing enterprises rather than by tilling the soil. Although the urban-dwelling portion of the U.S. population would not exceed 50 percent until 1920, the trend toward urbanization had revealed itself by the end of the nineteenth century.[54]

This demographic reality, coupled with the decline in the small family farm, threatened the tenets of the Dawes Severalty Act and late-nineteenth-century federal Indian policy. Whereas non-Indian people struggled to acquire the skills of the Industrial Age, the Indian Office insisted that the way to "assimilate" Indian people was to force them to farm, often on allotments far removed from their aboriginal territory and ill suited to agriculture. During this period the Pacific Northwest became economically important as a supplier of raw resources to eastern manufacturers. Large-scale mining, timber, and agricultural enterprises sprang up in the Coeur d'Alene region. As competition for northwestern resources intensified, the lands set aside for tribal people—particularly in resource-rich areas—attracted more covetous attention.[55]

Within this environment, the historical protections assimilation policy had afforded the Coeur d'Alene farming consolidation in Hangman's Valley gradually eroded. Changes in the nature of American work led to changes in leisure; as more people moved to urban areas, they began to value the West's less populated regions as a source of relaxation and sport.[56] With its beautiful lake, raging rivers, and primeval forests, the Coeur d'Alene region became the vacation destination of choice for Spokane's urban dwellers. In 1888 the *Spokesman Monthly Review* featured Lake Coeur d'Alene as a "natural beauty spot" and predicted that "it will become the most fashionable watering place within the territory of the great West." In 1891 the *Spokesman-Review* characterized Lake Coeur d'Alene as the "ideal summer resort" and in 1893 announced that the Coeur d'Alene region was becoming "widely known" as a tourist attraction, partly because of its exposure in national publications such as *Scientific American*.[57]

Pleasure seekers took advantage of the Northern Pacific Railroad's "excursion trains," which ran regular summer hours from Spokane to Coeur d'Alene during the 1890s. At Coeur d'Alene City, travelers boarded luxurious steamboats for cruises on the lake and journeys up the "shadowy" St. Joseph River—much of which remained within the borders of the Coeur d'Alene Reservation. Sightseers camped on the river's shores and cut wood for their fires. Famed for its dramatic scenery, swift water, and unrivaled trout fishing, the St. Joe attracted honeymooners, families, adventurers, and amateur photographers. Boardinghouses sprang up on Lake Coeur d'Alene's shores, and the deserted Cataldo Mission became a favorite location for vacation photographs.[58]

From the late 1890s through the 1910s, the Indian Office received repeated requests from picnickers and tourists to use reservation lands and resources. These usually came from official organizations or individuals with ties to local or state governments, suggesting that many ordinary citizens did not bother to ask for permission. Camp 99 of the Woodmen of the World asked to "hold an excursion and picnic at Chatcolet." The group also secured permission from "Chief of the Indians, Moctomal" (probably Subchief Peter Moctelme) to use his grounds and boats in exchange for fifty dollars, suggesting that tribal members tried to procure payment directly from tourists.[59] United States Deputy Marshal G. L. Ide informed Indian Agent Anderson that he and a friend were "anticipating a hunt, which will probably take us onto the Indian Reservation near Tekoa."[60] The Indian Office usually granted such requests, as long as the parties agreed not to bring alcohol onto the reserve or to steal or damage resources while there.

As tourists became the most recent invaders of Coeur d'Alene Reservation lands, the federal government pressured Schitsu'umsh leaders for land cessions. In 1891, for example, a few settlers illegally seized forty acres near the mouth of the Coeur d'Alene River—within reservation boundaries—and organized a town site. Claiming they did not initially know the boundary's location, the citizens petitioned President Benjamin Harrison to remove their town—which they named Harrison—from within the preserve. Characteristically, the settlers did not offer to move their town; they wanted the reservation boundary changed. Citing the 1887/1889 dual agreement, the Interior Secretary's Office confirmed Coeur d'Alene ownership of the Harrison town site. Again, Congress authorized appropriations for the negotiation of a land cession, and in 1893 a commission met with Chief Seltice and other tribal leaders. The negotiators told the chief there had been a "mistake" in the land cession boundary as described in the 1889 agreement. When the commissioners suggested that the tribe surrender the land without pay, Seltice refused to release the town site, and the negotiations disintegrated. The Indian Office persisted, however, and appointed a special agent to conduct further negotiations with the Coeur d'Alenes in 1894. At the ensuing council, the tribe reluctantly agreed to release Harrison for the sum of $15,000, despite the special agent's manipulative efforts to convince the leaders that "duty" compelled them to cede the lands without compensation. Congress approved legislation ratifying the agreement and authorizing payment a few months later.[61]

Local whites, as the Indian Office had predicted, also objected to what they viewed as unfair privileges accorded the Liberty, Boutelier, Nixon, and Peavy families. Throughout the 1890s the Indian Commissioner's Office investigated allegations of corruption and illegal activity brought against Liberty by local whites. Farmington businessman F. A. English wrote to the Indian Office decrying what he considered "a very serious state of affairs on the Coeur d'Alene Reservation on account of the debauchery of certain French and Irish parties located thereon." In 1898 the commissioner determined that for more than a decade Liberty—along with the other whites Seltice had adopted—had exercised undue influence over Coeur d'Alene tribal affairs, illegally supplied reservation residents with liquor, and used vigilante tactics to terrorize both Indian and non-Indian reservation residents. Indian Agent Albert Anderson had met with tribal members in spring of 1898 and found that "the Indians had no knowledge of consenting to the enrollment" of the white families. The Indian Office demanded that the local Indian agent forcibly remove, "in the interests of morality and decency and the welfare of the Indians," Liberty, the Nixons, the Bouteliers (Butlers), and the Chamberlaines from the reservation.[62]

Liberty moved to Spokane, where in 1896 he became a member of the Spokane Society of Pioneers. Removal from the reservation did not, however, stop Liberty and the others from receiving a percentage of the Coeur d'Alenes' wealth. The white families relentlessly pursued their claim for tribal funds, and several parties moved back onto the reservation after removal. The Department of the Interior reviewed the case in 1909. Assistant Secretary Jesse E. Wilson ruled that the Libertys and the three other families had been officially adopted by the tribe in the provisions of the 1887/1889 agreement and that they should "be accorded all rights and privileges that go with membership in the Coeur d'Alene Tribe of Indians."[63]

By 1902 the Interior Pacific Northwest was a changed place from the Native-dominated land that had characterized Andrew Seltice's childhood and early adulthood. Blind and sickened by age, his reservation under attack from new non-Indian invaders, his people divided over cultural and religious issues, Seltice spent his final months in Spokane receiving care at the Sisters of Providence Sacred Heart Hospital (now Sacred Heart Medical Center, one of the largest medical facilities in the Northwest). Seltice's final year was consumed with health crises and communications with Indian Agent Albert Anderson at the Colville Agency. Among his concerns were tribal divisions and crime on the reservation, collection of unpaid debts, and his health. "My sickness and my wifes [sic]," Seltice wrote in January 1902, "has been a source of great trouble and expence [sic] to me." "I greatly need you," he informed Anderson, and requested that the agent assist him in collecting the more than $2,000 a white man in the Tekoa area owed the chief.[64]

In a separate letter, mailed two weeks later from the Hotel Grand in Spokane, Seltice expressed regret that the agent had not met with him "before you left for Washington, D.C." and asked that the agent "see to it" that two Coeur d'Alene men, Bonemetsei and Louie Antelope, be "reprimanded" by the commissioner of Indian affairs for disrupting affairs on the reservation. The two men opposed Seltice's authority and were attempting to gather supporters to go to Washington to protest Coeur d'Alene land cessions and monetary payments. Seltice also blamed them for turning "half of the tribe" against reservation officials. Their efforts had become more successful in Seltice's absence from the reservation, and the tribal leader feared his health limited his ability to maintain control of reservation affairs. Seltice reiterated his position on tribal identity and reservation occupancy: "With us all the people that are on the reservation wether [sic] they are mixed blood or other wise if they are good people we want them protected for we feel that we are all one."[65] The efforts of the troublesome anti-Seltice faction threatened the chief's authority and represented those who still openly opposed the tribal leadership's assimilation policies. Seltice's letters from this period were penned by his son, Peter.

Chief Andrew Seltice died the evening of April 20, 1902. Peter Seltice informed the Colville Indian agent of his father's passing in a formal but deeply sad letter: "He will be buried this morning [April 22], of course the blow was a hard one for all of us, but poor mother she is in a pitifull [sic] condition." The letter expressed gratitude to the tribal people who had come to gather in the chief's honor and for the "ladies of Farmington" who brought the family bouquets of flowers.[66]

Seltice's passing created a vacuum in Coeur d'Alene leadership and altered local whites' mental maps of the Coeur d'Alene Reservation. Peter Wildshoe succeeded Seltice, but some tribal members believed the position should have gone to Peter Moctelme. When Wildshoe died in 1907, the role passed to Moctelme, but the controversy temporarily weakened the chieftainship.[67] The respect accorded Seltice by non-Indians in the Pacific Northwest had a flip side. External opinions of Coeur d'Alene leadership declined with his death. Seltice served as head chief for nearly forty years, during which his assimilation policy and the tidy farms of Coeur d'Alene agriculturalists earned the respect of area settlers and government officials. Referring to the chief's "wise administration," the *Spokesman-Review* described Seltice's passing as a "severe loss to the whites."[68] The manager of *Northwest Magazine,* a monthly periodical, wrote to Agent Anderson asking for "a good photograph of Saltese [sic] as well as a photo of his home of [sic] some scene near where he has lived since becoming 'a good indian.'"[69] Widely recognized by contemporaries as "one of the most intelligent and influential chiefs in the Northwest," Seltice had defined the tribe for the world outside the reservation.[70] Seltice's bargaining skills, assimilation policy, relationship with the Jesuit mission, and conviction of leadership allowed the Coeur d'Alenes to retain the agricultural portion of their reservation despite the fact that it was a rich, fertile land coveted by whites. His death created a void in tribal authority, leaving the Coeur d'Alenes vulnerable to the designs of non-Indians.

Between 1805 and Andrew Seltice's death, interaction between the Schitsu'umsh people and outsiders—explorers, fur traders, Jesuit missionaries, and federal Indian agents—mapped new cultural and geographical entities in northern Idaho. The Coeur d'Alene Tribe of Indians—as defined, perceived, and recognized by non-Indians in the Interior Northwest and by Indian agents—emerged as the Schitsu'umsh leadership accepted Catholic Christianity and embraced an assimilation policy aimed at protecting tribal resources. The Coeur d'Alene Indian Reservation resulted from the imposition of federal Indian policy and negotiation of a series of agreements between tribal leaders and federal officials. The identity of the Coeur d'Alene people became intrinsically linked to the Jesuit mission, agriculture, and the so-called civilized habits of industry, sedentary lifestyle, and white clothing. Although assimilation policy protected the tribe from relocation to another reservation and allowed Seltice to maintain control of the fertile Palouse area and the St. Joe River Valley, it instituted a transferral of power from traditional authority to a modernizing, progressive core group associated with the mission. This meant a gradual decline in the relative power of "traditional" Schitsu'umsh and a change in gender roles and authority. Whereas women had once participated more openly in Schitsu'umsh consensus politics and contributed a significant amount to tribal subsistence, they now found authority through participation in the church and in domestic duties such as raising vegetable gardens. Assimilation policy also contributed to the tribe's willingness, when it found itself in the position of having to sell territory or face further invasion, to sell the northern portion of the reservation. The 1889 agreement stripped the tribe of most of its traditional village sites, two-thirds of Lake Coeur d'Alene, and land adjoining the Spokane and Coeur d'Alene rivers.

The transfer of land in 1889 dealt a final blow to Schitsu'umsh who continued to live in traditional lake and river locations—they were forced to relocate within the new reservation boundary or face non-Indian encroachment without the support of tribal leadership, the Jesuit mission, or the Indian agency. By the end of the century, reference to these peoples in government documents had ceased; some may have been identified as members of other tribal groups in government records. The agreement negotiations that formed the territorial boundaries of the Coeur d'Alene Indian Reservation also created boundaries of identity. Irish Catholic immigrant families became tribal members by virtue of their adoption into the tribe and residence on the reservation, whereas other tribal affiliates lost their tribal identity. The evolution of the Coeur d'Alene Indian Reservation contributes to the complexity of the historical record of reservation policy. The Coeur d'Alene reserve, rather than representing a clear imposition of federal will, was shaped by the interests of Jesuit priests, Schi̲tsu'umsh leaders, non-Indian mental maps of the Coeur d'Alene people and their land, and individual government agents with often contradictory goals. The end result created a construction of tribal identity as well as one of territory.

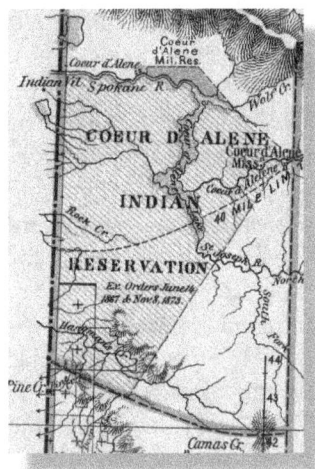

Epilogue

TODAY, COEUR D'ALENE COUNTRY REMAINS ONE OF THE MOST BEAUTIFUL PLACES in the Pacific Northwest. The region surrounding DeSmet, Idaho, still does not contain large cities or significant development. Driving through the Palouse on Highway 95, no strip malls, super-freeways, masses of steel and asphalt overpasses, or major airports appear. As the road crosses the reservation boundary, a sign welcomes visitors to the Coeur d'Alene Indian Reservation. Rolling hills painted with the bright yellow of rape seed or a golden shade of grain blend into stands of dark pine. DeSmet, Idaho, is a small town where tribal elders meet for lunch at the community center and the resident Jesuit priests say Mass and attempt to provide support for the problems associated with modern life, particularly modern life on a reservation. Around 1,840 people are enrolled members of the modern Coeur d'Alene Tribe, but not all are residents of the reservation.[1] The total reservation population in the 2000 census was 6,551, and nonnative residents outnumbered Coeur d'Alene tribal members.[2]

After leaving DeSmet, the two-lane road heads north to the tribe's headquarters near Plummer, Idaho. The headquarter's buildings sit on a hillside about six miles off the main road, in the heart of reservation land owned by the tribe and tribal individuals. The modern reservation is made up of a checkerboard of Indian and non-Indian landownership, a holdover from the period

167

following Andrew Seltice's death. Now the target of a tribal policy of repurchasing reservation lands, the checkerboard resulted from the imposition of severalty in the first decade of the twentieth century. Seltice's policy of protecting reservation resources by embracing civilization could not protect the tribe from allotment. The wealth amassed by the tribe through negotiated payments and agricultural success was stripped when Congress passed legislation in 1906 authorizing the interior secretary to break up tribal holdings and award 40-, 80-, or 160-acre allotments to Coeur d'Alene tribal members. Since some Coeur d'Alenes were among the most successful agriculturalists in the Northwest, the reform impulse underlying severalty—to turn Indians into farmers—did not apply to the Schitsu'umsh. In this instance allotment could not hide behind an altruistic motive; many Coeur d'Alene farmers cultivated more land than the standard 160 acres provided by allotment. Moreover, the arable land on the reservation could not support all tribal members, particularly as some Spokane bands were relocated to the reservation as a result of the 1887 and 1889 agreements.

The Coeur d'Alenes stridently opposed allotment, but local whites argued that the tribe—because of its high level of development—should receive its lands in severalty. Special Agent William B. Sams issued allotments totaling 104,077 acres, approximately one-fourth of the reservation, to 638 Coeur d'Alene Reservation enrollees during 1908 and 1909. Tribal members who cultivated more land than the allotments allowed were forced to give up the additional acreage. Moreover, because the Dawes Act limited allotments to agricultural and grazing land, Sams forbade tribal members to choose lake- or riverfront acreage susceptible to inundation during the spring runoff. Thus, in this important decisive action, allotment effectively isolated the Coeur d'Alene people from their reservation waterways. Allotment also highlighted the position of the reservation's white residents, who received sixty-six of the "choicest" farms.[3]

The General Land Office dispensed with remaining, or "surplus," reservation lands by holding a lottery in which more than 100,000 people registered. In May 1910 the lucky participants filed on 219,767 acres of the Coeur d'Alene Reservation. By 1934, when passage of the Indian Reorganization Act ended the misguided policies of severalty, Coeur d'Alene tribal holdings had been reduced to 62,400 acres—45,120 of which were leased to non-Indians. Severalty left the Coeur d'Alene people with only a fragment of their ancestral lands, separated them from traditional reservation waterways, and represented a low point in federal dealings with the Coeur d'Alenes. Allotment did not, however, change the boundaries of the reservation as amended by the 1889 agreement.[4]

The next stop on the modern map of the Coeur d'Alene reserve is Worley, the site of the Coeur d'Alene Tribe's impressive casino development. The casino, marked by a huge lighted sign, sits on Highway 95 and offers more than 1,000 sophisticated Vegas-style pull-tab machines. Five hundred people work at the site. Free shuttle service is provided from Spokane, Post Falls, and Coeur d'Alene. In addition to the casino, the tribe operates a resort and conference hotel and the Circling Raven Golf Club, which opened in August 2003. The $20 million in revenue generated by the tribe's gaming and tourism enterprises supports myriad social services on the reservation, including youth, elder, education, and economic development programs. Around 20 percent of the revenue is distributed as a per capita payment to individual tribal members.[5] The casino has been a source of controversy within the tribe, as some members view gaming as destructive to tribal culture whereas others insist that the money generated by gaming will enable the Coeur d'Alenes to reclaim "Indian identity."[6] These divisions recall those associated with Seltice's assimilation policy in the nineteenth century. Like that policy, the new progressive Coeur d'Alene gaming strategy has enabled the tribe to secure part of its land base—to repurchase reservation lands and revitalize social programming. At the same time, it has brought unprecedented change to Coeur d'Alene country.

Modern change is also apparent on the landscape itself, particularly as we leave Worley and approach the city of Coeur d'Alene. We leave the reservation when we cross the 1889 cession line near Rockford Bay. Suddenly the rolling hills are gone, replaced by hillsides covered with pine forests; the lake peeks out from the trees, a glorious sheet of blue water. Upscale housing developments and dramatic summer homes dot the shores of the lake as strip malls, theme restaurants, and motels pop up along the highway. Lake Coeur d'Alene is breathtakingly beautiful, a brilliant blue in a sea of dark green. The city, lake, and non-Indian resorts attract a significant proportion of Idaho's tourist dollars, a $2 billion economy that ranks third in the state behind manufacturing and agriculture.[7] Kootenai County, where the north shore's resort area is located, generates about 10 percent of Idaho's total tourist dollars (the reservation straddles two counties; DeSmet is located in Benewah County).[8] Central to non-Indian tourist operations is the five-star resort the Coeur d'Alene, ranked one of America's top resorts and home to the "world's only floating green"—a golf hole placed out in the lake. Golfers must be transported in small boats to the green if they are lucky enough to land on it.[9]

The lake's stunning beauty hides what the tribe has always known: that it is not in pristine condition. More than a century of mining in the Coeur d'Alene district dumped large amounts of lead, cadmium, and other heavy metals into Coeur d'Alene River, where they eventually made their way to the lake and currently reside in a muddy sludge at the bottom. As much as 468,000 metric tons of lead and 280 metric tons of mercury had washed into Lake Coeur d'Alene by the early 1990s.[10] As tribal biologist Phil Cernera explained in a 1997 interview, "People can't believe there's a problem here when it looks so good, but we've got levels of lead in the lower river that are 4,000 times background levels. Every beach is basically a redeposited tailings pile."[11] Local residents admit that few fish remain in the lake—which was once a great fishery—and that occasionally heavy spring runoff will contaminate the shoreline, leaving dead birds and plants in its wake.

Concerns that Idaho mismanaged the lake and its rivers prompted the Coeur d'Alene Tribe to sue the state during the early 1990s for the right to the lake's bed and banks. The case went to the Supreme Court in 1995, and in 1996 the Court ruled that the tribe could not bring suit against the State Land Board for control of Coeur d'Alene Reservation waterways because the Eleventh Amendment of the Constitution prohibits suits against state governments for quiet title to disputed property. But prior to the Supreme Court ruling, the Justice Department intervened on the side of the tribe, suing the State of Idaho to obtain ownership of the lower third of the lake for the Coeur d'Alenes. The Justice Department is obligated under the constitution to uphold the treaty and sovereignty rights of tribes. That case went to a Ninth Circuit Court of Appeals, where U.S. Federal District Judge Edward Lodge found that the portion of the lake within the boundaries of the reservation, as amended by the 1889 agreement, belonged to the tribe. Lodge argued that in negotiating with the tribe in 1889 the federal government recognized "that beneficial ownership of all land within the 1873 reservation, including submerged lands, had already passed to the Tribe." Therefore, the court found, Congress had "made very plain" its intent that the future State of Idaho would not absorb reservation lands and waterways upon statehood.[12] The courts' reaffirmation of Coeur d'Alene ownership of the lake enhances the tribe's ability to sue other entities, including power and mining companies, for their role in polluting the lake and rivers.

Leaving the city of Coeur d'Alene, we travel along the old Mullan Road route—now Interstate 90—to Cataldo Mission. As we approach the old mission site the interstate drops into the floodplain of the Coeur d'Alene River, where for thousands of years the Schitsu'umsh made their homes. By the early twentieth century the beautiful handcrafted church had fallen into disrepair; early-twentieth-century tourists often posed for photographs at the building, and birds and other animals made their homes inside the structure. The state now maintains the site as Mission State Park, an eighteen-acre area that includes picnic facilities, and the church is listed on the Register of Historic Places. If we continued on I-90 we would drive through Kellogg and into the heart of the Coeur d'Alene lead and silver mining district. Kellogg has reinvented itself as a resort town, where travelers can be transported into an old gold mine in relative comfort. Instead of visiting the mines, we backtrack to Highway 3 and head southwest along Coeur d'Alene River. We cross back into the reservation at a point in the river known as Black Lake. The terrain changes, and we once again enter the Palouse—less watered and less crowded with trees and people. As we make our way back to DeSmet and the southeast entrance of the reservation, we have traced a rough map of the 1873 reservation. This is at once a modern and an ancient place, where the Coeur d'Alene people continue to use progressive means—now gaming, resorts, golf courses—to maintain their traditions and reaffirm their sovereignty.

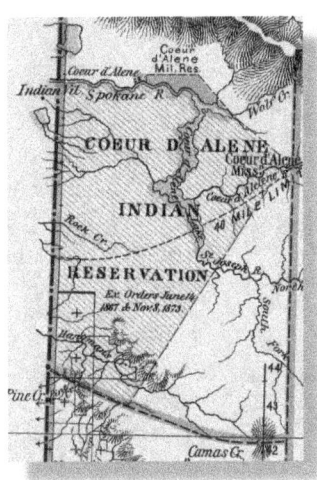

Notes

CA	Colville Agency
CDA	Coeur d'Alene Reservation
CIA	Commissioner of Indian Affairs
CT	*Coeur d'Alene Teepee*
GR	General Records
HED	House Executive Document
ICC	Indian Claims Commission
IS	Idaho Superintendency
LR	Letters Received
LRM	Letters Received, Miscellaneous
LS	Letters Sent
M	Microfilm
MASC	Manuscripts, Archives, and Special Collections
NA	National Archives
NA-PNR	National Archives—Pacific Northwest Region
PNWMC	Pacific Northwest Tribes Missions Collection
RG	Record Group
RIFJ	Reports of Inspections of the Field Jurisdictions
SC	Special Case
SED	Senate Executive Document
SHMP	Sacred Heart Mission Papers
SMD	Senate Miscellaneous Document
WS	Washington Superintendency

INTRODUCTION

1. Rodney Frey, in collaboration with the Schi̱tsu'umsh, *Landscape Traveled by Coyote and Crane: The World of the Schi̱tsu'umsh (Coeur d'Alene Indians)* (Seattle: University of Washington Press, 2001), 133–134.

2. I will use both the Native name of the tribe, Schi̱tsu'umsh, which translates as "the ones that were found here," and the contact-era French name, Coeur d'Alenes, to refer to the tribe. Tribal members initially resisted the non-Indian name but adopted it during the contact period and still use it today. Many variations of the Native spelling occur in historical documents, including "Skitswish," "Skeetshoo," "Sketsui," "Skitsuish," "Stchitsui," "Stietshoi," "Steel-shoi," "Skee-cha-way," "Skisamuq," "Skeetso-mish," and "Sket-so-mish." For a dictionary and grammar of the Coeur d'Alene language, see Lawrence G. Nicodemus, *Snchitsu'umshtsm: The Coeur d'Alene Language,* 2 vols. (Spokane, Wash.: Coeur d'Alene Tribal Council, 1975). Also see the Coeur d'Alene Indian Tribe's official website at www.cdatribe.org; Kimberly Rice Brown, "Overview of Coeur d'Alene History," in Joseph Seltice, *Saga of the Coeur d'Alene Indians: An Account of Chief Joseph Seltice,* ed. Edward J. Kowrach and Thomas E. Connolly, introduction by Ernest Stensgar (Fairfield, Wash.: Ye Galleon, 1990), 305, 325n; Albert W. Thompson, "Coeur d'Alene: The Names Applied to Tribe and Lake," *Idaho Yesterdays* 21 (Winter 1978): 11; Jack Dozier, "History of the Coeur d'Alene Indians to 1900" (M.A. Thesis, University of Idaho, 1961), 6.

3. Janet Campbell Hale, *Bloodlines: Odyssey of a Native Daughter* (New York: Random House, 1993), 1661–67.

4. Official Web site of the Coeur d'Alene Indian Tribe, www.cdatribe.org/overview.html, accessed August 26, 2002.

5. The research for this book was initially conducted for a dissertation completed in 1996 at Washington State University. A member of the Coeur d'Alene Indian Tribe served as a "de facto" member of the dissertation committee. Tribal historian Dixie Saxon provided helpful counsel. I shared lunch with tribal elders at the community center at DeSmet in spring of 1994.

6. This work builds on a growing body of literature that presents a more complex picture of federal Indian policy, Native identity, and the formation of Indian reservations during the second half of the nineteenth century. In his recent article, "They Mean to Be Indian Always: The Origins of Columbia River Indian Identity, 1860–1885," *Western Historical Quarterly* 32 (Winter 2001): 468–492, Andrew Fisher argues that the resistance of Columbia River groups to reservations and federal policy resulted in the formation of a new Indian identity in the region. See also Nicholas Thomas, *Colonialism's Culture: Anthropology, Travel and Government* (Princeton: Princeton University Press, 1994); Frederick E. Hoxie, *Parading Through History: The Making of the Crow Nation in America, 1805–1935* (Cambridge: Cambridge University Press, 1995); Brad Asher, *Beyond the Reservation: Indians, Settlers, and the Law in Washington Territory, 1853–1889* (Norman: University of Oklahoma Press, 1999); Jacki Thompson Rand, "Primary Sources: Indian Goods and the History of American Colonialism and the 19th-Century Reservation," in *Clearing a Path: Theorizing the Past in Native American Studies,* ed. Nancy Shoemaker (New York: Routledge, 2002), 137–157; Carol Devens, "'If We Get the Girls, We Get the Race': Missionary Education of Native American Girls," in *American Nations: Encounters in Indian Country, 1850 to the Present,* ed. Frederick Hoxie et al. (New York: Routledge, 2001), 157–171; James H. Merrell, *The Indians' New World: Catawbas and Their Neighbors From European*

Contact Through the Era of Removal (Chapel Hill: University of North Carolina Press, 1989); William T. Hagan, "Full Blood, Mixed Blood, Generic, and Ersatz: The Problem of Indian Identity," in *The American Indian: Past and Present*, 5th ed., ed. Roger L. Nichols (Boston: McGraw Hill, 1999), 1–10.

7. As stated by Gunlog Fur, "[A]ttention to various aspects of gender reveals a whole new universe of information contained in well-known sources." Fur, "'Some Women Are Wiser Than Some Men': Gender and Native American History," in *Clearing a Path*, ed. Shoemaker, 83; Lillian A. Ackerman, "The Effect of Missionary Ideals on Family Structure and Women's Roles in Plateau Indian Culture," *Idaho Yesterdays* 31 (Spring-Summer 1987): 64–73.

8. James H. Merrell, "The Indians' New World: The Catawba Experience," in Nichols, ed., *The American Indian*, 66.

9. "Mental mapping" refers to the abstractions people create to interpret geography, identity, and place. The notion is eloquently introduced and defined in Katherine G. Morrissey, *Mental Territories: Mapping the Inland Empire* (Ithaca: Cornell University Press, 1997).

10. Brad Asher found that "the great distribution of Indian resources that occurred at the turn of the century clarified many of the lines left indistinct by the failure of reservation policy, for it gave those who successfully fit themselves within the definition of *Indian* a specific set of group rights." Asher, *Beyond the Reservation*, 196.

11. For a discussion of technological advances in mapmaking, see Jeremy Black, *Maps and History: Constructing Images of the Past* (New Haven: Yale University Press, 1997), 48–50.

12. Ibid., 41–43.

13. On the use of maps and GIS (Geographic Information Systems) in history, see David Rumsey and Meredith Williams, "Historical Maps in GIS," in *Past Time, Past Place: GIS for History*, ed. Anne Kelly Knowles (Redlands, Calif.: ESRI, 2002), 1–18.

14. Richard White, *"It's Your Misfortune and None of My Own": A New History of the American West* (Norman: University of Oklahoma Press, 1991), 132.

CHAPTER 1

1. Joseph Seltice, *Saga of the Coeur d'Alene Indians: An Account of Chief Joseph Seltice*, ed. Edward J. Kowrach and Thomas E. Connolly (Fairfield, Wash.: Ye Galleon, 1990), 61.

2. Bryant used a variation of the name Oregon to refer to the Columbia River. William Cullen Bryant, "Thanatopsis," in *The Norton Anthology of American Literature*, 2nd ed., vol. 1, ed. Nina Baym, Ronald Gottesman, et al. (New York: W. W. Norton, 1985), 811.

3. The United States and Great Britain agreed to "joint occupation" of Oregon country at the Convention of 1818. Great Britain and the United States agreed to U.S. ownership of Oregon country south of the forty-ninth parallel in the Oregon Treaty of 1846. See Dorothy O. Johansen and Charles M. Gates, *Empire of the Columbia: A History of the Pacific Northwest* (New York: Harper and Brothers, 1957), 190–191.

4. For an examination of early-nineteenth-century non-Indian perceptions of the American West, see Anne Farrar Hyde, *An American Vision: Far Western Landscape and National Culture, 1820–1920*, American Social Experience Series, ed. James Kirby Martin (New York: New York University Press, 1990), esp. 23–47. See also William Dietrich, *Northwest Passage: The Great Columbia River* (Seattle: University of Washington Press,

1995), 74–81; Carlos Schwantes, *The Pacific Northwest: An Interpretive History* (Lincoln: University of Nebraska Press, 1989), 12, 32–33, 46; *Idaho Atlas and Gazetteer: Topo Maps of the Entire State* (Freeport, Maine: DeLorme Mapping, 1992), 1, 5, 50–51. For a brief overview of Jefferson's policy regarding western lands, see James A. Henretta and Gregory H. Nobles, *Evolution and Revolution: American Society, 1600–1820* (Lexington, Mass.: D. C. Heath, 1987), 206–207; White, *"It's Your Misfortune and None of My Own,"* 69–70.

5. Columbia Basin Sahaptin-speaking peoples include the Kittitas, Yakima, Klikitat, Wayampum, Umatilla, Cayuse, Walula, Wanapum, Wauyukma, Palouse, and Nez Perce. Salish speakers include the Lakes, Kalispel, Coeur d'Alene, Spokane, Colville, Chewelah, San Poil, Nespelem, Southern Okanogan, Methow, Chelan, Wenatchi, and Columbia. Verne F. Ray, "Native Villages and Groupings of the Columbia Basin," *Pacific Northwest Quarterly* 27 (1936): 102, 105, 107.

6. Paula Bock, "A Kinder, Gentler Archaeology," *Pacific Magazine: The Seattle Times Magazine* (May 28, 1995), 15.

7. For a recent and thorough anthropological study of Schitsu'umsh, see Frey, *Landscape Traveled by Coyote and Crane*, 1, 58–59.

8. James A. Teit, "The Coeur d'Alene," in facsimile reproduction of *The Salishan Tribes of the Western Plateaus*, 45th Annual Report of the Bureau of American Ethnology, 1927–1928, ed. Frank Boas (Seattle: Shorey Book Store, 1973), 37; Deward E. Walker Jr., *Indians of Idaho*, Anthropological Monograph of the University of Idaho, ed. Roderick Sprague (Moscow: University of Idaho Press, 1978), 63; Ray, "Native Villages," 116 (map).

9. Archaeological finds in Wilson Butte Cave, near Dietrich, Idaho, suggest the presence of ancient human habitation in the Interior Northwest dating from 13,000 B.C. Controversy exists over the entry points and dates of arrival for humans in the Western Hemisphere. Carbon dating also has difficulties; older carbon dates did not take into account fluctuating carbon 14:carbon 12 ratios and therefore must be "calibrated." Jared Diamond discusses these issues in *Guns, Germs, and Steel: The Fates of Human Societies* (New York: W. W. Norton, 1998), 35–43, 94–97. For evidence of prehistoric artifacts in Coeur d'Alene country, see Donald R. Tuohy, "Horseshoes and Handstones: The Meeting of History and Prehistory at the Old Mission of the Sacred Heart," *Idaho Yesterdays* 2 (Summer 1958): 20–27; Tom O. Miller, "Four Burials From the Coeur d'Alene Region, Idaho," *American Antiquity* 19 (July 1953): 389–390. For an explanation of archaeological periods in prehistoric Idaho, see Leonard J. Arrington, *History of Idaho*, vol. 1 (Moscow and Boise: University of Idaho Press and the Idaho State Historical Society, 1994), 23–32. See also B. Robert Butler, *A Guide to Understanding Idaho Archaeology (Third Edition): The Upper Snake and Salmon River Country* (Boise: Idaho State Historic Preservation Office, 1978); Frey, *Landscape Traveled by Coyote and Crane*, 5.

10. Pre-contact North American population figures vary widely, but recent figures are summarized in D. H. Ubelaker, "North American Indian Population Size, A.D. 1500 to 1985," *American Journal of Physical Anthropology* 77 (November 1988): 289–294. See also Dean R. Snow, "Microchronology and Demographic Evidence Relating to the Size of Pre-Columbian North American Indian Populations," *Science* 268 (June 16, 1995): 1601–1604; Walter Nugent, *Into the West: The Story of Its People* (New York: Alfred A. Knopf, 1999), 22–23; Teit, *Salishan Tribes*, 39–40.

11. Teit, *Salishan Tribes*, 39; Frey, *Landscape Traveled by Coyote and Crane*, 57. For a discussion of virgin soil epidemics and population decline, see Diamond, *Guns, Germs, and*

Steel, 210–212, and Alfred W. Crosby, *Ecological Imperialism: The Biological Expansion of Europe, 900–1900* (New York: Cambridge University Press, 1986), 196–216.

12. Teit's "chief informant" was tribal elder Kruto Nicodemus. Reichard assembled her work with information provided by Dorothy Nicodemus, Julia Antelope Nicodemus, Susan Antelope, Maurice Antelope, Tom Miyal, and Lawrence Nicodemus. Maurice Antelope also aided Ray in his research. Many individuals—both Coeur d'Alene and white—contributed to Chalfant's report, including Lawrence Nicodemus, Stanislaus Aripa, and Andrew Aripa. Teit, *Salishan Tribes*, 25, 95; Gladys A. Reichard, *An Analysis of Coeur d'Alene Indian Myths*, Memoirs of the American Folklore Society, Vol. 41 (Philadephia: American Folklore Society, 1947), 2, 3; Ray, "Native Villages," 99n; Stuart A. Chalfant, "Historical Material Relative to Coeur d'Alene Indian Aboriginal Distribution," in *Interior Salish and Eastern Washington Indians*, vol. 1, Garland Series of American Indian Ethnohistory, ed. David Agee Horr (New York: Garland, 1974), 61, 71, 117, 121, 130, 137.

13. Stuart Chalfant's field notes, compiled from oral interviews, provide a large primary source of tribal reminiscences. Because of its unique nature, notes referring to this section of Chalfant's work will note "Field Material"; the other sections, "Historical Material" and "Ethnological Analysis," will also be distinguished in the notes. Chalfant, "Field Material," *Interior Salish*, 123, 139–140; Walker, *Indians of Idaho*, 65; Richard Scheuerman and John Clement, *Palouse Country: A Land and Its People* (College Place, Wash.: By the authors, 1994), 10–11.

14. Teit, *Salishan Tribes*, 91; Chalfant, "Field Material," *Interior Salish*, 140–141, 148.

15. These conical structures were common to all tribes of the southern Columbia Plateau. Walker, *Indians of Idaho*, 70; Harvey S. Rice, "Native American Dwellings of the Southern Plateau," in *Spokane and the Inland Empire: An Interior Pacific Northwest Anthology*, ed. David H. Stratton (Pullman: Washington State University Press, 1991), 83, 89.

16. Quoted in Chalfant, "Field Material," *Interior Salish*, 139, 140, 142.

17. Walker, *Indians of Idaho*, 70; Sven Liljeblad, *The Idaho Indians in Transition 1805–1960* (Pocatello: Idaho State University Museum, 1972), 12–13; Morrissey, *Mental Territories*, 73. Ramona Ford discusses female authority in North American Native societies in "Native American Women: Changing Statuses, Changing Interpretations," in *Writing the Range: Race, Class, and Culture in the Women's West*, ed. Elizabeth Jameson and Susan Armitage (Norman: University of Oklahoma Press, 1997), 42–68.

18. For a table listing the Latin and Coeur d'Alene names of vegetal foods found in Coeur d'Alene country and a detailed explanation of food preparation, see Teit, *Salishan Tribes*, 88–95. Joseph Seltice inherited his father's narrations, to which he added his own oral interviews and readings in history. Seltice wrote two manuscript versions of the story before his death in 1949, when the collection passed to his daughter, Marceline Seltice Kevis. Kevis gave the records to Edward J. Kowrach, archivist of the Spokane Catholic Diocese, who, with the help of Jesuit priest Thomas E. Connolly, edited the manuscript for publication. Given its provenance, the Seltice account is an important but problematic source. See Bruce G. Miller, Review of Seltice, *Saga of the Coeur d'Alene Indians*, in *American Indian Quarterly* 16 (Fall 1992): 586, for an analysis of the scholarly difficulties associated with this account. Seltice, *Saga of the Coeur d'Alene Indians*, 10, 60.

19. Frey, *Landscape Traveled by Coyote and Crane*, 43.

20. Ibid., 36–37.

NOTES: CHAPTER 1

21. Quotes from Reichard, *Analysis of Coeur d'Alene Indian Myths*, 42; Rice, "Native American Dwellings," 84–89; Walker, *Indians of Idaho*, 70.

22. Ray's findings generally correspond to the organization of nineteenth-century Coeur d'Alene villages as recounted to Stuart Chalfant by Stanislaus Aripa and Louis Luke. Chalfant, "Field Material" and "Ethnological Analysis," *Interior Salish*, 118, 124–126, 140–141; Ray, "Native Villages," 116, 130–133; Frey, *Landscape Traveled by Coyote and Crane*, 42.

23. Reichard, *Analysis of Coeur d'Alene Indian Myths*, 42.

24. The chieftainship was determined by a combination of tribal status, wealth, marriage, and political consensus. Teit, *Salishan Tribes*, 152; Seltice, *Saga of the Coeur d'Alene Indians*, 42; Frey, *Landscape Traveled by Coyote and Crane*, 44–45.

25. Frey, *Landscape Traveled by Coyote and Crane*, 48.

26. Ibid., 46. On evaluating female authority in Native American societies, see Devon A. Mihesauh, "Commonality of Difference: American Indian Women and History," *American Indian Quarterly* 20 (Winter 1996): 15–28; Ford, "Native American Women," 42–68; Albert L. Hurtado, "Settler Women and Frontier Women: The Unsettling Past of Western Women's History," *Frontiers* 22 (September 2001): 1–6; Lillian A. Ackerman, "Sexual Equality on the Colville Indian Reservation in Traditional and Contemporary Contexts," in *Women in Pacific Northwest History: An Anthology*, ed. Karen J. Blair (Seattle: University of Washington Press, 1988), 152–169.

27. Morrissey, *Mental Territories*, 70.

28. Carl Waldman, *Atlas of the North American Indian*, rev. ed. (New York: Checkmark Books, 2000), 64.

29. Alvin M. Josephy Jr., *The Nez Perce Indians and the Opening of the Northwest* (Boston: Houghton Mifflin, 1997), 28; Crosby, *Ecological Imperialism*, 182–183; Frank Bergon, ed., *The Journals of Lewis and Clark* (New York: Penguin Books, 1989), 403–404; Clifford E. Trafzer and Richard D. Scheuerman, *Renegade Tribe: The Palouse Indians and the Invasion of the Inland Pacific Northwest* (Pullman: Washington State University Press, 1986), 6.

30. Between 1872 and 1874, 3.7 million bison were destroyed on the Great Plains. By 1889 only about twenty-five remained. For Coeur d'Alene accounts of the buffalo hunts, see Chalfant, "Field Material," *Interior Salish*, 119, 120, 121, 123; Seltice, *Saga of the Coeur d'Alene Indians*, 13, 14, 20. For the circumstances leading to the slaughter of the Plains bison, see Robert M. Utley, *The Indian Frontier of the American West, 1846–1890*, Histories of the American Frontier Series, ed. Ray Allen Billington (Albuquerque: University of New Mexico Press, 1984), 173–174, 227–230; White, *"It's Your Misfortune and None of My Own,"* 216–220. Rodney Frey gives 1876 as the last year in which the hunt took place because of diminishing bison herds. Frey, *Landscape Traveled by Coyote and Crane*, 56.

31. "Pemmican" was a high-calorie food of shredded, dried meat mixed with fat or bone marrow and stored in rawhide bags sometimes sealed with tree sap. See Teit, *Salishan Tribes*, 94, 151–152; Brown, "Overview of Coeur d'Alene History," 306.

32. Lillian A. Ackerman found that among the Plateau groups of eastern Washington women did not lose power with the advent of the buffalo hunts. See Ackerman, "Sexual Equality on the Colville Indian Reservation," 152–169; Liljeblad, *Idaho Indians in Transition*, 14–18. On the power structure within Plains groups, see Ford, "Native American Women," 58–59; James Wilson, *The Earth Shall Weep: A History of Native America* (New York: Grove, 1998), 247–260.

33. Gary E. Moulton, ed., *The Journals of the Lewis and Clark Expedition*, vol. 5 (Lincoln: University of Nebraska Press, 1988), 206–207, 209, 223, 226–227; Arrington, *History of Idaho*, vol. 1, 74–76.

34. Nicholas Biddle, ed., *The Journals of the Expedition Under the Command of Capts. Lewis and Clark*, vol. 2 (New York: Heritage, 1962), 450 (qtn.); James P. Ronda, *Lewis and Clark Among the Indians* (Lincoln: University of Nebraska Press, 1984), 32, 222–223, 228–230.

35. Biddle, *Journals of the Expedition*, 450.

36. Ibid.

37. Spellings of "Skeetsomish" vary in the Lewis and Clark journals, maps, and edited volumes.

38. Reuben G. Thwaites, ed., *Original Journals of the Lewis and Clark Expedition, 1804–1806*, vols. 4, 5, 6 (New York: Dodd, Mead, 1905), 363, 365; 93–94; 119.

39. Ibid., vol. 4, 363.

40. Although the journals refer to "Waytom Lake," the 1814 map of the exploration, based on the official sketches and journals, identified the lake as "Wayton Lake." Map analyzed using the David Rumsey Historical Map Collection, www.davidrumsey.com. Meriwether Lewis, William Clark, Nicholas Biddle, and Paul Allen, "Map of Lewis and Clark's Track, Across the Western Portion of North America," in *History of the Expedition Under the Command of Captains Lewis and Clark, to the Sources of the Missouri, Thence Across the Rocky Mountains and Down the River Columbia to the Pacific Ocean* (Philadelphia: Bradford and Inskeep, 1814); David Rumsey, "Image Data" for "Map of Lewis and Clark's Track," David Rumsey Historical Map Collection, www.davidrumsey.com.

41. Manual Lisa, whose fort on the Big Horn represents the first post for what became known as the "mountain trade," employed Colter. Colter was involved in wars with the Blackfeet because Lisa's firm angered the tribe by building a post in Blackfeet country in 1810. William Clark as quoted in Bergon, *Journals of Lewis and Clark*, 471; White, *"It's Your Misfortune and None of My Own,"* 119–121; Bernard DeVoto, *Across the Wide Missouri*, with a foreword by Mae Reed Porter, American Heritage Library (Boston: Houghton Mifflin, 1975), 387.

42. Richard White, *The Middle Ground: Indians, Empires, and Republics in the Great Lakes Region, 1650–1815* (Cambridge: Cambridge University Press, 1991), 477–478; Schwantes, *The Pacific Northwest*, 55–56; David H. Chance, *The Kootenay Fur Trade and Its Establishments, 1795–1871* (Seattle: U.S. Army Corps of Engineers, 1981), 90; Donald W. Meinig, "Spokane and the Inland Empire: Historical Geographic Systems and a Sense of Place," in *Spokane and the Inland Empire*, ed. Stratton, 5–6; Ronald H. Bailey and others, *The Old West*, ed. George Constable, with a foreword by Robert Utley, Time-Life Books (New York: Prentice-Hall, 1990), 60.

43. Because Thompson ordered his employee Jaco Finley to advance the fur trade into Coeur d'Alene country and Finley instead established Spokane House, Jack Dozier argued that the employee feared the Coeur d'Alenes too much to attempt to establish the post among them. See Dozier, "History of the Coeur d'Alene Indians to 1900," 18–19.

44. Ross Cox, *The Columbia River*, ed. Edgar I. Stewart and Jane R. Stewart (Norman: University of Oklahoma Press, 1957), 262 (qtn.); Thompson, "Coeur d'Alene," 12; Elizabeth Mary Andrews, "Fort Spokane and Spokane House" (M.A. Thesis, University of Washington, 1924), 33, 38, 42; James P. Ronda, *Astoria and Empire* (Lincoln: University of

Nebraska Press, 1990), 240–241; Jerome Peltier, *A Brief History of the Coeur d'Alene Indians, 1806–1909* (Fairfield, Wash.: Ye Galleon, 1982), 23.

45. Thompson, "Coeur d'Alene," 12.

46. The "trade origin" explanation of the tribe's name has been widely accepted and is replicated in most modern works. Albert W. Thompson argued, however, that this explanation is inaccurate because the tribe already possessed the nickname when David Thompson, the first trader with direct ties to the Coeur d'Alenes, arrived in the Pacific Northwest. A. Thompson contends that the name originated with eastern Indians who traveled West with the fur trade or with unfriendly tribes in buffalo country. Ibid., 11–15. For examples of the confrontational trade explanation, see Frey, *Landscape Traveled by Coyote and Crane*, 12 (qtn.); Brown, "Overview of Coeur d'Alene History," 306; Peltier, *Brief History of the Coeur d'Alene Indians*, 22–23; Wilfred P. Schoenberg, S.J., *Paths to the Northwest: A Jesuit History of the Oregon Province* (Chicago: Loyola University Press, 1982), 26; Dozier, "History of the Coeur d'Alene Indians to 1900," 6–7; Tuohy, "Horseshoes and Handstones," 22.

47. Seltice, *Saga of the Coeur d'Alene Indians*, 43.

48. J. B. Tyrell, ed., *David Thompson's Narrative of His Explorations in Western America, 1784–1812* (Toronto: Champlain Society, 1916), 410.

49. Ibid., 415.

50. Arrington, *History of Idaho*, 88.

51. Map analyzed using the David Rumsey Map Collection, www.davidrumsey.com. Aaron Arrowsmith, "A Map Exhibiting All the New Discoveries in the Interior Parts of North America, Inscribed by Permission to the Honorable Governor and Company of Adventurers of England Trading Into Hudsons Bay" (London: A. Arrowsmith, 1795, 1811); David Rumsey, "Image Data" for "New Discoveries in the Interior Parts of North America, 1811," David Rumsey Historical Map Collection, www.davidrumsey.com.

52. Map analyzed using the David Rumsey Map Collection, www.davidrumsey.com. Arrowsmith, "A Map Exhibiting All the New Discoveries"; Rumsey, "Image Data" for "New Discoveries."

53. DeVoto, *Across the Wide Missouri*, 68–71; Chalfant, "Field Material," *Interior Salish*, 120, 158; Schwantes, *The Pacific Northwest*, 64; Charles Sellers, *The Market Revolution: Jacksonian America, 1815–1846* (New York: Oxford University Press, 1991), 411.

54. Chalfant, "Field Material," *Interior Salish*, 148; Walker, *Indians of Idaho*, 144; Beverly Hungry Wolf, *The Ways of My Grandmothers* (New York: Quill, 1982), 68–69; Seltice, *Saga of the Coeur d'Alene Indians*, 14. Coeur d'Alene involvement in territorial battles probably accounts for the Jesuit observation that they were "a fierce and warlike tribe until the coming of the Blackrobes." See Robert Ignatius Burns, S.J., "Pere Joset's Account of the Indian War of 1858," *Pacific Northwest Quarterly* 38 (October 1947): 287.

55. Chalfant, "Field Material," *Interior Salish*, 148–149; Seltice, *Saga of the Coeur d'Alene Indians*, 192–198; 288n.

56. Chalfant, "Field Material," *Interior Salish*, 153–154.

57. The Nez Perce were the most populous group in the Coeur d'Alene neighborhood, and their territorial range of approximately 27,000 square miles brought them into conflict with several tribes. Alvin M. Josephy Jr., *The Nez Perce Indians and the Opening of the Northwest* (New Haven: Yale University Press, 1965), 20; Walker, *Indians of Idaho*, 70; Chalfant, "Field Material," *Interior Salish*, 111.

58. Teit, *Salishan Tribes*, 101.

59. Seltice, *Saga of the Coeur d'Alene Indians*, 42.

60. Chalfant, "Ethnological Analysis," *Interior Salish*, 182–183; Walker, *Indians of Idaho*, 123; Frey, *Landscape Traveled by Coyote and Crane*, 296–299n.

61. Trafzer and Scheuerman, *Renegade Tribe*, 26; Department of Interior, Bureau of Indian Affairs Planning Support Group, *Coeur d'Alene Indian Reservation: Human and Natural Resource Supportive Data*, Report no. 238 (Billings, Mont.: BIA Planning Support Group, 1976), 8.

62. Frey, *Landscape Traveled by Coyote and Crane*, 73; Charles A. Geyer, "Transcript of Charles A. Geyer's account of his visit to Spokane House and the Tshimikan Mission in the winter of 1843," (Charles A. Geyer Papers, Eastern Washington University, Cheney, Washington).

63. Ibid., 299n.

64. The Flathead people have a similar "Black Robe" prophecy. For a discussion of the role of prophecy among the Coeur d'Alenes and the Roman Catholic Church's position on Native prophecy, see Edward J. Kowrach, "Epilogue on Prophecy," in Seltice, *Saga of the Coeur d'Alene Indians*, 289–296. For accounts of Circling Raven's prophetic visions, see Seltice, *Saga of the Coeur d'Alene Indians*, 13–17, 19, 27, 33, 268n; Frey, *Landscape Traveled by Coyote and Crane*, 62; Hale, *Bloodlines*, xv.

CHAPTER 2

1. Quoted in Seltice, *Saga of the Coeur d'Alene Indians*, 33.

2. Robert Ignatius Burns, S.J., *The Jesuits and the Indian Wars of the Northwest* (New Haven: Yale University Press, 1966), 55; Schoenberg, *Paths to the Northwest*, 57.

3. Burns, *Indian Wars of the Northwest*, 36.

4. On the history and influence of the modern Society of Jesus, see www.jesuit.org.

5. Schoenberg, *Paths to the Northwest*, 17–18, 21–22; Peter J. De Smet, S.J. *New Indian Sketches* (New York: P. J. Kennedy, 1904; facsimile reprint, Seattle: Shorey Book Store, 1971), 62; Robert Donald Weaver, "A Preliminary Study of Archaeological Relationships at the Mission of the Sacred Heart of Jesus to the Coeur d'Alene Indians" (M.A. Thesis, University of Idaho, 1976), 13, 14.

6. Ted Fortier, *Religion and Resistance in the Encounter Between the Coeur d'Alene Indians and Jesuit Missionaries*, Native American Studies no. 10 (Lewiston, N.Y.: Edwin Mellon, 2002), 48–49 (qtn.).

7. The Jesuits did not found the first Catholic mission in the Pacific Northwest. Francis Norbert Blanchet and Modeste Demers established a mission north of Fort Vancouver in 1838. Schwantes, *The Pacific Northwest*, 81–82; Donald W. Meinig, *The Great Columbia Plain: A Historical Geography, 1805–1910*, Emil and Kathleen Sick Lecture Book Series in Western History and Biography (Seattle: University of Washington Press, 1968), 125–128; Howard L. Harrod, *Mission Among the Blackfeet* (Norman: University of Oklahoma Press, 1971), 23; Frederick E. Hoxie, "The Curious Story of the Reformers and the American Indians," in *Indians in American History: An Introduction*, ed. Hoxie (Arlington Heights, Ill.: Harlan Davidson, 1988), 214–215; Carlos A. Schwantes, *In Mountain Shadows: A History of Idaho* (Lincoln: University of Nebraska Press, 1991), 34–35.

8. White, *"It's Your Misfortune and None of My Own,"* 71–72; Schoenberg, *Paths to the Northwest*, 3–4.

9. Robert H. Ruby and John A. Brown, *Half-Sun on the Columbia: A Biography of Chief Moses* (Norman: University of Oklahoma Press, 1965), 7–8, 24; William T. Hagan, "How the West Was Lost," in *Indians in American History*, ed. Frederick E. Hoxie, 180–181; Schoenberg, *Paths to the Northwest*, 2, 22.

10. Weaver, "Preliminary Study of Archaeological Relationships," 7–8; Jacqueline Peterson with Laura Peers, *Sacred Encounters: Father DeSmet and the Indians of the Rocky Mountain West* (Norman: The DeSmet Project, Washington State University in Association with the University of Olkahoma Press, 1993), 28, 84; "Reductions of Paraguay" from "The Catholic Encyclopedia," www.newadvent.org.

11. Point's drawing of Coeur d'Alene village appears in Nicolas Point, S.J., *Wilderness Kingdom: Indian Life in the Rocky Mountains, 1840–1847: The Journals and Paintings of Nicolas Point, S.J.*, trans. and with an introduction by Joseph P. Donnelly, S.J. (Chicago: Loyola University Press, 1967), 58–59. For an illustration and discussion of Point's drawing of the first envisioned reduction, see Peterson, *Sacred Encounters*, 84, 92. Also Weaver, "Preliminary Study of Archaeological Relationships," 10, 15–16; Burns, *Indian Wars of the Northwest*, 41–42.

12. As discussed in Chapter 1, Twisted Earth's father, Circling Raven, experienced a prophetic vision in about 1740 that foretold of the coming of the Black Robes. See Seltice, *Saga of the Coeur d'Alene Indians*, 17, 33 for a full transcript of Twisted Earth's fabled speech to De Smet. Joseph Joset's account of the first direct contact between the Jesuits and Coeur d'Alenes refers to the lack of an interpreter. See "History Manuscript of the Sacred Heart [Old] Mission," Joseph Joset, S.J. Collection, Microfilm [M] A8136 (Roll 32), the Pacific Northwest Tribes Missions Collection of the Oregon Province Archives of the Society of Jesus [PNWMC], Microforms and Newspapers, Suzzallo Library, University of Washington, Seattle; Schoenberg, *Paths to the Northwest*, 24–25; Chas. J. Kress to Joseph Cataldo, undated, Joseph M. Cataldo, S.J. Collection, M-A8136 (Roll 28), PNWMC.

13. See "Father Joset's Distance Map of the Early Mission Network, 1849" and "The Interior, 1840–1880," in Burns, *Indian Wars of the Northwest*, 47.

14. Neither Jesuit nor Coeur d'Alene sources offer a clear picture of tribal leadership at the time of Point's arrival. The use of Christian names in Jesuit histories further confuses the matter. Point refers to Chief Twisted Earth as "Stellam," meaning "Thunderer." Twisted Earth, or Stellam, should not be confused with Joseph Stellam, a minor chief who, according to the Seltice history, "was a hold-out to Christianity and a renegade." Seltice, *Saga of the Coeur d'Alene Indians*, 268n; Nicolas Point, S.J., *Wilderness Kingdom*, 47–50; Robert C. Carriker, *Father Peter John DeSmet: Jesuit in the West*, Oklahoma Western Biographies, ed. Richard W. Etulain (Norman: University of Oklahoma Press, 1995), 59.

15. Joset's recounting of the incidence of traditional activities contradicts Point's assertion. Point, *Wilderness Kingdom*, 53, 54, 56, 62, 67; Cornelius M. Buckley, S.J., *Nicolas Point: His Life and Northwest Indian Chronicles* (Chicago: Loyola University Press, 1989), 213–215; Joset, "History Manuscript of Sacred Heart [Old] Mission," PNWMC; Carriker, *Father Peter John DeSmet*, 77; Fortier, *Religion and Resistance*, 7.

16. Frey, *Landscape Traveled by Coyote and Crane*, 62.

17. Indeed, a saying that "five Blackfeet will run from one Flathead" emerged among tribal people in the region. Isaac I. Stevens, "Report of an Exploration of the Country From the Heads of Navigation of the Missouri River to the Pacific Ocean and in the Territory of Washington," 1854-32706, Special Series A, General Records [GR] (1907–1939), Record

Group [RG] 75, National Archives [NA]; Peterson, *Sacred Encounters*, 97–98; Ruby and Brown, *Half-Sun on the Columbia*, 24; Olga Weydemeyer Johnson, *Flathead and Kootenay: The Rivers, the Tribes and the Region's Traders* (Glendale, Calif.: Arthur H. Clark, 1969), 278–279.

18. Certain methods of Jesuit instruction, such as the Catholic Ladder, took advantage of the appeal of Catholicism's ritualistic elements. See Buckley, *Nicolas Point*, 217, 230; Peterson, *Sacred Encounters*, 23–24.

19. Fortier, *Religion and Resistance*, 38.

20. Ibid., 60 (first qtn.), 61 (second qtn.).

21. Frey, *Landscape Traveled by Coyote and Crane*, 36–37, 41, 68. See Carol Devens, *Countering Colonization: Native American Women and the Great Lakes Missions, 1630–1900* (Berkeley: University of California Press, 1992).

22. Peterson, *Sacred Encounters*, 99; Schoenberg, *Paths to the Northwest*, 26; Seltice, *Saga of the Coeur d'Alene Indians*, 35.

23. Joset, "History Manuscript of the Sacred Heart [Old] Mission," PNWMC; Schoenberg, *Paths to the Northwest*, 26; Point, *Wilderness Kingdom*, 56 (qtn.); Frey, *Landscape Traveled by Coyote and Crane*, 73; Buckley, *Nicolas Point*, 217.

24. Schoenberg, *Paths to the Northwest*, 26.

25. For clarity I use the name "Sacred Heart" in referring to all early mission sites in the Coeur d'Alene region, but the sites have differing historical names. Point christened the first site on the St. Joseph River "Sacred Heart Mission," but later it became known as St. Joseph's Mission. When Joset moved the mission to the Cataldo site in 1846, known in Jesuit histories as "Joset's Knoll," the mission name reverted to "Sacred Heart." For an explanation of the varying usages, see Chas. J. Kress to Joseph Cataldo, undated, Joseph M. Cataldo, S.J. Collection, M-A8136 (Roll 28), PNWMC.

26. Peterson, *Sacred Encounters*, 98; Buckley, *Nicolas Point*, 234, 235, 240; Schoenberg, *Paths to the Northwest*, 27, 47–48, 57.

27. The church, now known as the Cataldo Mission of the Sacred Heart, is the oldest standing structure in the state of Idaho. In 1975 the Old Mission became a state park. Joset, "History Manuscript of the Sacred Heart [Old] Mission," PNWMC; Schoenberg, *Paths to the Northwest*, 27, 57–58; Seltice, *Saga of the Coeur d'Alene Indians*, 48–52; Cort Conley, *Idaho for the Curious: A Guide* (Cambridge, Idaho: Backeddy, 1982), 453–457.

28. Joset, "History Manuscript of the Sacred Heart [Old] Mission," PNWMC.

29. Schoenberg, *Paths to the Northwest*, 58, 64.

30. The measles epidemic resulted in the deaths of nearly one in two Cayuse tribal members. Two recent scholarly studies of Narcissa Whitman have provided new insight into this enigmatic woman's experiences. See Julie Roy Jeffrey's "Narcissa Whitman: The Significance of a Missionary's Life," *Montana: The Magazine of Western History* 41 (Spring 1991): 3–15, and her *Converting the West: A Biography of Narcissa Whitman* (Norman: University of Oklahoma Press, 1991). See also John D. Unruh Jr., *The Plains Across: The Overland Emigrants and the Trans-Mississippi West, 1840–60* (Chicago: University of Illinois Press, 1982), 304–306; Schwantes, *The Pacific Northwest*, 69–77; Patricia Nelson Limerick, *The Legacy of Conquest: The Unbroken Past of the American West* (New York: W. W. Norton, 1987), 37–41; White, *"It's Your Misfortune and None of My Own,"* 72–73, 101.

31. Robert H. Ruby and John A. Brown, *The Spokane Indians: Children of the Sun*, with a foreword by Robert L. Bennett (Norman: University of Oklahoma Press, 1970), 66–67, 77–82, quote on 80; Johnson, *Flathead and Kootenay*, 280–282.

NOTES: CHAPTER 2

32. St. Mary's remained closed for sixteen years. The closure of St. Mary's Mission resulted in disaffection with the reduction system De Smet had envisioned in the Pacific Northwest. Johnson, *Flathead and Kootenay,* 279–280; Schoenberg, *Paths to the Northwest,* 47–48.

33. Seltice, *Saga of the Coeur d'Alene Indians,* 37.

34. Charles A. Geyer, "Tshimakain Mission, ca. 1843," Papers of Elkanah and Mary Richardson Walker, 1821–1938, WSU 186, Cage 57, Manuscripts, Archives, and Special Collections, Holland Library, Washington State University, Pullman, Washington.

35. Tuohy, "Horseshoes and Handstones," 27.

36. Point, *Wilderness Kingdom,* 180–181.

37. Ibid., 174–175, 178, 180–181.

38. Either Point did not understand the spiritual significance of post-hunting rituals or he chose to ignore it. Rituals attending the hunt represented respect for the animals and an awareness of dependence on nature for survival and were conducted to maintain balance and to help ensure future success. Point may have recognized that forced removal of traditional practices would do more spiritual harm than good. Point, *Wilderness Kingdom,* 178, 180; Walker, *Indians of Idaho,* 162–163.

39. For an analysis of Coeur d'Alene mythology dealing with food scarcity and dispensation, see Reichard, *Analysis of Coeur d'Alene Indian Myths,* 40–41, 51–52.

40. Point, *Wilderness Kingdom,* 50; Joset, "History Manuscript of Sacred Heart [Old] Mission," PNWMC.

41. John Mullan, *Report on the Construction of a Military Road From Fort Walla-Walla to Fort Benton* (Fairfield, Wash.: Ye Galleon, 1998); originally published as U.S. Senate, Senate Executive Document 43, 37th Cong., 3rd sess., 1863, 42.

42. For a description of early Coeur d'Alene farming practices, see Seltice, *Saga of the Coeur d'Alene Indians,* 158–161.

43. Joset, "History Manuscript of the Sacred Heart [Old] Mission," PNWMC.

44. Seltice, *Saga of the Coeur d'Alene Indians,* 158–161.

45. Joset, "History Manuscript of the Sacred Heart [Old] Mission," PNWMC; Joset quoted in De Smet, *New Indian Sketches,* 63–64.

46. Five Cayuse men gave themselves up in June 1850 to an Oregon territorial court, where they quickly received a guilty verdict and death by hanging despite a lack of evidence regarding each man's location during the murders. Coeur d'Alene tribal history indicates that members disapproved of the Cayuse trial and believed Marcus Whitman was partially to blame for events at Waiilatpu. For two contemporary, anti-Catholic accounts of the massacre, see William Henry Gray, *A History of Oregon, 1792–1849* (New York: The American News Company, 1870; reprinted as part of the Far Western Frontier Series, New York: Arno, 1973), and Nelson A. Miles, *Personal Recollections and Observations of General Nelson A. Miles,* with an introduction by Robert Wooster (Chicago: Werner, 1896; reprint, Lincoln: University of Nebraska Press, 1992), 391–396 (page references are to reprint edition); Trafzer and Scheuerman, *Renegade Tribe,* 27–30.

47. Schoenberg, *Paths to the Northwest,* 43–44; Weaver, "Preliminary Study of Archaeological Relationships," 48.

48. Seltice, *Saga of the Coeur d'Alene Indians,* 53; print drawing as reproduced in Peterson, *Sacred Encounters,* 100.

49. E. L. Stevens, Acting Commissioner, to Sidney D. Waters, Indian Agent, June 16,

1884, Letters Received [LR], Commissioner of Indian Affairs [CIA], Colville Agency [CA], Coeur d'Alene Reservation [CDA], RG 75, National Archives and Records Administration—Pacific Northwest Region [NA-PNR].

50. Seltice, *Saga of the Coeur d'Alene Indians*, 42.

51. Washington achieved territorial status in 1853 after settlers north of the Columbia River requested separation from the Willamette Valley. See Kent D. Richards, *Isaac I. Stevens, Young Man in a Hurry: Washington's First Territorial Governor, 1853–1857* (Pullman: Washington State University Press, 1993), 96–98, 127, 153–154; Stevens, "Report of an Exploration," NA.

CHAPTER 3

1. As quoted in Joset, "Manuscript of the 1858 War," Joseph Joset, S.J. Collection, M-A8136 (Roll 32), PNWMC.

2. Isaac I. Stevens to George Manypenny, December 26, 1853, LR, WS [Washington Superintendency], M-234 (Roll 907), RG 75, NA-PNR.

3. The United States and Mexico went to war in 1846. A victorious United States negotiated the Treaty of Guadalupe Hidalgo in 1848. By agreeing to the terms of the treaty Mexico accepted the Rio Grande as the southern boundary of Texas and ceded New Mexico, California, and all the territory between them to the United States. An 1846 treaty with Great Britain gave the United States all of Oregon to the forty-ninth parallel but awarded Vancouver Island to Great Britain. The material in this chapter has been influenced by the History 422 (History of the Pacific Northwest) lectures of Dr. David H. Stratton at Washington State University.

4. Numbers from Unruh, *The Plains Across*, 84–85.

5. Johansen and Gates, *Empire of the Columbia*, 290–292.

6. Charles F. Wilkinson, *American Indians, Time and the Law: Native Societies in a Modern Constitutional Democracy* (New Haven: Yale University Press, 1987), 54–55.

7. "Annual Report of the Commissioner of Indian Affairs," November 6, 1858, reproduced in Francis Paul Prucha, ed., *Documents of United States Indian Policy*, 2nd ed. (Lincoln: University of Nebraska Press, 1990), 92–95; Johansen and Gates, *Empire of the Columbia*, 306–307.

8. The most comprehensive biography of Stevens is Richards, *Isaac I. Stevens*. A favorably biased portrait of Stevens appears in his son's work, Hazard Stevens, *The Life of Isaac Ingalls Stevens*, 2 vols. (Boston: Houghton, Mifflin, 1900). See also Schwantes, *The Pacific Northwest*, 104–105.

9. Stevens initially listed six tribes east of the Cascades: Coeur d'Alienes [sic], 200; Upper Pend Oreilles [Kalispel], 480; Lowerds, 520; Rock Island, 300; Colville, 320; Okanagan [sic], 250. Isaac I. Stevens to Commissioner of Indian Affairs, "Memorandum in Regard to the Indians on the Upper Missouri and West of Minnesota and in the Territory of Washington," May 10, 1853, LR, Washington Superintendency [WS], National Archives Microfilm Publications, M-234 (Roll 907), RG 75, NA-PNR; Isaac I. Stevens to Commissioner of Indian Affairs, "Report on Condition of Indians From Fort Benton to Olympia," December 6, 1853, LR, WS, M-234 (Roll 907), RG 75, NA-PNR; Schoenberg, *Paths to the Northwest*, 51.

10. *A Comprehensive, Explanatory, Correct Pronouncing Dictionary and Jargon Vocabulary*, 2nd ed. (Portland, Oregon Territory: S. J. M'Cormick, 1853), 11–12, reprinted in

NOTES: CHAPTER 3

Thomas Vaughan, ed., *Paul Kane, the Columbia Wanderer: Sketches, Paintings and Comment, 1846–1847* (Portland: Oregon Historical Society, 1971), 58; Isaac I. Stevens to George Manypenny, December 26, 1853 NA-PNR.

11. Oregon Territory's official census for 1850 showed a population north of the Columbia River of 1,049; in 1853 approximately 4,000 non-Indian people lived in scattered Puget Sound and Cowlitz River settlements. Isaac I. Stevens to George Manypenny, December 26, 1853, NA-PNR; Johansen and Gates, *Empire of the Columbia*, 300–301.

12. Isaac I. Stevens to George Manypenny, December 26, 1853, NA-PNR.

13. Richards, *Isaac I. Stevens*, xi, 178, 195–196. John Unruh estimated that between 1840 and 1860, Indians killed approximately 362 emigrants while emigrants killed 426 Indians along the overland trails. Unruh, *The Plains Across*, 144.

14. Conley, *Idaho for the Curious*, 451–453; Richards, *Isaac I. Stevens*, 323–325.

15. Isaac I. Stevens to B. E. Bonneville, March 28, 1854, LR, WS, M-234 (Roll 907), RG 75, NA-PNR.

16. Isaac I. Stevens to George Manypenny, June 8, 1854, LR, WS, M-234 (Roll 907), RG 75, NA-PNR.

17. "Governor's Message: Delivered to the Legislative Assembly in Joint Session," December 5, 1854, LR, WS, M-234 (Roll 907), RG 75, NA-PNR; quoted in Arthur J. Brown, "The Promotion of Emigration to Washington, 1854–1909," *Pacific Northwest Quarterly* 36 (January 1945): 10.

18. The Treaty of Fort Laramie was negotiated by David D. Mitchell with the Sioux, Cheyennes, Arapahos, Crows, Assiniboins, Gros Ventres, Mandans, and Arikaras. Robert A. Trennert Jr., *Alternative to Extinction: Federal Indian Policy and the Beginnings of the Reservation System, 1846–51* (Philadelphia: Temple University Press, 1975), 3, 31; William T. Hagan, *American Indians*, rev. ed., Chicago History of American Civilization Series, ed. Daniel J. Boorstin (Chicago: University of Chicago Press, 1979), 68–72; Richards, *Isaac I. Stevens*, 190–192; Francis Paul Prucha, *The Great Father: The United States Government and the American Indians*, unabridged ed., vol. 1 (Lincoln: University of Nebraska Press, 1984), 315–318.

19. Isaac I. Stevens to Andrew Bolon, March 23, 1854, Records of the Washington Superintendency (1853–1874), National Archives Microfilm Publications, M-5 (Roll 1), RG 75, NA; R. W. McClellan to Commissioner of Indian Affairs, August 9, 1854, LR, WS, M-234 (Roll 907), RG 75, NA-PNR; Richards, *Isaac I. Stevens*, 212–213.

20. Trafzer and Scheuerman, *Renegade Tribe*, 62; Burns, *The Jesuits and the Indian Wars of the Northwest*, 126.

21. Isaac I. Stevens to George Manypenny, June 14, 1855, LR, WS, M-234 (Roll 907), RG 75, NA-PNR; Trafzer and Scheuerman, *Renegade Tribe*, 46, 48–50.

22. For a legal-historical discussion of treaty making between U.S. officials and Native American groups, see Fay G. Cohen, *Treaties on Trial: The Continuing Controversy Over Northwest Indian Fishing Rights*, Report Prepared for the American Friends Service Committee (Seattle: University of Washington Press, 1986), 32–38. See also Trafzer and Scheuerman, *Renegade Tribe*, 58 (qtn.); Jerry M. Scott, "A History of the Formation of the Colville Indian Reservation" (M.A. Thesis, Washington State University, 1992), 48–49.

23. Isaac I. Stevens to George Manypenny, July 16, 1855, LR, WS, M-234 (Roll 907), RG 75, NA-PNR; Ruby and Brown, *The Spokane Indians*, 91–92.

24. Joset, "Manuscript of the 1858 War," PNWMC; Schoenberg, *Paths to the Northwest*, 61. An edited version of Joset's manuscript appears in Burns, "Pere Joset's Account of the Indian War of 1858," 285–314.

25. Isaac I. Stevens to George Manypenny, June 16, 1855, LR, WS, M-234 (Roll 907), RG 75, NA-PNR; Schoenberg, *Paths to the Northwest*, 61; Richards, *Isaac I. Stevens*, 225–226.

26. Isaac I. Stevens to George Manypenny, June 16, 1855, NA-PNR.

27. For an extensive account of these negotiations, see Burns, *Indian Wars of the Northwest*, 96–123; Ruby and Brown, *The Spokane Indians*, 92.

28. During its early years Fort Colville was referred to as "Fort Colvile" in honor of Lord Andrew Wedderburn Colvile, an English deputy governor of the Hudson's Bay Company. I have used the modern spelling except when quoting original sources. An overview of the establishment and administration of Fort Colville is found in Scott, "History of the Formation of the Colville Indian Reservation," 11–15. Accounts of regional mining activity are in W. Hudson Kensel, "Inland Empire Mining and the Growth of Spokane, 1883–1905," *Pacific Northwest Quarterly* 60 (April 1969): 84; William J. Trimble, "The Mining Advance Into the Inland Empire: A Comparative Study of the Beginnings of the Mining Industry in Idaho and Montana, Eastern Washington and Oregon, and the Southern Interior of British Columbia; and of Institutions and Laws Based Upon That Industry," Ph.D. Diss., *Bulletin of the University of Wisconsin* 683 (1914): 15, 16.

29. Clifford E. Trafzer, "The Palouse Indians: Interpreting the Past of a Plateau Tribe," in *Spokane and the Inland Empire*, ed. Stratton, 65; Isaac I. Stevens to George Manypenny, August 30, 1855, LR, WS, M-234 (Roll 907), RG 75, NA-PNR.

30. Qualchan's name also appears as "Qualchin" in government documents and manuscript sources. Robert M. Utley and Wilcomb E. Washburn, *Indian Wars* (Boston: Houghton Mifflin, 2002), 181; Richards, *Isaac I. Stevens*, 236–237, 420 note 3; J. Ross Browne to Commissioner of Indian Affairs, December 4, 1857, in U.S. Congress, House Executive Document [HED] 38, 35th Cong., 1st sess., Serial 955, 12; Trafzer and Scheuerman, *Renegade Tribe*, 62; White, *"It's Your Misfortune and None of My Own,"* 101.

31. Many versions of the start of the Yakima War have appeared in historical writings. Those sympathetic to the Yakima tribe include Richards, *Isaac I. Stevens*, 239–242, and Trafzer and Scheuerman, *Renegade Tribe*, 62–64. Other historians have blamed the Yakimas and Chief Kamiakin for inciting the bloodshed. Robert Ruby and John Brown subscribe to the latter theory, as represented in *The Spokane Indians*, 94–95, and *Half-Sun on the Columbia*, 32–35. J. Ross Browne's comments are found in a report he submitted to the Commissioner of Indian Affairs, December 4, 1857, in HED 38 10.

32. Isaac I. Stevens to George Manypenny, December 22, 1855, LR, WS, M-234 (Roll 907), RG 75, NA-PNR.

33. Burns, *Indian Wars of the Northwest*, 132.

34. Ibid., 133.

35. Isaac I. Stevens to Jefferson Davis, February 19, 1856, in U.S. Congress, Senate Executive Document [SED] 66, 34th Cong., 1st sess., Serial 822, 5.

36. Antoine Plante was a Hudson's Bay Company employee who became one of the Spokane Valley's first settlers. He operated a ferry ten miles above Spokane Falls; the site became a well-known landmark. Isaac I. Stevens to George Manypenny, December 22, 1855, NA-PNR; Joset, "Manuscript of the 1858 War," PNWMC.

37. Joset, "Manuscript of the 1858 War," PNWMC (qtn.); Burns, "Pere Joset's Account of the Indian War of 1858," 290–291 note 10.

38. Regular army forts remained poorly manned and widely dispersed throughout the antebellum era. No more than 8,000 officers and enlisted men reported for duty in the 2 million square miles comprising the western territories prior to the Civil War. See Utley, *Indian Frontier of the American West*, 53–54.

39. John E. Wool to Isaac I. Stevens, February 12, 1856; Isaac I. Stevens to Jefferson Davis, February 19, 1856, both in U.S. Congress, SED 66, 34th Cong., 1st sess., Serial 822, 37–39 [Wool to Stevens]; 6–7 [Stevens to Davis]. Kent Richards discusses Isaac Stevens's relationship with U.S. Army personnel in "Isaac I. Stevens and Federal Military Power in Washington Territory," *Pacific Northwest Quarterly* 63 (July 1972): 81–86.

40. Trafzer and Scheuerman, *Renegade Tribe*, 71–74; Richards, "Isaac I. Stevens," 86; Ruby and Brown, *The Spokane Indians*, 104–105.

41. Helen Addison Howard, "The Steptoe Affair," *Montana: The Magazine of Western History* 19 (April 1969): 30.

CHAPTER 4

1. Hale, *Bloodlines*, 1.

2. HED 1, 34th Cong., 3rd sess., Serial 894, 169; Trimble, "Mining Advance Into the Inland Empire," 22; Utley and Washburn, *American Heritage History of the Indian Wars*, 203.

3. Isaac I. Stevens to William Craig, March 14, 1857, Records of the Washington Superintendency (1854–1874), M-5 (Roll 3), RG 75, NA.

4. Trimble, "Mining Advance Into the Inland Empire," 32; Jack Dozier, "The Coeur d'Alene Indians in the War of 1858," *Idaho Yesterdays* 5 (Fall 1961): 23–24; Peltier, *Brief History of the Coeur d'Alene Indians*, 30.

5. Joset, "Manuscript of the 1858 War," PNWMC; Burns, "Pere Joset's Account of the Indian War of 1858," 292–294 note 21.

6. Vincent, as stated in Chapter 3, was also known to the Coeur d'Alenes as "Bassa." Joset, "Manuscript of the 1858 War," PNWMC; Burns, "Pere Joset's Account of the Indian War of 1858," 292–294 note 19.

7. Tilcoax later admitted that he had for two years conducted raids against whites in the Walla Walla Valley and had campaigned for intertribal involvement in a general Indian war. Peter De Smet to Captain A. Pleasonton, May 25, 1859, HED 65, 36th Cong., 1st sess., Serial 1015, 141; Burns, "Pere Joset's Account of the Indian War of 1858," 293 note 21; Dozier, "The Coeur d'Alene Indians in the War of 1858," 23.

8. John Fahey, *Saving the Reservation: Joe Garry and the Battle to Be Indian* (Seattle: University of Washington Press, 2001), 72.

9. Howard, "The Steptoe Affair," 30; Unknown to Anderson, February 22, 1908, Chloris Anderson Papers, File 2, Cage 274, Manuscripts, Archives and Special Collections [MASC], Holland Library, Washington State University, Pullman; Erasmus D. Keyes, *Fighting Indians in Washington Territory* (Fairfield, Wash.: Ye Galleon, 1988; originally published in *Fifty Years' Observation of Men and Events*, New York: Scribner, 1884), 21 (page numbers refer to reprint edition); Trafzer and Scheuerman, *Renegade Tribe*, 77; Burns, "Pere Joset's Account of the Indian War of 1858," 296 note 31; Joset, "Manuscript of the 1858 War," PNWMC (qtn.).

10. Covered up at the time and blamed on Paiute tribal people, the massacre has continued to engender controversy and has generated numerous historical interpretations. The classic account is Juanita Brooks, *The Mountain Meadows Massacre* (Norman: University of Oklahoma Press, 1970); more recent interpretations include Will Bagley, *Blood of the Prophets: Brigham Young and the Massacre at Mountain Meadows* (Norman: University of Oklahoma Press, 2002), and Sally Penton, *American Massacre: The Tragedy at Mountain Meadows, September 1857* (New York: Knopf Publishing Group, 2003). For a general history of the Mormons, see Leonard J. Arrington and Davis Bitton, *The Mormon Experience: A History of the Latter-day Saints* (New York: Alfred A. Knopf, 1979), esp. 164–168.

11. Anti-Mormon sentiment persisted in the Pacific Northwest throughout the nineteenth century. When the state of Idaho drafted its constitution, it disenfranchised Mormons on the basis of polygamy. For accounts of Mormon migration and Mormon persecution, see Limerick, *Legacy of Conquest*, 280–288; White, *"It's Your Misfortune and None of My Own,"* 163–169; Johansen and Gates, *Empire of the Columbia*, 412. Regarding Mormon arms supply to Interior Northwest Native peoples, see Browne to Commissioner of Indian Affairs, HED 38, 12; Howard, "The Steptoe Affair," 30. For an examination of the Mormon church's expansion beyond the Salt Lake Basin, see M. Guy Bishop, "'We Are Rather Weaker in Righteousness Than in Numbers': The Mormon Colony at San Bernardino, California, 1851–1857," in *Religion and Society in the American West: Historical Essays*, ed. Carl Guarneri and David Alvarez (Latham, Md.: University Press of America, 1987), 171–193. On the theology of the Mormon faith, see the church-sanctioned LeGrand Richards, *A Marvelous Work and a Wonder* (Salt Lake City: Deseret, 1976), esp. 72–75.

12. Joset, as noted earlier, did not want to make the voyage from Sacred Heart to Walla Walla in part because he feared he would miss crucial watering spots. See Burns, "Pere Joset's Account of the Indian War of 1858," 293 note 19. Steptoe quoted in Howard, "The Steptoe Affair," 30.

13. Trafzer and Scheuerman, *Renegade Tribe*, 77; Seltice, *Saga of the Coeur d'Alene Indians*, 99 (qtn.).

14. McBane, the spouse of a Nez Perce tribal member and son of a Hudson's Bay Company factor, apparently knew of the dangers inherent in crossing the Snake. In Stevens's report to Jefferson Davis regarding the 1855 Spokane Council, the ultimatum was not mentioned. Howard, "The Steptoe Affair," 31; Joset, "Manuscript of the 1858 War," PNWMC; Isaac I. Stevens to Jefferson Davis, February 19, 1856, SED 66, 5.

15. Timothy's message was either delivered in the Nez Perce language or translated from the Nez Perce tongue, a Sahaptian family language the Coeur d'Alenes, whose language descended from the Salish family, would not necessarily have understood. The Nez Perce and Coeur d'Alene dialects are as different as German and Spanish. Walker, *Indians of Idaho*, 21–25.

16. Quotes in Joset, "Manuscript of the 1858 War," PNWMC; also in Burns, "Pere Joset's Account of the Indian War of 1858," 294–295.

17. Seltice, *Saga of the Coeur d'Alene Indians*, 100.

18. Peter De Smet to Alfred Pleasonton, May 28, 1859, HED 65, 36th Cong., 1st sess., Serial 1051, 148.

19. Joset, "Manuscript of the 1858 War," PNWMC; Seltice, *Saga of the Coeur d'Alene Indians*, 100–102; Carl P. Schlicke, *General George Wright: Guardian of the Pacific Coast* (Norman: University of Oklahoma Press, 1988), 148.

20. Joset, "Manuscript of the 1858 War," PNWMC.

21. Joset, "Manuscript of the 1858 War," and Keyes, *Fighting Indians in Washington Territory*, 26, 27; Seltice, *Saga of the Coeur d'Alenes*, 102–105; Edward Steptoe to W. W. Mackall, May 23, 1858, reproduced in T. C. Elliott, "Steptoe Butte and Steptoe Battlefield," *Washington Historical Quarterly* 18 (October 1972): 249–250.

22. Joset, "Manuscript of the 1858 War," PNWMC; Seltice, *Saga of the Coeur d'Alene Indians*, 102–105.

23. The site of Steptoe's "last stand" should not be confused with the regionally familiar landmark known as "Steptoe's Butte." See Elliott, "Steptoe Butte and Steptoe Battlefield," 243–245, 248; Edward Steptoe to W. W. Mackall, May 23, 1858, in ibid., 251 (qtn.); Burns, *Indian Wars of the Northwest*, 228–229.

24. Keyes, *Fighting Indians in Washington Territory*, 21.

25. Ye Galleon Press Staff (?) to Chloris Anderson, February 22, 1908, Chloris Anderson Papers, 1905–1909, File 2, Cage 274, MASC, Washington State University; George W. Fuller, *A History of the Pacific Northwest With Special Emphasis on the Inland Empire*, 2nd rev. ed. (New York: Alfred A. Knopf, 1960), 248; Seltice, *Saga of the Coeur d'Alene Indians*, 109 (qtn.), 109–110; Frey, *Landscape Traveled by Coyote and Crane*, 79–78; Trafzer and Scheuerman, *Renegade Tribe*, 82–83.

26. Fahey, *Saving the Reservation*, 73.

27. Seltice, *Saga of the Coeur d'Alene Indians*, 112 (qtn.); Fuller, *History of the Pacific Northwest*, 249; John Mullan, "Topographical Memoir and Map of Colonel Wright's Campaign Against the Indians of Oregon and Washington," SED 2, 35th Cong., 2nd sess., Serial 984, 59–60.

28. Burns, *Indian Wars of the Northwest*, 229.

29. Ibid., 230; Joset, "Manuscript of the 1858 War," PNWMC.

30. Burns, *Indian Wars of the Northwest*, 230; Joset, "Manuscript of the 1858 War," PNWMC.

31. The Jesuits were considering abandoning Sacred Heart Mission because of Coeur d'Alene involvement in the battle with Steptoe. Newman S. Clarke to Joseph Joset, June 27, 1858, Joseph Joset, S.J. Collection, M-A8136 (Roll 32), PNWMC (qtn.); Trafzer and Scheuerman, *Renegade Tribe*, 84; Fuller, *History of the Pacific Northwest*, 251; Peltier, *Brief History of the Coeur d'Alene Indians*, 33.

32. Seltice, *Saga of the Coeur d'Alene Indians*, 117 (Vincent qtn.); Joset, "Manuscript of the 1858 War," PNWMC.

33. Seltice, *Saga of the Coeur d'Alene Indians*, 125; Keyes, *Fighting Indians in Washington Territory*, 26, 27.

34. For a detailed account of the Wright battles, see Burns, *The Jesuits and the Indian Wars of the Northwest*, 287–309; see also Johansen and Gates, *Empire of the Columbia*, 312. The Wright campaign is drawn from three primary sources: Joset, "Manuscript of the 1858 War," PNWMC; Keyes, *Fighting Indians in Washington Territory*, 21–27 (qtns. on 26 and 27, respectively); and Seltice, *Saga of the Coeur d'Alene Indians*, 120–129, 129 (qtn.).

35. Keyes, *Fighting Indians in Washington Territory*, 27–28.

36. Jesuit historian Robert Ignatius Burns has written that, in essence, Wright "had lost the war." Burns credits Father Joset for convincing the Indians to discontinue fighting. See Burns, *Indian Wars of the Northwest*, 297, 301. Conversely, in his biography of General

George Wright, Carl P. Schlike describes the Wright campaign as an unqualified military success. See Schlike, *General George Wright*, 175.

37. Dozier, "The Coeur d'Alene Indians in the War of 1858," 28–29; Joset, "Manuscript of the 1858 War," PNWMC; Keyes, *Fighting Indians in Washington Territory*, 28–29.

38. George Wright to Joseph Joset, September 10, 1858, Joseph Joset, S.J. Collection, M-A8136 (Roll 32), PNWMC.

39. Seltice, *Saga of the Coeur d'Alene Indians*, 130–131.

40. The original treaty resides in the Joseph Joset, S.J. Collection of the Oregon Province Archives of the Society of Jesus, Foley Center Library, Gonzaga University, Spokane, Washington. Published copies are in the Government Document Serial Sets. "Preliminary Articles of a Treaty of Peace and Friendship Between the United States and the Coeur d'Alene Indians," Joseph Joset, S.J. Collection, M-A8136 (Roll 32), PNWMC; "Preliminary Articles of a Treaty of Peace and Friendship Between the United States and the Coeur d'Alene Indians," HED 65, 36th Cong., 1st sess., Serial 1051, 89; Seltice, *Saga of the Coeur d'Alene Indians*, 337–339; Burns, *Indian Wars of the Northwest*, 309–310.

41. Descriptions of the treaty council appear in Seltice, *Saga of the Coeur d'Alene Indians*, 140–150; Keyes, *Fighting Indians in Washington Territory*, 30–31; Joset, "Manuscript of the 1858 War," PNWMC; Peltier, *Brief History of the Coeur d'Alene Indians*, 42–44.

42. Burns, *Indian Wars of the Northwest*, 310.

43. The insertion of Andrew Seltice's name above Vincent's "x-mark" on the Coeur d'Alene peace treaty in published government document versions accounts for the admission by some scholars, such as James A. Teit, that Seltice, not Vincent, was head chief during the 1858 war. See Burns, "Pere Joset's Account of the War of 1858," 304 note 68; Teit, *Salishan Tribes*, 153.

44. Joset, "Manuscript of the 1858 War," PNWMC; Keyes, *Fighting Indians in Washington Territory*, 32–35; Fuller, *History of the Pacific Northwest*, 257–259.

45. George Wright to Joseph Joset, September 19, 1858, Joseph Joset, S.J. Collection, M-A8136 (Roll 32), PNWMC; Keyes, *Fighting Indians in Washington Territory*, 30.

CHAPTER 5

1. Mullan, *Report on the Construction of a Military Road*, 52.
2. Prucha, *The Great Father*, 479–483.
3. William Harney to General Winfield Scott, October 24, 1858, George Wright to Alfred Pleasonton, October 28, 1858, HED 65, 36th Cong., 1st sess., Serial 1051, 86, 88.
4. Stevens's treaties were Medicine Creek (December 1854), Point Elliott (January 1855), Point No Point (January 1855), Neah Bay (January 1855), Walla Walla (June 1855), Yakima (June 1855), Nez Perce (June 1855), Hell Gate (July 1855), and Blackfeet Peace Treaty (October 1855). See Prucha, *The Great Father*, 404–406.
5. Ibid., 404–406, 408; Seltice, *Saga of the Coeur d'Alene Indians*, 155.
6. William Harney to Winfield Scott, June 1, 1859, Peter De Smet to Alfred Pleasonton, May 25, 1859, HED 65, 140–141; Carriker, *Father Peter John DeSmet*, 157.
7. Peter De Smet to Alfred Pleasonton, May 25, 1859, HED 65, 143; For a copy of the peace treaty signed by Coeur d'Alene chieftains and U.S. military officials in September 1858, see HED 65, 36th Cong., 1st sess., Serial 1051, 89.
8. De Smet's efforts on behalf of the Coeur d'Alenes and Sacred Heart Mission, and the emergence of the tribe as "civilized" following the 1858 hostilities, appear in stark

contrast to the postwar experiences of Kamiakin's Yakima band and the Palouse Tribe. See Trafzer and Scheuerman, *Renegade Tribe,* 91, 94–95, 102; Peter De Smet to Alfred Pleasonton, May 25, 1859, HED 65, 141–143; Burns, "Pere Joset's Account of the Indian War of 1858," 304 note 67 (qtn.).

9. Peter De Smet to Alfred Pleasonton, May 25, 1859, William Harney to Winfield Scott, June 1, 1859, HED 65, 140–141; De Smet quoted in Peltier, *Brief History of the Coeur d'Alene Indians,* 50; Brown, "Overview of Coeur d'Alene History," 307, 313.

10. Seltice, *Saga of the Coeur d'Alene Indians,* 9; Fahey, *Saving the Reservation,* 78–79.

11. Carriker, *Father Peter John DeSmet,* 160.

12. William Harney to Winfield Scott, June 1, 1859, HED 65, 140 (qtn.); Schoenberg, *Paths to the Northwest,* 72; Brown, "Overview of Coeur d'Alene History," 312. The original photos of the Fort Vancouver delegation, as well as the manipulated versions, are housed in the Oregon Province Archives of the Society of Jesus, Foley Center Library, Gonzaga University, Spokane, Washington.

13. Peter De Smet to Alfred Pleasonton, May 28, 1859, HED 65, 148. The letter also appears in De Smet, *New Indian Sketches,* 141–146, 146 (qtn.).

14. Ibid.

15. De Smet correspondence as analyzed in Carriker, *Father Peter John DeSmet,* 157–158.

16. Alfred Pleasonton to Peter De Smet, June 1, 1859, in De Smet, *New Indian Sketches,* 136; Scheuerman and Clement, *Palouse Country,* 21; James M. McPherson, *Battle Cry of Freedom: The Civil War Era* (New York: Oxford University Press, 1988), 532.

17. John Mullan, Report on the "Military Road Expedition," November 1, 1860, HED 29, 36th Cong., 2nd sess., Serial 1097, 80 (qtn.).

18. Joset, "Manuscript of the 1858 War," PNWMC; Burns, "Pere Joset's Account of the Indian War of 1858," 306 notes 76, 77; Conley, *Idaho for the Curious,* 451–453; Schoenberg, *Paths to the Northwest,* 58–59.

19. Map enclosures in Mullan, *Report on the Construction of a Military Road,* especially "Map of Military Road" and "Map of the Mountain Section."

20. William N. Bischoff, S.J., "The Coeur d'Alene Country, 1805–1892: An Historical Sketch," in *Interior Salish and Eastern Washington Indians,* vol. 1, Garland Series American Indian Ethnohistory, ed. David Agee Horr (New York: Garland, 1974; originally produced as part of Indian Claims Commission Docket 81, 1956), 204–205, 208; Johansen and Gates, *Empire of the Columbia,* 323–324.

21. Jos. S. Wilson, Commissioner, to Hon. W. T. Otto, Acting Secretary of the Interior, June 6, 1867, in Charles J. Kappler, ed., *Indian Affairs: Laws and Treaties,* vol. 1 (Washington, D.C.: Government Printing Office, 1903), 836–837; Merle W. Wells, "The Creation of the Territory of Idaho," *Pacific Northwest Quarterly* 40 (April 1949): 117, and "Caleb Lyon's Indian Policy," *Pacific Northwest Quarterly* 61 (October 1970): 193; Schwantes, *In Mountain Shadows,* 58, 64–65.

22. Joseph Seltice's family history lists the location of Coeur d'Alene extended families in 1863 as follows: "four families on the shores of Lake Coeur d'Alene, two families at Hayden Lake, some four families on the south side of the Spokane River and three families along the north side, one family at the crossing, now called Spokane Bridge, two families at Liberty Lake, one at Seltice Lake, one family at Rathdrum, one family at Spangle, two families at Oakesdale, one family at Colfax, two families at Potlatch, two families around De Smet, one family at Benewah Lake, two families some four miles south of Plummer,

one at Plummer, and a few families at Che-mee-wes in the St. Joe River Valley." Seltice, *Saga of the Coeur d'Alene Indians*, 178–179.

23. Ibid., 176–177.

24. Ibid., Wildshoe as quoted in Seltice, 177.

25. See Frey, *Landscape Traveled by Coyote and Crane*, 247–254, on the cultural importance of ceremonial giving and hospitality in Schi̱tsu'umsh life. Seltice, *Saga of the Coeur d'Alene Indians*, 175, 183–184, 202 (Joset as quoted in Seltice, 175; Vincent as quoted in Seltice, 183).

26. Peterson, *Sacred Encounters*, 100; Seltice, *Saga of the Coeur d'Alene Indians*, 202.

27. Seltice, *Saga of the Coeur d'Alene Indians*, 212 (qtn.), 214.

28. Andrew Seltice and Others, Chiefs, to Sidney Waters, April 20, 1884, MLR [Miscellaneous Letters Received], Colville Agency, RG 75, NA-PNR; "DeSmet 60 Years Ago," *Coeur d'Alene Teepee* [CT] 1, no. 1 (November 1937): 6; "DeSmet 60 Years Ago," CT 1, no. 2 (December 1937): 13; Alberta Murray, *These My Children* (Fairfield, Wash.: Ye Galleon, 1976), 43; Burns, *Indian Wars of the Northwest*, 379.

29. From verse 10, line 184, of the poem "Song of Myself," from Walt Whitman's *Leaves of Grass*, published during 1891 and 1892. Whitman's works mirrored trends in postbellum America. See Donald McQuade et al., *The Harper American Literature*, vol. 2 (New York: Harper and Row, 1987), 29–33, 41.

30. For a discussion of post–Civil War economic expansion in the North and West, see Eric Foner, *Reconstruction: America's Unfinished Revolution, 1863–1877*, New American Nation Series, ed. Henry Steele Commager and Richard B. Morris (New York: Harper and Row, 1988), 460–469. An overview of the Republican land bills of 1862 appears in White, *"It's Your Misfortune and None of My Own,"* 142–147.

31. Wells, "Caleb Lyon's Indian Policy," 193; *The Idaho Almanac: Territorial Centennial Edition, 1863–1963* (Boise: Idaho Department of Commerce and Development, 1963), 624.

32. Wells, "Caleb Lyon's Indian Policy," 193, 196, 200 (qtn. from J. S. Reynolds, *Idaho Statesman*, June 14, 1866); Arrington, *History of Idaho*, vol. 1, 220–223.

33. Arrington, *History of Idaho*, vol. 1, 223.

34. Schwantes, *The Pacific Northwest*, 106–108; Bischoff, "The Coeur d'Alene Country," 209–210.

35. Boundaries as quoted in Jos. S. Wilson to W. T. Otto, June 6, 1867, in Kappler, *Indian Affairs*, 836.

36. Johansen and Gates, *Empire of the Columbia*, 331–332; Nathaniel G. Taylor to Orville H. Browning, May 23, 1867, Jos. S. Wilson to W. T. Otto, June 6, 1867, W. T. Otto to Andrew Johnson, June 13, 1867, Andrew Johnson, Executive Order, June 14, 1867, all in Kappler, *Indian Affairs*, 835–837; E. Richard Hart, "The Tribal Claim to Lake Coeur d'Alene," Paper presented at the 1995 Biannual Meeting of the American Society of Environmental History, March 11, 1995, Las Vegas, Nevada, 7.

37. "Sketch of Coeur d'Alene Reservation, West Boundary," Map 356, Tube 290, Idaho—Coeur d'Alene 110, Central Map Files, Cartographic Records of the Bureau of Indian Affairs, National Archives, Washington, D.C.

CHAPTER 6

1. John P.C. Shanks to Thomas Bennett and Henry W. Reed, August 14, 1873, Senate Miscellaneous Document [SMD] 32, 43rd Cong., 1st sess., Serial 1601, 5.

2. Burns, *Indian Wars of the Northwest*, 306–309.
3. Scheuerman and Clement, *Palouse Country*, 21–24.
4. Arrington, *History of Idaho*, vol. 1, 294–295; Schwantes, *In Mountain Shadows*, 68.
5. Prucha, *The Great Father*, 586–589.
6. Thomas J. McKenny to Lewis V. Bogy, April 10, 1867, LR, WS, M-234 (Roll 909), RG 75, NA-PNR.
7. Harvey quoted in Ruby and Brown, *Half-Sun on the Columbia*, 51–53.
8. Kappler, *Indian Affairs*, vol. 1, 915–916; Scott, "History of the Formation of the Colville Indian Reservation," 85–87.
9. Kappler, *Indian Affairs*, vol. 1, 915–916; Scott, "History of the Formation of the Colville Indian Reservation," 87–88; Ruby and Brown, *Half-Sun on the Columbia*, 56.
10. The actual date of the move to the prairie is uncertain.
11. Quoted in Seltice, *Saga of the Coeur d'Alene Indians*, 185.
12. Gary B. Palmer, "Indian Pioneers: The Settlement of Ni'lukhwalqw (Upper Hangman Creek, Idaho) by the Schitsu'umsh (Coeur d'Alene Indians)," *Oregon Historical Quarterly* 102 (2001): 30–36; Seltice, *Saga of the Coeur d'Alene Indians*, 184–189, 234–236.
13. Joset quoted in Ackerman, "Women's Roles in Plateau Indian Culture," 72. For an examination of the influence of agriculture and western ideas of "womanhood" on gender roles in Native societies, see Lisa E. Emmerich, "'Right in the Midst of My Own People': Native American Women and the Field Matron Program," in *American Nations*, ed. Hoxie et al., 143–155.
14. "Senate Resolution," SMD 36, 50th Cong., 1st sess., Serial 2516; J.D.C. Atkins to Secretary of the Interior, February 7, 1888, SED 76, 50th Cong., 1st sess., Serial 2510, 2–4; Palmer, "Indian Pioneers," 26–27.
15. Joseph Joset, "History Manuscript of Sacred Heart [Old] Mission," PNWMC, 56.
16. Seltice, *Saga of the Coeur d'Alene Indians*, 235–236.
17. Quoted in ibid., 235.
18. Frey, *Landscape Traveled by Coyote and Crane*, 89, 255–258.
19. Unknown photographer "passing thru the Indian reserve," "View of tepee in clearing among trees," Negative no. l96-87.60, Northwest Museum of Arts and Culture, University of Washington Libraries Digital Collections, http://content.lib.washington.edu/.
20. John A. Simms to E. P. Smith, October 31, 1874, LR, WS, M-234 (Roll 913), RG 75, NA.
21. Seltice, *Saga of the Coeur d'Alene Indians*, 173.
22. James O'Neill, Report of Colville Agency, July 26, 1879, in Annual Report of the Commissioner of Indian Affairs to the Secretary of the Interior for the Year 1879, 141–144, University of Washington Libraries Digital Collections, http://content.lib.washington.edu/.
23. Seltice, *Saga of the Coeur d'Alene Indians*, 83.
24. The petition did not reach the secretary of interior until March 7, 1873. "Petition of the Chiefs of the Coeur d'Alene Tribe," November 18, 1872, LR, WS, M-234 (Roll 912), RG 75, NA-PNR. A copy of the petition is also housed as part of "The Coeur d'Alene Tribe of Indians v. the United States of America," Claimant's Exhibit 90, Docket no. 81, Records of the Indian Claims Commission [ICC], RG 279, NA.
25. Ibid.
26. Ulysses S. Grant, "Fifth Annual Message," December 1, 1873, in James D. Richardson, ed., *A Compilation of the Messages and Papers of the Presidents, 1789–1902*, vol. 7

(Washington, D.C.: Bureau of National Literature and Art, 1904), 252. On Grant's "peace policy," see Prucha, *The Great Father*, 479–483, and Hagan, *American Indians*, 110–112.

27. "Petition of the Chiefs of the Coeur d'Alene Tribe," November 18, 1872, NA.

28. George Sanford to Assistant Adjutant General, Department of the Columbia, June 1, 1872, LR, WS, M-234 (Roll 912), NA-PNR.

29. Edward R.S. Canby to J. M. Schofield, August 20, 1872, J. M. Schofield to Adjutant General's Office, Washington, D.C., September 24, 1872, William Belknap to Columbus Delano, September 30, 1872, all in LR, WS, M-234 (Roll 912), RG 75, NA-PNR.

30. "Report of Inspection of Fort Colville, W.T.," E. H. Ludington, August 11, 1872, William Belknap to Francis A. Walker, September 17, 1872, both in LR, WS, M-234 (Roll 912), RG 75, NA-PNR.

31. For a detailed history of the military transfer movement, see Prucha, *The Great Father*, 549–560. See also Stuart, *The Indian Office*, 56–59.

32. Office of the Commissioner of Indian Affairs to John A. Simms, July 8, 1872, John A. Simms Papers, Cage 213, Box 1, Folder 4, MASC, Holland Library, Washington State University, Pullman; John A. Simms to Robert H. Milroy, October 30, 1872, Letters Sent [LS], WS, RG 75, NA-PNR; John A. Simms to Robert H. Milroy, November 20, 1872, John A. Simms Papers; Robert H. Milroy to Francis A. Walker, December 15, 1872, Council Minutes of Council held November 1872, Garry and Seltice quotations in Council Minutes enclosed in Milroy to Walker, Council held November 1872, "The Coeur d'Alene Tribe of Indians v. the United States of America," Claimant's Exhibit 91, Docket No. 81, ICC, RG 279, NA; Simms to R. H. Milroy, Nov. 20, 1872, John A. Simms Papers.

33. Charles Ewing to Columbus Delano, June 5, 1873, LR, WS, M-234 (Roll 912), RG 75, NA-PNR.

34. John P.C. Shanks, Thomas W. Bennett, and Henry W. Reed to Edward P. Smith, November 17, 1873, SMD 32, 43rd Cong., 1st sess., Serial 1601, 2; Wilkinson, *American Indians*, 138 note 3.

35. The original orders provided that Oregon Superintendent of Indian Affairs Odenal accompany Agent Monteith to meet with the Coeur d'Alenes. Federal elimination of Oregon superintendency, however, meant Odenal could not accompany the Nez Perce agent. See Stuart, *The Indian Office*, 76–77.

36. Edward P. Smith to Columbus Delano, January 13, 1874, SMD 32, 43rd Cong., 1st sess., Serial 1601, 1–2; John Monteith to Edward P. Smith, August 6, 1873; "Petition of the Coeur d'Alene Indians," both in Docket 81, RG 279, NA; "Names, Post-office Addresses, Occupations, and Seats of Members of the House of Representatives," *Congressional Record*, 43rd Cong., 1st sess., vol. 2, part 6 (Washington, D.C.: Government Printing Office, 1874).

37. John Monteith to Edward P. Smith, August 6, 1873, "The Coeur d'Alene Tribe of Indians v. the United States of America," NA.

38. The St. Maries River was also designated as the South Fork of the St. Joe River on contemporary maps.

39. "Agreement Made and Entered Into on This 28th Day of July, A.D., 1873 at Latah or Hangman's Creek, in the Territory of Idaho," LR, Idaho Superintendency [IS], M-234 (Roll 341), RG 75, NA.

40. Ibid.; John Monteith to Edward P. Smith, August 6, 1873, "The Coeur d'Alene Tribe of Indians vs. the United States of America," NA; Dozier, "History of the Coeur d'Alene Indians to 1900," 89–91.

41. John P.C. Shanks to Thomas Bennett and Henry W. Reed, August 14, 1873, SMD 32, 4–7.

42. Ibid., 5.

43. Jay Cooke, one of the Northern Pacific's early financiers, was also the leading individual contributor to President Grant's presidential campaigns. See Foner, *Reconstruction*, 466–467; Kappler, *Indian Affairs*, vol. 1, 837; Edward Smith to Columbus Delano, November 14, 1873, Sacred Heart Mission Papers [SHMP], M-A8136 (Roll 16), PNWMC, Microforms and Newspapers, University of Washington, Seattle.

44. John P.C. Shanks, Thomas Bennett, and Henry Reed to Edward P. Smith, November 17, 1873, SMD 32, 2–3; Columbus Delano to Edward P. Smith, January 14, 1874, LR, IS, M-234 (Roll 341), NA; "Census of the White Inhabitants Residing Between the Spokane and Columbia Rivers, Together With the Whole Amount of Assessable Property of Those Owning Real Estate," in SMD 32, 10–11.

45. Seltice, *Saga of the Coeur d'Alene Indians*, 233, 236–237.

46. Ibid., 234–236.

47. One of Seltice's farms was located near present-day Tekoa, west of the Idaho/Washington territorial boundary and thus not on the reserve. Confusion over the actual location of the boundary line may have led Seltice to believe this operation was within reservation boundaries. See ibid., 205–210, 230–231; Joset, "History Manuscript of Sacred Heart [Old] Mission," PNWMC.

48. "Spokane and the Coeur d'Alene Indians at Tensed," photograph showing DeSmet Mission in background, L86-1300, American Indians of the Pacific Northwest Photographic Collection, University of Washington Libraries Digital Collections, Seattle, Washington; Dorothy Dahlgren and Simone Carbonneau Kincaid, *In All the West No Place Like This: A Pictorial History of the Coeur d'Alene Region* (Coeur d'Alene: Museum of North Idaho, 1991), 4–11.

49. Sister Ameilee, Superintendent of Providence of Mary Immaculate Girls' School to S. D. Waters, July 23, 1884, MLR, CA, RG 75, NA-PNR.

50. Although only the Wallowa Nez Perce bands were pulled into the conflict, whites did not make any distinction between Nez Perce bands or sometimes even between people of different tribes.

51. Schwantes, *The Pacific Northwest*, 120–122.

52 James Ewart to the Catholic Priests at Cour d'Alene [sic] Mission, June 27, 1877, Joseph Joset, S.J. Collection, M-A8136 (Roll 32), PNWMC, 845–846; Burns, *Indian Wars of the Northwest*, 383.

53. Schoenberg, *Paths to the Northwest*, 111–112.

54. Burns, *Indian Wars of the Northwest*, 395–397.

55. J. Joset to James Ewart, July 4, 1877, J. Joset to John Simms, U.S. Indian Agent, July 4, 1877, James Ewart to Father Joseph, July 5, 1877, J. M. Grunstrut, Capt. Palouse Rangers, to the Priest at Hangman Mission, July 27, 1877, all in Joseph Joset, S.J. Collection, MA8136 (Roll 32), PNWMC, 844–850, 862–863; Burns, *Indian Wars of the Northwest*, 395–397.

56. Citizens of Pine Creek to the Priests and Chiefs of the Coeur d'Alene Indians, June 17, 1877, LR, 1885-6939 (Inclusion 2), RG 75, NA.

57. "Petition of the Citizens of Idaho and Washington Territories," August 25, 1877, LR, 1885-6939 (Inclusion 1), RG 75, NA. Cataldo's notes are quoted in Robert Ignatius

Burns, S.J., "The Jesuits and the Spokane Council of 1877," *Pacific Historical Review* 21, no. 1 (1952): 65–75.

CHAPTER 7

1. Andrew Seltis [sic] and Others to John Simms, October 21, 1883-20347, LR, RG 75, NA, and (copy) MLR, CA, CDA, RG 75, NA-PNR.

2. James O'Neill, "Annual Report of Resident Farmer," August 6, 1880, MLR, CA, CDA, RG 75, NA-PNR.

3. The city's 1881 articles of incorporation designated the name "Spokane Falls," but the community increasingly referred to itself as "Spokane" throughout the 1880s and exclusively after 1890. N. W. Durham, *History of the City of Spokane and Spokane Country, Washington, From Its Earliest Settlement to the Present Time*, vol. 1 (Spokane: S. J. Clarke, 1912), 329, 332, 334, 362; Meinig, "Spokane and the Inland Empire," 13.

4. The state of Idaho retains the divisions created by its territorial boundaries even today. U.S. Highway 95, a mountainous two-lane road, remains the only connection between north and south. Schwantes, *The Pacific Northwest*, 107.

5. Scheuerman and Clement, *Palouse Country*, 24–27; Walker, *Indians of Idaho*, 63–65.

6. Fort Coeur d'Alene's allocation of land occurred outside reservation boundaries. The presence of military forces near Indian lands provided protection to tribes as well as settlers and helped maintain the integrity of reservation boundaries. Ruby El Hult, *Steamboats in the Timber* (Portland: Binfords and Mort, 1952), 20; Dahlgren and Kincaid, *No Place Like This*, 153, 155; Prucha, *The Great Father*, 548–549.

7. Inspector Bannister, "Report of Inspection," May 29, 1886, 1886-14875, Reports of Inspection of the Field Jurisdictions of the Office of Indian Affairs [RIFJ], CA, M-1070 (Roll 7), RG 48, NA; Inspector Ward, "Report of Inspection," January 21, 1884, 1884-2471, RIFJ, CA, M-1070 (Roll 7), RG 48, NA (qtn.).

8. Commissioner of Indian Affairs to Indian Agent John Simms, January 10, 1880, 1879-926, LR, CIA, CA, CDA, RG 75, NA-PNR.

9. Prucha, *The Great Father*, 723–726. For a discussion of OIA corruption centered on the agent's office, see William E. Unrau, "The Civilian as Indian Agent: Villain or Victim?" *Western Historical Quarterly* 3 (October 1972): 405–420. For an analysis of the Indian Service's spoils system on the Colville Agency during the 1870s, see Scott, "History of the Formation of the Colville Indian Reservation," 80–85.

10. Inspector Bannister, "Report of Inspection," May 29, 1886, NA.

11. The annual reports of Colville Agency farmers can be located in MLR, Colville Agency Records, RG75, NA-PNR.

12. O'Neill, "Annual Report of Resident Farmer," NA-PNR.

13. For a brief explanation of the duties of field inspectors and the organization of the Inspection Division of the Indian Service, see Edward E. Hill, *American Indians: Guide to Records in the National Archives of the United States Relating to American Indians* (Washington, D.C.: National Archives and Records Service, General Services Administration, 1981), 121. Stuart gives an expanded analysis of inspections and agency affairs in *The Indian Office*, 87–99.

14. Inspector Robert A. Gardner, "Report of Inspection," November 18, 1882, 1882-22981, RIFJ, CA, M-1070 (Roll 7), RG 48, NA.

15. The Dawes Act served as the guiding principle for Indian reservation management until 1934, when the Indian Reorganization Act outlawed severalty. See Frederick E. Hoxie, *A Final Promise: The Campaign to Assimilate the Indians, 1880–1920* (Lincoln: University of Nebraska Press, 1984). For the act itself, see General Allotment Act, *Statutes at Large*, vol. 24 (1887), 388–391.

16. Prucha, *Documents of United States Indian Policy*, 171.

17. Patricia Nelson Limerick has characterized the Dawes Act as an example of agrarian idealism and the unfortunate belief that in the West, Americans "could declare their independence of a flawed past and make a fresh start." See Limerick, *Legacy of Conquest*, 196–199. For a classic discussion of "the agrarian myth," see Richard Hofstadter, *The Age of Reform: From Bryan to F.D.R.* (New York: Vintage, 1955), 23–36. Robert H. Wiebe gives an account of the effect of urbanization in the late nineteenth century in *The Search for Order, 1877–1920*, The Making of America Series, ed. David Donald (New York: Hill and Wang, 1967), 11–43.

18. Inspector Gardner, "Report of Inspection," November 18, 1882, NA.

19. "Report of Northwest Indian Commission," June 29, 1887, in SED 14, 51st Cong., 1st sess., Serial 2679, 50–51.

20. Sidney Waters to Spokane Falls Mayor and Common Council, May 30, 1884, MLR, CA, CDA, RG 75, NA-PNR.

21. Asher, *Beyond the Reservation*, 172.

22. Hiram Price to Sidney Waters, November 24, 1883, 1883-21283, LR, CIA, CA, CDA, RG 75, NA-PNR.

23. The Spokane group originally refused to share a reserve with the Coeur d'Alenes, demanding the creation of their own reservation. Finally, in an agreement concluded with the Coeur d'Alenes in 1887 by U.S. commissioners John V. Wright, Jarred W. Daniels, and Henry W. Andrews and ratified in March 1891 (see following chapters), provision was made for the "Middle and Upper Bands of Spokane Indians" to remove to the Coeur d'Alene Reservation. Andrew Seltice and Others, Chiefs, to Sidney Waters, April 20, 1884, NA-PNR; Father Cataldo to John Mullan, January 10, 1886, 1886-9353, LR, RG 75, NA; "Message From the President of the United States, Transmitting a Letter of the Secretary of the Interior Relative to the Purchase of a Part of the Coeur d'Alene Reservation," SED 14, 51st Cong., 1st sess., Serial 2679, 68.

24. Inspector Ward, "Report of Inspection," January 21, 1884, NA.

25. Inspector Newell, "Report of Inspection," December 12, 1884, 1884-24656, RIFJ, CA, M-1070 (Roll 7), RG 48, NA.

26. James O'Neill, "Annual Report of Resident Farmer," July 26, 1884, MLR, CA, CDA, RG 75, NA-PNR.

27. Sidney Waters, "Monthly Report of Indian Agent," November 3, 1884, MLR, CA, CDA, RG 75, NA-PNR.

28. Sidney Waters per James O'Neill, "Monthly Report of Indian Agent," December 1, 1884, MLR, CA, CDA, RG 75, NA-PNR.

29. With this animal-powered mill, it took nearly twenty-five minutes to cut each board. For a description of this device and others like it, see Seltice, *Saga of the Coeur d'Alene Indians*, 48; Florence E. Sherfey, *Eastern Washington's Vanished Gristmills* (Fairfield, Wash.: Ye Galleon, 1978), 18–20.

30. Hiram Price to John A. Simms, March 30, 1882, 1882-5593, LR, CIA, CA, CDA,

RG 75, NA-PNR.

31. Congress passed no general legislation regulating timber cutting on Indian reservations until February 16, 1889, when congressional action permitted the sale of dead and fallen timber only. Prucha, *The Great Father*, 889; Hiram Price to John A. Simms, July 15, 1882, 1882-12298, LR, CIA, CA, CDA, RG 75, NA-PNR (qtn.).

32. Hiram Price to John A. Simms, October 26, 1882, 1882-19161, LR, CIA, CA, CDA, RG 75, NA-PNR.

33. Inspector Gardner, "Report of Inspection," November 18, 1882, NA.

34. William A.J. Sparks to L.Q.C. Lamar, December 4, 1885, 1886-1844, LR, RG 75, NA; M. J. Haley to Commissioner of the General Land Office, November 9, 1885, 1886-1844, LR, RG 75, NA.

35. In 1889 Seltice signed a title of abstract stating that he sold Post land in 1871. In 1894 Post received title from the government for the 289 acres that had become the townsite of Post Falls. Dahlgren and Kincaid, *No Place Like This*, 128, 130.

36. Hiram Price to Sidney Waters, March 14, 1885, 1885-3364, LR, CIA, CA, CDA, RG 75, NA-PNR; Zaccheus Lewis to Sidney Waters, March 30, 1885, MLR, CA, CDA, RG 75, NA-PNR, also in LR, 1885-7683, RG 75, NA.

37. Sidney Waters to Hiram Price, April 2, 1885, 1885-7683, LR, RG 75, NA.

38. Sidney Waters to Frederick Post, March 23, 1885, 1885-7683, LR, RG 75, NA.

39. Frederick Post to Sidney Waters, March 30, 1885, MLR, CA, CDA, NA-PNR; Dahlgren and Kincaid, *No Place Like This*, 128–129.

40. Dahlgren and Kincaid, *No Place Like This*, 22; James O'Neill, "Annual Report of Resident Farmer," July 26, 1884, MLR, CA, CDA, RG 75, NA-PNR.

41. B. A. Brouillet to Hiram Price, August 20, 1881, 1881-14739, LR, RG 75, NA.

42. John A. Simms to Hiram Price, July 31, 1882, 1882-14824, LR, RG 75, NA (qtn.); William P. Chandler to John A. Simms, NLR, CA, CDA, RG 75, NA-PNR.

43. Kappler, *Indian Affairs*, vol. 1, 837.

44. A survey chain is equal to 66 miles, so Baker changed the boundary by 4441.8 feet. Darius F. Baker, "Field Notes," April 5, 1883, 1887-30379, LR, RG 75, NA.

45. Andrew Seltis [sic] and Others to John Simms, October 21, 1883, NA.

46. F. Ross Peterson, *Idaho: A Bicentennial History* (Nashville: American Association for State and Local History, 1976), 101, 105; *Idaho Almanac*, 419; Schwantes, *The Pacific Northwest*, 139, 172. Schwantes includes a map of the Northern Pacific Railroad's route on p. 156.

47. Dahlgren and Kincaid, *No Place Like This*, 153; Hult, *Steamboats in the Timber*, 21, 28, 30, 31; Kensel, "Inland Empire Mining and the Growth of Spokane," 84–85.

48. Lucile Fargo, *Spokane Story* (New York: Columbia University Press, 1950), 151; Bischoff, "The Coeur d'Alene Country," 213–215.

49. Alex C. McGregor, "From Sheep Range to Agribusiness: A Case History of Agricultural Transformation on the Columbia Plateau," *Agricultural History* 54 (January 1980): 11–13.

50. Sidney Waters to Hiram Price, March 29, 1884, 1884-6671, LR, RG 75, NA (emphasis in original).

51. Ibid.

52. Sidney Waters to Hiram Price, May 1, 1884, 1884-9185, LR, RG 75, NA.

53. B. J. Hatch to J. N. Dolph, April 26, 1884, 1884-8664, LR, RG 75, NA.

54. Sidney Waters to Hiram Price, May 11, 1884, 1844-8955, LR, RG 75, NA.
55. Sidney Waters to Hiram Price, April 30, 1884, 1884-8955, LR, RG 75, NA.
56. T. F. Singisen to Secretary of the Interior, April 25, 1884, 1884-8588, LR, RG 75, NA.
57. Hiram Price to Sidney Waters, September 29, 1884, Hiram Price to Sidney Waters, November 18, 1884, both in 15610-1884, LR, CIA, CA, CDA, RG 75, NA-PNR.
58. Hiram Price to Sidney Waters, May 21, 1884, 1884-15610, LR, CIA, CA, CDA, RG 75, NA-PNR.
59. Andrew Seltis [sic] and Others to James O'Neill, August 16, 1884, MLR, CA, CDA, RG 75, NA-PNR.
60. John Atkins to Sidney Waters, April 22, 1885, 1885-6872, LR, CIA, CA, CDA, RG 75, NA-PNR; John Sweeney to Sidney Waters, March 28, 1885, John Sweeney to Sidney Waters, April 29, 1885, both in MLR, CA, CDA, RG 75, NA-PNR.
61. John A. Sweeney to Sidney Waters, June 25, 1885, MLR, CA, CDA, RG 75, NA-PNR.
62. Ibid.
63. Sidney D. Waters to John D.C. Atkins, December 26, 1885, SED 122, 49th Cong., 1st sess., serial 2340, 7.
64. "Trade and Intercourse Act," June 30, 1834, reproduced in Prucha, *Documents of United States Indian Policy*, 64–68; Prucha, *The Great Father*, 653–655.
65. H. M. Lazelle, "Report," July 27, 1886, 1886-21307, LR, RG 75, NA.
66. John T. Wallace to John D.C. Atkins, October 4, 1886, 1886-27104, LR, RG 75, NA; Robert McFarland to John D.C. Atkins, June 23, 1886, 1886-17184, LR, RG 75, NA.
67. Rickard D. Gwydir, *Recollections From the Colville Indian Agency, 1886–1889*, ed. and with an introduction by Kevin Dye (Spokane: Arthur H. Clark, 2001), 109.
68. Ibid., 109–110.
69. Ibid., 14–17.

CHAPTER 8

1. "Agreement With Coeur d'Alene," March 26, 1887, SED 14, 51st Cong., 1st sess., Serial 2679, 68.
2. By "extractive economy" I mean an industrial system dependent on the extraction of natural resources and their salability on the open market. This economy created a culture that valued resources mainly as a source of profit.
3. Bischoff, "The Coeur d'Alene Country," 218–219; Fahey, *Hecla*, 4–5; William S. Greever, *The Bonanza West: The Story of the Western Mining Rushes, 1848–1900* (Norman: University of Oklahoma Press, 1963), 275; John Fahey, *The Inland Empire: Unfolding Years, 1879–1929* (Seattle: University of Washington Press, 1986), 176.
4. For an overview of federal mineral laws, see Carl J. Meyer and George A. Riley, *Public Domain, Private Dominion: A History of Public Mineral Policy in America* (San Francisco: Sierra Club, 1985).
5. White, *"It's Your Misfortune and None of My Own,"* 398; Fahey, *Hecla*, 4; Schwantes, *The Pacific Northwest*, 172.
6. Bischoff, "The Coeur d'Alene Country," 217–220; William S. Shiach, Harry B. Averill, and John M. Henderson, *An Illustrated History of North Idaho Embracing Nez Perces, Idaho, Latah, Kootenai, and Shoshone Counties in the State of Idaho* (Western Historical Publishing Company, 1903), 1040.

7. Earlier, similar subsurface mining enterprises in the West, such as Nevada's famed Comstock Lode in Virginia City, proved devastating to the surrounding landscape. By 1873 Virginia City's water system pumped 2.2 million gallons of mountain water per day. See White, *"It's Your Misfortune and None of My Own,"* 234; Douglas McDonald, *Virginia City and the Silver Region of the Comstock Lode* (Las Vegas: Stanley Paher, Nevada Publications, 1982), 104–105.

8. The defining phrase of prior appropriation is "first in time, first in right." For a discussion of modern legal interpretations of prior appropriation in relation to Indian reservations, see Wilkinson, *American Indians,* 70–71. For an excellent presentation of the process by which California courts overturned riparian for prior appropriation rights, see Donald J. Pisani, *To Reclaim a Divided West: Water, Law, and Public Policy, 1848–1902,* Histories of the American Frontier, ed. Ray Allen Billington (Albuquerque: University of New Mexico Press, 1992), 11–32.

9. Bischoff, "The Coeur d'Alene Country," 263–264.

10. William A.J. Sparks to L.Q.C. Lamar, December 4, 1885, 1886-1844; A. F. Leach to Commissioner of the General Land Office, October 27, 1892, 1893-3191; quotations from A. F. Leach to Commissioner of the General Land Office, November 15, 1892, 1893-3191; M. J. Sexton to A. F. Leach, November 15, 1892, 1893-3191; W. M. Stone to Secretary of the Interior, January 21, 1893, 1893-3191; John M. Noble to Commissioner of Indian Affairs, January 24, 1893, 1893-721; all in LR, RG 75, NA. As described in Chapter 7, Congress did not pass general timber legislation for Indian reservations until 1889. After 1889 the "principle developed that the establishment of a reservation for use and occupancy of the Indians conveyed to the Indians a title in the timber . . ." (Prucha, *The Great Father,* 889).

11. William A.J. Sparks to L.Q.C. Lamar, December 4, 1885, 1886-1844; A. F. Leach to Commissioner of the General Land Office, October 27, 1892, 1893-3191; A. F. Leach to Commissioner of the General Land Office, November 15, 1892, 1893-3191; M. J. Sexton to A. F. Leach, November 15, 1892, 1893-3191; W. M. Stone to Secretary of the Interior, January 21, 1893, 1893-3191; John M. Noble to Commissioner of Indian Affairs, January 24, 1893, 1893-721; all in LR, RG 75, NA.

12. Sidney Waters to Father Tossi [sic], January 13, 1885, SHMP, M-A8136 (Roll 16), PNWMC.

13. John M. Reed, J. N. Batthis, and D. B. Conrad to C. S. Voorhees, December 26, 1885, 1886-4616, LR, RG 75, NA.

14. H. Cartmill to Lucius Q.C. Lamar, December 2, 1885, 1885-29998, LR, RG 75, NA.

15. As historian Patricia Limerick stated, "[W]hether the target resource was gold, farmland, or Indian souls, white Americans went West convinced that their purposes were as commonplace as they were innocent." When nature or Indians interrupted the rewards most white emigrants believed their due as a result of hand work and innocent motives, they felt "aggrieved." Limerick, *Legacy of Conquest,* 41–42.

16. James O'Neill to Colville Agent Benjamin Moore, January 2, 1886, Benjamin Moore to John D.C. Atkins, January 4, 1886, both in 1886-1179, LR, RG 75, NA.

17. Commissioner Atkins listed several specific instances in which the dead and fallen timber rule was exploited, such as the practice of profit seekers in Wisconsin and Minnesota of setting fire to green timber on reservations to classify it as dead. John D.C.

NOTES: CHAPTER 8

Atkins to Benjamin Moore, January 25, 1886, 1886-1179, LR, CIA, CA, CDA, RG 75, NA-PNR.

18. "Under the general regulation announced in Department letter to this office, of May 19, 1882, (Circular copy of which should be on the files of your office) the Indians occupying the Coeur d'Alene reserve are privileged to cut, haul and sell the *dead and fallen* timber, but are prohibited (under the decision of the U.S. Supreme Court in the George Cook case—copy enclosed), from cutting *live* timber on the reservation, except for individual use, or to clear the land for farming purposes." Acting Commissioner A. B. Upshaw to Benjamin Moore, September 22, 1886, 1886-17691, LR, CIA, CA, CDA, RG 75, NA-PNR.

19. For an extended treatment of Whitman County's fairs, see Laura Woodworth-Ney, "Whitman County Fairs, 1887–1944: A Reflection of Agricultural Development in the Palouse Country," *Bunchgrass Historian: Journal of the Whitman County Historical Society* 20 (1992): 5–24. Also Scheuerman and Clement, *Palouse Country*, 27–29; Fahey, *Inland Empire*, 27, 39; Keith Williams, "The Agricultural History of Latah County and the Palouse: An Overview and Three Case Studies," M.A. Thesis, Washington State University, 1984, 24; quotation from (Colfax) *Commoner*, October 7, 1887, 5, November 7, 1890, 2.

20. Andrew Seltis [sic] and Others to the President of the United States, March 23, 1885, 1885-6939 (Inclusion 3), LR, RG 75, NA.

21. Ibid.

22. Ibid.

23. Ibid.

24. John A. Sweeney to Sidney Waters, March 23, 1885, MLR, CA, CDA, RG 75, NA-PNR; James O'Neill to Sidney Waters, March 26, 1885, in 1886-9044, LR, RG 75, NA. Emphasis in original; see note 25 for citation.

25. James O'Neill to Sidney Waters, March 26, 1885, Sidney Waters to Hiram Price, March 26, 1885, both in 1886-9044, LR, RG 75, NA.

26. To the Honorable Senate and House of Representatives of the Forty-Ninth Congress From the Freeholders of Spokane and Whitman County, Wash. T., and Nez Perce County, Idaho, "A Petition Asking for the Opening of the De Smet Mission With-Hold and Allotment of Lands to the Indians in Severalty," circa 1886, SHMP, M-A8136 (Roll 16), PNWMC. The petition is also reprinted in Lawrence Palladino, S.J., *The Coeur d'Alene Reservation and Our Friends the Coeur d'Alene Indians*, with the title "Petition of Freeholders of Spokane and Whitman County, Wash. T., and Nez Perce County, Idaho" (Montana: St. Ignatius, 1886; reprint, Fairfield, Wash.: Ye Galleon, 1967), 1–12 (page numbers are to reprint edition).

27. Ibid.

28. Reprinted in Palladino, *The Coeur d'Alene Reservation*, 2–11 (qtns. on 3, 7, and 9).

29. Reprinted in Palladino, *The Coeur d'Alene Reservation*, 2–11 (qtn. on 11).

30. Traveler, "The Coeur d'Alene Indians: Why Their Reservation Should Not Be Thrown Open," *Coeur d'Alene Sun*, April 6, 1886, 1; a copy also resides in SHMP, M-A8136 (Roll 16), PNWMC.

31. Reprinted in Palladino, *The Coeur d'Alene Reservation*, 1–26, quotes on 10, 19.

32. "Wildshoe" is probably an Anglicized form of the chieftain's name, which also appears as "Welsho" in government documents and Jesuit correspondence.

33. Joseph M. Cataldo to Captain John Mullan, January 10, 1886, House Report 1109, 51st Cong., 1st sess., Serial 2810, 46.

34. John Mullan to the Bureau of Catholic Indian Missions, February 5, 1886, House Report 1109, 51st Cong., 1st sess., Serial 2810, 35–38.

35. The commission originally consisted of Wright, Daniels, and Major C. F. Larabee. After the group completed negotiations with Minnesota tribes, Larabee was replaced by Andrews. H. L. Muldrow, Acting Interior Secretary, to the President Pro Tempore of the Senate, April 9, 1886, SED 122, 49th Cong., 1st sess., Serial 2340, 1; "Ratification of Coeur d'Alene Indian Treaties in Idaho," House Report 1109, 51st Cong., 1st sess., Serial 2810, 2–4; L.Q.C. Lamar to President Cleveland, December 30, 1887, HED 63, 50th Cong., 1st sess., Serial 2557, 1–3; Peltier, *Brief History of the Coeur d'Alene Indians*, 55.

36. John Mullan to J. M. Cataldo, July 12, 1886, SHMP, M-A8136 (Roll 16), PNWMC.

37. "Report of Northwest Indian Commission," June 29, 1887, SED 14, 44–49.

38. "Ratification of Indian Treaties," House Report 1109, 13–15 (qtn. on 15); Ruby and Brown, *The Spokane Indians*, 190–193.

39. "Report of Northwest Indian Commission," June 29, 1887, SED 14, 49–50 (qtn.).

40. Ibid., 50.

41. Ibid.

42. Ibid.

43. Ibid., 51 (all qtns.).

44. Ibid., 52.

45. Ibid., 52–53 (qtns.). Also in "Agreement With Coeur d'Alene," March 26, 1887, SED 14, 67–70.

46. The Bouteliers later Americanized their name, changing it to "Butler." The most complete history of the four white families Seltice adopted was written by the wife of George N. Murray, one of Patrick Nixon's great-grandsons. Although the family history is favorably biased toward those families, it admits that association with the tribe made the families wealthy. Murray, *These My Children*, 51–72.

47. S. E. Liberty to Sidney Waters, July 23, 1885, MLR, CA, CDA, RG 75, NA-PNR.

48. Murray, *These My Children*, 61, 68, 93, 96.

49. A. B. Upshaw, Acting Commissioner, to B. P. Moore, U.S. Indian Agent, October 23, 1886, 27435-1886, LR, CIA, CDA, CA, RG 75, NA-PNR.

50. Liberty quoted in Jesse E. Wilson, Assistant Secretary, to the Commissioner of Indian Affairs, "Statement Relative to the Enrollment of Stephen Liberty, Patrick Nixon, Joseph Peavy, et al., Among the Coeur d'Alene Indians," February 20, 1909, Central Classified Files, Coeur d'Alene Jurisdiction, Decimal File 053, 83454-07, NA.

51. An example is contained in Dolph Boutellier to the Indian Department, February 6, 1889, 1889-5671, LR, RG 75, NA.

52. Murray, *These My Children*, 65.

53. "Report of Northwest Indian Commission," June 29, 1887, SED 14, 54.

54. Ibid., 52.

55. "General Allotment Act," February 8, 1887; "Annual Report of the Commissioner of Indian Affairs," October 1, 1889; reproduced in Prucha, *Documents of United States Indian Policy*, 171–174, 177.

56. "Report of Northwest Indian Commission," June 29, 1887, SED 14, 48.

CHAPTER 9

1. "Council Minutes of the Coeur d'Alene Indian Commission," SED 14, 9.

2. Schwantes, In Mountain Shadows, 124–125; Idaho Almanac, 146.

3. Idaho experienced an average population growth of 94.2 percent every ten years between 1870 and 1920. See Idaho Almanac, 228, 231; Fahey, Hecla, 10–11.

4. John Atkins to Rickard D. Gwydir, July 8, 1887, 1887-16596, John Atkins to Rickard D. Gwydir, September 19, 1887, 1887-24472, both in LR, CIA, CA, CDA, RG 75, NA-PNR.

5. T. Holmes, Resident Farmer, to R. D. Gwydir, July 17, 1887, MLR, CA, CDA, RG 75, NA-PNR.

6. Andrew Seltice to John D.C. Atkins, September 18, 1886, 1886-13973, Special Case [SC] 186, RG 75, NA; "Agreement Between the Coeur d'Alene Indians and the Washington and Idaho Railroad Company," December 29, 1886, 1888-12968, SC 186, RG 75, NA.

7. Ibid.

8. Benjamin Moore to John D.C. Atkins, April 5, 1887, 1887-8795, Andrew Seltice to G. W. Truax and J. Galland, April 18, 1888, 1888-12968, T. R. Tannatt to Senator J. H. Mitchell, May 8, 1888, 1888-12968, all in SC 186, RG 75, NA.

9. Rickard Gwydir to John D.C. Atkins, June 24, 1887, 1887-17688, LR, RG 75, NA.

10. Rickard Gwydir to John D.C. Atkins, August 15, 1888, 1888-21377, SC 186, RG 75, NA.

11. Lee Affidavit, August 17, 1888, 1888-21377, SC 186, RG 75, NA.

12. Fleet [Fleet spelling mistakenly used in affidavit] Affidavit, September 14, 1888, 1888-24309, SC 186, RG 75, NA.

13. William F. Vilas, Secretary of the Interior, to Frank C. Armstrong, Indian Inspector, October 1, 1888, 1888-24666, SC 186, RG 75, NA.

14. Heyburn was elected to the U.S. Senate from Idaho in 1903; he died in office in 1912.

15. "Coeur d'Alene Council Proceedings," October 22, 1888, 1888-27282, SC 186, RG 75, NA.

16. Quin A Mo Say Affidavit, December 8, 1888, 1889-782, SC 186, RG 75, NA.

17. Mars Asellah Clis Clis Tah Affidavit, December 8, 1888, 1889-782, SC 186, RG 75, NA.

18. Mulvern Affidavit, January 9, 1889, 1889-782, SC 186, RG 75, NA.

19. James N. Glover to William F. Vilas, November 21, 1888, 1888-29268, RG 75, NA.

20. Cowley Affidavit, November 27, 1888, SC 186, 1888-29328 (Inclusion 8), Special Case 186, RG 75, NA.

21. Bischoff, "The Coeur d'Alene Country," 254.

22. Detailed treatment of these topics appears in Merle W. Wells, "Idaho's Season of Political Distress: An Unusual Path to Statehood," Montana: The Magazine of Western History 37 (Autumn 1987): 58–67; Wells, "The Idaho Anti-Mormon Test Oath, 1884–1892," Pacific Historical Review 24 (August 1955): 235–252. Dubois wrote his own account: Louis J. Clements, ed., Fred T. Dubois's The Making of a State (Rexburg: Eastern Idaho Publishing, 1971). See also Arrington, History of Idaho, vol. 1, 371–373, 375–380; Schwantes, In Mountain Shadows, 124–125.

23. "Senate Resolution," SMD 36, 1.

24. Coeur d'Alene tribal and governmental population statistics differed throughout the 1870s and 1880s. The Coeur d'Alenes consistently listed their number at more than 500, whereas government sources indicated that the tribe consisted of fewer than 500 persons. J.D.C. Atkins to Secretary of Interior, February 7, 1888, SED 76, 2–4.
25. Morrissey, *Mental Territories*, 80.
26. J.D.C. Atkins to Secretary of Interior, February 7, 1888, SED 76, 6–7.
27. Seltice quoted in John A. Sweeney to Sidney Waters, June 25, 1885, NA-PNR. See also Morrissey, *Mental Territories*, 80.
28. J.D.C. Atkins to Secretary of Interior, February 7, 1888, SED 76, 7.
29. T. J. Morgan to John W. Noble, December 7, 1889, House Report 1109, 51st Cong., 1st sess., Serial 2810, 26–29.
30. Joseph M. Cataldo to John Mullan, May 10, 1889, Andrew Seltice, Regis Captain, and Peter Wildshoe to President Benjamin Harrison, April 30, 1889, both in 1889-14388, LR, RG 75, NA.
31. John Mullan to the President, May 28, 1889, 1889-14388, John W. Noble to John H. Oberly, June 18, 1889, 1889-16405, both in LR, RG 75, NA.
32. Andrew Seltice and Others, Chiefs, to Sidney Waters, April 20, 1884, NA-PNR; "DeSmet 60 Years Ago," CT 1, no. 1 (November 1937): 6; "DeSmet 60 Years Ago," CT 1, no. 2 (December 1937): 13.
33. Murray, *These My Children*, 43.
34. "Report of the Coeur d'Alene Indian Commission," September 1889, 1889-26974, Benjamin Simpson to Thomas Morgan, August 8, 1889, 1889-21998, "Council Minutes of the Coeur d'Alene Indian Commission," August 14–September 8, 1889, 1889-26974, all in LR, RG 75, NA. The council minutes also appear in "Report of Coeur d'Alene Indian Commission, Appointed March 2, 1889," SED 14, 51st Cong., 1st sess., Serial 2679, 5–13.
35. "Council Minutes of the Coeur d'Alene Indian Commission," SED 14, 8.
36. Ibid.
37. Ibid., 9.
38. Ibid.
39. Ibid.
40. Ibid., 10 (qtn.), 11; Telegram from Benjamin Simpson, N. B. Humphrey, and J. H. Shupe to Thomas Morgan, September 2, 1889, 1889-24564, LR, RG 75, NA.
41. "Report of Coeur d'Alene Indian Commission, Appointed March 2, 1889," SED 14, 11.
42. Ibid., 11, 12 (qtns.), 13.
43. Ibid., 11, 12 (qtns.), 13.
44. It is not clear if M. S. Monteith is a relation of the former Nez Perce Indian agent John B. Monteith.
45. "Council Minutes of the Coeur d'Alene Indian Commission," August 14–September 8, 1889, NA, 12–13.
46. "Agreement," September 9, 1889, 1889-26974, LR, RG 75, NA.
47. T. J. Morgan to Secretary of the Interior, December 7, 1889, SED 14, 51st Cong., 1st sess., Serial 2679, 2–3.
48. Ibid.
49. Thomas Morgan to Hal Cole, October 17, 1889, 1889-29111, R. V. Belt, Acting Commissioner, to Hal Cole, October 1, 1890, 1890–1901, both in LR, CIA, CA, CDA, RG

NOTES: CHAPTER 9

75, NA-PNR; "Memorandum in Explanation of the Bill to Ratify Agreements With the Coeur d'Alene Indians," May 8, 1890, 1890-19614, LR, RG 75, NA; John W. Noble to Benjamin Harrison, December 16, 1889, SED 14, 51st Cong., 1st sess., Serial 2679, 1; Dozier, "Coeur d'Alene Country," 7.

50. J. H. Franklin, Acting Auditor, to Hal J. Cole, Indian Agent, March 21, 1892, LR, CIA, CA, CDA, RG 75, NA-PNR; Murray, *These My Children*, 29n, 51, 63.

51. Mark C. Armstrong, Acting Commissioner, to John W. Bubb, February 17, February 23, and May 7, 1894, Andrew Seltice and Pierre Whyhilshow [sic] to Lyman E. Barnes, Stephen Liberty, interpreter, February 3, 1894, LR, CIA, CA, CDA, RG 75, NA-PNR.

52. *Congressional Record*, 51st Cong., 1st sess., vol. 21, part 1 (Washington, D.C.: Government Printing Office, 1889), 260; *Constitution of the State of Idaho, Adopted in Convention at Boise City, August 6, 1889* (Boise: Statesman Printing, 1889). Section 8, article 9 addresses the "Location and Disposition of Public Lands," whereas section 1, article 15 declares the "Use of Water a Public Use." For a legal and historical analysis of Idaho's constitution, see Dennis C. Colson, *Idaho's Constitution: The Tie That Binds* (Moscow: University of Idaho Press, 1991); Howard R. Lamar, "Statehood for Washington: Symbol of a New Era," in *Washington Comes of Age: The State in the National Experience*, ed. David H. Stratton (Pullman: Washington State University Press, 1992), 115–118; Arrington, *History of Idaho*, vol. 1, 421–423; Schwantes, *In Mountain Shadows*, 133–134; Johansen and Gates, *Empire of the Columbia*, 411–413.

53. In 1998 U.S. District Judge Edward Lodge ruled that, by virtue of the 1873 executive order and subsequent agreements, the tribe maintained ownership of the southern third of the lake, which had been taken over by the state of Idaho at the turn of the century. Ken Olsen, "Third of Lake Is Tribe's," *Idaho Spokesman-Review*, July 29, 1998, B1; Wilkinson, *American Indians*, 93–96, 102–103; Vine Deloria Jr. and Clifford M. Lytle, *American Indians, American Justice* (Austin: University of Texas Press, 1983), 203–209, 214–215, 223; *The Constitution of the United States* (Philadelphia: National Constitution Center, 1994), 14, 23–24; Idaho v. Coeur d'Alene Tribe of Idaho (no. 94-1474), 1996 WL 290997, Petitioner's Brief (U.S.S.CT. 1996), 11–12; A. C. Tonner, Acting Commissioner, to Albert M. Anderson, Colville Indian Agent, August 8, 1902, 1902-46912, LR, CIA, CDA, RG 75, NA-PNR.

54. For an overview of the ways in which industrialization impacted the work habits of nineteenth-century Americans, see Herbert G. Gutman, "Work, Culture, and Society in Industrializing America, 1815–1919," in *Work, Culture and Society in Industrializing America: Essays in American Working-Class and Social History*, ed. Herbert G. Gutman (New York: Vintage, 1977), 3–78. See also Paul Boyer, *Urban Masses and Moral Order in America, 1820–1920* (Cambridge: Harvard University Press, 1978), 123–125, 189; Alan Dawley, *Struggles for Justice: Social Responsibility and the Liberal State* (Cambridge: Harvard University Press, 1991), 19–20.

55. The challenge of small farming in an industrializing economy led to the creation of farmers' alliances and cooperatives and provided the impetus for the late-nineteenth-century Populist movement. See Gene Clanton, *Populism: The Humane Preference in America*, Social Movements Past and Present Series, ed. Irwin T. Sanders (Boston: Twayne, 1991), esp. 1–23.

56. For a history of tourism in the American West, see Earl Pomeroy, *In Search of the Golden West: The Tourist in Western America* (New York: Knopf, 1957; reprint, Lincoln: University of Nebraska Press, 1990).

57. *Spokesman Monthly Review,* June 21, 1888, 3; *Spokesman-Review,* August 9, 1891, 9, April 6, 1893, 2.

58. Arthur A. Hart, *Camera Eye on Idaho: Pioneer Photography, 1863–1913* (Caldwell, Idaho: Caxton, 1990), 51–52; Dahlgren and Kinkaid, *No Place Like This,* 186–187, 195, 200, 212.

59. Adolph Hunter, Spokane Camp No. 99 Woodmen of the World, to Captain A. M. Anderson, Indian Agent, July 16, 1901, MLR, CA, CDA, 1897–1904, RG 75, NA-PNR.

60. G. L. Ide, Deputy Marshal, District of Washington, to Major A. M. Anderson, Indian Agent, August 30, 1901, MLR, CA, CDA, 1897–1904, RG 75, NA-PNR.

61. The People of Harrison, Idaho, to President Benjamin Harrison, September 4, 1891, 1891-34538, First Assistant Secretary to John Noble, September 18, 1891, 1891-34538, Hoke Smith to Daniel M. Browning, December 15, 1893, 1893-46760, John Lane to Daniel M. Browning, February 10, 1894, 1894-7250, all in SC 200, RG 75, NA; "Letter From the Secretary of the Interior," HED 158, 53rd Cong., 2nd sess., Serial 3226, 1–18.

62. F. A. English to Albert M. Anderson, October 8, 1898, MLR, CA, CDA, RG 75, NA-PNR; C. N. Bliss to Commissioner, August 24, 1898, MLR, CA, CDA, RG 75, NA-PNR; W. A. Jones, Commissioner, to Albert M. Anderson, Indian Agent, August 25, 1898, 1898-57842, LR, CIA, CA, CDA, RG 75, NA-PNR; quoted in C. N. Bliss to Commissioner, August 24, 1898, MLR.

63. Murray, *These My Children,* 64; Jesse E. Wilson, Assistant Interior Secretary, to the Commissioner of Indian Affairs, February 20, 1909, Central Classified Files, Coeur d'Alene Jurisdiction, Decimal File 053, RG 75, NA.

64. Andrew Seltice, Chief of the Coeur d'Alene, to Major Albert M. Anderson, January 25, 1902, MLR, CA, CDA, 1897–1904, RG 75, NA-PNR.

65. Andrew Seltice, Pierre Willdcho [Wildshoe], Sol Louie, and Peter Seltice to Major Albert M. Anderson, February 8, 1902, MLR, CA, CDA, 1897–1904, RG 75, NA-PNR.

66. Peter J. Seltice to Major Albert M. Anderson, U.S. Indian Agent, April 22, 1902, MLR, CA, CDA, 1897–1904, RG 75, NA-PNR.

67. Thomas R. Cox, "Tribal Leadership in Transition: Chief Peter Moctelme of the Coeur d'Alenes," *Idaho Yesterdays* 23 (Spring 1979): 2–9, 25–31.

68. Quoted in Brown, "Overview of Coeur d'Alene History," 321.

69. Frederic L. Seixas to Albert H. Anderson, April 24, 1902, MLR, CA, CDA, 1897–1904, RG 75, NA-PNR.

70. Ernest L. Stensgar, introduction to Seltice, *Saga of the Coeur d'Alene Indians,* 9.

EPILOGUE

1. Schitsu'umsh, "Overview," Official Web Site of the Coeur d'Alene Tribe, http://www.cdatribe.org.

2. U.S. Census Bureau, *Population, Housing Units, Area, and Density: 2000,* Census 2000 Summary File 1, Idaho—American Indian Area, http://factfinder.census.gov.

3. Ross R. Cotroneo and Jack Dozier, "A Time of Disintegration: The Coeur d'Alene and the Dawes Act," *Western Historical Quarterly* 5 (October 1974): 409–412; Acting Commissioner to William Sams, March 16, 1908, 1908-17109, William Sams to Francis E. Leupp, April 5, 1908, both in GR, Decimal Classification 313, CDA, RG 75, NA; Murray, *These My Chidren,* 53.

4. For an overview of the Coeur d'Alene land lottery, see Jack Dozier, "The Coeur d'Alene Land Rush, 1909–1910," *Pacific Northwest Quarterly* 53 (October 1962): 145–150; Cotroneo and Dozier, "A Time of Disintegration," 412–413, 418. The findings of the Indian Claims Commission, a body appointed by Congress in 1946 to hear Indian tribes' grievances, recognized the supremacy of the 1887 agreement. In 1950 the Coeur d'Alene tribe filed a claim with the Indian Claims Commission. In 1958 the commission awarded the Coeur d'Alene tribe $4,342,778.03 as compensation for the "unjust" amount originally paid to the tribe, as part of the 1887 agreement, for aboriginal lands. Wight, Mitchell, and Schmidt, *Indian Reservations of Idaho, Oregon, and Washington*, 5–6. The Indian Claims Commission documents pertaining to the Coeur d'Alene tribe are housed as "The Coeur d'Alene Tribe of Indians v. the United States of America," NA.

5. "Circling Raven Golf Club" and "Luxurious Resort Hotel," http://www.cdacasino.com; Schitsu'umsh, "Overview," http://cdatribe.com; Fortier, *Religion and Resistance*, 94–96.

6. Fortier, *Religion and Resistance*, 95.

7. David Buford, "Tourism Benefits Significant," *Coeur d'Alene Press*, May 14, 2003, reproduced by Montana Associated Technology Roundtables, http://www.matr.net.

8. "Interview With Carl Wilgus, Tourist Director, State of Idaho," February 24, 2003, The Spokesman-Review.com, Spokane, Washington, http://www.spokesmanreview.com.

9. "Coeur d'Alene Resort Golf Course," Coeur d'Alene Tourism Web site, http://www.coeurdalene.org.

10. Gail and John Nord, "Sediment in Lake Coeur d'Alene, Idaho," *Mathematics Teacher* 91 (April 1998): 292–293.

11. Knight-Ridder News Service, "Paradise Polluted: Tribe Sues Mining Company for $600 Million," *Times-News*, January 2, 1997, B-2.

12. U.S. Court of Appeals for the Ninth Circuit, *State of Idaho v. United States of America*, Case no. 98-35831, Filed 05/02/00, 4736, 4742, http://www.ca9uscourts.gov.

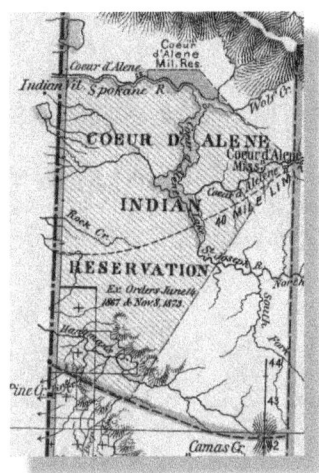

Selected Bibliography

PRIMARY SOURCES

UNPUBLISHED MATERIALS

MANUSCRIPT COLLECTIONS

Chloris Anderson Papers, 1905–1909, Cage 274, Manuscripts, Archives, and Special Collections, Holland Library, Washington State University, Pullman, Washington.

The Pacific Northwest Tribes Missions Collection of the Oregon Province Archives of the Society of Jesus, Microfilm A8136, Microforms and Newspapers, Suzzallo Library, University of Washington, Seattle:
    Joseph M. Cataldo, S.J. Collection, Roll 28.
    Joseph Joset, S.J. Collection, Roll 32.
    Sacred Heart Mission Papers, Roll 16.

Miles Poindexter Papers, Manuscripts and University Archives, University of Washington, Seattle, Washington.

Papers of Elkanah and Mary Richardson Walker, 1821–1938, WSU 186, Cage 57, Manuscripts, Archives, and Special Collections, Holland Library, Washington State University, Pullman, Washington.

John A. Simms Papers, Cage 213, Manuscripts, Archives, and Special Collections, Holland Library, Washington State University, Pullman, Washington.

NATIONAL ARCHIVES—PACIFIC NORTHWEST REGION, SEATTLE, WASHINGTON

Records of the Bureau of Indian Affairs, Record Group 75

Census Rolls, Northern Idaho Indian Agency, 1908–1934.
Farming and Grazing Lease Case Files, Northern Idaho Indian Agency, 1909–1944.
Letters Received, Miscellaneous, Colville Indian Agency, 1879–1904.
Letters Received from the Commissioner of Indian Affairs, Colville Indian Agency, 1865–1909.
Letters Received from the Superintendent of Indian Affairs, Washington Territory, Colville Agency, 1865–1878.
Letters Sent to the Superintendent of Indian Affairs, Washington Territory, Colville Agency, 1866, 1868, 1872–1876.

NATIONAL ARCHIVES, WASHINGTON, D.C.

Records of the Office of the Secretary of the Interior, Record Group 48

General Records of the Office of the Secretary of the Interior, Bureau of Indian Affairs, Coeur d'Alene, 1907–1936.
Letters Received by the Indian Division, 1849–1907.
Letters Sent by the Indian Division, 1849–1907.

Records of the Bureau of Indian Affairs, Record Group 75

General Records of the Bureau of Indian Affairs, 1907–1939, Coeur d'Alene Jurisdiction, Decimal Classified Files:
    000. General and Statistical, 010.–068.
    300. Lands, 303.–339, 370.–377.
Letters Received by the Office of Indian Affairs, 1881–1907, Coeur d'Alene Reservation, Coeur d'Alene Indians.
Letters Sent by the Office of Indian Affairs, 1881–1907, Coeur d'Alene Reservation, Coeur d'Alene Indians, Land Division.
Office of Indian Affairs Special Case 79, Coeur d'Alene Jurisdiction.
Office of Indian Affairs Special Case 143, Coeur d'Alene Jurisdiction.
Office of Indian Affairs Special Case 179, Coeur d'Alene Jurisdiction.
Office of Indian Affairs Special Case 186, Coeur d'Alene Jurisdiction.
Office of Indian Affairs Special Case 200, Coeur d'Alene Jurisdiction.
Report of Isaac I. Stevens to the Commissioner of Indian Affairs Regarding Exploration of Washington Territory, 1854, Special Series "A," Entry 126.

Records of the Indian Claims Commission, Record Group 279

Docket No. 81, "The Coeur d'Alene Tribe of Indians v. the United States of America."

Records of United States Army Continental Commands, Record Group 393

Brief Histories of the United States Army Commands and Descriptions of Their Records, Fort Sherman, Idaho.
Letters and Telegraphs Received, Fort Sherman.
Letters and Telegraphs Sent, Fort Sherman.
Letters Received by the Department of Oregon, 1858–1861, Coeur d'Alene.
Letters Sent by the Department of Oregon, 1858–1861, Coeur d'Alene.

Cartographic Records of the Bureau of Indian Affairs
Central Map Files, Idaho—Coeur d'Alene 110.

MICROFILM PUBLICATIONS OF THE NATIONAL ARCHIVES

Records of the Office of the Secretary of the Interior, Record Group 48
Reports of Inspection of the Field Jurisdictions of the Office of Indian Affairs, 1873–1900, Microfilm 1070:
    Colville Agency, Roll 7.
    Idaho Superintendency, Roll 20.
    Washington Superintendency, Roll 56.

Records of the Bureau of Indian Affairs, Record Group 75
Letters Received by the Office of Indian Affairs, 1824–1881, Idaho Superintendency, Microfilm 234, Rolls 337–353; Washington Superintendency, Microfilm 234, Rolls 907–920.
Records of the Washington Superintendency, 1853–1874, Microfilm 5:
    Copies and Drafts of Letters Sent, 1853–1874, Rolls 1–6.
    Letters From the Commissioner of Indian Affairs, 1853–1874, Rolls 7–8.
    Letters From Employees Assigned to the Colville Agency, 1854–1874, Roll 20.
Superintendents' Annual Narrative and Statistical Reports From Field Jurisdictions of the Bureau of Indian Affairs, 1907–1938, Coeur d'Alene Jurisdiction, Microfilm 1011, Roll 22.

Records of the Office of the Adjutant General, Record Group 94
Letters Received by the Office of the Adjutant General (Main Series), 1881–1889, "Papers and Copies of Reports Relating to White Intruders on the Coeur d'Alene Reservation, Idaho," File 2889 AGO 1887, Microfilm 689, Roll 533.

PUBLISHED SOURCES

GOVERNMENT DOCUMENTS

Constitution of the State of Idaho, Adopted in Convention at Boise City, August 6, 1889. Boise: Statesman Printing, 1889.
The Constitution of the United States. Philadelphia: National Constitution Center, 1994.
General Allotment Act. *Statutes at Large.* Vol. 24 (1887), 388–391.
U.S. Congress. *Congressional Record.* Vol. 2, part 6. Washington, D.C.: Government Printing Office, 1874.
———. *Congressional Record.* Vol. 21, part 1, index. Washington, D.C.: Government Printing Office, 1889.
———. Senate. "Indian Disturbances in the Territory of Washington and Oregon." Executive Document 66. 34th Cong., 1st sess., Serial 822, 1–68.
———. House. "Annual Report of the Secretary of War, 1856." Executive Document 1. 34th Cong., 3rd sess., Serial 894, 3–405.
———. House. "Indian War in Oregon and Washington Territory." Executive Document 38. 35th Cong., 1st sess., Serial 955, 1–66.

———. Senate. "Topographical Memoir and Map of Colonel Wright's Campaign Against the Indians of Oregon and Washington." Executive Document 2. 35th Cong., 2nd sess., Serial 984, 1–60.

———. House. "Correspondence With General Harney, Relating to Affairs in the Department of Oregon." Executive Document 65. 36th Cong., 1st sess., Serial 1051, 1–269.

———. House. "Indian Depredations in Oregon and Washington." Executive Document 29. 36th Cong., 2nd sess., Serial 1097, 1–90.

———. House. "Proposed Indian Reservations in Idaho and Washington Territories." Executive Document 102. 43rd Cong., 1st sess., Serial 1601, 1–11.

———. Senate. "Letter From the Secretary of the Interior, in Relation to a Bill to Create a Reservation in the Territory of Washington for the Coeur d'Alene and Other Indian Tribes." Miscellaneous Document 32. 43rd Cong., 1st sess., Serial 1601, 1–11.

———. House. "Report From the Chief of Engineers of an Examination of Coeur d'Alene Lake and River, and of Saint Joseph's River, Idaho." Executive Document 178. 48th Cong., 2nd sess., Serial 2303, 1–3.

———. Senate. "Correspondence on Claims of Certain Indians for Compensation for Lands." Executive Document 122. 49th Cong., 1st sess., Serial 2340, 1–7.

———. House. "Report on the Washington and Idaho Railroad Company." Report No. 4133. 49th Cong., 2nd sess., Serial 2501, 1–2.

———. House. "Report on the Spokane and Palouse Railway Company." Report no. 4134. 49th Cong., 2nd sess., Serial 2501, 1–2.

———. House. "A Communication From the Secretary of the Interior, With Accompanying Papers, Relating to the Reduction of Indian Reservations." Executive Document 63. 50th Cong., 1st sess., Serial 2557, 1–57.

———. Senate. "In Response to Senate Resolution of January 25, 1888, Information About the Coeur d'Alene Indian Reservation, in Idaho." Executive Document 76. 50th Cong., 1st sess., Serial 2510, 1–7.

———. Senate. "Resolution." Miscellaneous Document 36. 50th Cong., 1st sess., Serial 2516, 1.

———. House. "Ratification of Coeur d'Alene Indian Treaties in Idaho." Report 1109. 51st Cong., 1st sess., Serial 2810, 1–46.

———. House. "Ratification of Coeur d'Alene Indian Treaties in Idaho." Report 2988. 51st Cong., 1st sess., Serial 2815, 1.

———. Senate. "Message From the President of the United States, Transmitting a Letter of the Secretary of the Interior Relative to the Purchase of a Part of the Coeur d'Alene Reservation." Senate Executive Document 14. 51st Cong., 1st sess., Serial 2679, 1–90.

———. Senate. "Letter of the Secretary of the Interior Transmitting Correspondence in Relation to the Ratification and Confirmation of Certain Agreements Between the United States and the Coeur d'Alene Indians in Idaho Territory." Miscellaneous Document 95. 51st Cong., 1st sess., Serial 2698, 1–4.

———. House. "Letter From the Secretary of the Interior." Executive Document 158. 53rd Cong., 2nd sess., Serial 3226, 1–18.

BOOKS

Bergon, Frank, ed. *The Journals of Lewis and Clark*. New York: Penguin, 1989.

Clements, Louis J. *Fred T. Dubois's The Making of a State*. Rexburg: Eastern Idaho Publishing, 1971.

Cox, Ross. *The Columbia River*. Ed. Edgar I. Stewart and Jane R. Stewart. Norman: University of Oklahoma Press, 1957.

De Smet, Peter J., S.J. *New Indian Sketches*. New York: P. J. Kennedy, 1904; facsimile reprint, Seattle: Shorey Book Store, 1971.

Geyer, Charles A. "Transcript of Charles A. Geyer's account of his visit to Spokane House and the Tshimikan Mission in the winter of 1843." Charles A. Geyer Papers, Eastern Washington University, Cheney, Washington.

Glover, Richard, ed. *David Thompson's Narrative, 1784–1812*. Publications of the Champlain Society. Toronto: Champlain Society, 1962.

Gray, William Henry. *A History of Oregon, 1792–1849*. New York: 1870; reprinted as part of the Far Western Frontier Series, New York: Arno, 1973.

Gwydir, Rickard D. *Recollections From the Colville Indian Agency, 1886–1889*. Ed. and with an introduction by Kevin Dye. Spokane, Wash.: Arthur H. Clark, 2001.

Hult, Ruby El. *Steamboats in the Timber*. Portland: Binfords and Mort, 1952.

Kappler, Charles J., ed. *Indian Affairs: Laws and Treaties*. Washington, D.C.: Government Printing Office, 1903.

Keyes, Erasmus D. *Fighting Indians in Washington Territory*. Fairfield, Wash.: Ye Galleon, 1988; originally published in the author's *Fifty Years' Observation of Men and Events*. New York: Scribner, 1884.

Miles, Nelson A. *Personal Recollections and Observations of General Nelson A. Miles*. With an introduction by Robert Wooster. Chicago: Werner, 1896; reprint, Lincoln: University of Nebraska Press, 1992.

Moulton, Gary E., ed. *The Journals of the Lewis and Clark Expedition*. Vol. 5. Lincoln: University of Nebraska Press, 1988.

Mullan, John. *Report on the Construction of a Military Road From Fort Walla-Walla to Fort Benton*. Fairfield, Wash.: Ye Galleon, 1998. With maps.

Palladino, Lawrence, S.J.. *The Coeur d'Alene Reservation and Our Friends the Coeur d'Alene Indians*. Montana: St. Ignatius, 1886; reprint, Fairfield, Wash.: Ye Galleon, 1967.

Point, Nicolas, S.J. *Wilderness Kingdom: Indian Life in the Rocky Mountains, 1840–1847: The Journals and Paintings of Nicolas Point*. Trans. and with an introduction by Joseph P. Donnelly, S.J. Chicago: Loyola University Press, 1967.

Prucha, Francis Paul, ed. *Documents of United States Indian Policy*. 2nd ed. Lincoln: University of Nebraska Press, 1990.

Richardson, James D., ed. *A Compilation of the Messages and Papers of the Presidents, 1789–1902*. Vol. 7. Washington, D.C.: Bureau of National Literature and Art, 1904.

Seltice, Joseph. *Saga of the Coeur d'Alene Indians: An Account of Chief Joseph Seltice*. Ed. Edward J. Kowrach and Thomas E. Connolly. With an introduction by Ernest Stensgar. Fairfield, Wash.: Ye Galleon, 1990.

Thwaites, Reuben G., ed. *Original Journals of the Lewis and Clark Expedition, 1804–1806*. Vols. 4, 5, 6. New York: Dodd, Mead, 1905.

NEWSPAPERS

Coeur d'Alene Sun, April 6, 1886.

Coeur d'Alene Teepee (DeSmet, Idaho), 1937–1940.

Selected Bibliography

Commoner (Colfax, Washington), 1887–1890.
Spokesman Monthly Review (Spokane, Washington), June 21, 1888.
Spokesman-Review (Spokane, Washington), August 9, 1891; April 6, 1893; October 29, 1995; July 29, 1998.
Times-News, January 2, 1997.

Legal Documents

Idaho v. Coeur d'Alene Tribe of Idaho (no. 94-1474), 1996 Westlaw, U.S. Supreme Court, 1996:
    Petitioner's Brief, WL 290997.
    Amicus Curiae Brief, WL 288987, 291048, 376980, 376981, 376983.
    Respondent's Brief, WL 380391.
    Reply Brief, WL 439249.
    Supreme Court Official Transcript, WL 604993.

SECONDARY SOURCES

UNPUBLISHED MATERIALS

Andrews, Elizabeth Mary. "Fort Spokane and Spokane House." M.A. Thesis, University of Washington, 1924.
Dozier, Jack. "History of the Coeur d'Alene Indians to 1900." M.A. Thesis, University of Idaho, 1961.
Hart, E. Richard. "The Tribal Claim to Lake Coeur d'Alene." Paper presented at the 1995 Biannual Meeting of the American Society of Environmental History, March 11, 1995, Las Vegas, Nevada.
Scott, Jerry M. "A History of the Formation of the Colville Indian Reservation." M.A. Thesis, Washington State University, 1992.
Weaver, Robert Donald. "A Preliminary Study of Archaeological Relationships at the Mission of the Sacred Heart of Jesus to the Coeur d'Alene Indians." M.A. Thesis, University of Idaho, 1976.
Williams, Keith. "The Agricultural History of Latah County and the Palouse: An Overview and Three Case Studies." M.A. Thesis, Washington State University, 1984.

PUBLISHED SOURCES

Periodicals

Bock, Paula. "A Kinder, Gentler Archaeology." *Pacific Magazine: The Seattle Times Magazine* (May 28, 1995), 15.
Brown, Arthur J. "The Promotion of Emigration to Washington, 1854–1909." *Pacific Northwest Quarterly* 36 (January 1945): 3–17.
Burns, Robert Ignatius, S.J. "The Jesuits and the Spokane Council of 1877." *Pacific Historical Review* 21, no. 1 (1952): 65–75.
———. "Pere Joset's Account of the Indian War of 1858." *Pacific Northwest Quarterly* 38 (October 1947): 285–314.
Cotroneo, Ross R., and Jack Dozier. "A Time of Disintegration: The Coeur d'Alene and the Dawes Act." *Western Historical Quarterly* 5 (October 1974): 405–419.

Cox, Thomas R. "Tribal Leadership in Transition: Chief Peter Moctelme of the Coeur d'Alenes." *Idaho Yesterdays* 23 (Spring 1979): 2–9, 25–31.
Dozier, Jack. "Coeur d'Alene Country: The Creation of the Coeur d'Alene Indian Reservation in North Idaho." *Idaho Yesterdays* 6 (Fall 1962): 2–7.
———. "The Coeur d'Alene Indians in the War of 1858." *Idaho Yesterdays* 5 (Fall 1961): 22–32.
———. "The Coeur d'Alene Land Rush, 1909–1910." *Pacific Northwest Quarterly* 53 (October 1962): 145–150.
Elliott, T. C. "Steptoe Butte and Steptoe Battlefield." *Washington Historical Quarterly* 18 (October 1972): 243–253.
Howard, Helen Addison. "The Steptoe Affair." *Montana: The Magazine of Western History* 19 (April 1969): 28–36.
Jeffrey, Julie Roy. "Narcissa Whitman: The Significance of a Missionary's Life." *Montana: The Magazine of Western History* 41 (Spring 1991): 3–15.
Kensel, W. Hudson. "Inland Empire Mining and the Growth of Spokane, 1883–1905." *Pacific Northwest Quarterly* 60 (April 1969): 84–97.
McGregor, Alex C. "From Sheep Range to Agribusiness: A Case History of Agricultural Transformation on the Columbia Plateau." *Agricultural History* 54 (January 1980): 11–27.
Miller, Tom O. "Four Burials From the Coeur d'Alene Region, Idaho." *American Antiquity* 19 (1953): 389–390.
Palmer, Gary B. "Indian Pioneers: The Settlement of Ni'lukhwalqw (Upper Hangman Creek, Idaho) by the Schitsu'umsh (Coeur d'Alene Indians)." *Oregon Historical Quarterly* 102 (2001): 22–47.
Ray, Verne F. "Native Villages and Groupings of the Columbia Basin." *Pacific Northwest Quarterly* 27 (1936): 99–152.
Richards, Kent. "Isaac I. Stevens and Federal Military Power in Washington Territory." *Pacific Northwest Quarterly* 63 (July 1972): 81–86.
Snow, Dean R. "Microchronology and Demographic Evidence Relating to the Size of Pre-Columbian North American Indian Populations." *Science* 268 (June 16, 1995): 1601–1604.
Thompson, Albert W. "Coeur d'Alene: The Names Applied to Tribe and Lake." *Idaho Yesterdays* 21 (Winter 1978): 11–15.
Trimble, William J. "The Mining Advance Into the Inland Empire: A Comparative Study of the Beginnings of the Mining Industry in Idaho and Montana, Eastern Washington and Oregon, and the Southern Interior of British Columbia; and of Institutions and Laws Based Upon That Industry." Ph.D. diss. *Bulletin of the University of Wisconsin* 683 (1914).
Tuohy, Donald R. "Horseshoes and Handstones: The Meeting of History and Prehistory at the Old Mission of the Sacred Heart." *Idaho Yesterdays* 2 (Summer 1958): 20–27.
Ubelaker, D. H. "North American Indian Population Size, A.D. 1500 to 1985." *American Journal of Physical Anthropology* 77 (November 1988): 289–294.
Unrau, William E. "The Civilian as Indian Agent: Villain or Victim?" *Western Historical Quarterly* 3 (October 1972): 405–420.
Wells, Merle W. "Caleb Lyon's Indian Policy." *Pacific Northwest Quarterly* 61 (October 1970): 193–200.

———. "The Creation of the Territory of Idaho." *Pacific Northwest Quarterly* 40 (April 1949): 106–123.

———. "The Idaho Anti-Mormon Test Oath, 1884–1892." *Pacific Historical Review* 24 (August 1955): 235–252.

———. "Idaho's Season of Political Distress: An Unusual Path to Statehood." *Montana: The Magazine of Western History* 37 (Autumn 1987): 58–67.

Woodworth-Ney, Laura. "Whitman County Fairs, 1887–1944: A Reflection of Agricultural Development in the Palouse Country." *Bunchgrass Historian: Journal of the Whitman County Historical Society* 20 (1992): 5–24.

Books

Arrington, Leonard J. *History of Idaho.* 2 Vols. Moscow and Boise: University of Idaho Press and the Idaho State Historical Society, 1994.

Arrington, Leonard J., and Davis Bitton. *The Mormon Experience: A History of the Latter-day Saints.* New York: Alfred A. Knopf, 1979.

Asher, Brad. *Beyond the Reservation: Indians, Settlers, and the Law in Washington Territory, 1853–1889.* Norman: University of Oklahoma Press, 1999.

Baym, Nina, Ronald Gottesman, Laurence B. Holland, Francis Murphy, Hershel Parker, William H. Pritchard, and David Kalstone, eds. *The Norton Anthology of American Literature.* Vol. 1, 2nd ed. New York: W. W. Norton, 1985.

Beal, Merrill D. *"I Will Fight No More Forever": Chief Joseph and the Nez Perce War.* Seattle: University of Washington Press, 1963.

Bischoff, William N., S.J. "The Coeur d'Alene Country, 1805–1892: An Historical Sketch." In *Interior Salish and Eastern Washington Indians.* Vol. 1. Garland Series American Indian Ethnohistory, ed. David Agee Horr, 197–296. New York: Garland, 1974; originally published as part of the Coeur d'Alene Petition Before the Indian Claims Commission, Docket 81, 1956.

Bishop, M. Guy. "'We Are Rather Weaker in Righteousness Than in Numbers': The Mormon Colony at San Bernardino, California, 1851–1857." In *Religion and Society in the American West: Historical Essays,* ed. Carl Guarneri and David Alvarez, 171–193. Lanham, Md.: University Press of America, 1987.

Black, Jeremy. *Maps and History: Constructing Images of the Past.* New Haven: Yale University Press, 1997.

Boone, Lalia. *Idaho Place Names: A Geographical Dictionary.* Moscow: University of Idaho Press, 1988.

Boyer, Paul. *Urban Masses and Moral Order in America, 1820–1920.* Cambridge: Harvard University Press, 1978.

Brooks, Juanita. *The Mountain Meadows Massacre.* Norman: University of Oklahoma Press, 1970.

Buckley, Cornelius M., S.J. *Nicolas Point: His Life and Northwest Indian Chronicles.* Chicago: Loyola University Press, 1989.

Burns, Robert Ignatius, S.J. *The Jesuits and the Indian Wars of the Northwest.* New Haven: Yale University Press, 1966.

Carriker, Robert C. *Father Peter John DeSmet: Jesuit in the West.* Oklahoma Western Biographies, ed. Richard W. Etulain. Norman: University of Oklahoma Press, 1995.

Chalfant, Stuart A. "Historical Material Relative to Coeur d'Alene Indian Aboriginal Distribution." In *Interior Salish and Eastern Washington Indians*. Vol. 1. Garland Series of American Indian Ethnohistory, ed. David Agee Horr, 37–196. New York: Garland, 1974.

Chance, David H. *The Kootenay Fur Trade and Its Establishments, 1795–1871*. Seattle: U.S. Army Corps of Engineers, 1981.

Clanton, Gene. *Populism: The Humane Preference in America*. Social Movements Past and Present Series, ed. Irwin T. Sanders. Boston: Twayne, 1991.

Cohen, Fay G. *Treaties on Trial: The Continuing Controversy Over Northwest Indian Fishing Rights*. Report prepared for the American Friends Service Committee. Seattle: University of Washington Press, 1986.

Colson, Dennis C. *Idaho's Constitution: The Tie That Binds*. Moscow: University of Idaho Press, 1991.

Confederation of American Indians. *Indian Reservations: A State and Federal Handbook*. Jefferson, N.C.: McFarland, 1986.

Conley, Cort. *Idaho for the Curious: A Guide*. Cambridge, Idaho: Backeddy, 1982.

Crosby, Alfred W. *Ecological Imperialism: The Biological Expansion of Europe, 900–1900*. New York: Cambridge University Press, 1986.

Dahlgren, Dorothy, and Simone Carbonneau Kincaid. *In All the West No Place Like This: A Pictorial History of the Coeur d'Alene Region*. Coeur d'Alene: Museum of North Idaho, 1991.

Dawley, Alan. *Struggles for Justice: Social Responsibility and the Liberal State*. Cambridge: Harvard University Press, 1991.

Deloria, Vine, Jr. and Clifford M. Lytle. *American Indians, American Justice*. Austin: University of Texas Press, 1983.

Department of the Interior, Bureau of Indian Affairs Planning Support Group. *Coeur d'Alene Indian Reservation: Human and Natural Resource Supportive Data*. Report no. 238. Billings, Mont.: BIA Planning Support Group, 1976.

DeVoto, Bernard. *Across the Wide Missouri*. With a foreword by Mae Reed Porter. American Heritage Library. Boston: Houghton Mifflin, 1975.

Durham, N. W. *History of the City of Spokane and Spokane Country, Washington, From Its Earliest Settlement to the Present Time*. Vol. 1. Spokane: S. J. Clarke, 1912.

Fahey, John. *The Inland Empire: Unfolding Years, 1879–1929*. Seattle: University of Washington Press, 1986.

———. *Saving the Reservation: Joe Garry and the Battle to Be Indian*. Seattle: University of Washington Press, 2001.

Fargo, Lucile. *Spokane Story*. New York: Columbia University Press, 1950.

Foner, Eric. *Reconstruction: America's Unfinished Revolution, 1863–1877*. The New American Nation Series, ed. Henry Steele Commager and Richard B. Morris. New York: Harper and Row, 1988.

Fortier, Ted. *Religion and Resistance in the Encounter Between the Coeur d'Alene Indians and Jesuit Missionaries*. Native American Studies no. 10. Lewiston, N.Y.: Edwin Mellon, 2002.

Fradkin, Philip L. *Sagebrush Country: Land and the American West*. Tucson: University of Arizona Press, 1989.

Frey, Rodney. *Landscape Traveled by Coyote and Crane: The World of the Schitsu'umsh (Coeur d'Alene Indians)*. Seattle: University of Washington Press, 2001.

Fuller, George W. *A History of the Pacific Northwest With Special Emphasis on the Inland Empire.* 2nd rev. ed. New York: Alfred A. Knopf, 1960.

Fur, Gunlog. "'Some Women Are Wiser Than Some Men': Gender and Native American History," in *Clearing a Path: Theorizing the Past in Native American Studies,* ed. Nancy Shoemaker. New York: Routledge, 2002.

Greever, William S. *The Bonanza West: The Story of the Western Mining Rushes, 1848–1900.* Norman: University of Olkahoma Press, 1963.

Gutman, Herbert G. "Work, Culture, and Society in Industrializing America, 1815–1919." In *Work, Culture and Society in Industrializing America: Essays in American Working-Class and Social History,* ed. Herbert G. Gutman. New York: Vintage, 1977.

Hagan, William T. *American Indians.* Rev. ed. Chicago History of American Civilization Series, ed. Daniel J. Boorstin. Chicago: University of Chicago Press, 1979.

———. "Full Blood, Mixed Blood, Generic, and Ersatz: The Problem of Indian Identity," in *The American Indian: Past and Present,* ed. Roger L. Nichols. Boston: McGraw Hill, 1999, 1–10.

Hale, Janet Campbell. *Bloodlines: Odyssey of a Native Daughter.* New York: Random House, 1993.

Hampton, Bruce. *Children of Grace: The Nez Perce War of 1877.* New York: Avon, 1994.

Harrod, Howard L. *Mission Among the Blackfeet.* Norman: University of Oklahoma Press, 1971.

Hart, Arthur A. *Camera Eye on Idaho: Pioneer Photography, 1863–1913.* Caldwell, Idaho: Caxton, 1990.

Henretta, James A., and Gregory H. Nobles. *Evolution and Revolution: American Society, 1600–1820.* Lexington, Mass.: D. C. Heath, 1987.

Hill, Edward E. *American Indians: Guide to Records in the National Archives of the United States Relating to American Indians.* Washington, D.C.: National Archives and Records Service, General Services Administration, 1981.

Hofstadter, Richard. *The Age of Reform: From Bryan to F.D.R.* New York: Vintage, 1955.

Hoxie, Frederick E. *A Final Promise: The Campaign to Assimilate the Indians, 1880–1920.* Lincoln: University of Nebraska Press, 1984.

Hungry Wolf, Beverly. *The Ways of My Grandmothers.* New York: Quill, 1982.

Hyde, Anne Farrar. *An American Vision: Far Western Landscape and National Culture, 1820–1920.* The American Social Experience Series, ed. James Kirby Martin. New York: New York University Press, 1990.

The Idaho Almanac: Territorial Centennial Edition, 1863–1963. Boise: Idaho Department of Commerce and Development, 1963.

Idaho Atlas and Gazetteer: Topo Maps of the Entire State. Freeport, Maine: DeLorme Mapping, 1992.

Jeffrey, Julie Roy. *Converting the West: A Biography of Narcissa Whitman.* Norman: University of Oklahoma Press, 1991.

Johansen, Dorothy O., and Charles M. Gates. *Empire of the Columbia: A History of the Pacific Northwest.* New York: Harper and Brothers, 1957.

Johnson, Olga Weydemeyer. *Flathead and Kootenay: The Rivers, the Tribes and the Region's Traders.* Glendale, Calif.: Arthur H. Clark, 1969.

Josephy, Alvin M., Jr. *The Nez Perce Indians and the Opening of the Northwest.* Boston: Houghton Mifflin, 1977.

———. *Now That the Buffalo's Gone: A Study of Today's American Indians.* Norman: University of Oklahoma Press, 1984.
Knowles, Anne Kelly, ed. *Past Time, Past Place: GIS for History.* Redlands, Calif.: ESRI, 2002.
Kowrach, Edward J. "Epilogue on Prophecy." In Joseph Seltice, *Saga of the Coeur d'Alene Indians,* ed. Edward J. Kowrach and Thomas E. Connolly, 289–296. Fairfield, Wash.: Ye Galleon, 1990.
Lamar, Howard R. "Statehood for Washington: Symbol of a New Era." In *Washington Comes of Age: The State in the National Experience,* ed. David H. Stratton, 113–133. Pullman: Washington State University Press, 1992.
Limerick, Patricia Nelson. *The Legacy of Conquest: The Unbroken Past of the American West.* New York: W. W. Norton, 1987.
McDonald, Douglas. *Virginia City and the Silver Region of the Comstock Lode.* Las Vegas: Stanley Paher, Nevada Publications, 1982.
McPherson, James M. *Battle Cry of Freedom: The Civil War Era.* New York: Oxford University Press, 1988.
McQuade, Donald, et al. *The Harper American Literature.* Vol. 2. New York: Harper and Row, 1987.
Meinig, Donald W. *The Great Columbia Plain: A Historical Geography, 1805–1910.* Emil and Kathleen Sick Lecture Book Series in Western History and Biography. Seattle: University of Washington Press, 1968.
———. "Spokane and the Inland Empire: Historical Geographic Systems and a Sense of Place." In *Spokane and the Inland Empire: An Interior Northwest Anthology,* ed. David H. Stratton, 1–31. Pullman: Washington State University Press, 1991.
Merk, Frederick. *Manifest Destiny and Mission in American History: A Reinterpretation.* New York: Vintage, 1966.
Merrell, James H. *The Indians' New World: Catawbas and Their Neighbors From European Contact Through the Era of Removal.* Chapel Hill: University of North Carolina Press, 1989.
Meyer, Carl J., and George A. Riley. *Public Domain, Private Dominion: A History of Public Mineral Policy in America.* San Francisco: Sierra Club, 1985.
Morrissey, Katherine G. *Mental Territories: Mapping the Inland Empire.* Ithaca: Cornell University Press, 1997.
Murray, Alberta. *These My Children.* Fairfield, Wash.: Ye Galleon, 1976.
Nichols, Roger L., ed. *The American Indian: Past and Present.* 5th ed. Boston: McGraw Hill, 1999.
Nicodemus, Lawrence G. *Snchitsu'umshtsm: The Coeur d'Alene Language.* 2 vols. Spokane, Wash.: Coeur d'Alene Tribal Council, 1975.
Nugent, Walter. *Into the West: The Story of Its People.* New York: Alfred A. Knopf, 1999.
Peltier, Jerome. *A Brief History of the Coeur d'Alene Indians, 1806–1909.* Fairfield, Wash.: Ye Galleon, 1982.
———. *Warbonnets and Epaulets.* Montreal: Payette Radio Limited, n.d.
Peterson, F. Ross. *Idaho: A Bicentennial History.* Nashville: American Association for State and Local History, 1976.
Peterson, Jacqueline, with Laura Peers. *Sacred Encounters: Father DeSmet and the Indians of the Rocky Mountain West.* Norman: The DeSmet Project, Washington State University in association with the University of Oklahoma Press, 1993.

Pisani, Donald J. *To Reclaim a Divided West: Water, Law, and Public Policy, 1848–1902.* Histories of the American Frontier, ed. Ray Allen Billington. Albuquerque: University of New Mexico Press, 1992.

Pomeroy, Earl. *In Search of the Golden West: The Tourist in Western America.* New York: Knopf, 1957; reprint, Lincoln: University of Nebraska Press, 1990.

Prucha, Francis Paul. *The Great Father: The United States Government and the American Indians.* Unabridged ed. 2 vols. Lincoln: University of Nebraska Press, 1984.

———. *Indian Policy in the United States.* Lincoln: University of Nebraska Press, 1981.

Reichard, Gladys A. *An Analysis of Coeur d'Alene Indian Myths.* Memoirs of the American Folklore Society. Vol. 41. Philadelphia: American Folklore Society, 1947.

Rice, Harvey S. "Native American Dwellings of the Southern Plateau." In *Spokane and the Inland Empire: An Interior Pacific Northwest Anthology,* ed. David H. Stratton, 83–108. Pullman: Washington State University Press, 1991.

Richards, Kent D. *Isaac I. Stevens, Young Man in a Hurry: Washington's First Territorial Governor, 1853–1857.* Pullman: Washington State University Press, 1993.

Ronda, James P. *Astoria and Empire.* Lincoln: University of Nebraska Press, 1990.

———. *Lewis and Clark Among the Indians.* Lincoln: University of Nebraska Press, 1984.

Ruby, Robert H., and John A. Brown. *Half-Sun on the Columbia: A Biography of Chief Moses.* Norman: University of Oklahoma Press, 1965.

———. *The Spokane Indians: Children of the Sun.* With a foreword by Robert L. Bennett. Norman: University of Oklahoma Press, 1970.

Scheuerman, Richard, and John Clement. *Palouse Country: A Land and Its People.* College Place, Wash.: By the authors, 1994.

Schlicke, Carl P. *General George Wright: Guardian of the Pacific Coast.* Norman: University of Olkahoma Press, 1988.

Schoenberg, Wilfred P., S.J. *Paths to the Northwest: A Jesuit History of the Oregon Province.* With a foreword by Thomas R. Royce, S.J. Chicago: Loyola University Press, 1982.

Schwantes, Carlos. *In Mountain Shadows: A History of Idaho.* Lincoln: University of Nebraska Press, 1991.

———. *The Pacific Northwest: An Interpretive History.* Lincoln: University of Nebraska Press, 1989.

Sellers, Charles. *The Market Revolution: Jacksonian America, 1815–1846.* New York: Oxford University Press, 1991.

Sherfey, Florence E. *Eastern Washington's Vanished Gristmills.* Fairfield, Wash.: Ye Galleon, 1978.

Shiach, William S., Harry B. Averill, and John M. Henderson. *An Illustrated History of North Idaho Embracing Nez Perces, Idaho, Latah, Kootenai, and Shoshone Counties in the State of Idaho.* Western Historical Publishing Company, 1903.

Shoemaker, Nancy, ed. *Clearing a Path: Theorizing the Past in Native American Studies.* New York: Routledge, 2002.

Stevens, Hazard. *The Life of Isaac Ingalls Stevens.* 2 vols. Boston: Houghton, Mifflin, 1900.

Stratton, David H., ed. *Spokane and the Inland Empire: An Interior Pacific Northwest Anthology.* Pullman: Washington State University Press, 1991.

Stuart, Paul. *The Indian Office: Growth and Development of an American Institution, 1865–1900.* Studies in American History and Culture, no. 12. Ann Arbor, Mich.: University Microfilms International Press, 1978.

Svingen, Orlan J. *The Northern Cheyenne Indian Reservation, 1877–1900.* Niwot: University Press of Colorado, 1993.

Taylor, Theodore W. *The Bureau of Indian Affairs.* Boulder: Westview, 1984.

Teit, James A. "The Coeur d'Alene." In facsimile reproduction of *The Salishan Tribes of the Western Plateaus.* 45th Annual Report of the Bureau of American Ethnology, 1927–1928, ed. Frank Boas, 23–396. Seattle: Shorey Book Store, 1973.

Trafzer, Clifford E., and Richard D. Scheuerman. *Renegade Tribe: The Palouse Indians and the Invasion of the Inland Pacific Northwest.* Pullman: Washington State University Press, 1986.

Trennert, Robert A., Jr. *Alternative to Extinction: Federal Indian Policy and the Beginnings of the Reservation System, 1846–51.* Philadelphia: Temple University Press, 1975.

Unruh, John D., Jr. *The Plains Across: The Overland Emigrants and the Trans-Mississippi West, 1840–1860.* Chicago: University of Illinois Press, 1982.

Utley, Robert M. *The Indian Frontier of the American West, 1846–1890.* Histories of the American Frontier Series, ed. Ray Allen Billington. Albuquerque: University of New Mexico Press, 1984.

Utley, Robert M., and Wilcomb E. Washburn. *Indian Wars.* Boston: Houghton Mifflin, 2002.

Vaughan, Thomas, ed. *Paul Kane, the Columbia Wanderer: Sketches, Paintings and Comment, 1846–1847.* Portland: Oregon Historical Society, 1971.

Walker, Deward E., Jr. *Indians of Idaho.* Anthropological Monographs of the University of Idaho, ed. Roderick Sprague. Moscow: University of Idaho Press, 1978.

White, Richard. *"It's Your Misfortune and None of My Own": A New History of the American West.* Norman: University of Oklahoma Press, 1991.

———. *The Middle Ground: Indians, Empires, and Republics in the Great Lakes Region, 1650–1815.* Cambridge Studies in North American Indian History, ed. Frederick Hoxie. Cambridge: Cambridge University Press, 1991.

Wiebe, Robert H. *The Search for Order, 1877–1920.* The Making of America Series, ed. David Donald. New York: Hill and Wang, 1967.

Wight, E. L., Mary Mitchell, and Marie Schmidt, eds. *Indian Reservations of Idaho, Oregon, and Washington.* Portland: United States Department of the Interior, Bureau of Indian Affairs, 1960.

Wilkinson, Charles F. *American Indians, Time, and the Law: Native Societies in a Modern Constitutional Democracy.* New Haven: Yale University Press, 1987.

Web Sites

"Bureau of Indian Affairs, U.S. Department of the Interior." http://www.doiu.nbc.gov/orientation/bia2.cfm.

"The Catholic Encyclopedia." www.newadvent.org.

Circling Raven Golf Club" and "Luxurious Resort Hotel." http://www.cdacasino.com.

"Coeur d'Alene Resort Golf Course," Coeur d'Alene Tourism Web site. http://www.coeurdalene.org.

"David Rumsey Historical Map Collection." www.davidrumsey.com.

"Montana Associated Technology Roundtables." http://www.matr.net.

"National Archives and Records Administration." http://www.archives.gov.

"Office of the Circuit Executive: United States Courts for the Ninth Circuit." http://www.ce9.uscourts.gov/.

"Official Web Site of the Coeur d'Alene Tribe." http://www.cdatribe.org/.
"The Spokesman-Review.com, Spokane, Washington." http://www.spokesmanreview.com/.
"Supreme Court of the United States." http://www.supremecourtus.gov/.
"University of Washington Libraries Digital Collections." http://content.lib.washington.edu/.
"U.S. Census Bureau." http://www.census.gov.
"U.S. Court of Appeals for the Ninth Circuit, *State of Idaho v. United States of America*, Case no. 98-35831, Filed 05/02/00, 4736, 4742." http://www.ca9uscourts.gov.

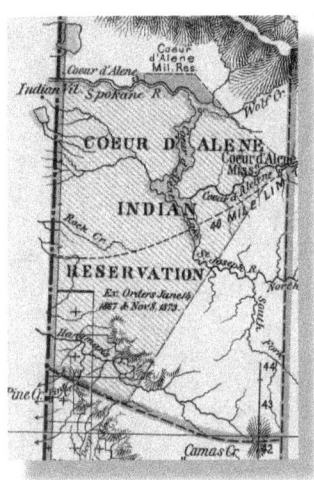

INDEX

Adolescents, 21
Aeneas, 111
Agriculture, 21, 33, 40, 46, 89, 90, 108, 116, 124, 144, 161, 206(n55); on Coeur d'Alene Reservation, 108, 110, 111, 129–30, 154, 168; Jesuits and, 26, 30, 36–37; Andrew Seltice's campaign for, 88, 106; as tribal policy, 37–38. *See also* Farms
Alcohol trade, 80, 89, 100–101; on Coeur d'Alene Reservation, 120–22
Allen, Paul, 16
Allotment, 109, 168
Almota Creek, 61
Amelia Wheaton (steamboat), 116
American Board of Commissioners for Foreign Missions, 25, 33
American Fur Trading Company, 19
Americans: settlers, 38, 43–44, 45, 46–47, 71; traders, 13, 19. *See also* Homesteaders; Miners
Anderson, Albert, 164
Andrews, Harry W., 135, 136, 138
Antelope, Louie, 164
Aripa, Stanislaus, 10
Armstrong, Frank C., 147, 148

Arrowsmith, Aaron, 18
Assimilation, 40, 161; Coeur d'Alenes and, 103, 149, 151, 168; Jesuits, 24, 41; Andrew Seltice and, 122, 143, 164–65; as tribal policy, 37–38
Astor, John Jacob, 17
Astorians, 17
Atkins, John D.C., 129, 130, 145, 149–50, 151
Authority, 31, 74; political, 39–40; spiritual, 12–13; women's, 23, 30, 89

Baker, Darius F., 114–15
Ballard, David W., 81, 82, 86
Ballard, James M., 158
Barnabee, Christine, 140
Bartelmy, 111; Spokane, 109, 110; villages and, 11–12
Bartholomew, Louis, 157
Bartholomew, Pierre, 139(fig.)
Basil (Bazil), 108, 111, 157
Basile, 145
Bassa. *See* Vincent, Chief
Batthis, J. N., 127, 128
Battles: with Blackfeet, 19–20; Steptoe campaign, 62–64; Wright campaign, 66–67
Belknap, William, 93, 94

223

Index

Benewah County, 169
Bennett, Thomas W., 86, 95, 96, 99
Biddle, Nicholas, 16
Bitterroot Mountains, 8, 10, 116
Bitterroot Valley, 23
Blackfeet, 16, 51; conflict with, 19–20, 26, 29, 33–34, 47, 48, 182(n17)
Black Lake, 170
Black Robe: Jesuit missionaries and, 25–26; oral tradition of, 21, 23, 27, 28, 29, 182(n12)
Blanchet, Francis, 27
Boarding schools, 101
Bogy, Lewis V., 86
Boise, 81, 144
Boise Basin, 77
Bolon, Andrew J., 49, 52, 53
Bonaventure, 74
Bonemetsei, 164
Bonneville, B. E., 47
Boundaries, reservation, 3–4, 87, 88, 96, 99–100, 104, 114–15, 117–18, 120–21, 128, 130, 150, 151, 155
Boutelier (Butler), Adolph, 157, 160
Boutelier (Butler), Alfred, 157
Boutelier (Butler), Jerry, 157
Boutelier, Julien, 138, 139, 140
Boutelier, Mary Elizabeth, 140
Boutelier, Pauline (Sister Joseph Mary), 140
Boutelier, Rosilda Liberty, 160
Boutelier (Butler) family, 163, 203(n46)
Bowen, Thomas M., 86
British, trade, 13, 17–18
Brouillet, B. A., 114
Brown, Father, 19–20
Browne, J. Ross, 53
Bryant, William Cullen, 7
Buffalo: hunting, 13–14, 19, 26; treaty rights and, 51, 52
Bunker Hill claim, 124
Bureau of Catholic Indian Missions, 114, 134
Bureau of Indian Affairs, 1, 25, 82; reformers in, 92–93; and reservation administration, 107–8. *See also* Office of Indian Affairs
Burke, 125
Butler family. *See* Boutelier family
Butte City, 123

California, 24, 126
Camas root, 10, 14; digging areas, 88, 102
Camille, Ignace, 20
Campbell, Amasa B. (Mace), 144

Camp Chopunnish, 15
Camp 99, 162
Canby, R. S., 93
Canoes, 10
Canyon Creek, 124, 125
Captain, Regis, 152
Cartmill, H. B., 128
Cartography, 4–5
Caruana, Father, 80
Cash crops, 129–30
Casino and resort, 168–69
Cataldo, 13
Cataldo, Joseph (J. M.), land claims negotiations, 92, 93, 103, 134, 135, 136, 147, 152
Cataldo Mission (Old Mission), 12, 31, 32, 40, 162, 170, 183(nn25, 27)
Catholicism, 3, 30, 41, 89, 95, 140, 165; conversion to, 31–32; missions, 25–26, 28–29, 46, 181(n7); and native spirituality, 23–24; Andrew Seltice and, 79–80, 91; tribal policy and, 37–38
Cattle growers, 116. *See also* livestock raising
Cayuse, 38, 183(n30), 184(n46); conflict with, 54, 55; negotiations with, 50, 58; and Protestant missions, 25, 29, 33
Central Organization of the Farmers Protective Association of Whitman County, 127–28
Cernera, Phil, 169
Chalfant, Stuart A., 9, 10, 20
Chamberlaine, Mary Elizabeth, 140
Chamberlaine family, 163
Chandler, William, 114
Chantilly, Battle of, 76
Chatcolet, 162
Chewelah, 105, 107
Chiefs, 12; political organization and, 39, 40, 46; succession of, 20–21, 79, 164–65
"Chiefs of the Coeur d'Alene When Sacred Heart, the Second Rocky Mountain Mission, Was Founded" (Point), 39
Child rearing, 30
Chopunnish. *See* Nez Perce
Christianity, 25
Church of Jesus Christ of Latter-day Saints, 60; politics and, 144, 149, 189(n11)
Circling Raven, 21, 29, 182(n12)
Circling Raven Golf Club, 169
Civil War, 71, 76, 79
Clark, William, 3, 4, 8, 14, 15, 16, 25
Clarke, Newman S., 58, 65, 72
Clarkia, 10

Clearwater Range, 10
Clearwater River, 8, 11, 77, 101, 114; Lewis and Clark on, 14–15
Cleveland, Grover, 130, 141, 160
Coeur d'Alene (city), 12, 132, 162, 169
Coeur d'Alene, Lake, 1, 8, 9, 11, 12, 15, 22, 31, 35, 75, 77, 106, 160, 162, 192(n22); claims for, 96, 151; and Coeur d'Alene Reservation, 83, 85, 118, 149, 150, 156, 165; maps of, 18, 19; pollution of, 169–70; steamboats on, 116, 130
Coeur d'Alene (steamboat), 117, 120
Coeur d'Alene Indian Reservation, 1, 90, 97(fig.), 103, 125, 144, 159(fig.), 167–71; administration of, 107–8; agriculture on, 129–30; alcohol trade on, 120–21; boundaries of, 99–100, 104, 114–15, 117–18, 120–21; and Colville Indian Agency, 116–17, 119–20; creation of, 2–3, 87, 96, 98–99; economics of, 136–37; federal inspections of, 110–11; Idaho territory and, 82–83; incursions on, 118–19; land cessions and, 162–63, 165–66; land claims for, 132–35; land negotiations for, 151–56; land rights on, 127–28, 138–39, 141–42, 206(n51); land transfers on, 158, 160; Simpson commission cession of, 156–58; opposition to, 87–88, 93–94; railroad, 145–48; resources on, 149–50; Spokane Indians and, 109–10, 198(n23); timber cutting, 112–14, 127–29; tourism, 161–62; trespassing on, 115–16
Coeur d'Alene Mountains, 9, 130
"The Coeur d'Alene Reservation" (Palladino), 133–34
Coeur d'Alene River, 9, 11, 12, 19, 22, 31, 75, 78, 105, 130; land claims to, 91, 145; miners on, 81–82, 123, 124, 125–26; reservation boundaries and, 96, 155, 156
Coeur d'Alene Steam Navigation Company, 117
Coeur d'Alene Tribal Police, 145
Coeur d'Alene Tribe, 2, 46, 48, 57, 69, 72, 77, 82, 111, 136–37, 143, 149, 163, 166, 167, 170, 180(n46), 185(n9), 192(n22), 205(n24); casino, 168–69; as civilized, 45, 85–86, 102–3, 104; and Colville Reservation, 87–88; and Father De Smet, 73–74; and homesteaders, 132–33; land claims of, 91–92, 94, 95, 98, 131–32; land concession and, 157–58; land rights of, 78–79, 133–34, 154–55; land usage by, 150–51; leadership in, 164–65; negotiation with, 51, 52, 54, 58, 68, 151–52; non-Indians in, 138–40; as nontreaty tribe, 50–51; progressive and nonprogressive, 90–91; railroads and, 145–48; relocation of, 88–89, 94; territory of, 8–9, 75; and U.S. Army campaigns, 61, 63–64, 65, 66, 67; waterways used by, 160–61
Coeur d'Alene Valley, 28
Cole, Hal, 154
Colfax (Wash.), 86, 102, 113, 129
Colter, John, 16, 19
Columbia Plateau, 13, 87
Columbia River, 7, 8, 18, 77, 88
Columbia Tribe, 61, 87
Colville District, 87
Colville Indian Agency, 80, 86, 87, 90, 105, 115, 123, 127, 140, 146, 154; and Coeur d'Alene Reservation, 110–13, 116–17, 131, 145, 158, 164; management of, 107–8, 119
Colville Reservation, 88, 98, 107, 136
Colville Tribe, 20, 45, 51, 52, 61, 72, 74, 80, 87, 96, 185(n9); land rights of, 94, 103
Colville Valley, 57–58
Conflict, 180(n57); with Blackfeet, 47, 48; Indian-White, 57–58; with Yakima, 53–54. *See also* Massacres; Warfare
Congiato, Nicholas, 24, 59, 65
Conrad, D. B., 127, 128
Conversions: Catholic, 31–32; Protestant, 33
Cooske, H. R., 52
Corps of Discovery, 14
Cowley, M. M., 148
Cox, Ross, 17
Coyote cycle, 1
Craig, William, 58

The Dalles, 8, 65
Dances, 29
Daniels, Jarred W., 135, 136, 203(n35)
Dawes Severalty Act, 109, 141, 142, 143, 150, 156, 161, 168, 198(nn15, 17)
Deboos, 62
Deer, winter hunting of, 35
Delano, Columbus, 93, 94, 95, 99
Demers, Modeste, 27
Democratic party: in Idaho, 144, 149, 160; in eastern Washington, 77, 78
De Moy, Victor C., 64
Deseret, State of, 60
DeSmet, 167, 169
DeSmet Mission, 90, 101, 104, 105, 121, 126, 127, 128, 132, 146, 192(n22); land rights, 124, 131, 133; Northwest Indian Commission,

225

INDEX

137–38, 141; Simpson commission and, 153, 154
De Smet, Peter John, 23, 25, 26, 29, 33, 62, 83; and Coeur d'Alene missions, 27, 28, 31; on land rights, 75–76; peace efforts, 73–74
Department of the Columbia, 93
Department of Oregon, 72
Diomedi, Alexander, 89
Diseases, 26, 31; epidemic, 9, 21, 183(n30)
Divorce, 30
Dolph, J. N., 117
Donation Land Law, 44
Doty, James, 48, 49
Dubois, Fred T., 149, 151, 160

Eagle City, 116, 123
Economic activities: seasonal, 9–11, 35; reservation-era, 111–14, 131, 136–37, 146; and reservation use, 153–54
Economies, 200(n2); Coeur d'Alene tribal, 150–51; food redistribution, 36–37; Idaho Territory, 143–45; Stevens' observations of, 45–46; subsistence, 34–35
Eells, Cushing, 33
Eells, Myra, 33
Elites, Jesuits as, 24
Elk, 11
English, F. A., 163
English Syndicate No., 3, 134
Epidemics, 9, 21, 33
Etienne, 39
Ewart, James, 102
Ewing, Charles, 95

Factionalism: of Coeur d'Alene Tribe, 147, 149, 161
Families, extended, 11, 30
Farmers Protective Association, 127, 128
Farmington, 119, 127, 132, 136, 146
Farmington Landing, 117
Farms, 146, 196(n47); in Hangman's Valley, 100, 104, 106; and Simpson commission cession, 156, 157; tribal, 3, 90, 111. *See also* Agriculture
Feast of the Assumption of the Blessed Virgin Mary, 79
Feasts, 35, 79
Federal policy, 2, 71–72; protection of Indian land rights, 75–76
Felt, Robert, 147
Feuds, 61

Finch, John A., 144
Firearms, 20, 30; Jesuits and, 38–39, 41, 60; suppliers of, 59–60
Fisher, Jesse, 126
Fisher, John, 126
Fisher, William, 126
Fishing, 12, 34, 35, 36, 94, 111
Flathead Reservation, 136
Flathead tribe, 8–9, 13, 16, 19, 25, 48, 74; missionaries, 23, 26, 34, 38–39; as nontreaty tribe, 50–51; Stevens negotiation with, 51–52; warfare with Blackfeet, 29, 182(n17)
Flathead Treaty, 51–52
Flett, Robert, 139(fig.)
Food, 178(n31); gender roles in procurement of, 88–89; seasonal, 10–11, 35
Fort Benton, 47, 48, 76
Fort Coeur d'Alene, 106, 197(n6)
Fort Colville, 52, 65, 87, 187(28); military inspection of, 93–94
Fortier, Ted, 25, 29
Forts, 188(n38); fur trading, 16–17
Fort Sherman, 130
Fort Spokane, 17, 21
Fort Vancouver, 27; peace delegations at, 74–75
Fort Walla Walla, 56, 58, 59, 65, 73, 76
Four Lakes, Battle of, 66
Fraser River, 58
Freeholders, land claims of, 132–33
French, trade, 13, 16–17
French-Canadians, in Coeur d'Alene Tribe, 138–40
Frey, Rodney, 11, 12, 90
Friends of the Indian, 109
Fur trade, 2, 16–18, 20–21

Gabriel, 28, 39
Gambling, Jesuit missionaries and, 29, 31
Gardner, Robert A., 108, 109, 112, 150
Garfield, Selucious, 87–88
Garry, Chief, 94, 135, 136, 139(fig.)
Gaston, William, 63, 64
Gazzoli, Gregory, 74, 92
Gem, 125
Gem-of-the-Mountains claim, 124
Gender roles, relocation of, 88–89
General Allotment Act, 109, 141
General Land Office, 168; Coeur d'Alene Reservation and, 82, 99, 100
General Sherman (steamboat), 116, 117
Geyer, Charles A., 21, 34

Gibson, James, 139(fig.)
Glover, James N., 148
Gold discoveries, rushes, 58, 77; Coeur d'Alene Reservation and, 115, 116, 121; North Fork Coeur d'Alene River, 105, 123; in Washington Territory, 52–53, 57
Gordon, G. W., 150
Grande Ronde massacre, 55
Grant, Ulysses S., 87, 88; and Coeur d'Alene Reservation, 98–99; peace policy, 71, 92
Great Britain, 7; and Oregon country, 38, 175(n3), 185(n3)
Great Plains, 14
Grizzly Mountain, 20
Groves, Maggie Hickey, 106
Guarani Indians, 26
Gwydir, Mary, 121
Gwydir, Rickard D., 121, 139(fig.), 145, 147

Hale, Janet Campbell, 1
Haller, Granville, 53
Hangman's (Latah) Creek, 9, 69, 83, 89, 91, 93, 95, 102, 126; agriculture in, 129–30; tribal farms in, 104, 150
Hangman's Creek agreement, 95, 96, 99
Hangman's Valley, 96, 161; and Coeur d'Alene Reservation, 101, 139; farms in, 100, 106
Harney, William S., 72, 73; and peace delegations, 74–75
Harrison, 127, 162–63
Harrison, Benjamin, 152, 162
Harrison, Samuel, 15
Harvey, George W., 87
Hayden Lake, 11, 12, 78, 85, 192(n22)
Healing, Jesuit missions and, 29
Hecla claim, 124
d'Herbomez, Louis, 49
Heredity, 12
Hickey, John, 106
History of the Expedition Under the Command of Captains Lewis and Clark, 15–16
Holland Land Company, 134
Holmes, T., 145
Homestead Act, 80, 136
Homesteaders, homesteads, 76, 88, 114, 158; land claims petitions, 132–33; Palouse country, 86, 123–24
Horse racing, 8, 10, 80, 89
Horses, 13–14
Hostages, Coeur d'Alene, 73
Howard, Oliver O., 101, 102, 103

Hudson's Bay Company, 17–18, 19, 21, 38, 45, 52, 54, 187(n28); firearms, 59–60
Huet, Charles, 28, 30, 34
Humphrey, Napoleon, 151–52
Hunting, 11–12, 34, 35, 36, 111, 162, 184(n38); buffalo, 13–14, 26; winter, 37–38
Huybrechts, Francis, 32

Idaho, 7, 10, 15, 170; Coeur d'Alene tribe in, 1, 9; statehood movement, 143, 149, 160
Idaho City, 81, 106
Idaho Territory, 85, 86, 106, 189(n11); creation of, 77–78; extractive economy of, 143, 144–45; mining camps in, 81–82
Idaho Test Oath, 144, 149
Ide, G. L., 162
Identity: Coeur d'Alene, 2, 3–4, 18, 77, 83, 102–3, 138–39, 151, 166; Spokane, 109–10
Ignace, 39
Indian agents, 95; corrupt, 86–87. *See also* Colville Indian Agency; *agents by name*
Indian Appropriations Act, 95, 135, 151
Indian fighters, 54–55
Indian Reorganization Act, 168, 198(n15)
Indian Service, 107
Institution of the Society of Jesus. *See* Jesuit Order
Interior Department, 87, 161, 163; land claims and, 91–92, 93, 94
Isolation, Coeur d'Alene, 24, 27, 32, 107

Jackson, Andrew, 48
Jefferson, Thomas, 8
Jesuit Archives, 1, 2
Jesuit Order: resurrection of, 24–25
Jesuits, 76, 77, 78, 85, 89, 101, 132, 138, 151; agriculture and, 36–37, 90; Coeur d'Alene relations with, 28–29, 30–32, 51, 69, 190(n31); firearms and, 38–39, 60; land claims and, 91, 124, 133–34, 141; as missionaries, 3, 23–24, 25–26, 33–34, 46; Paraguay mission model of, 26–27; peace negotiations, 55, 75; and Andrew Seltice, 79–80; teaching of, 35–36
Johnson, Andrew, 82
Joseph, Chief, 101–2
Joseph Mary, Sister (Pauline Boutelier), 140
Joset, Father Joseph, 2, 24, 31, 54, 55, 77, 86, 88, 89, 102, 183(n25), 189(n12); firearms, 38–39, 60; intertribal negotiations, 58–59; land rights, 78, 79, 92; and Palouse Valley, 82–83;

227

peace efforts of, 67, 69; protection of travelers, 64–65; and Steptoe campaigns, 61, 62, 63; and winter hunt, 37–38
Justice Department, 170

Kaizemet, Louis, 130
Kalispel (Pend Oreille) tribe, 8, 13, 20, 26, 46, 48, 51, 61, 74, 87, 185(n9); land, 52, 94, 96, 103. *See also* Lower Kalispel
Kamiah (Idaho), 15
Kamiakin, 50, 52, 53, 58, 66
Kellogg, 170
Kellogg, Noah B., 124
Kettle Falls, 10
Keyes, Erasmus D., 65, 66–67, 69
King and Monaghan, C. B., 116, 117, 120
Kinship, bilateral, 11
Kootenai (Kootenay), 13, 52
Kootenai County, 81, 113, 126, 144, 169
Kullyspell House, 16, 18
Kutenai, 19

Lakes Indians, 72, 87, 96
Lamar, Lucius Q.C., 130
Land: cessions of, 162–63; changes in use of, 88–89; Coeur d'Alene, 27, 78, 99–100, 146; compensation for, 158, 160; negotiations over, 76, 134, 135, 151–55; northern Idaho, 144–45; protection of Indian rights, 83, 124, 127–28, 138–39, 141–42; reservation, 49, 167–68; severality, 108–9; Simpson commission cession of, 155–58; U.S. policies for, 43–44, 71–72, 75–76, 80–81; in Washington Territory, 48, 52
Land claims, 95–96, 103; for Coeur d'Alene Reservation, 133–35, 141–42, 151; petitions on, 130–33; Andrew Seltice and, 91–92, 130; military and, 93–94
Landscape, relationship to, 22
Lapwai, 25, 38
Latah County, 129, 144
Latah Creek, 10, 69
Lazelle, H. M., 120
Lead deposits, 123, 124–25
Leadership, 12–13, 39; Coeur d'Alene, 59, 69, 74, 79, 164; Andrew Seltice's, 74, 153, 165
Lee, Jason, 25
Lee, Louis, 147
Leo, 111
Lewis, Charles, 111
Lewis, Meriwether, 3, 4, 8, 14, 15

Lewis, Peter, 111
Lewis, Samuel, 15
Lewis, Sebastian, 111
Lewis, Zaccheus, 113
Lewis and Clark expedition, 8, 14–15; maps, 4, 15–16
Lewiston, 81
Liberty, Edmond, 157
Liberty, Joseph Edmond, 140
Liberty, Mary, 140
Liberty, Stephen, 2, 138–39, 140, 147, 149, 151, 153, 157, 158, 160, 163
"Liberty Clause," 140
Liberty family, 163
Liberty Lake, 12, 74, 78, 85, 139, 192(n22)
Liquor. *See* Alcohol trade
Little Falls, 113
Littler North Fork, 11
Little Spokane River, 20, 135–36
Livestock raising, 46, 26, 100, 106, 116; Palouse country, 86, 123–24
Lodge, Edward, 170, 206(n53)
Lodges, 11
Louis band (Spokane tribe), 134
Louis Joseph, 39
Louise, 39
Louisiana Purchase, 8
Lower Kalispel, 51, 52, 72, 185(n9)
Lower Spokane Reservation, 136
Lower Union Flat, 86
Loyola, Ignatius, 24
Ludington, E. H., 93–94
Lumber. *See* Timber industry
Lyon, Caleb, 81

McBane, John, 61, 189(n14)
McDonald, Angus, 54
McGregor, Alex, 116
McGregor, John, 116
McKenny, Thomas J., 86–87
Magdeline, 20
Manifest Destiny, 5, 43, 48
Manypenny, George, 47–48, 51
Mapmaking, 4–5
Maps: Interior Pacific Northwest, 18–19; Lewis and Clark's, 15–16; national, 4–5
Marriage, 8, 41; Jesuit missions and, 29, 30
Mars Asellah Clis Clis Tah, 147–48
Marshall Court, 44
Marthe, 39
Martin, Nelson, 145

Mason, Billy, 139(fig.)
Massacres: Grande Ronde, 55; Mountain Meadows, 60, 189(n10); Ward, 46
Meadows, 9
Measles, epidemics, 33, 183(n30)
Medicine bundles, Jesuit missionaries and, 29, 31
Melkapsi, 62, 68
Menetry, Joseph, 50
Mental maps, Coeur d'Alene identity and, 2, 3
Methodist Church, 25
Methow tribe, 72, 87
Middle Spokane band, 135
Milkapsi, 59, 73
Milo Creek, 125
Milroy, Robert H., 94
Miners, 125, 158; on Coeur d'Alene reservation, 100, 105, 120, 123, 124; in Washington Territory, 52, 53, 57–58, 76, 77–78
Mining, 144, 161, 201(n7); pollution, 169–70; on South Fork Coeur d'Alene River, 124–25; timber cutting and, 126–27; water rights, 125–26
Mining camps, 58, 77, 123; lawlessness in, 81–82
Mining Law (1872), 124
Missionaries, missions, 2, 46, 49, 55, 181(n7); acceptance of and resistance to, 29–30; and firearms, 38–39, 60; Jesuit, 3, 23–24, 25–26, 28–29, 30–32, 33–34, 35–36; Paraguay model for, 26–27
Mission of the Sacred Heart. *See* Sacred Heart Mission
Mission State Park (Idaho), 170
Missouri River, 76
Missouri Vice Province, 25
Mix, Charles E., 44
Mobility, geographic, 14
Moctelme (Moctomal), Peter, 162, 164
Monaghan, James, 120–21
Montana, 7, 9, 23, 52, 78, 160
Monteith, John B., 195(n35); Coeur d'Alene reservation and, 95–96, 98–99
Monteith, M. S., 157
Mool-le-men-kin, 80
Moore, Benjamin, 120–21, 128
Morgan, Thomas J., 141, 154
Mormons, 60, 144, 149, 189(n11)
Mormon War, 60
Morrill Act, 81
Moscow, 10

Moses band, 87
Moshell, 53
Mountain Meadows Massacre, 60, 189(n10)
Mullan, 125
Mullan, Elden, 77
Mullan, John, 2, 47, 48, 66, 76, 77, 135, 138; on land claims, 134–35, 142, 152
Mullan Road, 47, 76, 77, 106
Mulvern, Pat, 148
Muratori, Luigi A., *A Relation of the Missions of Paraguay*, 26
Murders, 53, 55
Murray, 123
Myrtle, 123

Natatkem, Zachary, 63
Negotiations: government, 50, 51, 53, 135–36; intertribal, 58–59
Nehlukteltshiye, James, 63
Nellie, 139(fig.)
Nesmith, James W., 72
Newell, Inspector, 111
Nez Perce, 8, 13, 19, 20, 48, 53, 63, 65, 72, 103, 105, 131, 180(n57), 189(n15); buffalo hunts by, 26, 51; negotiations, 50, 58; Lewis and Clark and, 14–15; Nez Perce War, 101–2; Protestant mission among, 25, 29
Nez Perce War, 101–2
Nichel, 39
Ni'Lukhwalqw, 88
Nixon, Benjamin, 140
Nixon, Bernard John, 140
Nixon, Mary Francis, 139–40
Nixon, Mary Liberty, 140
Nixon, Patrick, 138, 139–40, 157, 158
Nixon family, 160, 163
Noble, John W., 152–53
No Hand, 27
Northern Pacific Railroad, 80–81, 106, 115–16, 129, 130, 144, 162, 196(n43)
Northern Plateau War, 69
North Fork Coeur d'Alene River, 116, 123, 124
North West Company, fur trade, 16–17, 18, 19
Northwestern Improvement Company, 129
Northwest Indian Commission, 135–36, 137–38, 140, 141–42
Northwest Indian Commission Agreement, 123, 138–39, 140, 141–42, 149, 151
Northwest Ordinance, 44
Northwest Passage, 7, 8

Oberly, John H., 152
Oblate missions, 49, 60
Office of Indian Affairs (OIA), 2, 3, 108; land cessions, 162, 163; land rights, 127–28. *See also* Bureau of Indian Affairs
Ogden, Peter Skene, 38
OIA. *See* Office of Indian Affairs
Okanogan, 20, 51, 72, 87, 185(n9); negotiation with, 52, 54, 96
Okanogan River, 88
Omnibus Bill, 160
O'Neill, James, 2, 90, 107–8, 111, 112, 114, 118, 119, 131; on timber industry, 128, 129
Oral tradition, 1, 21, 27, 36; Blackfeet, 19–20
OR&N. *See* Oregon Railway and Navigation Company
Oregon, 7, 24, 186(n11)
Oregon Country, 7, 8, 24, 38, 175(n3), 185(n3); American settlers in, 43–44
Oregon Donation Land Act, 44
Oregon Railway and Navigation Company (OR&N), 146, 148
Oregon Territorial Legislature, 38
Oregon Territory, 44, 69, 72, 75
Oregon Trail, 43, 33, 72; Indian-settler conflict on, 46–47
Ore-or-no-go claim, 124
Orofino (Idaho), 15
Oro Fino Creek, 77
O'Rourke, Phil, 124
O'Sullivan, John L., 43
Overland emigrants, 33
Owhi, 68–69

Pacific Department (U.S. Army), 55
Pacific Railroad Act, 80–81
Palladino, Lawrence, "The Coeur d'Alene Reservation," 133–34
Palmer, Joel, 50, 55
Palouse (region), 3, 8, 78, 128, 129, 150, 167; Coeur d'Alene Reservation and, 82–83, 100, 103, 165; homesteads in, 86, 123–24; relocation to, 89–90
Palouse City, 86
Palouse Rangers, 102
Palouse River, 58, 130
Palouse Tribe, 10, 14, 26, 38, 72, 103; conflict with, 54, 59; negotiation with, 50, 56, 58, 68, 69; U.S. Army and, 61, 65, 66
Pandosy, Charles, 49
Paradise Valley, 86, 88, 102, 130

Paraguay model, reduction, 26–27, 75
Patriarchy, Jesuit, 24
Patronage, Indian Service positions, 107
Paulin, 39
Payette (Idaho), 81
Peace agreements, 1858, 71, 78
Peace camps, 33
Peace pact, 20
Peace proposals/councils, 65; at Fort Vancouver, 74–75; Wright and, 67–69
Peace policy, Grant's, 71, 92
Peavy (Pevey), John, 157
Peavy, Joseph, 138, 139, 140, 160
Peavy family, 163
Pend Oreille. *See* Kalispel tribe
Pend Oreille River, 87, 130
Peopeomoxmox, 55
Peow, Baptiste, 109
"Petition of Freeholders of Spokane and Whitman County, Wash. T., and Nez Perce County, Idaho," 132
Petitions, land claims, 130–33
Pierre Ignace, 39
Pine Creek, 86, 102, 103, 132
Plains tribes, 14, 21
"Plan du Villages des Coeurs-d'alenes" (Point), 26–27
Plante, Antoine, 54, 58, 130, 187(n36)
Pleasonton, Alfred, 73
Plummer, 127, 167, 192(n22)
Point, Nicolas, 24, 31, 36, 184(n38); "Chiefs of the Coeur d'Alene . . . ," 39; Coeur d'Alene mission, 28, 30; on native subsistence, 34–35; "Plan du Villages des Coeurs-d'alenes," 26–27
Pointed Hearts. *See* Coeur d'Alene Tribe
Polatkin, 27
Polatkin, Paul, 137
Political organization, 13; authority, 39–40; Stevens' view of, 45–46
Politics, Idaho, 144, 149
Polygamy, Jesuit missionaries and, 29, 31, 40
Poorman claim, 124
Population, 9, 144, 205(n24); Washington Territory tribes, 44–45
Post, Frederick, 113–14, 126
Post Falls (Idaho), 114
Potato farming, 21
Potlatch (Idaho), 10, 100, 192(n22)
Power, centralization of, 39–40
Price, Hiram, 112, 114, 117, 118, 120; and land claims, 131–32

Prichard, Andrew, 116
Prichard's Creek, 116
Prior appropriation, 125, 126, 201(n8)
Property ownership, 30, 33
Prophecy, 21; Black Robe, 23, 27, 28, 29, 182(n12)
Prosser, Special Agent, 113
Protestants, missions, 25, 29, 33, 34, 46

Qualchan, 52, 53, 63, 68–69, 187(n30)
Quin A Mo Say, 147
Quinmosee, 100–101

Radical Republicans, 82
Railroads, 115–16; on Coeur d'Alene reservation, 105, 145–48; land granted to, 80–81, 134; Stevens survey for, 44–45
Ranching, 86, 116
Rathdrum (Idaho Territory), 116
Ravalli, Anthony, 32, 50, 54
Ray, Verne F., 9, 11
Reduction model, for Jesuit missions, 26–27, 30, 31, 34, 36, 75
Reed, Henry W., 95, 99
Reed, John M., 127, 128
Regis, 111
Reichard, Gladys A., 9
A Relation of the Missions of Paraguay (Muratori), 26
Religion, 144. *See also* Catholicism; Spirituality
Religious organizations, reform, 92–93
Relocation: Coeur d'Alene Tribe, 88–90; Spokane Tribe, 135
Removal Bill (1830), 48
Republican party, 71, 77, 78, 82
Reservation(s), 49, 72, 75, 81, 93, 94, 109, 120; administration of, 107–8; boundaries of, 2–4, 96, 104, 114–15, 117–18, 128, 130, 150; creation of, 2, 87; economics, 111–13; formation of, 95, 98–99; Idaho territory and, 82–83, 85; incursions on, 118–19; land cessions, 162–63; mapping of, 4–5; Simpson commission and, 153–58; Stevens promotion of, 47–48, 52; timber cutting, 199(n31), 201(nn10, 17), 202(n18); trespass on, 100, 115–16
Resistance, to Jesuit missions, 29–30, 31
Ritchie, John, 102
Roads, 47, 48, 76, 77
Rock art, at the Dalles, 8
Rock Creek, 87

Rockford Landing, 117
Rocky Mountain Fur Trading Company, 19
Rocky Mountain Missions, 1, 24
Roots, 10
Rosalia, 63

Sacred Heart Mission, 28, 31, 32, 34, 41, 44, 46, 64, 73, 75, 76–77, 79, 80, 91, 183(n25), 190(n31); agriculture, 36, 37; and Coeur d'Alene Reservation, 85, 96; firearms at, 38, 39; as refuge, 81, 82; Isaac Stevens at, 40, 51, 53, 54, 57; U.S. Army campaigns and, 67–68, 69
Sahaptin speakers, 8, 189(n15)
St. Ignatius (Montana), 13, 134
St. Joe Boom Company, 160–61
St. Joseph (St. Joe) River, 9, 11, 12, 22, 75, 77, 78, 91, 130, 145; Coeur d'Alene control of, 160–61; Coeur d'Alene Indians on, 90, 192–93(n22); and Coeur d'Alene Reservation, 83, 85, 96, 118, 149, 150, 155, 165; Jesuit mission on, 28, 30
St. Louis, Nez Perce and Flathead trip to, 25–26
St. Maries, 12, 126
St. Maries River, 9, 96
St. Mary of the Rocky Mountains mission, 26, 29, 33, 34, 184(n32)
Salish speakers, 8, 9, 29, 33
Salmon (Idaho), 81
Salmon fisheries, fishing, 8, 10, 11
Salt Lake settlements, 60
Sams, William B., 168
Sanford, George, 93
San Francisco claim, 124
San Poel Tribe. *See* San Poil Tribe.
San Poil Tribe, 72, 87, 96
Sawmills, 198(n29); Coeur d'Alene acquisition of, 112, 113; operation of, 126–27
Scarcity cycles, 36
Schitsu'umsh, 1, 174(n2). *See also* Coeur d'Alene Tribe
Schoenberg, Wilfred, 32
Schofield, J. M., 93
Schools, on reservation, 112, 137
Seasonal activities, 9–11, 35, 111
Secretary of the Interior, 1
Seltice, Andrew, 2, 3, 11, 53, 68, 74, 78, 100, 102, 109, 110, 113, 115, 121, 122, 139(fig.), 143, 160, 191(n43); and adoption of non-Indians, 138–39; agriculture, 129–30, 196(n47); and "civilization," 85–86; and

Colville Agency, 119–20; land claims on, 91–92, 94, 95, 96, 103, 130, 133, 136; land negotiations, 152, 155–57, 163; land rights protection, 83, 106, 124, 154; leadership of, 79–80, 101, 151, 153, 164, 165; and Northwest Indian Commission, 140, 141; and railroads, 145–46, 148; on reservation incursions, 118–19; on relocation, 88, 89
Seltice, Joseph, 11, 18, 28, 37
Seltice, Moses, 74
Seltice, Peter, 164
Seltice family, 14, 62, 63, 64, 111
Settlers: American, 38, 43, 71–72, 76, 78, 102; Hudson Bay Company and, 45; Indian conflict, 46–47
Severalty, 108–9, 132, 168
Sexton, M. J., 112, 113; sawmill operated by, 126–27
Sexton and Cobb, M. J., 113
Shamans, 12–13, 31
Shanks, John P.C., 85, 95, 96, 98, 99
Sheep growers, 116
Sherman, William T., 106
Shoshone, 47
Shoshone-Bannock, 19
Shupe, John H., 151
Silver deposits, 123, 124–25
Simms, John A., 2, 90, 94, 98, 102, 112, 113, 114, 121
Simpson, Benjamin, 2, 151, 158
Simpson commission, 153–54; land cessions, 155–57
Singisen, T. F., 118
Sisters of Providence of Mary Immaculate (Sisters of Charity), 101
Siuwheemtuk, Louise, 39
Sketsomish. *See* Coeur d'Alene Tribe
Smena, Victor, 63
Smith, Elijah, 146
Snake River, 7, 8, 18, 189(n14); as protected area boundary, 58–59; Steptoe's campaign and, 61, 63
Snoqualmie Pass, 52
Soldiers of the Sacred Heart, 80, 102, 136, 145
South Fork Coeur d'Alene River, 127; mining on, 123, 124, 125, 126
Spalding, Eliza, 25
Spalding, Henry, 25, 38
Spirituality, and Roman Catholicism, 23–24, 29
Spokane Council, 54, 58, 68
Spokane County, land rights, 127–28

Spokane Falls (Spokane), 10, 15, 16, 106, 110, 126, 162, 163, 164, 197(n3); Northern Pacific Railroad and, 115–16
Spokane House, 16, 17
Spokane Plains, Battle of, 66–67
Spokane Prairie, 85
Spokane Reservation, 107, 121
Spokane River, 8, 9, 11, 19, 20, 22, 35, 54, 113, 165, 192(n22); crossing, 100–101; Coeur d'Alene reservation, 85, 96; ferry crossing, 58, 187(n36)
Spokane Tribe, 13, 20, 26, 48, 51, 72, 74, 87; and Coeur d'Alene Reservation, 109–10, 142, 198(n23); land claims, 94, 103, 134; negotiations with, 52, 53, 54, 58, 68, 96, 135–36; perceptions of, 109–10; Protestant missions among, 25, 33; and Steptoe campaign, 61, 62, 63, 64; and U.S. Army, 65, 66
Spokane Valley, 27, 78, 79, 88, 100; battle in, 66–67
Stanley, John Mix, 45
Steamboats, 145; and alcohol trade, 120–21; on Lake Coeur d'Alene, 116, 117, 130
Stellam (Twisted Earth), 21, 23, 31, 53, 73, 113, 182(n14); and Jesuit missionaries, 27, 28, 30–31; on reservation boundaries, 119–20
Stellam, Joseph, 53, 182(n14)
Stellam, Paschal, 62
Steptoe, Edward J., 56, 58, 59, 73; campaign of, 60–64, 101, 190(n31)
Steptoe Butte, 130
Stevens, Isaac I., 2, 43, 69, 72, 76, 185(n9); and Coeur d'Alenes, 57, 134; on Indians' political organization, 45–46; railroad survey, 44–45; as territorial governor, 40, 41; treaty negotiations by, 50–52, 138, 191(n4); on tribal removal, 47–48; and Yakima, 53, 54, 55–56
Subsistence, 9–10, 22, 27, 34–35, 89, 92, 154
Sullivan claim, 124
Survey: reservation boundary, 114–15, 117–18
Sweeney, John A., 119, 131, 151

Tammutsa. *See* Timothy, Chief
Tannatt, T. R., 146
Taylor, Oliver, 63
Tecomtee, 79
Teit, James A., 9
Tensed, 10
Territoriality, 17, 46
Territorial system, U.S., 44

Territory, 11, 43; Coeur d'Alene, 8–9, 18, 75, 78, 180(n54); maintaining, 78, 180(n57)
Thompson, David, 16, 17, 18
Thompson, David P., 86
Tiger claim, 124
Tilcoax, 58, 59, 61, 73, 188(n7)
Timber industry, 124, 126, 161, 199(n31), 201(nn10, 17), 202(n18); Coeur d'Alene Reservation and, 127–29, 155, 156; non-Indian settlers and, 144, 145; reservation-era, 112–14, 117
Timber resources, 27, 155
Timothy, Chief, 61, 63, 189(n15)
Toner, James, 124
Tosi, Paschal, 127
Tourism, 161–62, 170
Trade, 8, 10, 14, 16, 19, 20, 180(n46); for firearms, 59–60
Trade and Intercourse Act (1834), 120
Treaties, 72, 81, 95 191(n4); negotiation of, 50–52, 134–35, 138; U.S. Army–Coeur d'Alene, 68, 83
Treaty system, abolition of, 95
Treaty of Fort Laramie, 49, 186(n18)
Tribal delegations, to St. Louis, 25–26
Tribal policies, of assimilation, 37–38
Tribal removal, 47–48
Tribal succession, 20–21
Tshimakain, 33, 34
Twisted Earth. *See* Stellam
Twisted Hair, 15

Umatilla, 50
Union Pacific Railroad, 148
United States, 7–8, 25; Indian policies of, 48–49; land policies of, 43–44, 75–76; and Oregon Country, 38, 175(n3), 185(n3)
U.S. Army, 72, 73; land claims and, 93–94; Steptoe's campaign and, 60–64; as threat, 58, 59; and volunteers, 54–55; Wright's campaign, 65–68
U.S. Congress, 72, 82; land claims/rights, 135, 151, 154–55; reformers in, 92–93
U.S. Geological Survey of the Territories, 5
U.S. Senate, on Coeur d'Alene land claims, 135, 149
U.S. Supreme Court, 44, 129
Upper Columbia River, 52
Upper Spokane band, 135
Upper Union Flat, 86
Upshaw, A. B., 129, 140

Villages, 12; traditional, 89, 165; winter, 11, 154
Vincent (Bassa), Chief, 12, 20–21, 40, 62, 63, 65, 68, 74, 79, 191(n43)
Vincent Xwipep, 59
Vision seeking, 21

Waiilatpu, 33, 34, 38
Walker, Elkanah, 33
Walker, Francis, 87
Walker, Mary, 33
Wallace (Idaho), 125
Wallace, William R., 124
Walla Walla (town), 86
Walla Walla Council, 49, 50, 52
Walla Walla Tribe, 46, 50, 54, 72
Walla Walla Valley, 38, 45, 72, 77, 188(n7)
Wallowa Valley, 101
W&IRR. *See* Washington and Idaho Railroad
Ward, Inspector, 110
War Department, 1, 158
Ward massacre, 46–47
Wardner, 125
Warfare, 26, 38, 180(n54); American-Indian, 46–47, 53–56, 188(n7); with Blackfeet, 19–20, 29, 33–34, 182(n17); U.S. Army campaigns, 60–68, 69
Washington, 2, 7–8, 10, 160
Washington and Idaho Railroad (W&IRR): and Coeur d'Alene Tribe, 145–48, 153; and Andrew Seltice, 148–49
Washington Superintendency of Indian Affairs, 86–87
Washington Territory, 40, 49, 86, 185(n51); American-Indian conflict in, 46–47; gold rush in, 52–53; miners in, 77–78; reservations in, 75, 93, 105; settlement of, 72, 76; treaties in, 50–52; tribal removal from, 47–48; tribes in, 44–45
Water rights, 125–26, 201(n8)
Waters, Sidney (Sydney), 2, 110, 111, 119, 131; on boundary survey, 117–18; land claims petition and, 131, 132; suspension of, 120, 121; timber cutting, 113–14
Waterways: Coeur d'Alene Tribe control of, 160–61; navigable, 149, 150
Wayton Lake (Lake Coeur d'Alene), 15, 16, 179(n40)
Wealth, reservation-era, 111
Weapons. *See* Firearms
West Colville Reservation, 94, 96, 99
Wham-shen-mel, 100

233

Wheaton, Frank, 103
Wheat production, 36–37, 41
Wheyilshoo, 156
Whilcomte, 151
Whiskey, 101. *See also* Alcohol consumption
Whitman, Marcus, 25, 33, 38
Whitman, Narcissa, 25, 33, 38
Whitman County, 127–28, 129
Whitman County Agricultural Fair, 129
Wildshoe, Louis, 134, 135
Wildshoe, Peter, 63, 79, 100, 152, 164, 202(n32)
Wilkinson, Melville, 103
Willamette Valley, 25, 38, 72
Williams, W. C., 64
Wilson, Charles, 81–82
Winans, William Park, 87–88, 94, 96
Wolf Lodge Creek, 118, 155
Wolf Lodge district, 150
Women, 89; authority of, 10, 13, 23, 30
Woodmen of the World, 162

Wool, John E., 55, 57–58
Worcester v. Georgia, 44
Worley, 168–69
Wright, George, 2, 55, 72, 73, 83, 92, 93, 155; campaign of, 65–67, 101, 190–91(n36); peace negotiations, 68–69; at Sacred Heart Mission, 67–68
Wright, John V., 135, 136–37, 141, 203(n35)

Yakima River, 52
Yakima Tribe, 14, 60; conflict with miners by, 52–53, 54; negotiations with, 50, 51, 68, 69; missions, 46, 60; U.S. Army and, 61, 63, 65, 66
Yakima War, 53–54, 56
Youmas, Andrew, 66
Young, Brigham, 60

Zemplsenxul, Bonaventure, 64
Zulyatsot, Sebastian, 67

www.ingramcontent.com/pod-product-compliance
Lightning Source LLC
Chambersburg PA
CBHW071339080526
44587CB00017B/2888